Defensive Internationalism

Defensive Internationalism

Providing Public Goods in an Uncertain World

Davis B. Bobrow
&
Mark A. Boyer

The University of Michigan Press
Ann Arbor

Copyright © 2005 by Davis B. Bobrow and Mark A. Boyer
All rights reserved
Published in the United States of America by
The University of Michigan Press
Manufactured in the United States of America
♾ Printed on acid-free paper

2008 2007 2006 2005   4 3 2 1

No part of this publication may be reproduced,
stored in a retrieval system,
or transmitted in any form or by any means,
electronic, mechanical, or otherwise,
without the written permission of the publisher.

*A CIP catalog record for this book
is available from the British Library.*

Library of Congress Cataloging-in-Publication Data

Bobrow, Davis B.
Defensive internationalism : providing public goods in an uncertain world /
Davis B. Bobrow and Mark A. Boyer.
p.   cm.
Includes bibliographical references and index.
ISBN 0-472-09879-9 (cloth : alk. paper) —
ISBN 0-472-06879-2 (pbk. : alk. paper)
1. Internationalism. 2. Economic assistance. 3. Public goods.
4. Security, International. I. Boyer, Mark A. II. Title.

JZ1308.B63 2004
327.1—dc22   2004017197

To Gail & Sondra

CONTENTS

Preface and Acknowledgments	ix
Chapter 1. *Understanding Defensive Internationalism: Black, White, or Shades of Gray*	1
Chapter 2. *Clubs, Identities, and Institutions: A Tale of Overlapping Interests*	17
Chapter 3. *Domestic Support for Contributions: How Stable and Strong?*	48
Chapter 4. *International Development Assistance*	132
Chapter 5. *International Debt Management and Relief*	180
Chapter 6. *United Nations Peacekeeping Operations*	222
Chapter 7. *Pursuing International Environmental Quality*	270
Chapter 8. *A Global Prognosis of Muted Optimism?*	326
Notes	357
References	377
Index	407

PREFACE AND ACKNOWLEDGMENTS

This project has preoccupied us for nearly a decade. It began as a single conference paper presented at the 1995 annual meeting of the International Studies Association and evolved into this book. When we started looking into the questions raised in the following pages, nearly everyone thinking and writing about global affairs was still trying to understand the implications of the end of the Cold War and the apparent structural transformation of the global system. We now know a little bit more about that transformation and its political, economic, and military implications, but we are still far from certain about the future evolutionary trajectory of global politics.

The following chapters provide some clues about the direction and shape of that trajectory based on three assumptions. First, we believe that past policy actions by global political actors provide a useful indicator, albeit an imperfect one, of future actions and choices. We hold this belief because of the largely incremental way most policy is made and changed in developed societies. This belief is also based in notions of the political culture that develops and is at least partly reflected in domestic political interests within societies that provide boundaries for policy-making in both the short and long term.

Second, we also believe that in our globalizing world, policy actors (in our case, primarily states) are increasingly forced to deal with global forces whether or not the actors want to do so. Put simply, isolationist-type or even unilateralist policies can only "solve" an actor's policy problems for short intervals. To cope with problems over the long term, states must directly engage the world and the problems posed from outside domestic borders to solve problems that have domestic impacts. As the title of the book suggests, states are compelled to be internationalist for defensive reasons.

The aftermath of the 9/11 attacks and the ongoing tale of the invasion and occupation of Iraq have reinforced these convictions. For us, these unfinished stories affirm the motivational effects of defensive internationalism. These events have been and continue to be shaped by the tendencies of actors in international affairs to draw on established policy inclinations. These occurrences are rife with the rationales, opportunities, constraints, and indeed temptations presented to political elites by preexisting domestic political cultures. The siren song of unilateralism seems sooner rather than later to be drowned out by exigencies that require multilateral treatment.

Third, we believe that to understand contemporary global policy dynamics it is essential to incorporate both theory and data into our analysis, especially if the goal is to produce useful policy implications. The first two chapters focus on a number of conceptual and theoretical questions and bodies of literature to synthesize divergent schools of thought and to show how that synthesis helped lead us to our stance of defensive internationalism. Chapters 3–7 focus on the data that can help us determine the validity of the theoretical constructs and our thematic stance. Chapter 8 ties the theory and data together to provide a global prognosis about the prospects for international cooperation and lays out a number of expectations and policy needs for the coming years.

In getting to this stage of our project, especially after nearly a decade of work, we have many colleagues, students, and friends to thank for their help. We have been blessed with an excellent group of research assistants along the way, including Mary Caprioli, Erin Carriere, Becky Chaffee, Peter Jonason, Yasumasa Komori, Miyuki Kubo, James Na, Gergana Noutcheva, and Daniela Trajkovska. Most recently, Magnolia Hernandez did superlative "crunch-time" work in helping us update the data for the final version of the manuscript. Natalie Florea updated data and read the entire penultimate draft of the manuscript for factual errors and stylistic problems. She also had a wonderful eye for helping us make sure that what we wrote was understandable to others in our field (and hopefully even some people outside of it).

In addition, many colleagues have read or listened to various parts of the project along the way. Their comments, though not always heeded, were invaluable in helping us stay on track, especially in substantive policy areas where our detailed expertise was lacking. We are indebted to Hartmut Behr, Marijke Breuning, Mike Butler, Mario Carranza, Peter Dombrowski, Yale Ferguson, Betty Hanson, Joe Hewitt, Richard Higgott and his colleagues at the University of Warwick, Walter Isard, Bob Kudrle, Steve Lamy, Laura Neack, Lou Pauly, Rodger Payne, Bruce Russett, Todd Sandler, Siegmar Schmidt, Steve Smith and his colleagues at Aberystwyth, Herman Schwartz, Jennifer Sterling-Folker, the late Susan Strange, Tom Volgy, and several anonymous reviewers. A special note of thanks is owed to three institutions that generously provided Bobrow with free time from other duties and conducive settings for working on this project: the German Fulbright Commission, the Institut fur Politikwissenschaft of the Universitat Koblenz-Landau, and the Robert Schuman Centre for Advanced Studies of the European University Institute.

As any author knows, projects such as this are also made much easier, especially in the closing stages, through solid, reliable, and most importantly, cheerful support from those around us who provide administrative and editorial support. Donalyn Maneggia had the task of taking our double-edited final manuscript and getting it prepared for the University of Michigan Press. To her we are deeply in debt, especially since she continues to speak to both of us. MaryAnn Gebet also provided excellent support in earlier stages of the project as we pursued our dual-university collaboration, one that started just as the Internet wave was beginning to crest. We also thank Javier Morales-Ortiz for doing a great job on the index and the University of Connecticut Research Foundation for funding that portion of the project.

We should also note that a number of pieces of this book appeared in some form as journal articles or book chapters. A much earlier cut at the peacekeeping material in chapter 6 appeared in the *Journal of Conflict Resolution* 41 (6): 723–48 (December 1997); parts of an earlier version of chapter 2 were published by Mark Boyer in the book *Political Space*, edited by Yale H. Ferguson and R.J. Barry Jones (SUNY Press, 2002); and some portions of the data used in chapter 4 were published in the *Journal of International Relations* 4:84–111 (1997).

A very special word of thanks and acknowledgment must also go to Craig Boyer, whose creative mind and artistic abilities produced the concept for the cover of this book. In discussions with his father about the book, he crafted the idea of intertwined flags, drew several sketch possibilities, and allowed us to submit the drawings to the Press for consideration. Our editor and others at the Press liked the concept and agreed to use it on the cover, adding a true personal touch to the final product.

Finally, we thank our editors and staff at the University of Michigan Press. Jeremy Shine shepherded the manuscript in its early stages, and Jim Reische stepped in just before the production stage. In both cases we were in good hands, and we appreciate their patience with us as we took longer to finish up than we (and they) would have liked.

1 UNDERSTANDING DEFENSIVE INTERNATIONALISM
Black, White, or Shades of Gray

Some years ago, Harold Lasswell (1936) defined politics as "who gets, what, when, how." As we survey the world around us, however, a more appropriate definition of politics seemingly would place equal emphasis on "who *gives*, what, when, how." Giving affects what is received in all its connotations: providing, contributing, supplying, transferring, and even gifting. And what we expect to get back when we give to others affects what we give. For us, these conceptions of giving and receiving hold for international and domestic policy and politics as well as for interpersonal relations. We also believe that better understanding of "who gives, what, how, when" is at the heart of many current global policy challenges for states and other actors in the world system.

This position does not depend on an assumption that global actors are inherently generous. It does, however, involve embracing two fundamental views about global affairs. The first was well put by Stanley Hoffman (1989, 277) when he wrote that when "working in a field in which violence, deceit, injustice and oppression are in full display, beware of illusions, but never give up hope—by which I do not mean a faith in progress, only the modest belief that it is not impossible." This position underlies an expectation that we label *muted optimism*. In other words, we have hope about the prospects for coping with international and global problems, but that hope is tempered by a grounding in the reality of politics in a state-centric world.

The second position, which we label *defensive internationalism,* has its basis in Kenneth Boulding's *The Economy of Love and Fear* (1973). As he summarized the position some years later, "grants, that is, one-way transfers, have two sources. One is love, or at lower levels, respect, legitimation, and so on, but the other is fear, which is why I pay most of my income tax" (Boulding 1989, 111). Doing the "right thing" does not always result from unselfish motives but can also be a product of fear and concern about one's security, narrowly defined.

These positions on our part are ones we took before the 9/11 attacks and even before the articulation and application of the national security doctrines of the second Bush administration. As we finished this book in the contemporary context of the American invasion and occupation of Iraq, most of the systematic empirical data available predate those events. As we argue in the conclusion, those developments certainly cast further doubt on a view of international affairs that is characterized by humanity-embracing, generous philanthropy. Yet for us, these events make a commitment to muted optimism even more necessary and validate the practical importance of defensive internationalism.

We began our writing (all too long ago) with an interest in why rich countries with resources sufficient for large volumes of giving often end up reluctant to give with the quality or quantity widely thought necessary to reduce current problems experienced by large sections of the world. This pattern of undergiving seems to continue even when current problems could also apparently harm the globally rich themselves. Our initial question was why the North does what it does for the South, even if what is done is often not enough. This question in turn led to related questions. Why do some northerners give more than others? Why do countries increase or reduce what they give at different times? Why do they give with more or less generous terms? Why do they choose to give more to achieve certain goals or outcomes around the world rather than to achieve the many other worthy goals? Why do they direct their giving to some troubled populations and regions more than to others? In light of the answers to those questions, how clearly does recent history lead us to project one or another set of expectations about future giving?

Giving and getting in policy and politics are not, of course, just about the deliberate or inadvertent transfer of desirables, or "goods," but also concern the deliberate or inadvertent transfer of undesirables, or "bads." In fact, many contemporary headline stories and controversies in world affairs focus on such negative transfers—diseases from Africa, financial instability from open capital markets, or deaths in New York from Middle Eastern terrorists. Positive transfers are less likely to make the headlines but surely constitute part of the ongoing policy rhetoric and calls to action about such goals as accelerating economic development or promoting democracy and human rights.

Thus, our subject is about much more than academic concerns, although we will explore the topic in an academic way. Policy cooperation and conflict on transnational matters centrally involve who ought to, who has, and who will give and get what, when, and how. The centrality of giving and getting in contemporary global policy proposals is readily evident in the flood of rhetoric citing moral ideas and pragmatic expectations and recommending particular allocations of tangible resources.

The rationales we hear for global giving involve many of the same assumptions that underlie the arguments for and against domestic social welfare programs. For example, "moral hazard" arguments contend that some giving provides "perverse incentives"—that is, encourages behavior that compounds a problem (e.g., perpetual living off welfare payments) rather than promotes behaviors (e.g., seeking job training) that lessen the problems of the underprivileged. Other positions have more to do with motives for giving and how they impel similar or different behaviors about transfers of the same commodity. They too are familiar concerns in purely domestic settings (e.g., blood donations, as analyzed by Titmuss 1971). Other arguments concern the distributions of benefits and costs in the giving-getting relationship. We are all familiar with enjoinders capturing different judgments about distributions: "Beware of foreigners bearing gifts" versus "Do not look a gift horse in the mouth." We will explore how these different positions play out in approaches to global giving and appraisals of particular giving policies and situations. For now, we note only that numerous examples are available for different positions.

The broadening and deepening of global interdependence make transnational giving and getting matters of growing activity, controversy, and consequence. Whatever the weight of their good and bad aspects, internationalization and globalization technologies and processes have brought us far into a world of flows across national, international, and regional boundaries. Boundaries are not what they used to be, and distance is not what it once was. We think that attempts to reestablish traditional border security are likely to be very costly and eventually ineffective in critical ways.

Arnold Wolfers's now almost fifty-year-old observation about the impingement of a "milieu" condition on "possession" goals surely is even more apt in the contemporary world than it was during the height of the Cold War. He wrote that a participant in international affairs is

> selfish or shortsighted if he puts all his efforts into the accumulation and protection of his possessions while remaining indifferent to the peace and order, the public health and well-being of the community in which he resides or works. It is one thing to be in good physical or financial condition within an orderly and prosperous

community, but quite another thing to be privileged by the wealth of one's possessions in surroundings of misery, ill health, lack of public order, and widespread resentment. (1962, 75)

Many of our previous assertions are, then, hardly great discoveries. We also have no illusions about our ability to provide complete and fully satisfying answers to our questions, at least in terms of providing clear-cut evidence one way or another. Our aspirations are far more modest, and we thus will try to accomplish four things in sequence.

The first is to set out an approach integrating the implications for international giving from several intellectual frameworks of great current interest in the academic study of international relations. The central elements of each framework are drawn from, often in crude and oversimplified ways, policy debates and campaigns for adoption outside of the academy—in governments, the media, and interest group lobbying and citizen mobilization efforts (including those conducted by "public interest" groups). The theoretical frameworks are those of public goods theory and its variants, identity-based constructivism, and multilateral institutionalism. We think that the attention given to those several frameworks implies that each has some intrinsic merit as well as explanatory and predictive inadequacy. We want to exploit the strengths and compensate for the limitations of these approaches as they help us understand and analyze the subject at hand. Chapter 2 does just that.

The second is to characterize the domestic belief systems that provide incentives and disincentives for rich-country governments to engage in particular forms and degrees of giving. We think that competitors for high national office try to associate themselves and their policies with prevailing citizen beliefs and avoid contrary courses of action. That is not to deny the importance of domestic and transnational voluntary organizations (i.e., nongovernmental organizations) or private sector firms (e.g., multinational manufacturing and services companies). We do assume, however, that the impacts of nonstate actors depend on degrees of compatibility and contradiction between what they would have states do and what domestic publics prefer, tolerate, or oppose. Chapter 3 reports generally relevant beliefs, while those more specific to particular issues are considered in chapters 4, 6, and 7.

The third is to explore the fit between our conceptual expectations and prevalent domestic beliefs, on the one hand, and what has actually been given in four issue areas of international policy, on the other. The issue areas are those of international development assistance, debt management and relief, peacekeeping, and environmental protection. Those are surely not the only issue areas where international giving matters, and some observers certainly would argue that these are not the most important topics. For our purposes, it is not necessary to cover the entire waterfront of international giving and getting or to treat the issue areas currently of the greatest salience to major power elites and publics. What is necessary is that our issue areas have characteristics that make them useful for tracing and understanding the implications of our concepts and identified beliefs. It is obviously desirable that the issue areas manifest strong giving and getting interactions and matter for the well-being of much of the world in a way that is of more than fleeting or localized importance. We think that our chosen issues meet those criteria. Our four issue areas are examined in detail in chapters 4–7.

Finally, more speculatively and less rigorously, chapter 8 draws out what are for us the major implications of our analysis in terms of international giving and getting. This involves a summary of behavior in the relatively recent past as well as certain expectations this behavior suggests for future policies. We will in comparative fashion suggest implications for the three major international sources of giving relevant to our cases: the United States, the European Union and its members, and Japan. We will, however, pay somewhat more attention to the United States, not because we view it as the extreme outlier among the rich countries in terms of generosity or stinginess in international giving but rather in the spirit of the Mexican saying that living close to the United States is like sleeping in the same bed with an elephant. The elephant's movements, whatever their motivation, matter a great deal. Much of the world views itself for better or worse as living close to the United States in the sense of being profoundly affected by it. The American share of resources relevant to the transfer of goods and bads makes it the global elephant. Those realities may erode in the long run of history, but they surely characterize the recent past, the present, and the proximate future of global affairs.

STARTING POINTS

We began our work with some convictions. Readers can judge the extent that those convictions have biased our analysis. By now we also know what is in the following chapters. Accordingly, we will not engage in coy pretenses that we began with fully open minds or are ignorant of what our analyses have found.

We believe that most players in international affairs share two common preferences. The first is for basic order in the sense of sufficient regularity to enable predictions about what others do and the consequences of those actions. Actors are not attracted to surprises and uncertainty.

As opposed to a more chaotic policy environment, a context of regularity allows players to pursue progress (as they define it) and to avoid regression. By *progress,* we refer to improvements in actual and perceived conditions in fundamental terms—physical security, economic prosperity, ecological sustainability, and cultural continuity. Regression amounts to worsening conditions in one or more of those respects. Both involve combinations of probabilities (likelihoods) and absolute and relative conditions. Assessments of conditions involve historical retrospectives and forward-looking estimates of what is in fact happening to those fundamental conditions.

We also assume that most international affairs actors increasingly view their conditions as sensitive to and possibly determined by events and trends in a world outside of their national territory and/or citizenry. Thus, the regularities of substantial interest for these players are increasingly global yet remain significantly domestic and local. These recognitions spur efforts to form international clubs, groupings across borders intended to help assure regularity, facilitate progress, and limit regression from existing conditions. We expect that when formed, those clubs will play important roles in international giving and getting.

Our premises do not claim universal love of the status quo or uniformity of views about what will enhance global order and progress. Our assumptions do suggest that a policy line seen to have a reasonable chance of enhancing the prospects for both order and progress will often be chosen over alternatives seen as inferior in those respects. That applies with respect to achieving improvements, avoiding regression, and countering looming threats or precedents of disorder and shock. Most participants in international affairs, at least most of the time, will, within the limits of their understandings and capabilities, try to avoid negative capital formation and accumulation with the parochial and collective problems they involve (Keller, Lowi, and Gendlin 2000).[1] An illustration of our premises was the prevalent, although not universal, initial reaction to the September 11 events in the United States. The targets of those events in both physical and symbolic terms were two pillars of current international regularity, one economic (the World Trade Center towers) and one military (the Pentagon).

What different actors will do on behalf of regularity or to avoid regression and achieve progress in their conditions depends on a host of factors. We do not view most actors as dedicated, unselfish philanthropists. We also do not reject in principle the merits of "tough love" approaches. We do believe that those who find the current order and its projected path into the future more attractive than recognized alternatives will try to do something in its defense, expansion, or acceleration.

What they do, however, may be of large or small magnitude relative to their resources or even limited to encouraging what are thought to be conducive courses of action by others. This latter policy approach may be a selfish move of burden dodging, or it may follow from convictions that what others do will in large measure make the difference in outcomes. We expect those who have the greatest stakes in global order and progress and who perceive those stakes as threatened to be especially likely to exert themselves. If they also have large material and nonmaterial resources—as such countries often do—then they are capable of making large efforts directly and providing incentives and disincentives for others to follow even if those other players are less interested in the goals of order or progress.

If the real world meets those conditions in full, we then expect to see a positive spiral of international giving and getting. That will be especially true when in most countries there is consensus on the nature of some dramatic threat to order and progress and agreement on what course of action will effectively and efficiently lessen the threat. The real world surely falls short of meeting those conditions. Most obviously, some currently active players in international affairs see the regularities of the current global order as inherently worsening conditions. More often, there is serious disagreement on what are severe threats or barriers to order and progress, on their trends and timelines, and on efficacious treatments. Still more commonly, a general support of regularity and agreement on the nature of progress and regression coexists with different preferences for specific policy actions. While most governments and most of their citizens may well agree on general objectives—such as ending poverty in the world, forestalling genocide, preserving the environment—they still will bargain hard and long over who should get what share of the benefits, who should bear what share of the costs, and when those distributions should take effect (Fearon 1998).

For us, these factors make it unlikely that clearly virtuous spirals of international giving and getting will occur. Yet the widespread preferences for regularity and progressive policy movement make it likely that we have and will get movement of a progressive, albeit nonlinear and largely reactive, kind. Giving will tend to grow in terms of issue coverage, quality and quantity of global policy contributions, and country participation. Yet the resources committed to the policies that implement that movement will be rather small fractions of state resources and will be focused unevenly on one or another part of the world. States will differ in the allocated share of their resources and their geographical application. States will differ in the degree to which they are attracted to giving in the service of one opportunity or another for global progress and regularity or with the goal of limiting damage from one or another threat.

Our expectations for international giving and getting are neither white nor black, bright nor bleak, but a complex pallet of shades of gray. The following chapters set forth the conceptual basis for that position and consider evidence about the presence of beliefs and actions that fit or clash with that view.

UNDERSTANDING MUTED OPTIMISM THROUGH CONTRAST (AND SIMILARITY)

Our position of muted optimism can best be clarified by contrasting it with the other possibilities that it suggests. Muted pessimism, one counterpossibility, also features variety and nonlinearity in giving but sees the overall pattern of movement as declining in terms of issue coverage, quality and quantity of global policy contributions, and country participation. The sharper contrasts, however, are with the less qualified optimist and pessimist positions. Each has advocates in the large and complex literatures of hegemonic stability theory and of state decline. They offer arguments about what will happen down the road and, at least implicitly, about what should happen in normative terms.

In the hegemonic stability camp, pessimists argue that global order and progress become casualties of a withdrawal by the dominant great power (for now, the United States) from a role in world affairs characterized by activism, pro-progress giving, and pro-regularity policing. As such, the hegemon is indispensable as an underwriter and a disproportionately large formulator of the goals and provider of the resources conducive to order and progress. The current hegemon, faced with domestic preoccupations, superpower fatigue, and diminishing relative resources and possibly lacking a credible overarching adversary, reduces its giving, if reluctantly and in irregular ways. Moreover, other actors do not and possibly cannot do more to replace the curtailed contributions of the once-committed hegemonic power. As a result, a spiral of selfish, neoisolationist behavior harms the general welfare of the world's nations and populations.[2] Examples of this phenomenon include the Dark Ages after the fall of the Roman Empire and the "coming anarchy" (Kaplan 2000) after the decline of the United States. In this view, the U.S. activist reaction to 9/11 is just a temporary deviation from a more general trend.

The optimistic variant of the hegemonic stability literature and in particular of power transition theory focuses on the positive influence that unipolarity has had and can have on global order and progress (i.e., Rome in the past or the United States in the present).³ More specifically, a United States well into an era of unprecedented and sustainable superiority in hard and soft power assets will bring the world through "engagement and enlargement" to a new level of systemic order and progressively increasing well-being. The United States will do so by exporting economic forms (free markets), political institutions (democracy), and cultural styles (McWorld)—all under the umbrella provided by military dominance. There need be little anxiety about insufficient contributions by such an America because it de facto contributes by "doing its own thing." Being the hegemon, then, inherently enhances global order and progress, and others will more or less willingly follow down the path. At an extreme, the American empire in the twenty-first century is a desirable, feasible, and indeed the best available prescription for order and progress in the world. In this perspective, 9/11 was a wake-up call to America to do what was needed for global order and progress, and the subsequent response was at least a partial confirmation that it would be done.

A less extreme form of hegemonic optimism admits that great powers eventually do decline but also emphasizes that what they do for global order and progress does not end abruptly. Positive residual effects can continue. The prospects emphasized by hegemonic stability pessimists are rejected; those by full-bore optimists are moderated. The pro-regularity and pro-progress influence of even a declining hegemon can have an inherently long half-life. With the United States cast in that role, the particulars include the continued centrality of the dollar and American capital markets in world finance and in the international institutions related to international economic growth. Those and other "soft power" assets (Nye 1990) can continue to influence others to behave in pro-regularity and pro-progress ways. The widespread and continuing exportation of American ideas and institutions socializes others into the values and preferences that induce these others to act in such ways (e.g., Ikenberry and Kupchan 1990; Nau 1990). In effect, building on Goldstein (1993), the United States has already put much of the world on the right path through the transfer of ideas leading to a pro-regularity and pro-progress linkage abroad of widely held interests and the institutions to help sustain them into the future. The process remains incomplete but has gone so far that its fruits are sustainable even after eventual U.S. decline (Kupchan 1998). This perspective has strong relationships to that of muted optimism, and we will return to it later.⁴

In sum, both pessimistic and optimistic hegemonic stability strands attribute a key role to the United States The divide between these views hinges on whether the United States can and will maintain its influence and power either promptly or reluctantly and in a sustained or an episodic way (e.g., Steinbruner 1998). Following through on this logic, hegemonic optimists and pessimists tend to take a jaundiced view of the chances that others will step up and play a significantly larger giving role absent continuing American leadership.

Generally optimistic and pessimistic views can be also found in the state-decline literature. We discuss the various strands here without fully accepting their common premise that the state has become less powerful and central to world affairs.[5] Its pessimistic variant (e.g., Huntington 1993, 1996; Saideman 1997) emphasizes the potential negative impact of declining state power when it mixes with the rise of ethnonationalist or even transnational ideational forces (such as religious fundamentalism). The emergence of militant non-state-based identities and of exclusive communities in the wake of the state's decline amount to an increase in the numbers and capabilities of those opposed to prevailing regularities in international affairs and of those committed to notions of progress that run counter to those held by most international actors. What for most is progress is for them regression, and vice versa.

At best, such exclusivist emerging actors are too caught up in their "struggle" and too suspicious to find established patterns of international giving and getting attractive approaches to global interaction. At worst, they are drawn to rather than repelled by prospects for increased international turbulence and gain satisfaction from imposing harms on a broadly defined global other. Letting those with such agendas run free creates reduced global regularity and accelerated regression in basic conditions.

Two responses may follow from awareness of such developments by a majority of international affairs actors who see no attractive or readily available replacement for the current order. The first and preferred response focuses on eliminating the emerging, hostile actors by dedicating resources to that purpose and, in effect, defining success in that effort as necessary to save global regularity and block regression. This approach poses the possibility of a major, long-lasting diversion of resources from other aspects of global pro-regularity and pro-progress giving.[6] The second response is a milder one featuring a combination of quarantine and containment augmented by tardy, limited, and inconclusive interventions. Examples are international responses to conflicts in Bosnia, Chechnya, Kosovo, Somalia, and Rwanda. Diversion, then, might only be small and temporary.

The optimistic variant of state decline is most fully represented by what we might term socioeconomic globalists, who see an emerging world unified not so much by any political entity as by the new information and communications technology, economic and cultural globalization, and widely held beliefs about a shared human fate, moral obligation, and desired international role (e.g., Friedman 2000; Fukuyama 1992; Rosecrance 1999). At an extreme, those who see states as in absolute decline take heart from the passage of such inherently selfish and predatory actors and the rise of ones that are apparently less so. These globalist voices are in essence a cheering section for what Rosenau (1997) has called "fragmegration."

A more prevalent line of reasoning argues that decline will push states to act better in terms of international giving and getting. Increased benevolence will be a consequence of growing interdependency, of relevance surmounting distance, and of emerging transnational communities (e.g., Biersteker 1992; Held 1996; Zacher 1992). National governments—and the international organizations they form and control—are pushed to pursue opportunities to counter threats to global order and progress. Part of that effort involves transnational arrangements for collective action that broaden the range of issues under consideration and deepen policy capacity for collective action. Rather than doing less by way of international giving, most actors are propelled to do more because doing so is associated with getting more materially and psychically. Parenthetically, whatever its initial reluctance, the United States will also eventually do so, even if for no other reason than to preserve a domestically attractive self-image. In this brighter vision for the future, international giving will flourish because of the rewards flowing from globalized economic activity and transnational political cooperation. These incentives amount to a political version of an "invisible hand" promoting order and progress in global affairs.

To us, that is essentially the message of neoliberal institutionalism, with its emphases on diffused international norms and increasingly institutionalized cooperation (e.g., Keohane 1984; Krasner 1983; L. L. Martin 1999). It also fits with prospects held out by proponents of the "democratic peace" (e.g., Russett 1993) and even with arguments that hold out the essential requirement of multilateralism in a post-9/11 world (Nye 2002). Eventually, if slowly, these processes will reach out from the core of the current global system to include its periphery (e.g., Goldgeier and McFaul 1992). These views also have substantial connections to muted optimism.

WHERE MUTED OPTIMISM DIFFERS

All of the themes discussed thus far are espoused by highly respected advocates, all of whom can reasonably cite historical examples in support of their approaches and can pose conceivable futures based on current trajectories. Yet we find none of these arguments sufficiently compelling for us to join a particular bandwagon. We prefer muted optimism, which differs most distinctly from hegemonic pessimism, hard (as distinct from soft) hegemonic optimism, state-decline pessimism, and the profragmentation state-decline optimists. Our approach most resembles soft hegemonic optimism and the state-decline optimists, who suggest improved national government performance featuring cooperation in international institutions. Yet we differ with those perspectives in ways that we think have importance for international policies affecting regularity and progress. We ask readers to defer judgment on whether muted optimism is more or less flawed than the other alternatives until after considering the arguments and evidence in the following chapters.

We depart from hegemonic pessimism in several major respects. First, we do not accept that a dominant power is necessarily more forthcoming, effective, and efficient than others in what it does for global regularity and progress or even against regression. Such a power might be characterized this way at some points in time, but the longer-term reality of the country's role is not a given in global practice. If the hegemon has been less than outstanding in pro-regularity and pro-progress terms, its decline is not such a disaster. Second, we think the timelines of hegemonic decline are long rather than short and are subject to some slowing down depending on domestic characteristics and the preferences of foreigners. Accordingly, there can be time and opportunity to compensate for adverse implications of the decline. There also may be domestic and international coalitions willing and able to act in ways that defer the decline. Third, we see no general reason to expect that the first wave of hegemonic retrenchment will directly reduce the great power's pro-regularity, pro-progress, or antiregression activities. Prevailing domestic coalitions may see such activities as at the core of their self-conception and try hard to preserve them as a form of national self-realization. Further, support from foreigners to defer decline may seem to hinge on continuing and even upgrading such activities. That possibility is more likely if the foreigners that matter value relevant giving highly (our first reservation). Defensive internationalism can be part of a great-power program to defer decline. Sustained or increased giving can also occur by others with separate motives of national self-realization and defensive internationalism.

Hard hegemonic optimism exaggerates what a dominant power can and will do for global order and progress and the stemming of regression. On the "what is possible" side of measuring hegemonic power and influence, great powers have always had limited capabilities. In the past, these restrictions often resulted from less than universal spatial reach. Now, the limitations may be more a result of limited abilities to prevent damage to the homeland and of foreign presence in a world of international flows. On the "hegemonic will" side of the equation, there is no inherent reason to believe that the hegemon's most empowered domestic coalition will choose to allocate resources—as hard hegemonic optimists would prefer—to an effective level of quantity or quality. Whether the hegemon does so depends on prevailing domestic factors working for or against such priorities. Indeed, the more confident the adherents of guaranteed allocation are in a great power, the more vulnerable they may make it to ineffectiveness, inefficiency, and shortfalls in its allocations. What the great power holds as most conducive to global order and progress may amount to counterproductive arrogance. Arrogance can spiral upward under several conceivable conditions. When foreigners are apparently bandwagoning with great-power prescriptions for regularity and progress, such apparent popularity may forestall desirable questioning. When foreigners are increasingly leaving regularity and progress to such a great power, it may see little reason to give them voice in determining what advances order and progress. When foreigners mobilize against the hegemon's chosen forms of activism, they can be seen as "part of the problem, not the solution" and thus as sources of support for regression and disorder to be treated accordingly. Given limitations of capability and will, any of these factors can have adverse implications for future giving to global order and progress and countering regression. The rejoinder that unipolar supremacy leads others to increase their giving probably applies more to situations where it seems possible that doing so will prevent the unfettered supremacy that hard hegemonic optimists recommend.

State-decline pessimists may seem to have been prophetic in the aftermath of 9/11. We accept their view of the growing emergence of exclusivist, anti-prevailing-regularity actors. We differ with them on the magnitude of that trend relative to countervailing ones. In other words, the correct answer is inherently an empirical matter. We see substantial evidence suggesting in global aggregate the growth of identities, interests, and clubs favoring pro-regularity activity and sharing in large measure a progress agenda. If we are right, the rise of negatively disposed actors will, if anything, generate an increase in giving by the positively disposed to contain and even roll back unwanted disorder and threats of regression. That tendency is, however, fragile. National societies and the international clubs they populate are prone to differ on the likely benefits for global order and progress from an exclusivist attack on the threatening actors with coercion as its largest element. They are likely to differ on the fit between such a response and their views of their own rights, obligations, and interests. Thus, like economic sanctions, the prospects for collective implementation of long duration are weak. Further, in the contemporary world, an exclusivist attack response will almost inherently have or be interpreted to involve "collateral damage"—that is, harm to those beyond the immediate targets. This increases the chances that the attack will enlarge as much as or more than it reduces the segment of international actors who see global regularity as leading to regression for them. We think these limitations and possible negative consequences will be recognized by enough international actors to make sole reliance on an eradication solution at most sustainable for only a short while.

Our case against state-decline fragmentation optimists is simple. We doubt that smaller communities will in general do more to assist outsiders than will larger ones. We do not believe that small communities have inherently less predatory inclinations than large ones. The small are not reliably more beautiful than the large in international affairs. The additional effort or transaction costs of reaching pro-regularity and pro-progress commitments to giving from a much larger number of actors may well go up faster than the resources to be gained. That is, there may be a classic diminishing marginal returns scenario as the number of actors in a collective grows while the resources of each additional member get smaller.

In contrast to the perspectives just discussed, muted optimism relies heavily on major elements of soft hegemonic and of neoliberal state-decline optimism. With respect to the former, we agree on the importance of soft assets and thus soft giving. Their direct importance in shaping global regularity and progressive or regressive conditions accompanies their indirect importance in affecting holdings and uses of military or hard assets. We agree that ideas and the interest-institution formations they encourage matter. We also agree that institutions conducive to pro-regularity and pro-progressive activity have taken root and are spreading in much of the world. While the United States is the origin and diffuser of some of those institutions, we see other sources (in particular other Organization for Economic Cooperation and Development members) as substantially important as well. We note that on occasion, American soft exports have done less than advance the results one associates with a benign great power. We also are not confident that the United States will devote its soft power assets on a sustained and systematic basis to pro-regularity, pro-progress, and counterregression policy directions in a timely and productive way. We think that the United States will use some assets in such ways some of the time and that prevailing domestic beliefs (self-realization) provide politicians with disincentives to act otherwise.

Consequently, we accept the importance of some of the mechanisms that soft hegemonic optimism emphasizes but do not associate them completely with the United States. Thus, we see prospects for international giving as dependent on the push provided by other actors based on their domestic politics and culture and their club memberships and agendas. At some times for some issues, those other actors will do more than the United States. At other times, for other issues, other actors will do less, even relative to their resources. After all, the others also exhibit some domestic parochialism and surely have fewer resources relative to those of the United States. On some but hardly all occasions, each possibility can provide the United States with defensively international incentives to increase or at least maintain its giving. Thus, we are on balance optimistic, but we think more mutedly so than soft hegemonic optimists. Policy talk does not always translate into policy action.

Overwhelming evidence generally supports the arguments advanced by neoliberal state-decline optimists that national governments will try to engage in more collective action to advance regularity and progress and counter regression. Such evidence also backs up the institutionalist positions that states will increasingly form clubs and that, again in general, those clubs will foster more of the sorts of activities central to our project than would otherwise be the case. The optimistic part of our perspective embodies these views. The muted part sees their operational activities as a long, hard slog marked by episodic defections.

Collective action and club broadening and deepening have and will be marked by lengthy pauses at particular stages, occasional reversions to unilateralism, incomplete issue and case coverage, constrained resources (financial, legal, and organizational), and limited international participation. Steps taken will often come only after substantial disorder and regression have occurred. When taken, they will on some salient occasions be viewed as having disappointing results, fostering internationally unfair distributions, and setting dubious precedents for regularity and progress. Those evaluations and their associated reservations about collective action and club evolution will sometimes be widely shared in the global system. At other times, evaluations will differ both inside and outside the Organization for Economic Cooperation and Development. The result will be at least a pause in the momentum envisioned by institutional optimists. Moreover, some parties previously committed to a particular collective and club action program will cancel or qualify their commitment. The strength of these possible developments will largely be determined within national political systems, systems with less than identical prevailing beliefs about appropriate world roles and diverse self-interest priorities. Differences in those nationally focused beliefs are likely to yield differences about policy-specific preferences for collective action and club programs. A world of limited clubs does not always set a firm floor under levels of international giving. Such a world does not guarantee that giving will be larger, fairer, faster, or more efficient. And such clubs do not always bring with them a simpler and more timely decision-making process for what should be done and who should pay for it.

In short, muted optimism is neither euphoric nor despairing about pro-regularity and pro-progress giving. This perspective recognizes the imperfections and pitfalls of an incrementalist, nonlinear view while believing that part of a loaf is better than none. It does expect creeping, erratic increases in the quantity of pro-progress and pro-regularity giving, including decreases in generating bads for others. The part of the loaf will grow over time. Our expectations can fairly be characterized as "ameliorist," with no illusions that amelioration provides the amount and immediacy of the global outcomes we would like to see.

Our preferred outcomes include justice on a global scale. We have often been asked how our muted optimism perspective relates to global justice. We answer that muted optimism stops short of directly addressing justice questions, with their host of weighing and enforcing issues regarding obligations, rights, responsibilities, and authoritative institutions. We of course recognize that some forms of movement toward global regularity (order) and progress and some doctrines proposed for each raise serious justice issues. For us, muted optimism with its emphasis on regularity versus chaos and progress in basic conditions of life versus deficits in them deals with some preconditions conducive to reaching justice goals. Giving as explored in the subsequent chapters deals with efforts to more fully achieve those several preconditions. Doing so, as we have already suggested and will amplify later, may have that and other motivations. We make no claim that regularity and progress as we stipulate them amount to the necessary and sufficient conditions for global justice. Our premise instead is that on balance and over time, a higher degree of achievement of each (not just order) provides a more fertile ground for global justice than would their opposites or than would taking them to be so assured that further giving is not needed.

2 CLUBS, IDENTITIES, AND INSTITUTIONS
A Tale of Overlapping Interests

Theoretical parsimony is always desirable though rarely achievable. That is certainly true for our approach to understanding the prospects for contributions to global order and progress in recent and coming years. We think the answer lies in the interplay between two sets of factors, and we thus turn away from single-lens parsimony. The first set involves the degree and content of overlapping interests embodied in state membership and behavior in international clubs. The second set features beliefs about the identities, rights, obligations, and interests ingrained or changing in states' domestic political cultures. Taken together, they yield for us a world that varies from issue to issue and over time in the degree that actors have discrete, overlapping, or sometimes identical incentives and disincentives to contribute to global order and progress.

Since many of the world's ills are concentrated in the global South, we are particularly interested in activities that largely affect that zone and hold promise for improving order and accelerating progress there. At the same time, those especially well resourced to undertake pertinent activities are often in the global North. Thus, cooperation and even contribution competition between the nations in the Organization for Economic Cooperation and Development (OECD) on activities assisting the global South must also be understood. We do not deny the importance of structural power in the international system, but we choose to focus on a period where it has been roughly constant—the years after the decline of U.S.-USSR bipolarity dating from the mid-1980s. We believe that the systemic structure that began to form at about that time will be with us for one or more decades to come.

Club theory provides our starting point. Our interest in it is the theoretical origin of the work presented in this book. It has become the conceptual spine that links and combines elements from several other bodies of theory, most notably identity-focused constructivism and institutionally and normatively focused multilateral liberalism and neoliberalism. The resulting synthesis enables us to take advantage of rational choice perspectives without being confined by presumptively neat and clear preference orderings and artificially parsimonious formal models. In our view, treating rational choice constructs along the lines laid out throughout this chapter takes into account many of the criticisms leveled against that frame in recent years (Cohn 1999; Green and Shapiro 1994). We believe this synthesis takes advantage of complementary insights about international cooperation in several bodies of theory in ways foregone by more purist and single minded advocates of each particular approach.

The price paid for this eclecticism is a sort of fuzziness or messiness relative to single-lens purists. Whether that price is worth paying is a judgment we ask readers to defer until after considering the arguments and evidence laid out in this and the following empirical chapters. For now, we suggest only that our attempts at synthesis are a useful way to deal with difficulties of explanation and anticipation regarding international cooperation and contributions to global order and progress. The fashionable single-lens approaches seen throughout contemporary international relations theorizing and policy analysis downplay the complexity of our subject and have elements of determinism about them that tend to emphasize only one or another narrow band of scenarios and determinants for the future of international relations.[1]

In effect, we think it makes sense to think in terms that span and relate both sides of what March and Olson (1998, 954) have called two "great divides." The first is between those who see actions as driven by a logic of anticipated consequences and prior preferences and those who see action as being spurred by a logic of appropriateness and a sense of identity. The second is between those who see history as efficient in the sense that it follows a course leading to a unique equilibrium dictated by exogenously determined interests, identities, and resources and those who instead see history as inefficient, following a meandering, path-dependent course distinguished by multiple equilibria and endogenous transformation of interests, identities, and resources. In trying to span the first divide, we echo the call of Finnemore and Sikkink (1998) to focus on connections between norms and rationality rather than by opposing the two. In trying to span the second divide, we focus on the multiple possibilities for what actions will be taken and on who will take them and when, either to cope with a given international state of affairs or to modify it. Those possibilities follow from the interpreted logic of international structures, the shocks from and interpretation of dramatic events, and campaigns by state and nonstate actors to change or preserve what have been held to be "givens" about global order, progress, and justice.

We agree with the classic realists, such as Morgenthau, that states pursue interests and wrestle with their multiple priorities—in particular, priorities for relative or absolute gains. We think, however, that such a position provides little in the way of explanation, anticipation, or prescription unless we can grasp the determinants of those judgments. As Keohane (2001, 8) puts it, "Understanding beliefs is not opposed to understanding interests. On the contrary, interests are incomprehensible without an awareness of the beliefs that lie behind them." More speculatively, we reason that the two sets of factors we choose to emphasize provide a conceptual basis for the feasibility and likelihood of contributions to global order and progress to an increasing degree in the contemporary world. This is not to say that the record of contributions will be unmarked by partial policy reversals, standstills, rationing, and selective applications but rather that contributions will increase over time, albeit unevenly. Later chapters in this volume address the extent to which our conjectures on that score are or are not supported by recent history for the range of beliefs and behaviors we examine.

PURE, IMPURE, AND CLUB GOODS: VARIATIONS ON THE PUBLIC GOODS THEME

Public goods theory is an umbrella category used to refer to one set of rational choice theories of political decisions about allocation problems. It is understandably convenient to lump discussions of club goods, impure public goods, and pure public goods into a single public goods theory treatment. We think such de facto theoretical homogenization is unhelpful, and we choose to follow recent writings that emphasize distinctions within the public goods framework with respect to products (the goods themselves or outcomes such as peace), their production (activities resulting in the goods, such as peacekeeping), and contributions to each (such as peacekeeping finances and personnel) (Kaul, Grunberg, and Stern 1999).

The familiar pure public goods conception provides a point of departure. By definition, pure public goods are nonrival and nonexcludable. Nonrivalry means that consumption of a public good by one actor does not diminish the amount of the good available for consumption by others. National defense is a common illustration. Ostensibly, one citizen can consume the national defense good without reducing the amount of that good available for consumption by other citizens. Nonexcludability refers to the inability of producers of a public good to exclude from consumption those not paying for it or otherwise contributing to its production. Once it is provided for one member of an unorganized or organized universe of consumers, it inherently is made available to all. That is, it becomes a collective good where membership in the collective does not require contributing to provision of the good. For example, even if a citizen pays little or no taxes, he or she cannot be denied the benefits national defense expenditure provides as long as his or her residency (or possibly incarceration for tax evasion) is within the boundaries of the defended state.

The pure public goods notion can be extended to apply in terms of nonrivalry and nonexcludability to pure public bads. That is, once such bads are produced, exposure to them (consumption) may not appreciably reduce the amount available to which others may be exposed (the nonrival condition). They are nonexcludable in that once they are produced, even those who did not contribute to that production cannot be excluded from its consequences. Environmental degradation is one of the primary examples put forth as an illustration of the creation of public bads within particular policy spaces. As the label implies, global warming affects the global policy space, while localized pollutants do not. Some types of goods and of bads can be produced at each of several levels of governance (local, national, regional, and international) (Cook and Sachs 1999). We are interested in goods where production and consumption take place in more than one country—international and sometimes even global public goods and bads.

Pure public goods and bads carry with them pernicious incentives for collective well-being. For the former, these take the form of the familiar free-rider problem as laid out in Mancur Olson's classic work, *The Logic of Collective Action* (1965). Given nonrivalry and nonexcludability, members of a consumer collective have reason to ride for free on the public goods production others supply. The strong version of the free-rider problem expects that no one in the collective will contribute to the production of the public good—all making the same free-rider calculation—so that there is no provision. A weaker version holds that some contributions will be made, but they will be far from enough for a desirable level of production. In strong and weaker versions, undersupply of contributions and thus public good provision will be a chronic problem. Some members may not contribute at all, and others will contribute less than their fair share, all the while assuming that someone else will fill the gap. The traditional fair-share yardstick is one of relative ability to contribute to provision. Given the origins of the theory in economics, ability is usually treated as a function of economic resources (relative to gross domestic product or gross national product).

For public bads, the incentives are pernicious for contributions that would restrain their production and thus limit growth in or even reduce their supply. The negative incentives can feature the direct and the opportunity costs contributions would involve. The result will be at least suboptimal levels of restraint or reduction, and perhaps none at all. Again, the fair-share notion invokes economic ability, if only in relation to that share of bads an actor has been providing or is willing to help to reduce. For public bads, oversupply is the chronic problem. Contributions to ameliorate the bad will be so small as to allow excessive production and thus excessive provision.

Olson did, however, leave a theoretical escape hatch. It involves the possible existence of privileged groups—that is, some subset of actors who have the will and resource capacity to provide a public good or reduce a public bad even if others behave in more opportunistic fashion. In its most extreme form, a single actor perceives so attractive a benefit-to-cost ratio for consuming the good or avoiding the bad that the actor takes on the whole burden involved. That possibility—some might say necessity—underlies hegemonic-stability interpretations of international affairs during and since the Cold War era (Gilpin 1981; Mearsheimer 1993). A privileged actor contributes disproportionately either on its own or by forming a group of associated supporters and followers. If the capacity or will of such an actor and group shrinks or evaporates, contributions will decline in aggregate. Changed circumstances can lead such an actor or group to recalculate its benefit-to-cost ratio with a less conducive result for provision, assuming no substitute steps forward. The consequence will be a cut in contributions toward provision of public goods and a weakening in restraints on production of public bads. As Nye (2001, 95) puts it, "If the largest beneficiary of a public good (such as international order) does not take the lead toward its maintenance, nobody else will." Others, however, argue that hegemonic decline in effect cuts the benefits from free riding and increases the likelihood of collective action by forcing states to cooperate to achieve favorable outcomes (Snidal 1985).

The previous reasoning is, of course, relevant only to conduct in international affairs within prevailing conceptions of the public goods or bads supply chain—that is, what are public goods and bads, efficient and effective means of increasing or reducing their production, and conducive contributions to those ends.[2] Conceptions on those matters may never be a matter of global consensus, and the degree of consensus and the prevailing conception among subsets of actors in international affairs can change with knowledge and circumstances. Further, the participants in international affairs may or may not see themselves as members of the privileged group and change their evaluation of membership for themselves in that respect. Variety and volatility can also mark current members' judgments about the appropriateness of membership for others already in the group and those outside of it who seek membership. Even with global consensus on the public goods and bads supply chain and stable appraisals of membership value, the nonrival and nonexcludable conditions must be met within the privileged group for the inferred consequences to appear in practice.

All of these requirements pose serious application problems for the pure variant of public goods theory and suggest that we need to look elsewhere for theoretical guidance about international cooperation and contributions. The general reasons for this position and how we choose to act on it are discussed in the remainder of this chapter. Subsequent and more empirical chapters demonstrate that our reservations are warranted at least in the context of the four substantive policy areas we examine.

In international reality, many matters that are reputedly public goods and are discussed in those terms exhibit some rivalry in consumption or excludability from consumption or provide "joint products" (i.e., both private [national] goods for the contributors and producers and public goods for them as a whole and for others) (Sandler 1999). All of these possibilities have substantial "impurities" in public goods terms. If consumption of the goods involves rivalry without exclusion, a consequence may be actions increasing public bads, such as deterioration of air or ocean quality. Such goods, with their resulting crowding, congestion, or exhaustion, have been addressed under the concept of common pool resources (Gardner, Ostrom, and Walker 1990; Ostrom, Gardner, and Walker 1994). They are prone to be limited in provision, because the incentives are even weaker than for pure public goods (Aggarwal and Dupont 1999).

Still other goods have little or only partial rivalry but a substantial degree of excludability, at least potentially.[3] Their consumption may be controlled by limited membership clubs, domestic or international. Often called club goods, the supply chain incentives for club members are stronger than for pure public goods, pure public bads, or common pool resources.[4] These incentives are especially weak for those outside of the relevant club, unless they are associated with future membership. For example, security alliances or economic integration areas are selective about membership and can exclude outsiders from some of the public goods available to members. They also can take in new members, as with G-7, North Atlantic Treaty Organization (NATO), or European Union enlargement. In such situations, current members are in part wagering on what will be the net effect of adding new members on the public goods and bads supply chain. If candidates see the benefits of future membership and its probability as sufficiently large, they have incentives to make contributions to goods production or to bads reduction as a strategy to gain admission.

Such clubs are increasingly common features of the international landscape. Some of the goods they provide are at most public only within the club and are sometimes called "patented goods" (Aggarwal 1996). By extension, one can also conceive of club bads, where the suppliers can exclude themselves from consumption but others cannot. For those, supplier amelioration incentives are especially weak but are especially strong for the nonmember consumers to coalesce to seek more restraint in supplier behavior. Yet other club contributions to the supply chains can have "adoption spillovers"—that is, have weaker excludability characteristics. In those cases with less than full excludability, increased provision of a club good can reach at least some nonmembers. Indeed, in some instances, such prospective spillovers may come to the club and not just from it. Relevant nonmembers, as contributors or producers of public goods or ameliorators of public bads, may offer prospects encouraging members of a small privileged club not so much to disband as to seek to create larger, overlapping clubs (e.g., a G-10 or a G-22 as a complement to the G-7 or, after adding Russia, G-8).

Finally, joint products may well offer stronger incentives for contributions than do products that are more purely public for the world at large or even for all members of a club. Because of the joint public and private good produced in these instances, self-interest (in the form of pursuing jointly produced private goods) can then stimulate contributions advancing collective interest—that is, a collective engine powered by selfishness. Other things being equal, the prospects for supply activity (contributions and production) are greater for club goods and joint product goods than for pure public goods and common pool resources. Similar reasoning applies for incentives to contribute to the amelioration of bads—that is, to containment and reduction of bads exhibiting club and joint properties.

In addition to differences in the characteristics of products with diverse implications for incentives to contribute to production and amelioration, the variety of internationally relevant at least impurely public goods and bads suggests that there is no one single best (efficient and effective) contribution strategy. United Nations Development Program and World Bank publications have come to emphasize three contribution strategies with different degrees of promise for producing enhanced provision of one or another public good or reduced provision of one or another public bad (Kaul, Grunberg, and Stern 1999; World Bank 2001a). The distinctions drawn are between best-shot, weakest-link, and summation approaches to provision. Given the incentives to undercontribute to goods and overcontribute to bads, the strategy choice is an important one.

For best-shot strategies, the efforts of the largest contributor determine the provision outcome. The contributions and production usually center on technical competence and scale economies. Attention then centers on the "biggest guy on the block" in terms of technical competence and the incentives and resources that player provides to technical communities. Relevant examples might include the development of an AIDS vaccine or the food strains for a green revolution. For weakest-link strategies, the situation is the opposite—the efforts of the actor contributing least to good production or to bad amelioration determine the outcome. There usually are very large negative externalities whose reduction hinges on modifying or eliminating the behavior of the weakest-link actor. Examples here might be states with lax controls over stocks whose diffusion would foster proliferation of weapons of mass destruction or failed states whose territories provide sanctuaries and operating bases for international terrorists. For summation approaches, production and provision are determined by the total contributions made. Examples might include reducing greenhouse gases, stabilizing emerging market financial systems, or achieving food abundance.

Each type of strategy presents unique collective action problems. Best-shot contributions and production improve provision outcomes only with appropriate use by consumers other than their contributors or producers (Jayaraman and Kanbur 1999). Weakest-link approaches can lead other international actors to "limit their contributions to that of the weakest member because anything above that may well prove to be wasted" (Kaul, Grunberg, and Stern 1999, 487). Summation raises the free-rider problem in obvious ways and is closest to the classic pure public goods theory formulation.

The distinctions between various types of pure and impure public goods, bads, and strategies clearly pose complex analytic issues about what has and will be done for global order and progress. Many combinations and permutations are possible, and which ones are operating in international affairs is often contested or uncertain. Yet it is clear that rather than an international system primarily characterized by purely public provision, we face an international system where many goods and bads are significantly rival or excludable or both but are not completely and permanently so. The incentives for free riding and underprovision are usually present to some degree but not with the strength posited in Olson's original conception.⁵ Yet it also is the case that what international actors actually do and have done about the goods and bads supply chains often defies readily consensual, transparent, and obvious classification as one or another type of public good or bad.

If we are reasonably on the mark with these judgments, the implications of public goods theory for global order and progress are not as bleak as the initial conception suggests but rather are contingent on a variety of factors to be discussed later—particularly beliefs within societies and international club and institution formation. As a transition to a direct discussion of those matters, we suggest five aspects of current and likely international reality that argue against the most bleak supply chain expectations.

First, in many areas of international policy, the production of public goods (and their variants) is the unintended result of the production of private goods or reduction of private bads. In addition, private goods are many times the by-product of the production of public goods and reduction of public bads. The result of this joint production of public and private goods can be the creation of incentives that increase likelihood of provision of impure public goods and reduction of impure public bads. The private goods element brings to bear a degree of motivation that might otherwise be lacking.⁶ This is most obviously true within clubs.⁷ As we will see in chapter 6, contributions (monetary and human) to peacekeeping operations are at least partly motivated by the monies paid to participants. For many developing world contributors, the payment per soldier is higher than the marginal cost for the country involved. Thus, the public good of peacekeeping is partly motivated by the private good of financial benefit.

Second, conditions central to a prisoner's dilemma choice situation are often avoidable. The traditional pure public goods construct resembles a prisoner's dilemma game where the two players are destined to arrive at a suboptimal outcome (Hardin 1982). That outcome follows from the structure of payoffs in the game and the inability of the players to communicate to develop over time the coordination and trust to give them confidence that better outcomes are within their individual and collective reach. Having that ability in a world of extended, multiround play improves the chances for cooperation; thus, a more rewarding result is possible, even when the structure of payoffs is unchanged from the classic prisoner's dilemma construct (Axelrod 1984). We do not contend that the contemporary world manifests the ideal communication between all parties, the clarity in message transmission and reception, and the full transparency that help to reduce the risks of cooperation and to build a foundation of trust. We do suggest that a variety of social and technological developments have moved and continue to move us toward those conditions. Of course, one can also readily conceive of international affairs situations where the structure of payoffs does not resemble that of prisoner's dilemma games, whatever the degree of communication and iteration (Aggarwal and Dupont 1999).

Third, if we start from the assumption that a world of egoistic actors provides an insufficient ability to cooperate, we unrealistically slight the effects of commonly held values, goals, and senses of affiliation within a growing population of clubs and the emergence of relatively if incompletely inclusive collectives. Commonly held values and goals, ceteris paribus, may increase the estimated benefits associated with contributions to public goods provision and public bads reduction and may even decrease estimates of costs.

Lumsdaine's (1993) work on foreign aid programs of advanced industrialized societies since World War II provides a relevant example. He demonstrates an emerging sense of collective interest in provision to such programs and a coherence in them that simple unilateral values and goals would not produce. More generally, Nau (1990), Nye (1990), and Ikenberry and Kupchan (1990) have emphasized the degree to which the values of American hegemonic power became internalized in many other actors in the system during the Cold War era (and, we would add, since then). The collection of essays on security communities in Adler and Barnett (1998) lends credence to this argument even beyond the narrow impact of American values and hegemony.

Fourth, unlike the initial public goods discussions, the reality of international affairs usually places considerations of provision of any one good or reduction of any one bad in a context of provision and reduction issues about others. Growing interdependence between actors and between issues provides a context rich in possibilities for trading across actors and issue-relevant contributions toward the production of public and private goods and reduction of public and private bads, in contrast to a setting demanding "case-by-case bilateral reciprocity" (Ruggie 1996, 20). The possibilities for "bargaining linkages" and "package deals" and the joint products associated with them make for far more complex and on occasion far more robust incentives than the initial pure public goods construct envisions (Aggarwal 1998).

Those incentive structures may be more conducive to contributions with public-goods-providing and public-bads-reducing elements when we also recognize that actors differ in the efficiency and ease with which they can make different sorts of contributions. That is, there may well be significant opportunities for efficiency gains when actors specialize in the production of some public goods and reduction of some public bads (Boyer 1993). With multiple goods and bads placed on the bargaining table, division of labor becomes a possibility at least sometimes substantially competitive with free riding.

Beyond purely economic efficiency gains, there are possibilities to take advantage of differential political costs and gains. The financial price of a contribution surely is not the only price associated with it. Consider the costs associated with breaking away from policy habits and the institutional structures embodying them or the difficulties of securing internal consent within a potential contributor. For example, American political leaders for the last half century have found it easier in terms of public support and opposition to contribute to order and progress in military ways rather than in foreign economic aid ways. Japanese political leaders have faced the opposite situation. For reasons discussed later, making public goods contributions of a particular kind may even provide private benefits to the sponsoring set of officeholders. In short, near-simultaneous consideration of multiple types of provision and reduction by multiple actors offers opportunities to realize efficiency gains and exploit policy inclinations beyond those available in a simpler policy setting.

Fifth, unlike most of the club goods writing, a single club often exists not in isolation but rather in a state of interaction and overlap with other current or potential clubs. This sort of complex interdependence is at least as fundamental to our understanding of contemporary international relations as is egoistic anarchy (Milner 1991). The choices any one actor or club of actors makes are conditioned and constrained by the actions taken and anticipated on the part of others in a world of linked issues and clubs. Those others, in addition to clubs, include independent states, statehood movements, and private and third-sector (i.e., nongovernmental organization) actors. Each of them can take steps to form their own clubs, join existing ones, and stimulate existing clubs and their members to form new collectives or add missions and members to established collectives.

Whatever one's evaluation of the positive and negative consequences, globalization processes will, if anything, increase the prevalence of these phenomena, albeit in a nonlinear and less than universal fashion. Yet all five aspects involve factors outside the main focus of public goods theory. They hinge on matters of interpretation and estimation and thus on normative and pragmatic beliefs and ideas about the roles in, contents of, and prospects for the supply chains discussed previously. Some of those beliefs and ideas concern the merits and demerits and capabilities and limitations of international clubs and institutions (formalized clubs). They also involve the actual functioning of those multilateral arrangements.

BRINGING IN BELIEFS ABOUT SELF, OTHERS, AND INSTRUMENTS

Public goods theory, at root an economic theory of behavior, assumes that decisions about contributions to provide impure public goods and reduce bads follow from rational calculations similar to those made by participants in markets. That leaves to be understood the sources of the utilities and the judgments that lead to conclusions that one or another level and mix of contributions will produce the desired result at an acceptable level of risk. We think those sources to an important extent lie in beliefs within national societies of three kinds. Put in rational choice terms, on what will possible contributors draw to arrive at contribution preferences?

- Understandings of how best to achieve desired outcomes at an acceptable level of risk, taking into account limited resources and information. These understandings are largely based on beliefs (norms and ideas) that lead to categorizing outcomes, production processes, and contributions in terms of the types of public goods and bads and strategies introduced earlier. Relevant beliefs include cause-and-effect opinions about how the world works with respect to connections between contribution, production, and provision for the outcome under consideration.
- Normative justifications (rights and obligations) for making contributions with more or less of a private element to provision of a recognized public good or amelioration of a recognized public bad.
- Images about ties of shared identity, affinity, and interest with particular foreigners (e.g., along national, ethnic, racial, religious, or class lines) and with multilateral arrangements.

By giving these matters importance, we are in effect saying that the application of public goods thinking will provide more insight into concrete international affairs situations if we integrate it with what is now commonly termed a constructivist perspective (Wendt 1994, 1999).

That integration does not require assuming that any single construction is always superior in terms of stimulating contributions to goods provision or bads reduction. A broad collective interest construction, compared to a narrow self-interest one, will not necessarily yield greater contributions to global order and progress (cf. Wendt 1994, 386). That is partly because of the pro-contribution consequences that can result from joint product and club goods constructions. In part, it is because the collective interest construction does not inherently make for a wise choice or mix among the best-shot, weakest-link, and summation strategies. Nor is it clear that all collective interest constructions inherently feature what are from an outside perspective public goods and bads or embody an accurate grasp of who is appropriately in the collective.

Finally, some constructions of self-interest can generate substantial contributions to goods provision or at least bads amelioration. Actors centered on self-interest may do that if and when such contributions are seen as the road to self-interest realization—toward what they think they ought to be and want to be. For example, suppose we accept the mainstream economic view that international economic opening (with proper safeguards for orderly conduct) will contribute to an impurely public good of absolute economic gains. Shulman (2000) has shown that on occasion, intense nationalists (in Quebec, India, Ukraine) can push hard for such opening based on their self-interest priorities. Even more striking is the case of the quite expensive nineteenth-century British efforts to end slavery. Those efforts were pursued by domestic noncosmopolitans with little or no transnational interaction and a "parochial and religious imperative to reform their domestic society" (Kaufmann and Pape 1999, 632). Politicians signed onto this policy emphasis because they believed it advantageous to their quest to gain and hold high office (a distinctly private good).

Accordingly, we need to attend to a self-centered facet of identity formation—the preferred construction of national and group self-appraisal. Actors in international affairs (states, substates, nonstates, or trans-states) bring to situations standards of judgment about what is right and wrong, good and evil on their part. When situations are processed in terms of those standards, contributing acts—both of commission and omission—are scored as ethically appropriate and warranted or as their more troubling opposites.

Strong and prominent convictions about entitlements, rights, and obligations can provide strong incentives for at least impurely public-goods-producing and bads-reducing actions without having to get into arguments about the merits and feasibility of degrees of rivalry and excludability. Playing a consciously positive role in our supply chains need not be a central motivation to have at least the positive effects of adoption spillovers. There often are domestically well established and salient self-conceptions of proper role in international goods provision and bads amelioration. Some may be "moral rules" and others "taken-for-granted scripts," perhaps originally formulated as "utilitarian conventions" (Spruyt 2000, 67–70). Those, too, can short-circuit contribution and provision arguments. Such rules, scripts, and conventions tend to set the odds favorably for accepting evolving international norms and commitments that seem to fit well and for rejecting ones that clash. Nations and peoples can differ in the strength and content of such beliefs. That makes them likely to respond differently to newly proposed (or specified) norms and commitments with regard to participation in goods and bads supply chains. Whether or not they are lodged in a construct emphasizing collective interests, the content of salient normative and utilitarian principles (how we should behave and what behavior is effective) matters. In other words, such principles, "when violated, engender regret or a feeling that the deviation or violation requires justification" (Cortell and Davis 2000, 69). Thus, the advocates of deviation or violation face a special burden of justification and "must try to show that the facts are not as they seem to be; or that the rule, properly interpreted, does not cover the conduct in question; or that some other matter excuses nonperformance" (Chayes and Chayes 1995, 119, quoted in Cortell and Davis 2000, 69). Our premise is that prominent, widely held principles of appropriate national conduct are a nontrivial part of domestic politics and that politicians prefer to avoid the additional work and risks involved in departing from such principles.

Of course, the standards embodied in self-conceptions will differ across actors, given their varied histories, cultures, ideologies, theologies, and material situations. Actors should then differ in their proclivity to play particular roles with particular intensities in the supply chains for public goods provision and bads reduction (controlling for their national resources). A ledger drawn in these terms should show somewhat predictable leaders, laggards, sluggards, and abstainers. Keeping such ledgers over time could tell us where particular actors stand relative to others and could identify graduates into or dropouts from the more contributing categories.

While we do not accept the universal superiority of a collective compared to a "self" construction of interests, we surely agree that anteing up for collective action is more likely when it involves cooperation with others viewed as having identical or at least compatible interests. It is less likely and surely takes more selling domestically with others thought to have competitive or, even worse, antagonistic interests. For any particular collective action situation, we think the parties and their domestic constituents tend to apply a set of preconceived judgments about the others in relation to themselves and about others' character or reputation (behavioral tendencies). These amount to opinions about shared identity and affinity and about the likelihood of reciprocity or appreciation versus exploitation. Constructions emphasizing the presence of shared identity and affinity and the likelihood of reciprocity and appreciation ("fair" responses) make public goods provision and bads reduction seem likely to be a positive-sum game with the associated contribution incentives. Their opposites make it seem more of a zero-sum game prone to reneging, deception, defection, and waste.

Discussion of some extreme shared-identity possibilities can help make the link to public—particularly club—goods theory. Suppose actors adhere to a unique and distinct *I* identity and view all others as total outsiders (*They*). Such actors will see little in the way of common interests (i.e., recognize few goods and bads as publicly relevant even in club terms) and have little motivation to contribute to such public goods and bads except on the basis of humanitarian or other self-realization norms. Private goods and bads will dominate allocation decisions. Nonrivalry seems a fantasy and excludability a virtue. In a state-centric world with such an identity formation, states would see anything that redounds to the benefit of other states as at worst a loss and at best a distraction to be kept as temporary and cheap as possible. Cooperation tends to be criticized as a utopian delusion, although parallel action where each party pursues private benefits may not be.

Consider the other extreme. The prevailing identity construction of the world has only a homogenized *We* from which the *I* is indistinguishable and the *They* is an empty set. Stylized this way, there is a warrant for uniform treatment of individuals, groups, and organizations in the *We* regardless of nationality or issue. Other things being equal, we would expect an especially high propensity to make contributions and relatively little resistance to doing so. The notion that public goods and bads are inherently in tension with private goods and bads has less credibility. Efforts aimed at helping others reliably accrue benefits also benefit oneself. There is little reason to worry about the relative or absolute size of private goods elements for those in the inclusive collective. Norms of distributional equity become possible, minimizing rivalry and excludability.

Of course, international relations rarely approximates either the extreme of "exclusive nationalisms" or global society (Buzan 1993). Intermediate identity constructions predominate. Many of them involve generalized images of some others as well disposed to *Us* and in a loose sense being "close" to *Us*. In contrast to these affinity judgments are ones of still others as steeped in enmity toward *Us* and at opposite ends of political, cultural, and economic system typologies. The rich set of intermediate possibilities in effect provides a menu from which different selections have been and are being made between issues and situations in terms of *I/We/They* formulations and the assignment of particular others to each of the latter two categories. As new issues or others come onto an actor's international affairs view screen, there may well be a period of controversy and experimentation about shared identity in relation to these new phenomena. We live in such a time of transition and change, where the placement of another nation or nonstate actor between the exclusive and inclusive extremes often is uncertain or controversial.

Part of that uncertainty and controversy involves the character attributed to those we place in *We* or *They* categories and its immutability. After all, we know that national populations differ in the extent that fellow citizens are thought to be trustworthy or tricky, likely to reciprocate assistance or not, having or not having "some special commitment to one another and some special sense of their common life" (Walzer 1983, 61–62, quoted in Blaney and Inayatullah 2000, 51). Negative characterizations raise the possibility that contributions to the goods-providing and bads-reducing supply chains will be exploited by those others sooner or later, directly or indirectly. Positive characterizations dampen such concerns. Put differently, the expected value in private, club, and public terms of cooperation will be expected to be higher with others thought to have affinity and good character than with those profiled more negatively.

Further, all the elements of the public-goods-providing and bads-reducing supply chains involve some shadow of the future. Very little is truly instantaneous in international relations, and that surely applies to cooperation to provide public goods and reduce public bads. Such cooperation may take a long time since it often involves compounded bargaining games, diverse national resource allocation processes, and complex and extended implementation to get from a decision to contribute to outcomes of provision or amelioration. Accordingly, important aspects of judgments about shared identity, affinity, and character involve estimates of momentum and reversibility. These may deal with aggregate directions—for an increasing or decreasing share of international issues and actors is the prevailing identity formation increasingly a matter of *We* relative to *I* and *They*? For more specific crucial or pivotal actors (a possibly quite different subset for best-shot, weakest-link, and summation strategies), such estimates include trends in character and notions of *I/We/They*. Implications can differ positively or negatively from the status quo about prospects for goods provision and bads reduction. Our reasoning is that actors will tend to reduce the public element in their commitments and contributions or to increasingly surround it with conditions when they perceive that shared identity with other contributors or consumers is declining or their reputations have become less positive. The consequences will be domestic pressures among potential and current contributors to do less, not more, and to avoid contribution commitments whose private and public payoffs will come, if at all, only in quite distant and unlikely futures.

Much of the reasoning in the previous paragraphs suggest that crucial beliefs can make for a pro-cyclical bias in contributions to provision and amelioration. Strong and growing *We* constructions and attributions of more positive reputations soften a trade-off between public and private elements and lessen fears of free riding and exploitation of contributors. Conversely, perceived weakening of common identities and more salient attributions of bad character have the opposite effects. The first set can encourage a contribution bandwagon, and the second can encourage a rush for exits from our supply chains. The irony, of course, is that global order and progress may most need initiatives to enhance public goods provision and bads amelioration when a global shared fate is denied and actors of bad character abound.

BELIEFS, CLUBS, AND CONSEQUENCES

Self-realization and identity beliefs exhibit a relationship with international clubs that cuts two ways. We turn first to the ways that identity formations affect club behavior. The relationship in the other direction will be discussed later.

With respect to self-concepts, the inclination to form or join international clubs gains strength as internally held standards call for membership in collectives rather then a stand-alone posture and for participation in shaping some aspects of the world rather than in just adapting to it. A national self-concept emphasizing exemplary public goods provision to a world broader than the club has particularly interesting implications. Such members are likely to push their clubs to contribute more to goods provision and bads amelioration and indeed to make such activities an increasingly major part of the club agenda. Self-concepts of a contrasting nature have very different implications. They make for a reluctance to form or join clubs, an emphasis on retained autonomy, and even condemnation of public element provision (as perceived in an image of the United States as "Uncle Sucker" rather than "Uncle Sam"). They create an emphasis on private elements for the ambivalent member, foster rivalry within the club, and encourage an agenda focusing on highly excludable goods.

The relational aspects of identity have clear relevance for the creation of clubs, as nascent clubs require at a minimum some *We* notions of shared interests, even if primarily defined in a negative way against some notion of a *They*. The more comprehensive the *We* in issue terms, the broader the issue coverage members are willing to grant to a club. The more robust the momentum toward a *We* identity among club members and would-be members, the more likely are future expansions of club authority and membership, a declining propensity to free ride, and an increase in public element provision. At any given level of cooperation in a club, a low degree of reversibility reduces tendencies both to curtail club functioning and resources and to push the club to concentrate more on goods and bads private to a particular member.

Once again, international reality leads us to complicate our reasoning. In the real world of global politics, actors possess not one identity but rather a portfolio of identities. They usually have not put all their eggs in one identity basket, and their portfolio is not constant in its mix of holdings. This portfolio of identities notion suggests that actors in international affairs are not inclined to a uniform stance toward all conceivable multilateral arrangements but instead vary their stances about appropriate fellow members, authorities, conditionalities, and contributions—and even about whether to have a particular multilateral arrangement at all. The portfolio metaphor also suggests an inclination to pursue membership in more than one club. Actors may seek to have a portfolio of clubs in which the holdings differ in important respects. The result is likely to be patterns of affiliation that create a "layering and overlapping" of club memberships and identities (Ferguson and Mansbach 1996). A synoptic view would then see layers of collectives for particular issue baskets and regions in international affairs and substantially (but not universally) overlapping memberships across those issue and region segments. The layering and overlapping may include private- and third-sector parties as well as state and substate actors.

Clubs for us are venues for engaging in at least superficial multilateralism with a substantially voluntary element. International institutions are the subset of clubs that show some degree of formal organization. We see a continuum where the informal pole is marked only by the presence of some shared identity or attributed affinity.[8] There is a degree of confidence that the members will not engage in viciously predatory behavior toward each other (beggar thy fellow member). As a result, the notion of a public good or bad among them is credible. Those characteristics are most present for the functional issues and geographic spaces covered by the club. Coverage may be narrow or quite encompassing. As one moves from the informal pole to the other extreme of formal government, organization increases in terms of an institution's powers and abilities to grant or withhold membership, extract and allocate resources, secure and distribute information, and make rules and apply sanctions for noncompliance. Multilateral arrangements, like national public sectors, are supposed to fulfill roles that markets can fill only poorly, including remedying undersupply of public goods and oversupply of public bads for their citizens. Contemporary international affairs is, of course, amply populated along the intervening sections of the club continuum, arrangements labeled as dialogues, meetings, forums, groups, communities, organizations, and concerts.

In international affairs, movement along the continuum from informal affinity to formal government usually involves shifting the locus of authority for engaging in collective action away from states to multilateral arrangements. Indicators of movement toward the government pole also include a shift away from consensus to more majoritarian voting rules and from uniform shares of representation to ones more correlated with differentials in some resource variable (e.g., wealth, arms, population, oil reserves).

As such institutions become more like governments, one expectation is that contributions to provision of club goods and reduction of club bads will increase (Abbott and Snidal 1998; L. L. Martin 1992a, b, 1999; Snidal 1985), ostensibly because the prospects for nonrival and nonexcludable consumption are increased for those under the umbrella of the institutions and are decreased for those outside it. In addition, the appropriateness of free riding among members of the collective is reduced, and the sanctions to punish free riding increase in strength. Desires for increased cooperation and contributions then suggest creation of institutions more like governments. If preferences on normative or pragmatic grounds are for global provision versus more exclusive provision, there should be a preference for more universal rather than regionally limited institutions, a United Nations or a World Trade Organization over a European Union, NATO, or North American Free Trade Area. Multilateral institutionalism would then offer a significant portion of the solution to the undersupply and overconsumption problems introduced earlier.

Yet possibilities of greater contributions and cooperation are by no means guaranteed for several reasons. First, these institutional developments are likely to be far from linear and accelerating in their movement toward the government pole (Bobrow and Kudrle 1999). As with national and subnational governments, members may not view these institutions as having a reasonable degree of publicness in benefit-to-cost terms. The result may be powerful subcoalitions of members to arrest the movement of the institution toward the government pole. Multilateral institutions are often crafted mostly with an eye toward securing private goods and avoiding private bads for their members (e.g., Mattli 1999). Second, the public goods element high on a group's agenda may focus on averting a bad rather than providing a good. International institutions often emerge as a form of bulwark against some fearsome public bad, especially one that remains vivid in memory for many of the actors involved (e.g., war in Europe as a spur to NATO, collapse of the international liberal economy and financial system as a spur to Bretton Woods). The attractions and consequences of a large public element come later and often have to be proven in practice through incremental steps and pauses to ascertain and digest their consequences.

Provision by institutions using their own authorities or those delegated on a case-by-case basis by member states will then rise and decline as those experiences warrant and satisfaction of common values demands. The amount of unmet demands will also depend on the occurrence and clarity of situations that violate common values at least in precedent-setting terms. Rather than embodying a full commitment to collective action (the government pole), contemporary multilateral institutions often tend to present at most a promise to consider such a commitment. The states involved often reserve substantial authority to block particular contributions and retain options to limit and terminate provision as their private interests warrant or the stimulus of a feared public bad fades away. The devices found in most multilateral institutions (such as flexible geometries, concerted unilateral action, "red card" options, and reservations and exceptions) in effect are accommodations to the realities just noted.

Finally, most international institutions are neither fully inclusive or internally egalitarian. Instead they often are "institutions of the privileged, by the privileged, and all too often for the privileged" (Keohane 2001, 7). The result can be a tendency to favor what we have earlier called club goods over more globally public ones. Even within the club, there often is a tendency for one or a few large members to dominate determinations of priority, a sort of minilateralism within multilateralism (Ruggie 1993a, 34). This core group may well tilt policies toward ones that have an especially large private element for those members.

The limitations on global public goods provision and bads amelioration are serious but need to be kept in perspective relative to the possibilities for a world without multilateralism and imperfect international institutions. Minilateralism may be accompanied by greater acceptance of restraint on the pursuit of purely private benefits than would otherwise be the case, so-called self-binding. Breaking restraints and commitments to which the larger member or members previously assented might well entail a reputational loss, a private bad for them (Wallander, Haftendorn, and Keohane 1999). Further, their resistance to committing to contributions to a public element may be lessened by multilateral institutionalism. In a world of states with very asymmetric resources, multilateral institutions can increase the confidence of those with particularly abundant resources that they will not bear the full burden of the public element. Free riding may seem more constrained. If the large compete for influence in the international institution, they may find contributions to enhanced provision of public goods and amelioration of bads useful in gaining the support of smaller members. Excessive demands by larger members for privateness may foster possibilities of an alternative institution without them or the collapse of one in which their political leaders are invested. Such expectations may make enhancing the public element a more privately beneficial choice for them than being stingy about it (e.g., Bobrow 1999a). Even "undemocratic" international institutions may have procedures that enable smaller and weaker members to aggregate their influence and thus hold a stronger bargaining position than would otherwise be the case.[9] For smaller and weaker members, emphasizing and making public element contributions central to an institution's program may safeguard against or at least dilute the imposition of larger members' more privately inclined preferences.

Limited membership institutions, as contrasted with relatively universal membership ones, do not necessarily perform less well in terms of public goods provision and bads amelioration across their membership set or even for a broader slice of the world. The key lies in the values and commitments in place with regard to the public element. This is partly a "coalition of the willing" argument. Suppose at any given time the membership has already made a commitment to provide a given level of public goods on some timetable to those in it and for the broader world. Admission of others committed to less of a public element within the membership set would have adverse rather than positive effects from a public goods/bads view. Admission of others who might drain institutional resources would also have adverse implications. Suppose instead that the carrot of admission can be used to motivate the candidates to contribute to a higher level of public goods provision or bads amelioration. The consequences of admission after qualification would then be positive (Downs, Rocke, and Barsoom 1998).

Limited membership would seem a warranted concern from our perspective only if one or both of two conditions are met. First, a limited membership institution acts in ways that punish outsiders more committed to public goods provision or bads amelioration than current members. Second, the qualifications for membership give candidates incentives to reduce their public goods provision and increase their public-bads-producing contributions.

Many of the advantages and limitations of the range of multilateral arrangements obviously differ from case to case. What seems to be a common implication of the institutions is the way they can change domestic and bilateral interests and incentives among their members, even if only in limited ways. The existence of multilateral institutions and their associated public outputs allows for the possibilities of reneging and defection, but they also make promise breaking more noticeable globally. Existence also works to create and nourish stakeholders in member nations and a central cadre committed to collective action and a discourse featuring the publicness of goods and bads. Existence does offer the possibility of greater recognition of joint products and support for contributions to these products from government and nongovernment actors who want the private benefits involved. Previous actions by a multilateral entity can even strengthen the domestic influence of those who get private benefits from the joint products versus those who do not (e.g., firms and workers for whom trade is their lifeblood versus those who are import competing) (Mansfield and Milner 1997). And the entity itself and participation in it can become an important part of members' identity. Thus, a positive view of multilateral arrangements does not require believing that they force states to do what they would rather not do. It suffices to believe that such multilateralism induces citizens and leaders to see greater emphasis on the public element in impurely public goods provision and bads reduction as conducive to achieving their goals.

The chances for more or for less positive consequences from the existence of international clubs follow in part from the overlapping and nested nature of membership and issue coverage that mark contemporary multilateral arrangements. Many actors hold overlapping but to a varying extent different portfolios of memberships. Those portfolios are expanding for most states, firms, and third-sector organizations for all the reasons associated with a tide of internationalization and globalization (Solingen 1998). We think that expansion and its drivers have substantial implications for the magnitudes and degrees of purity of public goods provision and public bads reduction.

Examples of the overlapping and cross-cutting nature of contemporary international institutions appear in table 2.1. The inventory could be expanded at great length, but the examples in it suffice to illustrate our argument. Note the substantial overlaps in membership, particularly of the original G-7 countries. It suggests the possibility of at least some members in each club for whom the goods sought by other clubs are compatible and perhaps the same. Second, it suggests that at least some members of each club recognize that desired gains of private goods and amelioration of private bads cannot be satisfied by any one multilateral arrangement in isolation. Third, it suggests that each arrangement has at least some members whose common values and identity have some basis more fundamental than their memberships in multilateral arrangements. Fourth, each example has added members to its original roster, and several are in the process of further enlargement.[10] That pattern also marks more global arrangements, such as the United Nations and the World Trade Organization. There are two implications conducive to some club expansion. First, at least some possible candidates estimate that there is more in the way of private benefits to be had and attractive club goods to be gained from being inside rather than outside. Second, at least a preponderance

TABLE 2.1. Memberships of Overlapping International Clubs

Group of Eight (8 member states with the European Commission president included in annual meetings)	European Union (25 member states)
Canada, France, Germany, Italy, Japan, United Kingdom, United States, Russia, (European Union)	Austria, Belgium, Czech Republic, Cyprus, Denmark, Estonia, Finland, France, Germany, Greece, Hungary, Ireland, Italy, Latvia, Lithuania, Luxembourg, Malta, Netherlands, Poland, Portugal, Slovakia, Slovenia, Spain, Sweden, United Kingdom
NATO (26 members)	NAFTA (3 member states to date)
Belgium, Bulgaria, Canada, Czech Republic, Denmark, Estonia, France, Germany, Greece, Hungary, Iceland, Italy, Latvia, Lithuania, Luxembourg, Netherlands, Norway, Poland, Portugal, Romania, Slovakia, Slovenia, Spain, Turkey, United Kingdom, United States	Canada, Mexico, United States *Possible expansion to others in Western Hemisphere in near future.*
OECD (30 member states)	APEC (21 member economies with international organization observers)
Australia, Austria, Belgium, Canada, Czech Republic, Denmark, Finland, France, Germany, Greece, Hungary, Iceland, Ireland, Italy, Japan, South Korea, Luxembourg, Mexico, Netherlands, New Zealand, Norway, Poland, Portugal, Slovakia, Spain, Sweden, Switzerland, Turkey, United Kingdom, United States	Australia, Brunei, Canada, Chile, China, Hong Kong, Indonesia, Japan, South Korea, Malaysia, Mexico, New Zealand, Papua New Guinea, Peru, Philippines, Russia, Singapore, Taiwan, Thailand, United States, Vietnam (South Pacific Forum, ASEAN, Pacific Economic Cooperation Council)

Source: Data from various international organization web sites.

Defensive Internationalism

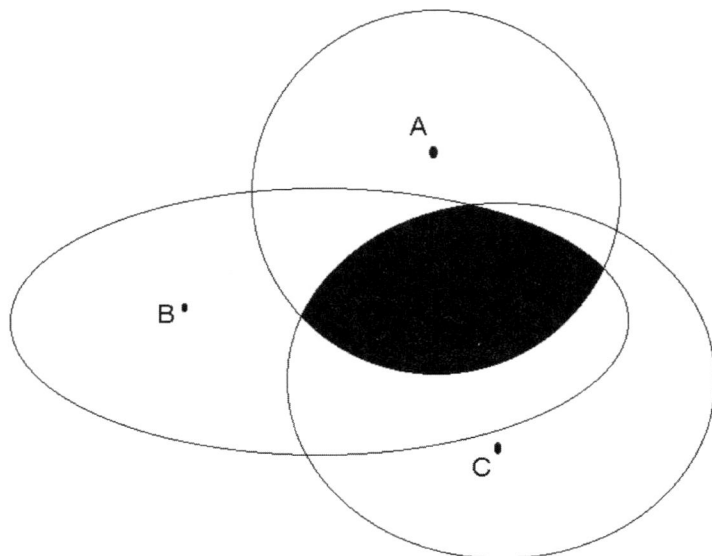

Fig. 2.1. Policy space with significant overlap

of the current members estimate that bringing some others in will have net positive joint product results.

The patterns just discussed do not directly address matters of what issues are covered by one or more multilateral arrangements. To explore that aspect, Venn diagrams of two stylized overlapping institutional arrangements seem helpful. These appear in figures 2.1 and 2.2, where for each of three clubs the point labeled with an A, B, or C represents its preferred international policy outcome.

The desired policy spaces in figure 2.1 overlap to a substantial although not to an ideal extent (the shaded area) indicating a nontrivial potential for cooperative contributions. If the overlapping members also exercise minilateral style control in each club, such contributions are particularly likely. Such a state of affairs supplements the intuitively greater likelihood for cooperation and agreement on what are public goods and bads as issues are located in the common policy space. But what about issues that lie outside the overlapping policy space? As cooperation emerges on issues within the area of overlap, club members have reason to make decisions on other policy issues that will avoid "getting in the way" of collective action on overlap issues. In effect, cooperation on overlap issues may produce a policy environment that reinforces the overlap by bringing outlying policies in line with the club

CLUBS, IDENTITIES, AND INSTITUTIONS

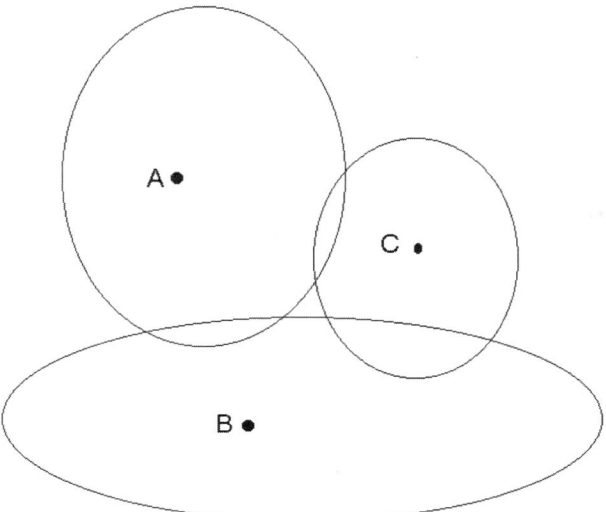

Fig. 2.2. Policy space with no collective overlap

overlap. The primary reason for doing so would be to make sure that outlying policies do not reduce the chances for collective action to get impure public goods provision and bads amelioration on standing club agenda policy issues.

These tendencies and their associated pro-contribution prospects are possible but not necessarily assured. The stylized situation is unrealistically general and static. The overlaps shown may only cover policies for short-lived salient situations rather than general policy goals. That is, their content may emphasize crisis responses (e.g., to an Asian financial collapse, a localized Balkan genocide, or even a 9/11 terrorist incident) rather than a broad and lasting outcome (such as financial stability, human rights, or elimination of terrorism). As the crisis situation loses salience, the policy overlap may then evaporate. After all, the point for the cooperating actors may have been to fix the crisis so that they could turn to other matters or at least to contain the crisis and avoid embarrassment from appearing to ignore it. In such cases, public element contributions may in a variety of ways (e.g., promises to domestic publics, discernible signals to fellow club members) seem to be only temporary expedients. The prospects for broadening and deepening collective action may be weaker than our general interpretation of figure 2.1 has argued.

More fundamentally, impermanence may follow from change from below because of evolving events and issues within the members or from above with external systemic changes. In the former, the conceptions of identities and interests held by national political elites may be caused to change from below by shifts in the views, priorities, and domestic influence of constituents. Overlap will decline if more purely domestic matters move to center stage or if previously central multilateral arrangements and overlapping issues decline in importance before others take their place. The contemporary simultaneous dynamics of state fragmentation and integration foster that possibility (Rosenau 1990).

What if the nature of the international system or conceptions about it are changing in fundamental ways? Then, an existing figure 2.1 pattern has increasingly weak implications for future cooperation and the public element of contributions to our supply chains. Even if the apparent pattern seems to continue—a possibility fostered by residual institutionalization—it may ring hollow. That is, cooperation may continue for a while in a declaratory way, but there will be increased difficulty in securing the contributions required for true collective policy action. The members are simply buying time to figure out an attractive replacement. More radically, a multilateral arrangement may dissolve with a hiatus before some new constellation of beliefs and influence generates different clubs and institutions—or at least ones so altered in membership and interests that the content of preferred outcomes and overlapping policy space change as well.

In periods of substantial domestic and international system change, as in ones of low degrees of interdependence, the lack of overlap shown in figure 2.2 merits consideration. Possibilities for cooperation, agreement on the nature of public goods and bads, consensus on what are key issues, and thus support for the public element of contributions are all severely limited in this world. Relationships between institutions or clubs are likely to be confrontational and difficult. Any successfully negotiated cooperation is likely to be narrow, shallow, and fragile. It will tend to be rationalized as a simple, non-precedent-setting, time-limited, and second-best adaptation to pressing but passing circumstances. Instead of a tendency to pull other issues into a cooperative space, there will be a tendency to pull issues out of that space.

It is not hard to find in current and earlier international affairs evidence that fits with figures 2.1 and 2.2. Each configuration and its implications are central, respectively, to well-established neoliberal and offensive realist views of international cooperation. There is, however, a third school with more qualified views: defensive internationalism.[11] In that framing of international relations, either figure 2.1 or figure 2.2 configurations can occur and flourish. There are, however, more possibilities for the figure 2.1 patterns and dynamics when the focus is on public or club bads amelioration rather than goods. In other words, clubs and the actors that form them focus primarily on avoiding lose-lose situations. Pure public bads in global or club terms pose precisely such situations.

INTERPRETING AND EXPLORING THE THREE SCHOOLS AND THEIR CONTRIBUTION PROSPECTS

The three schools (offensive realist, neoliberal institutionalist, and defensive internationalist) pervade discussions of international policy and, perhaps with different labels, have done so for a very long time. Each has a different vision of the prospects for global order and progress. Each tends to favor and oppose particular lines of conduct with respect to making the world "the best it can be." We think that the alternatives the three schools provide rest in large measure on different views of the sets of considerations discussed in previous sections of this chapter: public and impurely public goods and bads, belief constructions, and multilateral arrangements. These differences crystallize in each school's views about what issues are most important, about what are perceived as commitment problems, and about the chances for robust international commitments. A brief discussion of the schools provides us with a way to integrate the earlier parts of this chapter. Our discussion will, of course, not do justice to the more sophisticated, nuanced voices in each school. Yet that is not all bad. In the hurly-burly of application to policy and public discourse about policy, those voices are usually not the loudest—that is, their interpretations get simplified at best and even dumbed down. Our stylized discussion does suffice to suggest some empirical analyses of beliefs and international policy actions that will help us to understand better the prospects for impurely public contributions by global North clubs to global order and progress of some ultimate benefit to all or part of the global South.

The likelihood of reliable commitments has strong implications for what are warranted bets on international futures by public officials and interested citizens. Judgments about commitment, trust, and risk surely enter into the prospects for the multilateral arrangement configurations illustrated in figures 2.1 and 2.2. The political feasibility of acting in ways that create global commitments by a particular state and the confidence that others will make them are significantly influenced by domestic beliefs about self-realization, identity, and utilitarian effectiveness. The credibility of solutions to commitment problems has much to do with the likelihood of public goods provision and bads reduction, at least in terms of expectations about whether any of the strategies noted previously (i.e., best shot, weakest link, and summation) have a good chance of working.

Offensive realists tend to reject the possibility of reliable commitments, most certainly between those not bonded into a tight *We*. They are skeptics about the chances that transnational identities will dominate nation-state ones and are convinced that the world centers on competition among states. Their preoccupation is primarily with private goods and bads. While they may at times admit to the merits of concern with impure public goods, they will vigilantly defend a high level of private element as a sine qua non criterion for contributions. Excessive publicness is riskier than excessive privateness. These beliefs lead offensive realists toward the tendency to reject resource allocations to club or global goods production and bads reduction, except in the cases where those allocations seem likely to be cost-effective in enhancing national clout.

Neoliberal institutionalists do not deny the existence of commitment problems but believe that they can be controlled and diminished through multilateral institutionalism. Cooperation breeds cooperation; contributions stimulate complementary contributions. Domestic publics have or can be encouraged to have self-conceptions, identities, and cause-and-effect understandings that lessen tensions between what we have called private and public elements. While neoliberals on occasion recognize the relevance of pure public goods and bads, the more immediate agenda centers on club goods and joint products and on driving up the public element of each. For neoliberals, success in that direction will lead to a virtuous spiral of *We* and multilateral arrangements that enhance broadening and deepening of the collective. Since international affairs do not preclude those developments, it is feasible to enhance the size and share of the public element. Excessive privateness is a riskier course than excessive publicness.

Defensive internationalists take a more qualified and contingent position. The particulars of the issue and the relevant others matter a great deal. Depending on those factors, the greatest potential for risk reduction may lie with offensive realist or with neoliberal prescriptions. For the issue at hand, much depends on the inherent publicness as a practical matter—the chances for rivalry and excludability and what they mean for national absolute and relative gains. Defensive internationalists will be attentive to but will not automatically accept the possibility of a more positive private (national) outcome with contributions to our supply chains than would otherwise be available. That is, defensive internationalists will consider the arguments specified for particular policy areas put forward by proponents from each of the other schools. They will tend to accept collective action when one or a combination of two conditions is present: (1) excludability for their state from a particular class of bads is simply not possible; (2) contributions to goods-providing and bads-reducing supply chains can in principle reduce the harms others will otherwise impose on the contributor. Both conditions center on threat-reduction prospects.

Once defensive internationalists are convinced that one or both of the conditions applies, the size and nature of the favored contributions to supply chains depend on the persuasiveness of technical, evidential arguments that have two strands. The first involves the extent that relevant threats are serious and increasing. The second centers on evaluations of whether the proposed contributions—particularly their public elements—will be effective and efficient in reducing the threats. This suggests an openness to weighing the issue-specific merits of the production strategies introduced earlier (i.e., best shot, weakest link, and summation). It also suggests considerable concern with the linkages among national contributions, production, and outcomes. Judgments about the extent that those linkages are promising or highly problematic will be affected by general beliefs about the sorts of nonmarket efforts that have desired impacts and by images of others who play key roles in the supply chains. Those images will focus on the other actors' characters and reputations.

We think that defensive internationalists often play crucial swing roles in determining the contributions to our goods providing or bads reducing supply chains made by OECD countries and by the multilateral institutions within which they provide leadership and hold veto power. That swing role is, for us, especially likely when aggregate domestic opinion does not pressure politicians to behave in ways that uniformly conform to the offensive realist or neoliberal schools.[12] The implications of our assertions then go against any across-the-board pattern of increase or decrease in contributions to the supply chains for the large number of general goals that have been put forward as international public goods and bads by the United Nations, World Bank, and the Trilateral Commission (Kaul, Grunberg, and Stern 1999, 454–55; World Bank 2001a, 111–30; Trilateral Commission 2001).

We instead expect variation across contributors, issues, and policy instruments and nonlinear shifts in the absolute and relative size of the public element in their contributions. Defensive internationalists in the OECD countries may well differ in judgments about the relevant conditions discussed previously. Even when such differences do not exist, successful influence attempts will tend to be couched in ways that fit with nationally prevailing beliefs of the kinds discussed earlier or modified in the policy process to do so. Some of those beliefs are stable, while others change and alter the prospects for particular contribution policies. In addition, defensive internationalists, like all of us, are functioning in a world with changing knowledge. Salient interpreted experience can lead to discouragement or to intensified efforts. Newly salient experiences can also alter priorities among threats and political imperatives to allocate resources to lessen them.

The patterns we expect, with all their lack of uniformity and linearity, will show, however, that the floor under contributions is becoming a higher one—a zone of resistance to reductions. That would mean that intermittent declines never go as far down as historical levels. We expect that this zone of resistance will be rather sturdy for two main reasons. The first, along globalization lines, is that excludability from international bads is less and less possible and is more and more widely recognized as such. That applies across economic, security, and environmental outcomes. We also expect to see a pattern of episodic contribution increases spurred by newly imminent public bads where excludability hopes have taken a hard and dramatic blow. Those increases will also, on occasion, be stimulated by ostensibly new and more promising recipes for providing joint products. Further, the proliferation and enlargement of multilateral arrangements surely increases attention to impure public goods as bargaining foci and provides venues for trading in them.

It remains to be seen to what extent our arguments are compatible with what has, in fact, been happening in international affairs. Consequently, we first must ascertain the prevalence of domestically held beliefs lending themselves to support for or opposition to a state contributing to our international-goods-providing and -bads-reducing supply chains. Of particular importance are beliefs with arguable implications for the size and share of a public element in contributions. Those beliefs suggest more specific expectations of who will contribute more or less to one or another policy attempt to improve international outcomes. Second, those expectations and those suggested by impure public goods/bads thinking then need to be examined in light of actual supply efforts. Given our emphasis on impure public goods (in both their club and joint-product aspects), the issues we examine should have outcomes and contributions that are reasonably held to have some public element. Given our concern with global order and progress, we need to look at issues for contributions having major consequences for goods and bads production in the global South. Given our concern with OECD contributions, we also need to look at issues where there is an available over-time record of OECD contributions. Given our emphasis on multilateral arrangements, we must examine issues where some multilateral involvement has been central to achievement of collective policy goals.

As indicated in chapter 1, we have chosen four international policy issues that we think meet our needs—development aid, debt management and relief, peacekeeping, and environmental protection. The appropriateness of each in its public goods aspects, relevance to global order and progress and welfare of the South, importance of contributions by the North, and involvement of multilateral arrangements will be discussed in later chapters. The four issues have figured prominently in discussions about international public goods and bads. They surely are not the only pertinent ones. We do not suggest that any success our approach has in illuminating the four issues proves that it would enlighten us about the issues not considered. Our claim is a much more modest one. If our approach fares well in our four highly relevant issue cases, it should be a serious candidate for application to other international public goods/bads issues—especially those of enormous relevance to the global South and those requiring large, tangible northern contributions.

3 DOMESTIC SUPPORT FOR CONTRIBUTIONS
How Stable and Strong?

Like it or not, national government decisions about programs and budgets remain the central gatekeepers for contributions to global order and progress. Intergovernmental organizations (IGOs), nongovernmental organizations, and other nonstate actors matter but do so primarily insofar as they push states to contribute or as the delivery agents of state contributions. States will continue to provide (or withhold) mandates and resources for international institutions and encourage (or obstruct) contributions by nonstate actors. As a result, we make two primary assumptions: (1) state decisions are affected by domestic demand for, opposition to, and permissiveness about international contributions; and (2) public opinion provides one indication of current and prospective domestic demand, permission, and opposition to such policies. Accordingly, crude maps of public opinion across potential contributor states and over time help clarify the growth, stasis, or decline of global and club norms because they inform us about the diversity and modification of domestically supported policy options. They help us explore the possibility that domestic norms regarding international contributions have become or are becoming legitimate international norms as they relate to identity and club membership. Examining public opinion on identity and international policy can illuminate the extent that multilateralism is based not only on utilitarian self-interest but also on more globalized value structures that make contributions the right thing to do (Finnemore 1996, 338–39).[1]

The conceptual arguments in chapters 1 and 2 lead us to examine public opinion constructions of three general kinds. The first deals with identities and focuses on the diffusion of identity across conceptions of *I*, *We*, and *They* discussed in chapter 2. Pertinent *We* possibilities range from narrow, nationalistic sentiment about one's own country to broader sentiments embracing a club of countries or even global humanity. Those who see a broader common identity expect several consequences. Incentives for making contributions to international affairs will tend to exceed disincentives for international contributions. The distinction between private (i.e., national) and public goods will erode as the relevant consumer groups for these goods become broader. Finally, the attractiveness of collective action will grow in tandem with a willingness to rely on multilateralism, clubs, and international institutions as contribution makers and managers.

Based partly on recent strands in the international relations literature (e.g., Adler and Barnett 1998; Cronin 1999; Lapid 1995), the previous chapter emphasized the importance of the absolute and relative presence of world, club, national, group, and other identities for contributions to international projects. We will devote particular attention to clubs and loose groupings, such as "communities," "meetings," "North," "South," "First World," "advanced industrialized countries," "developing countries," and "democracies." We explore them in three distinct ways: (1) common club membership; (2) positive evaluations (i.e., conceptions that focus on such ideas as *friendly, trustworthy, ally, close*) that are suggestive of their being part of a *We* group; and (3) negative evaluations (i.e., *unfriendly, untrustworthy, distant, threat, hostile, enemy*) that suggest that countries are outside a club or loose grouping—that is, a *They*.

Social-psychological research has established that trust makes more likely cooperation to deal with collective action problems (Dawes 1980). Along lines emphasized in diplomatic studies and game theory, we think that trust in others and in collective institutions, while not a necessary condition, is conducive to international cooperation (Adler and Barnett 1998; Deutsch et al., 1957; Kydd 2000; Lieberman 1967; Maoz and Felsenthal 1987).[2] We think a sense of attachment to a broader entity than one's country is also worth examining to understand better the ties that may bind states together in common policy directions. Accordingly, we will try to gauge the presence or absence of "imagined communities" (Anderson 1991) and in-group as contrasted with out-group framings (A. Cohen 1985; Delanty 1995; Eisenstadt and Giesen 1995; Triandafylliou 1998; Waever 1996). Whether or not identity constructions precede recognition of shared interests of a pragmatic nature, such constructions can provide a context conducive to cooperation in some instances and with some other actors.

The second kind of public opinion construction involves national or club values and roles in the world that bear on what we previously referred to as self-realization. These constructs focus on views of national and club rights, obligations, and priorities thought to be warranted or unwarranted. Prevailing beliefs about these matters carry with them justifications for some contribution postures and place a heavy burden of persuasion on those who would have a state pursue a clashing course of action. If predominant self-conceptions emphasize international contributions and multilateral collective action, the burden of persuasion away from such approaches will fall on those who would avoid or cut contributions and opt for unilateralism. For us, self-conceptions that assume national superiority, reject accommodation to the interests of others, and cling to sovereignty instead place the burden of justification on the advocates of contributions and multilateralism.

The third type of public opinion construction involves appraisals of the costs and benefits of particular types of contributions and of management of international contributions by supranational institutions. Public opinion constructions of this type, like that of the second, relate to defensive internationalism as a motivation for international contributions and multilateral mechanisms. Because defensive internationalism emphasizes the private benefits generated by international contributions, the burden of policy justification rests on contribution advocates to show that a contribution will yield greater benefits than costs. The weighting and indeed categorization of what might be seen as benefits and costs are, of course, affected by identity and self-realization beliefs.

In chapter 2, we suggested that domestic support for contributions and cooperation will be greatest when public opinion manifests broad identities, conducive values and role conceptions, and perceptions of large net benefits from international policy management and contributions to more globalized policy goals. Domestic support will be least under the opposite set of circumstances. Shifts toward or away from elements of policy support can throw light on the presence or absence of internationalist momentum. Long-term stability of such profiles for particular countries leads us to expect continuity and sustainability in their contributions, be they great or small.[3] Public opinion constructions of all three kinds may bolster or counterbalance each other, but we do not view particular content of one sort as a necessary or sufficient condition for the others to have content similarly supportive or resistant to contributions. Indeed, the possibilities of mixed constructions—some supportive, some less so—provide a major part of the foundation for the muted optimist and pessimist positions discussed in chapter 1.

Within data constraints, we will explore aspects of salience, affect and evaluation, and behavioral choice (Sinnott 1996) as they bear on the domestic politics of international cooperation both individually and through interaction. State leaders have strong incentives to deliver international cooperation when the policy domain and cooperating parties are highly salient to the public, when they are associated with strongly positive affective evaluations, and when contributions have a history of being the normal behavior. Leaders have particularly strong disincentives to contribute under the opposite conditions. The grayness of mixed or neutral conditions suggests to us a substantial likelihood that contributions, if any, will be tardy, conditional, and intermittent, although that is better than the pessimists of chapter 1 would expect.

Subsequent sections of this chapter report public opinion constructions of identities, values, and roles and the costs and benefits of collective action with other states or international institutions. Later chapters focusing on foreign aid, United Nations peacekeeping operations, and environmental quality contributions will discuss public opinion specific to those issues.[4]

CAVEATS AND QUALIFICATIONS

Before turning to poll data on our interests, it seems important to clarify our views on the connection between public opinion and foreign policy and to point out some limits on reasonable interpretation of survey results.

Public Opinion and Policy

Long-standing controversy about the public opinion–foreign policy nexus has centered on three main issues: (1) the possible implications of public opinion for policy quality; (2) the nature of public opinion on international matters; and (3) the actual strength of the connection between opinion and policy. Advocates of negative impact (Lippman 1955; Morgenthau 1978) have argued that public opinion produces emotional, erratic, tardy, and ill-informed policy. It poses dangers of "disruption from below" of what would supposedly be rational, consistent, timely, and well-informed international endeavors if only left in elite hands. Others, at least since Lord Bryce, have argued that policy quality is at least as vulnerable to "derailment from above" by an elite whose preoccupations, information, and values are less than optimal (Nimcic 1992).

Much of this dispute rests on differing judgments about the nature of public opinion regarding international affairs. The negative position points to a "lack of intellectual structure and factual content . . . superficial psychic states not anchored in a set of explicit values and means ends calculations or traditional compulsions." This approach was most clearly asserted for the American public by Almond (1950, 69) and has been extended in a more qualified way to the European public by Rattinger (1991). On the more positive side, others view public opinion as stable, coherent, and responsive to information at least in the aggregate (Page and Barabas 2000; Page and Shapiro 1992). A substantial body of work supports that position for the American public (Chanley 1999; O. R. Holsti 1992, 1996; Murray 1996; Wittkopf 1986, 1990), and there are compatible findings for European and Japanese publics (Bobrow 1989; Gabel 1998).

Yet even the more positive position leaves open the question of the significance of public opinion for public policy. Three basic positions on its significance have been advocated (Foyle 1994). Elite control argues that there is little impact prior to decision making followed by intensive elite efforts to manipulate the public to support policies already chosen. The opposite position, public control, views political leaders as following specific policy preferences held by the public. The third and intermediate position views public opinion as a constraint. Public opinion sets the limits of politically serious options, even if it does not determine specific policy choices (Powlick 1991; Risse-Kappen 1992; Russett 1990; Sobel 2001).

Along constraint lines, we support a "permissive consensus" view believing that the behavior of national governments in advanced industrialized democracies is affected, not dictated, by aggregate citizen preferences on international policy issues (Lindberg and Scheingold 1970). Our constraint-oriented view implies that policymakers pay particular attention to the balance of support and opposition for possible contributions. Accordingly, we will make considerable use of net opinion scores focusing on the difference between the more conducive and less conducive public positions. In any event, our position should not be confused with the much bolder, rubber-stamp assertion that politicians simply mimic public pluralities and majorities. Our limited-influence premise (see Eichenberg 1998) gains support from recent observations that foreign policy decision makers take public preferences increasingly into account when making decisions to reject or back off from policies clashing sharply with predominant public opinion (O. R. Holsti 1992, 445–47; Powlick and Katz 1998). Responsiveness to opinion is, if anything, encouraged by the weakening of party loyalty among electorates, the increase in contested elections, divided-government splits in party dominance of national institutions, and a rise in single-issue voting.

Like Oppenheimer (1979) we do not assume that states are utility maximizers in international relations because of the problems of aggregating substate preference levels. Our position requires only a willingness to believe that foreign policy decision makers seek to satisfy a utility function that combines public preferences with personal views on national interests. To contend otherwise is to assert politicians' indifference to the risks of political suicide or of draining, avoidable vulnerabilities subject to exploitation by domestic competitors. Acceptance of the elite-control position leaves unexplained the substantial effort politicians in democratic societies (and most others, for that matter) make to manipulate and condition public opinion to produce support or at least toleration of policy positions.

Skepticism about our position on the stability and coherence of public opinion (e.g., Clark and Dautrich 2000) does not suffice to deprive public opinion of policy relevance but suggests only that politicians have an incentive to hedge their contribution stance in terms of clarity, magnitude, duration, conditionality, and reversibility of commitments. Volatility or finely drawn divisions in public opinion lead us to expect policy elite equivocation and incrementalism about international contributions. Such choices have important rather than trivial implications for international giving.

Another demur relies on evidence that policy elites misperceive public opinion (Kull and Destler 1999). Yet that does not suffice to reject responsiveness to signals from the public but instead identifies only poor signal reception. In our view, such misperception is less likely on matters the public overwhelmingly finds important and salient. Even when substantial distortion occurs, the possibility remains for correction of interpretations and thus the potential to shift political elite calculations about the demand for and resistance to international contributions.

We do not assume that all members of a polity exert equal influence. Elites within a society can provide especially strong incentives to politicians, are more likely to have opinions on a wider range of issues than the general public, and can be more attentive to international issues and pertinent national policies. Congruent elite and general public opinion has particularly strong implications for what makers of foreign policy will and will not do about contributions. When elites have clear predominant views and the general public grants little or no importance to an issue, we expect foreign policy decision makers to lean toward elite positions. If issues are salient to both segments of a population and predominant opinions clash, we expect a tendency toward inconsistent and even contradictory contribution policy moves in an attempt to appease both groups. When available, we will consider both elite and general public opinion.

Declared views in public opinion polls are, of course, not the only measure of public opinion for foreign policy officials. We expect constraints to operate with particular strength when foreign policy officials face mobilized activists whose signals go beyond answers to pollsters. Small activist minorities can have influence far greater than their numbers—for example, the intense opponents of the World Trade Organization (WTO), International Monetary Fund, and World Bank in recent years. For the issues discussed in the later chapters, we will consider self-reported activism when data are available.

Public Opinion Poll Realities

Public opinion polls are themselves constructions reflecting interests and culture, as is the case with most social statistics. Polls seldom if ever provide a full, unbiased opportunity for publics to express all their views on international contributions, regardless of the technical quality of a poll.[5]

Polls are commissioned by interested parties who fund the surveys in an effort to gain some benefit from their results. Polls are designed by experts and organizations who need a continuing flow of commissions based on sponsor satisfaction. What we have in the way of polls is shaped by fundamental inequalities in the capacity to commission them and largely reflects establishment interests, including those of well-heeled minorities. Funding sources for polls are often not reported.

The secondary analyst of polling data needs to be aware of the various benefits polls can provide. One is simply knowledge of public positions. Another is a better basis for policy marketing to the general or attentive publics. A third is to provide ammunition in intraestablishment maneuvering—for example, to provide a basis for arguing the political feasibility of a particular policy position or warning about looming problems of national division and resistance. A fourth is to appear relevant (newsworthy) to what media gatekeepers decide will interest audiences.

Whatever the priority of these benefits for survey sponsors and designers, a key consideration is to limit the risk of results that can harm, embarrass, or weaken the sponsor's desired policy position. One way to minimize that risk is through formal or informal prior screening—for example, Japanese government agencies formally screen questions and response alternatives posed in government-funded polls. Another is to focus exploration of public opinion on an issue and policy alternative dear to sponsors while taking care to avoid undermining the credibility of results. To a substantial extent, credibility depends on questions and response alternatives fitting well with what sponsors, respondents, and audiences conceive to be meaningful and relevant ways to think about a particular polling subject—in our case, international affairs.

In an ideal world of cross-national and longitudinal social science research, we could draw on a warehouse of survey research with the following properties. Polls across Organization for Economic Cooperation and Development (OECD) and developing states would have identical questions offering identical response alternatives repeatedly for more than the past decade. They would be available for elites and general publics. Subjects covered in those polls would systematically have included each of our three categories of opinions (i.e., identities, values and roles, and contribution benefits and costs). Queries would cover salience, affect and evaluation, and a range of behavioral choices. And questions would deal regularly with the four contribution issue areas we have singled out for attention—foreign aid, debt management and relief, United Nations peacekeeping, and environmental quality.

Research reality, however, falls far short of that ideal of data availability. Relevant poll data are largely limited to the advanced industrialized democracies belonging to the OECD, and even for them information is almost nonexistent for debt relief. Question and response wordings are far from uniform, and repetition at regular intervals is more the exception than the rule. With the partial exception of the United States, we lack repeated readings of elite views for most issues. The questions and answers available to us are limited by these factors. Although serious, these data inadequacies do not prohibit us from assembling mosaics (with more than a few missing tiles) of public opinion information about domestic support for some contributions of interest in those states best resourced to make them.

In the rest of this chapter, we use polls conducted by organizations of established technical competence and, unless otherwise noted, drawing on national adult populations. Due caution leads us to pay little attention to exact numerical responses and to small differences in those responses, and thus we do not report sample sizes that would enable calculations about statistically significant differences.[6] For our purposes, the absence of pronounced differences in time and space is as informative as their presence. We have greater confidence in patterns of responses in numerous polls to similar questions with similar response alternatives than in responses to a single query.

We begin the empirical part of this chapter with some broad comparative survey results and then discuss Western Europe, the United States, and Japan in turn. The first set of surveys deals with survey data that readily allow us to compare national publics in terms of breadth of identity, self-realization with respect to claimed superiority and its key contents, acceptance of foreign policy accommodation to the interests of others, and consent to international institutions having enforcement powers. The sections on Western Europe, the United States, and Japan also address many of these considerations but vary in emphasis and completeness because of the survey data available. That state of affairs of course may reflect the differences in sponsor concerns and international affairs cultures referred to earlier. In any event, those sections necessarily involve piecing together fragments of results from numerous polls.

SOME BROAD COMPARATIVE RESULTS

One measure of public support for international cooperation focuses on the primary identity declared by survey respondents. If respondents' identities focus beyond the state, we think that they will be relatively more supportive of policy choices involving cooperation and transnationalism. Geographically broad polling along these lines was conducted in 1990–93 in some forty countries (Inglehart, Basañez, and Moreno 1998). In none of them did more than 22 percent give first place to a "world/continent-subcontinent" identity rather than to a country or locality one. The level of 20 percent was reached only in Brazil, Italy, and Nigeria.[7]

Does the case for muted optimism gain strength if we shift the focus identity to notions of attachment to an institutionalized club, a geographic space, or even positive attitudes toward particular other countries and international institutions? We reason that prevalent attachment or even positive attitudes would be conducive to collective action and suggest at least the emergence of protoclubs. Lack of attachment and negative attitudes toward other international actors would suggest a lack of domestic permissiveness for collective action. Data are far richer on these matters than for direct probes of supranational identity.

Table 3.1 bears on these ideas with results from a twenty-four-country poll conducted in 1995. In all polled countries, publics feel substantially closer to their countries than to a broader space (columns A and B). Yet within that general pattern, there are interesting differences. Broader regional affinities are especially present in Japan, Italy, Spain, Austria, and the countries of Central-East Europe. A sense of superiority to other countries (column C) was especially lacking in both parts of Germany, Italy, the Netherlands, Spain, Sweden, and most of the Central-East European countries. Its opposite, pronounced national superiority, was especially present for the United States, Canada, Aus-

TABLE 3.1. Nationalism and Internationalism (in percentages)

	(A) Net Closeness to Country	(B) Net Closeness to Continent or Subcontinent	(C) Net National Superiority	(D) National Superiority Score	(E) Should Limit Imports	(F) Should Follow Own Interests	(G) IR Institutions Enforcement
United States	62	18	75	4.2	55	16	61
Canada	49	12	68	4.1	19	11	67
Australia	88	−28	79	4.1	67	17	46
New Zealand	87	8	73	4.1	28	26	56
Japan	90	52	79	4.3	−3	−41	61
Philippines	37	−31	41	3.6	49	−3	49
Norway	89	15	59	3.8	10	5	58
West Germany	58	17	−2	3.3	3	−23	79
East Germany	63	18	−3	3.4	36	−33	69
Ireland	85	10	57	3.8	44	40	48
Italy	75	38	1	3.1	39	−17	89
Netherlands	74	11	19	3.4	−14	−15	60
United Kingdom	41	−57	39	3.6	50	28	64
Spain	79	25	0	3.3	66	40	75
Austria	82	37	57	4.0	55	43	63
Sweden	66	−25	27	3.7	18	17	75
Bulgaria	83	74	54	4.1	77	63	56
Czech Republic	83	61	−21	3.1	26	−15	62
Hungary	93	89	−18	3.2	54	12	82
Latvia	73	−30	−11	3.5	62	5	35
Poland	88	41	6	3.7	55	16	72
Slovenia	86	39	−5	3.2	29	−22	75
Slovak Republic	79	63	−24	3.0	32	−36	50
Russia	64	−62	10	4.0	41	37	81

Source: Data from T. W. Smith and Jarkko 1998.

Note: The first question asked, "How close do you feel to your country?" and the second, "How close do you feel to your continent or subcontinent?" For each, entries were calculated by subtracting the sum of not very close and not close at all from the sum of very close and close. The national superiority question asked for agreement or disagreement with the statement that the respondent's country was a "better country than most other countries." The entries are the result when the sum of disagree strongly and disagree is subtracted from that of agree strongly and agree. The net score is the mean response of the national sample where agree strongly receives a score of 5, agree receives a 4, neither agree or disagree a 3, disagree a 2, and disagree strongly a 1. The net percentages for the last three columns were calculated in the same way as for the national superiority question. The statements posed were for imports and following interests with respect to the respondent's country, whether it should (a) "limit the import of foreign products in order to protect its national economy"; (b) "follow its own interests, even if it leads to conflict with other nations." The international institutions questions asked for agreement or disagreement with the statement, "For certain problems, like environmental pollution, international bodies (e.g., UN, EU, WHO) should have the right to enforce solutions."

tralia, New Zealand, Japan, Norway, Ireland, Austria, and Bulgaria.[8] Yet more optimistically in some other responses not shown here, only in Austria did a majority believe that "the world would be a better place if people from other countries were more like the people in my country." Only in Austria, Hungary, the Netherlands, Slovenia, the Philippines, and Spain did majorities deny that there were "some things about my own country today that make me feel ashamed."

Economic nationalism (limiting imports—column E) and, more generally, accepting the risk of international conflicts (column F) probe support for the pursuit of self-interest policies. Low-positive and negative scores imply a relative propensity for international cooperation. On protectionism, that procooperation stance was particularly noticeable in the publics of Canada, Japan, Norway, West Germany, the Netherlands, and Sweden. An anticooperation propensity was most marked in the publics of the United States, Australia, the United Kingdom, Spain, Austria, Bulgaria, Hungary, Latvia, and Poland. As for conflict avoidance, the publics of Japan, Norway, both parts of Germany, Italy, the Netherlands, the Czech Republic, Slovenia, and Slovakia stand out. They provide a contrast to the relative acceptance of the risk of conflict marking the publics of Ireland, Spain, Austria, Bulgaria and Russia. Others, including the United States, have small margins in favor of risking conflict. Yet only a few Eastern European countries found a majority agreeing with the statement that "people should support their country even if the country is in the wrong."

As for transferring elements of sovereignty to international institutions (column G), majorities accepted that position in most of the polled publics. Strong majorities of two-thirds or more were, however, present only in Canada, both parts of Germany, Italy, Spain, Sweden, Hungary, Poland, Slovenia, and Russia.

With regard to international contributions, we in general expect more public support in those countries where we found relatively high feelings of closeness to others beyond the borders, low senses of national superiority, low support for import limitations, low support for risking conflict by asserting interests, and high support for authoritative international institutions. Countries with such a profile on three or more of the indicators were Japan, Italy, Germany, Spain, the Netherlands, Sweden, the Czech Republic, Hungary, Poland, Slovenia, and Slovakia. Canada and Norway came close. We shall return to these initial expectations later.

Publics of some of the countries in table 3.1 were also asked to assess the benefits from their current or potential membership in their relevant regional associations (the European Union [EU] for Europeans,

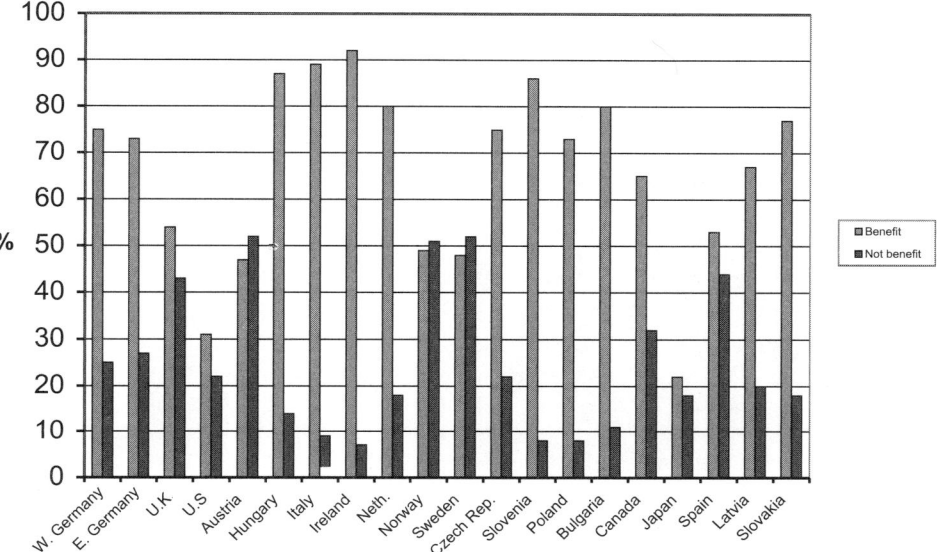

Fig. 3.1. Views of regional clubs: Perception of benefits. (Data from T. W. Smith and Jarkko 1998.)

North American Free Trade Area [NAFTA] for Americans and Canadians; and Asia-Pacific Economic Cooperation [APEC] for the Japanese). As figure 3.1 shows, except for Norway, Sweden and Austria, more of the public sees benefit than the opposite, although a plurality of American and Japanese respondents reserved judgment. Canadians were more prone to see NAFTA as beneficial than were Americans. For a still smaller number of European countries and for Canada and Japan, publics were asked whether their country "should do all it can to unite fully" with the regional association or "do all it can to protect its independence." Results from those publics resembled those in figure 3.1, with the interesting exception of the massive majority for uniting fully in Japan.

Another potential "community" with club good contribution incentives might center on alignment with and followership of the United States. The broad comparative information comes from U.S. government–sponsored polls in 1993 and 1994 (U.S. Information Agency 1995), a Gallup International poll taken shortly after 9/11 (Gallup International 2001), and a Pew Research Center poll taken in the second half of 2002 (Pew Research Center 2002c). In the U.S. Information Agency polls, public samples in forty-four countries and urban or elite

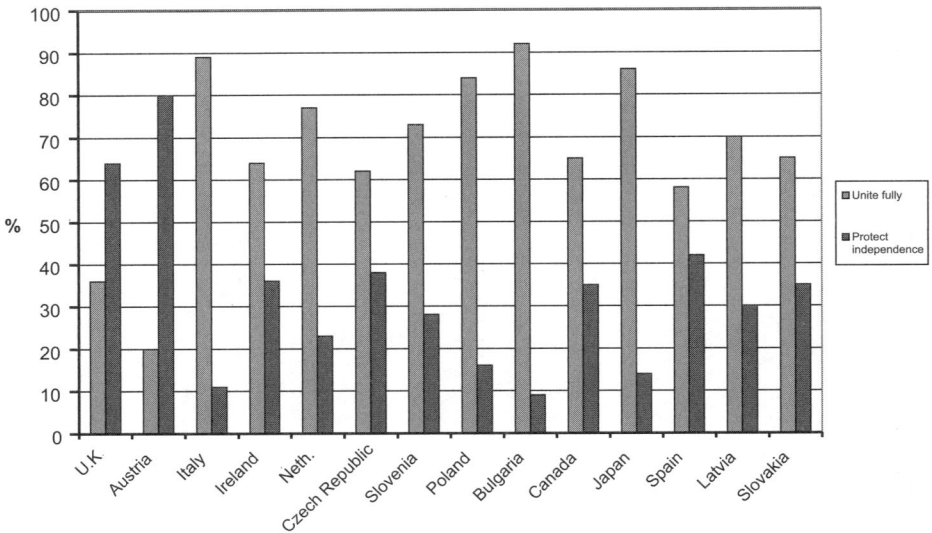

Fig. 3.2. Views of regional clubs: Unity or autonomy? (Data from T. W. Smith and Jarkko 1998.)

samples in thirteen others were asked questions allowing them to express positive or negative opinions of the United States.[9] In the Gallup International poll, public samples in thirty-seven countries were asked about preferences for U.S. policy, its effect on their country, and their country's cooperation with such policy.[10] All the questions were couched in the context of the recent terrorist events. In the Pew poll, public samples were interviewed in forty-four countries about a wide range of international and domestic matters.[11] While not all of the same countries were polled on each occasion, a substantial number were sampled on at least two occasions.[12]

For the most part, the United States received overwhelmingly positive ratings on a general favorability question asked in 1993–94 and 2002, as was also true in 1999–2000 U.S. Information Agency polling. Results in terms of broad bands of public opinion for more specific questions present a more differentiated picture that is more relevant to particular international cooperation policy issues. These findings appear in table 3.2.

In spite of the near universality of generally favorable views of the United States, the numerous entries in the last two columns hardly suggest massive, general, and comprehensive enthusiasm for American international leadership and behavior. The first section, shown in table

TABLE 3.2. Views of the United States (net % bands)

	Positive	Divided	Negative
	A. Treatment of Our Interests, Responsible Foreign Policy		
1994	Italy, Israel, Armenia, Russia	Germany, Georgia, Japan, Korea, Thailand	France, United Kingdom, Spain, Kazakhstan, Ukraine, El Salvador, Panama, Mexico, Peru, Colombia, Chile, Brazil
2001	Italy, Luxembourg, Portugal, United Kingdom, Norway, Czech Republic, Croatia, Estonia, Lithuania, Mexico, Israel, South Africa	Denmark, Finland, Germany, Netherlands, Switzerland, Bosnia, Bulgaria, Romania, Colombia, Ecuador, Zimbabwe	Austria, France, Greece, Spain, Ukraine, Argentina, Peru, Venezuela, India, South Korea, Pakistan
2002	Uzbekistan, Venezuela, Honduras, Guatemala, Peru, Vietnam, Philippines, Nigeria, Ivory Coast, Kenya, Uganda, Angola, South Africa, Mali, Tanzania, Ghana	Germany, United Kingdom, Bolivia, Indonesia, India	Canada, Italy, France, Poland, Ukraine, Czech Republic, Slovak Republic, Russia, Bulgaria, Jordan, Pakistan, Lebanon, Egypt, Turkey, Mexico, Brazil, Argentina, Japan, South Korea, Bangladesh, Senegal
	B. International Role		
Influence over our country (1994)	Romania	Germany, Bulgaria, Poland, Hungary, Czech Republic, Slovak Republic, Estonia, Lithuania, Latvia, Russia, Ukraine	France, United Kingdom, Italy, Spain, Turkey, Croatia, Albania, Macedonia, Israel
Appropriately activist (2002)	Germany, Czech Republic, Slovak Republic, Ukraine, Ivory Coast, Senegal, Philippines	Peru, United Kingdom, Italy, Bulgaria, Poland, Mali, Japan, South Korea, Jordan, Uzbekistan	Canada, Argentina, Bolivia, Brazil, Guatemala, Honduras, Mexico, Venezuela, France, Russia, Angola, Ghana, Kenya, Nigeria, South Africa, Tanzania, Uganda, Bangladesh, India, Indonesia, Vietnam, Egypt, Lebanon, Pakistan, Turkey

(continued)

TABLE 3.2—*Continued*

	Positive	Divided	Negative
Shaper of the rich/poor gap (2002)	Kenya, Nigeria	Ghana, Uganda, Philippines	Canada, Argentina, Bolivia, Brazil, Guatemala, Honduras, Mexico, Peru, Venezuela, United Kingdom, France, Italy, Germany, Bulgaria, Czech Republic, Poland, Russia, Slovak Republic, Ukraine, Angola, Ivory Coast, Mali, Senegal, South Africa, Tanzania, Bangladesh, India, Indonesia, Japan, South Korea, Vietnam, Egypt, Jordan, Lebanon, Pakistan, Turkey, Uzbekistan
Opponent of terrorism (2002)	Canada, Bolivia, Brazil, Guatemala, Honduras, Mexico, Peru, Venezuela, United Kingdom, France, Italy, Germany, Bulgaria, Czech Republic, Poland, Russia, Slovak Republic, Ukraine, Angola, Ghana, Ivory Coast, Kenya, Mali, South Africa, Tanzania, Uganda, India, Japan, Philippines, Vietnam, Uzbekistan		Argentina, Senegal, Bangladesh, Indonesia, South Korea, Egypt, Jordan, Lebanon, Pakistan, Turkey
Military partner against terrorism (2001)	Denmark, France, Germany, Italy, Luxembourg, Netherlands, Portugal, Spain, United Kingdom, Norway, Czech Republic, India, Israel	Bosnia, Lithuania	Austria, Finland, Greece, Switzerland, Bulgaria, Croatia, Estonia, Romania, Ukraine, Argentina, Colombia, Ecuador, Mexico, Panama, Peru, Venezuela, South Korea, Pakistan, South Africa, Zimbabwe

TABLE 3.2—*Continued*

	Positive	Divided	Negative
		C. Soft Power	
Role model to follow (1994)	Germany, Italy, Turkey, Kazakhstan, Uzbekistan, Russia, Israel, Kenya, Nigeria, Cameroon, Ghana, Senegal	Tanzania	United Kingdom
Spread of ideas and customs (2002)	Philippines, Japan, Nigeria, Ivory Coast	Bulgaria, Venezuela, Honduras, Uganda, South Africa, Ghana	Canada, Germany, United Kingdom, Italy, France, Poland, Ukraine, Czech Republic, Slovak Republic, Russia, Guatemala, Peru, Bolivia, Mexico, Brazil, Argentina, Vietnam, Indonesia, India, South Korea, Bangladesh, Kenya, Angola, Mali, Tanzania, Senegal, Uzbekistan, Jordan, Pakistan, Lebanon, Egypt, Turkey
Ideas about democracy (2002)	Canada, Poland, Ukraine, Czech Republic, Slovak Republic, Bulgaria, Venezuela, Honduras, Guatemala, Peru, Vietnam, Philippines, Indonesia, Japan, South Korea, Nigeria, Ivory Coast, Kenya, Uganda, Angola, South Africa, Mali, Tanzania, Ghana, Senegal, Uzbekistan	Germany, United Kingdom, Italy, Mexico, India, Bangladesh, Lebanon	France, Russia, Bolivia, Brazil, Argentina, Jordan, Pakistan, Turkey
Ideas about business practices (2002)	Poland, Ukraine, Slovak Republic, Russia, Bulgaria, Venezuela, Honduras, Guatemala, Peru, Philippines, Indonesia, India, South Korea, Nigeria, Ivory Coast, Kenya, Uganda, South Africa, Tanzania, Ghana, Uzbekistan, Lebanon	United Kingdom, Italy, Czech Republic, Mexico, Vietnam, Japan, Angola, Mali, Senegal, Jordan	Canada, Germany, France, Bolivia, Brazil, Argentina, Bangladesh, Pakistan, Egypt, Turkey

(continued)

TABLE 3.2—*Continued*

	Positive	Divided	Negative
Cultural exporter (1994) Popular culture (2002)	Germany, Italy, Poland, Uzbekistan Canada, Germany, United Kingdom, Italy, France, Poland, Ukraine, Czech Republic, Slovak Republic, Bulgaria, Venezuela, Honduras, Guatemala, Mexico, Brazil, Philippines, Indonesia, Japan, South Korea, China, Nigeria, Ivory Coast, Uganda, Angola, South Africa, Mali, Ghana, Senegal	United Kingdom, Slovak Republic Russia, Peru, Vietnam, Kenya, Tanzania	France, Czech Republic, Jordan, Turkey Bolivia, India, Bangladesh

Source: Data from U.S. Information Agency 1995; Gallup International 2001; Pew Research Center 2003.
Note:
Part A: The 1994 results are responses to "America expects [our nation] to give in to its wishes in matters that concern our two countries" and, if that not asked, to a query about "confidence that the U.S. deals responsibly with world problems [in Russia and the newly independent states], international/regional problems [in the Middle East and North Africa], problems in East Asia, [in East and Southeast Asia]." The 2001 question was, "Some say American foreign policy has contributed to this terrorism against the U.S. Generally do you think American foreign policy has a positive effect on [your country], a negative effect, or no effect." The 2002 opinions were in response to the statement "America expects [our country] to give in to its wishes in matters that concern our two countries." For each, positives are those with a more favorable view of U.S. behavior.
Part B: The 1994 opinions were in response to the statement, "The U.S. has too much influence over [our country]" and, in Russia and the NIS, "over [our country's] domestic affairs." The activism question asked, "In terms of solving world problems, does the U.S. do too much, too little, or the right amount in helping solve world problems?" Too much and too little are treated as negative opinions. The rich/poor gap question asked, "Do U.S. policies increase the gap between rich and poor countries, lessen the gap . . . or . . . have no effect on the gap?" Lessen the gap answers are treated as positive, increase the gap as negatives. The 2002 terrorism question asked if respondents favored or opposed the "U.S.-led efforts to fight terrorism." That in 2001 asked, "Some countries and all NATO member states have agreed to participate in any military action against the terrorists responsible for the [9/11] attacks or against those countries harboring the terrorists. Do you agree or disagree that [your country] should take part in military actions against terrorists with the U.S.?"
Part C: The role model query asked about "U.S. performance providing a good model for other countries to follow." The spread of ideas and customs asked about it being good or bad that "American ideas and customs are spreading here." The democracy and business practices questions asked whether respondents liked or disliked "American ideas," and that on popular culture asked about "American music, movies, and television." The 1994 cultural question asked about agreement or disagreement that "American culture is a threat to [our country's] culture."

3.2, part A, suggests that many—indeed, a growing number of—countries with major roles in international and regional affairs have publics lacking strong majorities convinced that the United States respects their interests or acts responsibly on the world scene. That pattern also holds for views of the U.S. international role, as shown in table 3.2, part B.

Negative judgments are especially prevalent with regard to the U.S. effect on economic inequality. Strikingly more majorities were positive about American leadership against terrorism, even if they were not positive about taking part in relevant U.S. military actions. The judgments about American soft power in table 3.2, part C suggest a complex mixture. On the one hand, most publics were attracted to an American model with respect to domestic politics, business, and popular culture, and in another 2002 question, almost all publics admired American science and technology. On the other hand, many publics predominantly expressed a sense of threat and loss from the international export of such American phenomena.

In public goods language, the implication is that substantial portions of the populations of many countries doubt that American foreign policy and international leadership seeks or results in benefits to them (i.e., provides them with club or public goods). Publics in many countries, including several "close allies," have shown at most a wary albeit continuing willingness to consider cooperation with the United States on a case-by-case basis, even if that cooperation can leave a residue of irritation and suspicion about what cooperation yields. Those views for aggregate national publics coexist with more positive judgments about other aspects of the American way of life but do not seem to transfer to the matters of primary concern to us about international cooperation. Drawing on the 2002 survey, that conclusion does not amount to a belief that the United States is inherently bad. Majorities in most of the polled publics viewed their disagreements as focusing on American policies, not American values. That conclusion also does not amount to support for a military rival to the United States, bringing a possible new era of bipolarity. Majorities in most of the polled publics thought the emergence of such a rival would make the world more rather than less dangerous. With respect to international cooperation, there is, then, not so much a desire to shrink American influence and activity as there is wariness about the policies that the United States seems inclined to pursue and an unwillingness to see them as inherently meritorious in collective interest terms.

A final set of multinational comparative data, again from the 2002 survey, suggests further reasons for that skepticism and doubt as well as a basis for selective cooperation, as table 3.3 demonstrates. The columns in that table are the shares of each national public reportedly experiencing a lack of means to buy food or medical care. The rows report what were seen by those publics as the first or second greatest danger to the world.

When we pay particular attention to what the publics perceived as

TABLE 3.3. Experienced Poverty and Perceived World Dangers, 2002

Greatest World Dangers	65% or More	45%–64%	25%–44%	Less than 25%
Nuclear weapons	Bolivia, Peru, *Angola*, Ghana, Uganda	Brazil, Mexico, **Venezuela**, *Bulgaria*, Senegal, South Africa, Tanzania, **Philippines**, Pakistan, *Turkey*	Argentina, Poland, Bangladesh	United States, United Kingdom, *Italy*, Slovak Republic, Japan, Lebanon
Religious and ethnic hatred	Ghana	Russia, Ivory Coast, **Nigeria**, India, Uzbekistan	Bangladesh, **Indonesia**, **Jordan**	United States, Canada, United Kingdom, France, *Italy*, Germany, Czech Republic, Slovak Republic, Lebanon
Infectious disease/ AIDS	Bolivia, **Peru**, *Angola*, **Ghana**, **Uganda**	*Brazil*, **Guatemala**, **Honduras**, **Mexico**, *Venezuela*, Russia, Ukraine, ***Ivory Coast***, **Kenya**, **Mali**, Nigeria, **Senegal**, **South Africa**, **Tanzania**, Uzbekistan	Vietnam	
Pollution, environment	Bolivia	Guatemala, Honduras, **Ukraine**, Philippines	**China**, *Vietnam*	Canada, Czech Republic, *Japan*, **South Korea**
Rich/poor gap		Bulgaria, **Kenya**, Mali, **India**, Pakistan, **Turkey**	Argentina, Poland, China, Indonesia, Jordan	France, *Germany*, South Korea

Source: Data from Pew Research Center 2002a.
Note: Columns reflect the percentage of respondents in the respective national publics who said that during the past year there were times when they "did not have enough money to buy food" or "to pay for medical and health care." The national percentages responding affirmatively average the responses to each query. Rows reflect the percentage of respondents in the respective national publics selecting that item as the first or second "greatest threat to the world today." When the most prevalent response was a majority it is in italicized bold; when the most prevalent response was not that of a majority it is in bold. When the second-most prevalent response was a majority, it is italicized. When it was not, it appears in roman type. Tied items are reported in the table. The empty cell of diseases on the part of well-off publics precedes SARS. In any event, to the extent that danger follows from poverty and pollution, contributions to alleviate those dangers might mitigate that posed by disease.

the greatest threat and their majority choices, we note several patterns in the data with potential implications for the perceived gains in public goods or reduction of public bads from international contributions. The dangers of disease, pollution, and economic inequality primarily have publics with high rates of experienced poverty; the danger of religious and ethnic hatred has publics with low rates of experienced poverty. Nuclear weapons dangers spread across the levels. Except for infectious diseases, the dangers were salient for at least some of the relatively well off publics and some of the less well off ones. There may well then be the possibility of cooperative contributions across North-South lines by differing de facto coalitions. It is also clear that the publics of the rich OECD states do not have a common view of what are the greatest dangers. That implies that our later chapters will find differences among these countries in contribution propensities. Those chapters directly bear on the rich-poor gap (development assistance and debt relief), pollution and the environment, and violent conflict that can be based along religious or ethnic lines (UN peacekeeping). Several of these issues indirectly bear on the infectious disease problem. The entries also suggest that the U.S. public does not attribute cardinal priority to any of those sorts of contributions relative to that of managing the threats posed by nuclear weapons.

WEST EUROPEANS

The possibility that there exists a European supranational identity has been probed repeatedly for EU member publics, and the results provide a similar message to that seen in earlier tables and figures. Data for the past decade support the conclusion for the 1983–91 period that "it is too soon to speak of the internationalization of identities. For the present, a European identity is a vanguard phenomenon . . . not a real community of belonging of the kind experienced in nation states" (Duchesne and Frognier 1995, 223).

In surveys taken from 1994 to 2002, EU publics were given the opportunity to indicate if they expected to see themselves "in the near future" as "European only."[13] Those opting for a solely European identity consistently reached double digits only for Luxembourg, France, and Belgium; others who reached the 10 percent level did so only in 1994 (Eurobarometer, various issues). The response alternative "predominantly European" (as well as national) was chosen by only slightly larger percentages and showed no general upward trend. These results offer some reason to be pessimistic about EU collective action to provide international contributions.

Relevant identity patterns are more promising for muted optimism if we moderate the criterion to one of multiple, nonexclusive identities. The selection of an identity with at least some European component relative to one of narrow nationality appears in figure 3.3. Data displayed

Defensive Internationalism

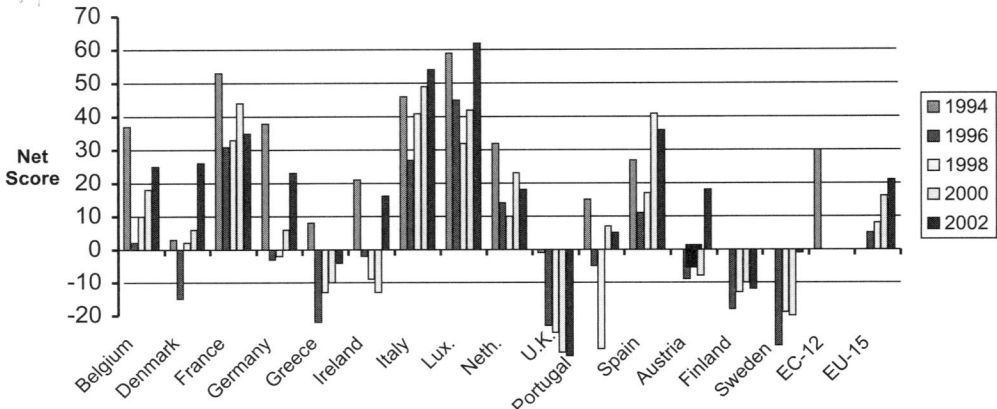

Fig. 3.3. Expected identity: A partly European wave? (Data from Eurobarometer, nos. 42, 43, 46, 47, 49, 50, 52, 53.)

are the sum of the answers with at least some European element minus that of nationality only. Positive numbers indicate the predominance of some degree of supranational identity; negative numbers indicate the predominance of a narrow national identity. The exclusively national identity was substantially greater in only two of the EU-15 in 2002 (the United Kingdom and Finland), with France, Italy, Luxembourg, and Spain showing the greatest overall Europeanness. Aggregate EU public responses at the right side of the figure show modestly "part European" results, which increased from 1996 on but did not achieve the 1994 level of the twelve members of the European Community (EC-12). By this less demanding measure, those who see identity as the driver of contributions would mute but not fully abandon pessimism about the EU as a contributor club.

That position might also cite responses to questions about European citizenship and common cultural identity. Europe as a citizenship choice fared better than the exclusively European identity choice discussed previously. Nonetheless, respondents providing that view were for the most part small minorities with no general pattern of growth over the period 1985–96.[14] In 1996, country citizenship predominated in all of the EU-15 countries. Responses, when queried in 1998 and 1999, were negative for most EU member publics with regard to a European cultural identity, although less so than those for European citizenship or identity in general.[15] As Jan Zielonka (1998, 220) has observed, "Amidst growing uncertainty, complexity and change, Europeans stick to the only solid binding factor: national identity."

DOMESTIC SUPPORT FOR CONTRIBUTIONS

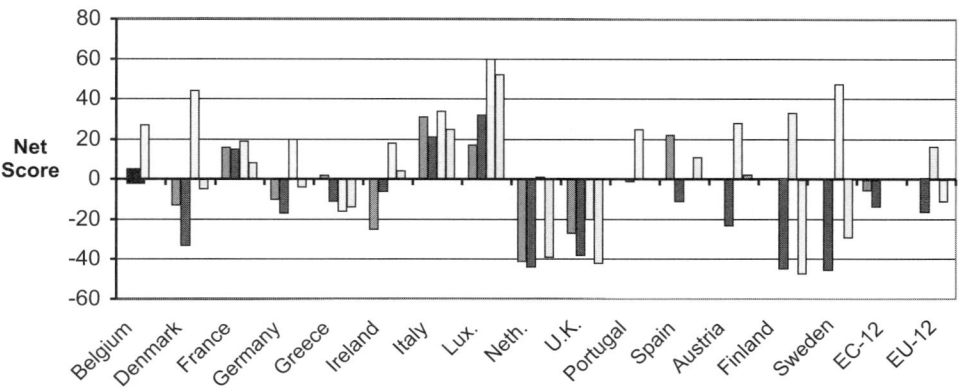

Fig. 3.4. Net attachment. (Data from Eurobarometer, nos. 30, 36, 40, 44, 50, 51.) *Note:* Net attachment scores were created by subtracting the sum of those "not very" and "not at all" attached from the sum of those "very" or "fairly" attached.

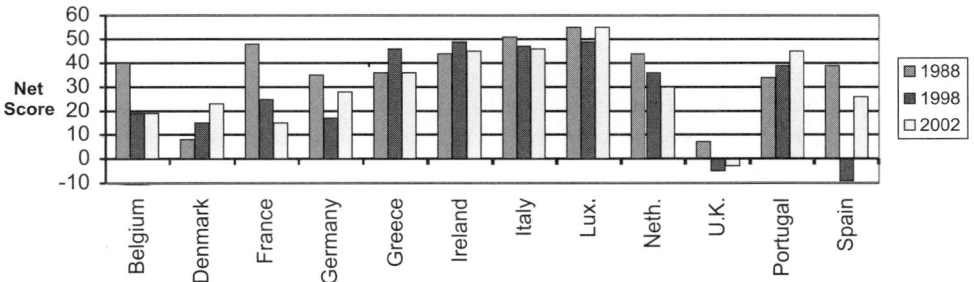

Fig. 3.5. Net dissolution regret. (Data from Eurobarometer, nos. 30, 36, 40, 44, 50, 51.) *Note:* The dissolution regret question asked, "If you were told tomorrow that the [EC/Common Market/EU] had been scrapped, would you be very sorry about it, indifferent, or relieved?" We subtract the percentage "relieved" from that for "very sorry."

At the same time, there is evidence that EU publics have somewhat volatile and mixed feelings about the EU. Figure 3.4 displays net attachment results, and figure 3.5 net dissolution regret scores. Attachment scores were generally higher at the end of the 1990s than at the beginning of the decade, having recovered from a prevailing decline at mid-decade. By 2002 they had turned in the other direction, with substantial attached majorities only in Italy, Luxembourg, and Spain. Yet the possibility of dissolution has predominantly been viewed with regret from 1988 through 2002, with the recurrent exception of the United Kingdom. The data in these figures and the identity findings suggest that

European publics tend to want to keep the EU while recurrently finding it a distant and chilling entity.

Trust in the EU can promote collective action, and feelings of trust did trend upward from 1976 to 1990 (Niedermayer 1995). Subsequent years do not provide data suggesting a high level of trust in the EU in general, in EU institutions, or in the peoples of other EU states.[16] Trust in the EU as a whole declined sharply from the fall of 1997 through the spring of 2002, by which time only publics in Belgium, Greece, Ireland, Italy, Luxembourg, the Netherlands, Portugal, and Spain had pluralities with trust in the EU. Distrust exceeded trust by a substantial margin in the United Kingdom, Finland, and Sweden. Only the Scandinavian publics (Denmark, Finland, Sweden) appeared to trust the peoples of the other members to any large degree. In 2001–2, the median percentage expressing trust in EU institutions hovered for most member publics around the 50 percent level, with the U.K. public persistently much less trusting. These views hardly signal endorsement of a blank check for EU collective action. Further, the still-lower trust scores given to the peoples of the candidate countries for future EU membership suggest that enlargement will work to reduce whatever trust-based endorsement for collective action has existed among the publics of the EU-15.[17] If anything, the level of trust in EU institutions may diminish with the entry of the accession countries. Their publics' median level of trust in EU institutions in 2002 was with one exception below a third (European Commission, "Candidate Countries Eurobarometer" 2002).

The EU as an Interest-Based Club

The rather iffy public opinion basis for EU collective action to this point may not be decisive. Even if clubs are not supported by common identities, they can be maintained because of the benefits—perceived and real—associated with membership. EU publics have repeatedly been given an opportunity to express their views about membership in the EU and the national benefits that accrue from membership.[18] Figures 3.6 and 3.7 demonstrate the difference between positive and negative appraisals for 1990–2002.

With respect to membership, data for 1990–2002 show a predominance of positive net evaluations but very thin ones for the United Kingdom and, until recently, relatively small ones for Austria and Sweden. The other publics have been enthusiasts for the whole period, although in the EC-12 countries the 2002 levels for the most part were below those of 1990. Most member publics seem to subject the EU to a continuing evaluation of the rewards provided by membership rather than granting it a firm and unconditionally positive verdict.

DOMESTIC SUPPORT FOR CONTRIBUTIONS

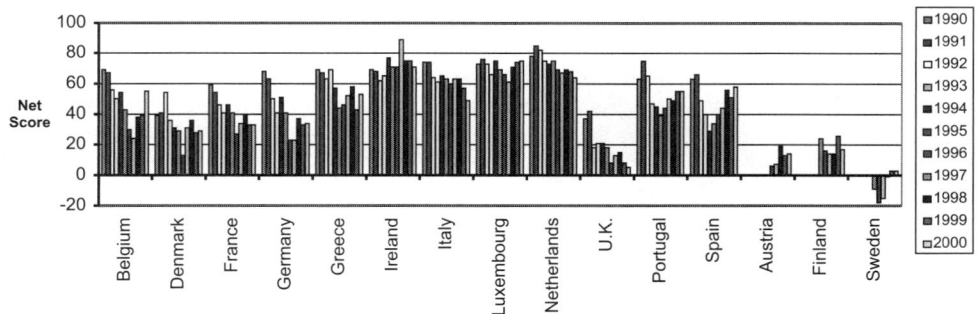

Fig. 3.6. Net evaluation of membership. (Data from Eurobarometer, nos. 34, 36, 38, 40, 42, 44, 46, 48, 50, 51, 54.)

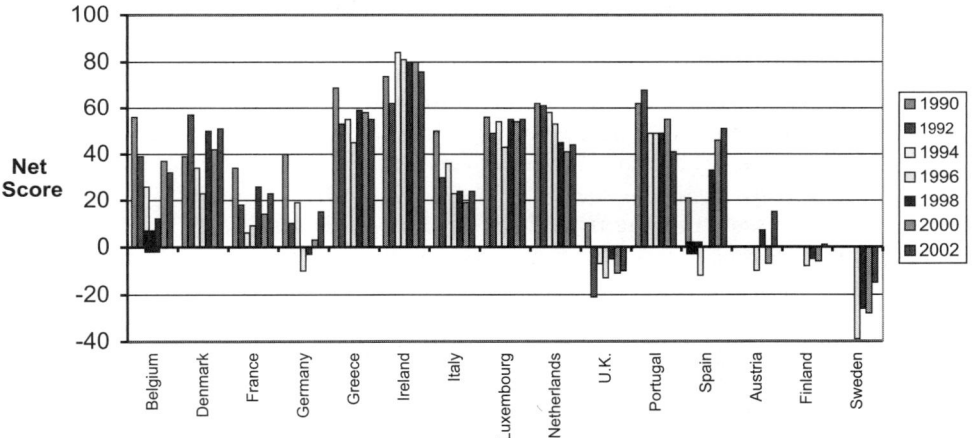

Fig. 3.7. Net national benefit evaluations. (Data from Eurobarometer, nos. 34, 36, 38, 40, 41, 42, 44, 46, 48, 50, 52, 54.)

With respect to perceived benefits, net positive evaluations predominate but are somewhat more modest than those for membership. Negative net perceptions are in the most recent years limited to the United Kingdom and the newer members (Austria, Finland, and Sweden), for which negative levels show recent reductions. For the most part, the positive margins for the EC-12 publics are smaller than they were in 1990. Support for EU multilateralism based on public perceptions of self-interest apparently has to be earned on an ongoing basis and remains fluid. Nevertheless, the verdict as of 2002 was clearly positive, a position supported by polling in a subset of current and of candidate EU members.[19]

Member country elites were also asked each question in 1996 (Spence 1996, A1, A3). Support for membership was uniformly and massively predominant with the exception of Sweden, which had a low net 75 percent score. As for benefits, only in Sweden did the net score fall below 50 percent. Several other members were below 75 percent—the United Kingdom (72 percent), Spain (67 percent), Austria (61 percent), and Finland (64 percent). The judgments of European elites suggest an enthusiasm not generally shared by their publics and significant skeptical elite minorities in several countries.

The Character of the EU Club

The members of any club confront choices about desirable club characteristics. Additional insights into EU or, indeed, any club phenomena can be garnered from opinions about integration and the "internationalization" of issues that are wholly or partly assigned to multilateral institutions for decision making. The strength of desires for accelerated integration and issue internationalization in a club imply the robustness of commitment to it as a vehicle for joint action. We turn first to opinions on the desired speed of European integration and compare them to the perceived current speed.[20]

On a scale ranging from 7 for "as fast as possible" to 1 for "standstill," desired-speed scores were in the 4 to 5.8 range for all member publics of the EU-15 in 2002. Scores were, however, lower than those reported for the EC-12 in 1986, and the margin over perceived current speed had shrunken further from the reduction already apparent by 1996 (Eurobarometer, nos. 50, 53, 56, 58). Those publics particularly in favor of a substantial acceleration (1 point greater than perceived current speed) had shrunk from all members of the EC-12 of 1986 to only France, Greece, Italy, and Portugal of the EU-15. Those preferring a slowdown were most evident in Denmark and Finland, and there was little appetite for more acceleration in Luxembourg or Sweden.

Support for greater integration also implies a willingness to share policy decision making between national and EU entities—that is, a jointness or internationalization of policy setting (Sinnott 1995b).[21] National differences are substantial in recent years and do not change very much when more issues are included in the internationalization bundle, as shown in table 3.4.[22] We report both the average level of support for jointness across issues and the percentage of issues queried where jointness was preferred.

In 2002, support of policy internationalization on both measures predominated in most of the national publics. Taking the opposite view were the publics of Denmark, the United Kingdom, Austria, Sweden, and Finland. Support for issue internationalization had increased from the late 1990s, especially in Greece and Portugal. Yet as the last column suggests, most publics wished to reserve a number of issues for national control. These results are compatible with muted but much less than full-blown optimism about the long-term commitment to collective action embodied in issue internationalization. They fit with the patterns of trust in EU institutions discussed previously and with the substantial majorities in all of the EU-15 polled in 2002 to retain national veto rights in a soon-to-be enlarged European Union.[23]

Elite opinion can help us better understand the drivers and prospects for issue internationalization within the EU. EU member country elites (elected politicians, civil servants, industrialists, media, and cultural intellectuals) were polled in 1996 (Spence 1996) on a series of fourteen issues and asked, "To what extent should each of the following policy areas be decided at the national or regional level and to what extent at the European level?" There was a high level of agreement between national elites on moving in the direction of internationalization. There were, however, clear differences about the desired degree of internationalization—that is, how much of the policy setting should be shifted to the European level. Support for a high degree of shifting was particularly limited in Denmark, Germany, Ireland, the United Kingdom, Finland,

TABLE 3.4. Issue Internationalization (in percentages)

	Average Level of Joint Support			Issues with Jointness Preferred		
	1997	2000	2002	1997	2000	2002
Belgium	55	58	58	83	68	67
Denmark	43	40	45	39	44	48
France	57	57	59	72	64	67
Germany	54	55	52	61	64	58
Greece	48	43	67	56	44	89
Ireland	50	46	56	56	52	58
Italy	65	63	65	94	80	74
Luxembourg	56	52	57	67	56	58
Netherlands	63	61	53	72	72	63
United Kingdom	38	32	40	28	20	37
Portugal	43	43	56	28	44	74
Spain	56	57	65	72	68	78
Austria	44	43	48	39	48	58
Finland	35	40	40	28	40	37
Sweden	40	37	40	28	32	37

Source: Data from Eurobarometer, nos. 47, 53, 58.

and Sweden. Support for a relatively full shift was strongest in Italy and Spain. In sum, there was no shared preference for further sovereignty shifting—beyond that already agreed to—that would allow central EU institutions to make more timely and binding collective action commitments.

A club's inclusiveness—that is, its openness to new members—also matters when assessing the prospects it offers for international cooperation. For current EU members, a more favorable attitude on enlargement suggests more openness to joint action with a broader set of continental states, and a more negative attitude suggests resistance to joint action. We look at attitudes on enlargement in two ways. The first is the average predisposition of the current members toward admission of candidate countries; the second is the average support for particular candidates.[24] Two possibilities, Norway and Switzerland (states that have not sought admission) had massive majority support for admission in all of the EU-15. Turkey, in spite of its manifest desire to get in, elicited the opposite reaction. The lack of variation across the current members on these three countries leads us to limit our attention to the remaining twelve candidates. The data appear in tables 3.5 and 3.6.

TABLE 3.5. Support for Enlargement

	Net Average Support for the 12 (%)			Enlarges with Majority Support/Opposition (n)		
	1997	2000	2002	1997	2000	2002
Belgium	−16	−10	−2	0/1	1/3	1/0
Denmark	23	40	38	8/0	10/0	11/0
France	−15	−23	−25	0/5	0/7	0/10
Germany	−13	−10	−4	1/3	0/2	1/2
Greece	26	19	38	7/0	9/0	12/0
Ireland	16	21	37	0/2	5/0	12/0
Italy	11	11	21	3/0	3/0	6/0
Luxembourg	−6	−13	20	1/0	0/4	8/0
Netherlands	25	19	14	8/1	4/0	7/0
United Kingdom	11	5	7	1/0	1/0	2/0
Portugal	11	12	17	0/0	0/0	0/0
Spain	31	30	48	6/0	5/0	12/0
Austria	−4	−19	3	1/1	1/6	3/2
Finland	13	18	27	6/0	6/0	9/0
Sweden	41	43	47	10/0	11/0	12/0

Source: Data from Eurobarometer, nos. 47, 53, 58.

Note: The first three columns are the average of support minus opposition scores for the 12 candidate countries in each of the current EU members. The last three columns provide the number of candidate countries of the 12 whose admission receives majority support or opposition from each current EU member public.

DOMESTIC SUPPORT FOR CONTRIBUTIONS

We find that most EU country publics fall into three groups: (1) those strongly disposed to admit a large number of candidates (Denmark, Greece, Ireland, Spain, and Sweden); (2) those moderately disposed, supporting the admission of a selected subset of candidates (Italy, Luxembourg, the Netherlands, the United Kingdom, Austria, and Finland); and (3) the negatively disposed toward enlargement (Belgium, France, and Germany). We reason that member states of each group are likely to engage in collective action jointly with the enlargement countries in declining order. Inclusiveness sentiment clearly reached a high in 2002.

As for particular candidates (table 3.6), by 2002 the twelve for the most part had substantial net support across the EU-15 and little in the way of strongly opposed member publics. The exceptions were Bulgaria, Romania, and Slovenia. After some declines in 2000, support reached a high in 2002. We reason that EU-15 propensities for collective action will be greater for the first group than for the second.

Affiliation openness and indeed the self-defined character of the EU are further illuminated by questioning in 1998, 2000, and 2001 about the extent to which various criteria are important for EU entry (Eurobarometers, nos. 50, 53, 56). Of the eight criteria posed, there was overwhelming emphasis (80 percent or more) among publics in each of the EU-15 for those of (1) respect for human rights and the principles

TABLE 3.6. Current Member Views

	Average Net Support for Admission (%)			Majority Support/Opposition by Current EU Members (n)		
	1997	2000	2002	1997	2000	2002
Bulgaria	3	10	7	2/1	2/5	5/3
Cyprus	12	18	25	2/0	6/1	10/1
Czechoslovakia	14	14	24	6/0	6/0	9/1
Estonia	10	9	19	4/1	3/2	8/1
Hungary	23	21	38	9/0	7/0	11/1
Latvia	12	8	18	4/1	3/1	8/1
Lithuania	2	8	16	4/1	3/2	7/1
Malta	21	18	32	7/0	9/0	12/0
Poland	19	15	23	7/1	7/1	9/0
Romania	−1	−5	2	2/3	1/5	3/3
Slovakia	3	5	15	3/1	3/3	7/1
Slovenia	0	1	8	1/1	3/3	6/1

Source: Data from Eurobarometer, nos. 47, 53, 58.
Note: The first three columns are the average support minus opposition scores for each candidate in the 15 current member publics. The last three columns contain the number of current member publics out of the 15 in which majorities supported or opposed admission of a particular candidate.

of democracy; (2) combating organized crime and drug trafficking; and (3) protecting the environment. With less robust majorities, all publics attached importance to the candidate being able to pay its share of the EU budget. Only the Danish, British, Finnish, and Swedish publics lacked majorities believing in the importance of the candidate being "prepared to put the interest of the EU above its own." These findings suggest that support for inclusiveness among EU member publics is largely contingent on political conversion and light expansion burdens for existing members.

The International Role of Europe and the EU

The views discussed thus far provide a setting for the types of international behavior that interest us the most. They do not, however, bear directly on European public and elite preferences for common EU international policies. As a result, we now turn from issues of club attachment and commitment in general to common foreign and security policy. Opinions on the internationalization of foreign and defense policy are an appropriate starting point. For the publics of the EC-12 and then the EU-15, substantial, relatively stable, and persistent majorities have favored internationalization in Western Europe of foreign policy since 1989 (Sinnott 1995b, 265–66; Eurobarometer, nos. 33–58). A distinction can be drawn, however, between persistent enthusiasts for such jointness with two-thirds or more supporting it (Belgium, Germany, France, Italy, Luxembourg, the Netherlands) and those with only thin or wavering supportive majorities (Denmark, Greece, Finland, Sweden, and the United Kingdom).

Internationalizing (more precisely, "EU-izing") foreign policy has received more support than doing the same for security and defense policy.[25] In aggregate, support for the latter has been frozen around the 50 percent level from 1989 through 2002, with the exception of a temporary surge in the spring of 1996.[26] For the aggregate EU public, defense has not been an especially favored area for policy internationalization. Only the Dutch public has had persistent enthusiasm for jointness in EU defense. Only persistent minorities have favored jointness in Denmark, Greece, Ireland, Austria, Portugal, Finland, Sweden, and the United Kingdom.[27] EU national elite attitudes on foreign and defense policy jointness had relatively the same degree of skepticism as their national publics (Spence 1996). Differences among national elites were more pronounced on defense than on foreign policy jointness.

More demanding questions have been asked of publics since the mid-1990s: questions about whether the EU "should have one common

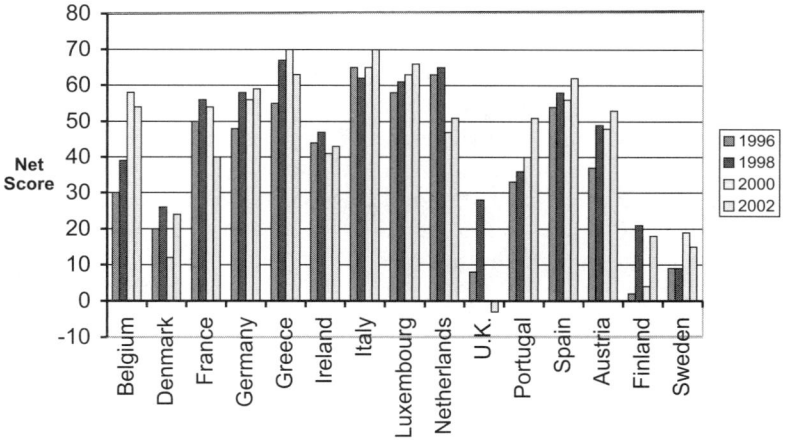

Fig. 3.8. Net support for common foreign policy. (Data from Eurobarometer, nos. 47, 50, 54.)

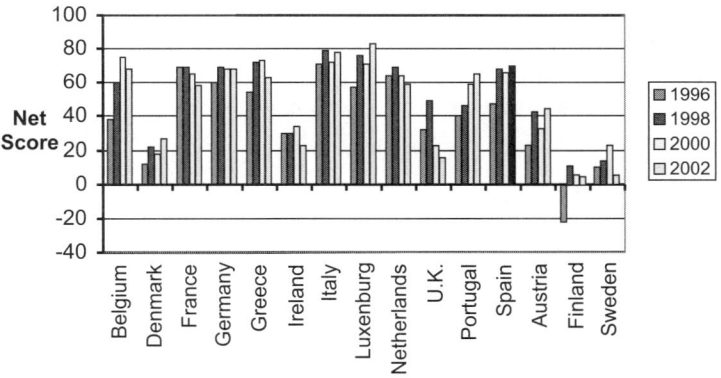

Fig. 3.9. Net support for common defense and security policy. (Data from Eurobarometer, nos. 47, 50, 54.)

foreign policy toward countries outside the European Union" and about support for "a common defense and military policy" or "defense and security policy." Net support data appear in figures 3.8 and 3.9.

All EU publics favored varying degrees of a common foreign policy in 1996–2002 with the exception of the United Kingdom. All favored a common defense/security policy (with the exception of Finland in 1996). The margin between support and opposition varied, however, being smaller in Denmark, the United Kingdom, Finland, and Sweden.

In the other countries, the margin by 2002 was quite massive. These results appear to provide much of what a mandate requires. Questions, however, remain about the stability of public support in the small margin states and the priority given to foreign and defense policy areas relative to others. We explore these aspects for all of the EU-15 publics through repeated polling over an extended period, polling in recent years of five current members and one accession member, and finally through a poll that asked a relatively unique set of questions of EU publics shortly after the events of 9/11.

In 1998 (Eurobarometer, no. 50), publics of the EU-15 were offered a list of twelve problems and asked to choose "which one . . . is the most important at the present time?" The possibility especially pertinent here was "getting Europe to speak with one voice in discussions with the Americans and Russians." In no country was that problem chosen by even 10 percent of respondents. A different question about public priorities for the EU was asked in 1998, 1999, 2000, 2001, and 2002 (Eurobarometer, nos. 50–53, 56, 58) and sought opinions about whether each of a variety of problems "should be a priority or not," a less demanding query in terms of prioritization. Three of the possibilities relate to the EU's international role: "asserting the political and diplomatic importance of the EU around the world"; "maintaining peace and security in Europe"; and enlargement—"welcoming new member countries."

The priority of asserting EU importance globally in no case ranked higher than tenth out of the twelve to fifteen issues posed and was usually lower. Other than Greece, this priority never received net majority support. It did, however, often have consistent net plurality support (in Greece, Spain, France, Ireland, Italy, Luxembourg, and the Netherlands). Support was thin or inconsistent in Austria and the United Kingdom and in a minority position in Germany, Finland, and Sweden. The priority accorded by the candidate countries in 2002 was similarly low (European Commission, "Candidate Countries Eurobarometer" 2002).

The regional security problem overwhelmingly received priority status (falling below 80 percent for only one country in one poll) and never ranked below fifth among the issues posed. This pattern stands in marked contrast to a Cold War query (Eurobarometer, no. 20, 1983) asked of EC-10 publics in which defense was ranked far down the list of priorities in 1983. Relatively low importance for this issue was also evident in the EC-12 of 1991 (Eurobarometer, no. 36). Notably, though, the recent priority given to regional security does not correlate with support for increased defense spending. When asked in 1999 in EU members Denmark, France, Germany, Italy, the United Kingdom, and

Finland, the predominant opinion in each country was for continuing the current level of spending with very substantial majorities for doing that or spending less ("Global Finance" 1999).[28]

Reactions to enlargement were almost opposite those for regional security (Eurobarometer, nos. 50–58). Persistent majorities against assigning priority to enlargement occurred in Belgium, France, Germany, Italy, Luxembourg, the Netherlands, the United Kingdom, Austria, and Finland. Only Denmark (majority) and Ireland and Sweden (pluralities) consistently reported priority, although they were joined by the Greek public in 2002.[29]

These findings suggest a high priority for collective action on regional security issues, but not through the enlargement mechanism. The findings also suggest modest support for a wider international role as long as it does not divert from more salient problems. A set of queries in 2002 about the fears of EU citizens allows for some sharpening of this conclusion.[30] Ten possibilities were posed, with the three involving conflicts in Europe relatively less feared. What was most feared was international terrorism and organized crime, followed by proliferation of weapons of mass destruction (WMD) and a nuclear power plant accident. The results suggest receptivity to antiterrorism and to countering WMD proliferation through international cooperation and contributions.

What those contributions might be is suggested by late 2001 polling on the then current crisis about terrorism and the U.S. campaign in Afghanistan (European Commission, "Europeans and the International Crisis" 2001). Prevailing majorities in all or most member publics found EU measures "essential" or "necessary" to limit the spread of the conflict, to provide humanitarian/economic reconstruction/democratization aid, to improve relations with Arab states and Arab populations, and to enhance transportation security and policy and court cooperation. Those are all, of course, essentially nonmilitary activities. When the questions inquired into providing national member security resources to U.S. efforts, most EU publics favored intelligence sharing, with somewhat fewer in support of allowing use of their domestic military bases. Those favoring combat troop commitments were even fewer than those in the poll a month earlier reported in table 3.2. All member publics predominantly opposed supplying "arms and equipment" to indigenous groups attempting to "overthrow governments protecting terrorists." Direct engagement in and active assistance to violent actions are not a generally preferred form of contributions.

A more integrated view of the EU's international role can be drawn from the 2002 polling of publics in six countries now or soon to be in the EU, five of which are likely to be among its largest voting power states. The countries were the United Kingdom, France, Germany, the Netherlands, Italy, and Poland.

What did the public majorities agree on? The EU should exert strong international influence relative to the United States and indeed become a superpower (albeit to cooperate rather than compete with the United States). Either in that context or more generally there was a lack of predominant support for increasing military spending. The EU was held to have more international influence than Russia or China but less than the United States. The EU was more important for the publics' countries than was the United States. It was in their interest to be active in world affairs and increasingly so in the Arab-Israeli conflict, even with associated costs. Their strength would rest far more on an economic than a military pillar, and using that strength to foster economic development in poor countries was the most preferred way to combat terrorism. As for possible threats to the countries' vital interests in the next ten years, majorities agreed with treating international terrorism as the most widely recognized and extremely important threat. They also agreed on a number of possible threats as not being extremely important (fewer than 30 percent in any public): political turmoil in Russia, economic competition from the United States, the development of China as a world power, and the impact of globalization.

What did they disagree on? Except for the U.K. public, the EU was judged to have more international influence than its major members. Unlike the others, the U.K. and Polish publics had more favorable views of the United States than of the EU. With the exception of France, the publics agreed with Europe specializing in "things like assisting poor countries develop their economies and trying to help reconstruct societies after a war," with the United States specializing in "military conflict."[31] Again with the exception of France, they would, however, not favor increased economic aid spending. As for threats, except for Poland, 40 percent or more of each public gave extreme importance to Islamic fundamentalism, global warming, and Israel-Arab military conflict. Differences were more widespread on the importance of immigration and refugees and India-Pakistan tension.

How do these patterns compare with earlier views of EU elites? When asked about EU dealings with great-power states (Spence 1996),[32] elites in no EU country thought that the current role was excessive, but preferences for a larger role varied widely. Enthusiasts (60 percent or more) were found in Belgium, Germany, Greece, Spain, France, Italy, Luxembourg, and the Netherlands. This support was countered by majorities with combined preferences for the status quo and role reduction in Portugal, Finland, Sweden, and the United Kingdom. The twenty-first-century EU publics seem to have greater appetites for international stature for Brussels.

The 1996 elite polling also provided some partial answers about what issues the current or enlarged role should concentrate on.[33] Eleven threats were posed: four focused on specific nonmember states and the remainder on general external possibilities (e.g., nuclear weapons proliferation; religious fundamentalism; nuclear accidents; and ethnic, nationalist, or territorial violence) or matters with obvious domestic consequences inside the EU (e.g., immigration from nonmembers and extreme nationalist movements in the EU countries). Results are reported in table 3.7.

When asked about threats from major powers (Russia, Japan, the United States, China), respondents in the EU aggregate placed Russia below the midpoint on a threat scale and the other three only slightly above it. A Russian military threat made the top five only for Swedish elites; an American economic threat placed in the top five only for Greek and Spanish elites; a Japanese economic threat made the top five only for Greek, Spanish, and Irish elites; and a threat from the "development of China as a world power" reached the top five only for the elites of Austria, Ireland, Luxembourg, the United Kingdom, and Portugal. In general, nation-specific threats received less importance than those from religious fundamentalism, nuclear proliferation, extreme nationalist movements outside the EU, and immigration. This finding is in general compatible with the more recent public views. A reasonable surmise is that intra-EU cooperation is more likely on those more highly ranked possibilities, a number of which were also prominent for publics more recently. That expectation also applies to international contributions. When member country elites were asked in 1996 about the most serious problems and issues facing the EU (Spence 1996, A5–6), three choices focusing on external relations made the top ten overall: enlarging the EU, external relations, and defense.[34] Yet enlargement received majority mention only in Denmark; external relations the most (only 32 percent) in Greece; and defense the most (only 23 percent) in Austria. Those numbers did not seem conducive to making the respective issues a collective action priority for the EU, and more recent public opinion has not changed that perception.

The public and elite opinions just discussed and the reservations about the United States evidenced in table 3.2 may provide politicians with some incentives for cooperative activity and international contributions that might counter interpretations of the EU as at most a follower and at worst a nonentity. These opinions surely argue against reductions, given the desire for a prominent international role with civil

TABLE 3.7. EU Elite Threat Preceptions

	B	DK	FR	GE	GR	IR	IT	LU	NL	UK	P	SP	AU	FI	SW	Mean Threat Score
Religious fundamentalism	3	1	2	4	3	4	1	1	5	4	1	1	3	2	8	6.2
New nuclear powers	5	2	3	3	9	1	2	2	6	1	2	8	2	5	2	6.2
Immigration from non-EU countries	4	3	5	1	6	9	3	6	3	8	5	4	9	6	6	5.9
Violent nationalist movements outside EU	2	4	1	2	7	8	6	4	1	5	8	6	4	3	5	5.9
Nuclear accident	7	5	4	5	2	2	4	3	7	7	4	10	1	1	3	5.8
Ethnic/territorial conflicts inside Europe	6	6	6	6	5	6	5	9	2	3	9	5	10	4	1	5.8
Nationalist movements in EU	1	10	8	8	8	10	7	11	4	6	10	9	11	8	9	5.4
Development of China	8	7	9	9	10	3	10	5	8	2	3	7	5	11	7	5.4
Economic power of United States	10	11	7	11	1	7	8	8	11	10	6	2	8	9	11	5.1
Economic power of Japan	9	9	11	10	4	5	9	7	9	9	7	3	6	10	10	5.1
Remaining military might of Russia	11	8	10	7	11	11	11	10	10	11	11	11	7	7	4	4.8

Source: Data from Spence 1996, 55–56.

Note: B = Belgium, DK = Denmark, FR = France, GE = Germany, GR = Greece, IR = Ireland, IT = Italy, LU = Luxembourg, NL = Netherlands, UK = United Kingdom, P = Portugal, SP = Spain, AU = Austria, FI = Finland, SW = Sweden. Participants were asked to arrange the eleven threats in rank order from least to most threatening (1–11).

The final column, "mean threat score," is the average score when each national elite sample was asked to rank each of the threats (rows) on a scale from 1 to 10, with ten being the worst. For example, in the first row 6.2 is the average for the polled country elites on the threat from religious fundamentalism. The earlier columns indicate the rank of the named threat in the row relative to other threats for the particular country elite (column). For the top cell in the first column, the entry of 3 indicates that the Belgian elite thought there were two threats more severe, judging by where they placed them on the 1 to 10 scale. Therefore, the final column is not generated from the entries in the earlier ones.

emphases. We do not, however, find public (or even necessarily elite) demand across EU members that would push the EU club to assume a comprehensive and dominant leadership role in contributions to global order and progress.

Europe in a World of Multiple Clubs

The implications of the previous EU opinion data for international cooperation depend in part on what accompanies them in terms of views on cooperation with international institutions that are not exclusively European (e.g., the United Nations, the North Atlantic Treaty Organization [NATO], or the WTO) and on cooperation with non-European major powers (especially the United States). At the end of the Cold War, opinions about these possibilities for international cooperation and contributions did not feature competition between them but rather were substantially independent of each other (Everts 1995, 420).

A comparative 1999 question (Eurobarometer, no. 51) found more trust in the United Nations than in the EU with the exceptions of Greece, Italy, and Portugal. Positive views on UN trustworthiness exceeded negative ones by 20 percent or more for the publics of Denmark, Ireland, Italy, Luxembourg, the Netherlands, the United Kingdom, Portugal, Spain, Finland, and Sweden. For Denmark, the Netherlands, the United Kingdom, Finland, and Sweden trust in the UN was much higher than trust in the EU. For them, collective action contributions may get more support if done through the UN or under its umbrella than if done directly by the EU. In 2002, massive majorities in the six-country polling discussed previously favored strengthening the UN (Chicago Council and Marshall Fund 2002).

As for NATO, publics in major EU member states hardly seem to have rejected it in the 1980s, 1990s, or early twenty-first century (Everts 1995, 426; Chicago Council and Marshall Fund 2002). Sinnott (1996) reports no sustained decline from 1989 in the high levels of percentage support in the United Kingdom (in the 70s), Germany (in the 60s) and even an upward trend in France (to about 60 percent) into 1995. In 1995, the British, French, and German publics all had high confidence in NATO, with only the French having greater confidence in the EU. For a somewhat larger set of European NATO members, the 1999 assessment also was positive but with diverse positions on replacement of NATO as the primary European defense vehicle. French and Italian publics were in favor; Danish, German, and British publics were opposed. The one EU but not NATO member polled (Finland) lacked a majority with a positive assessment but was evenly divided on replacement ("Global

Finance" 1999).³⁵ The general preference for multiple affiliations conforms to that reported by Sinnott (1995b) for surveys taken 1980, 1989, and 1991.³⁶ In 2002, in the context of the pro-EU attitudes of the six country publics, large majorities wanted to strengthen NATO and affirmed its importance. That same year, when asked to choose between placing decision authority for European defense with national governments, NATO, or the EU, majorities for the EU were present among the EU-15 publics only in Greece, Italy, and Luxembourg. Pluralities in Denmark and the United Kingdom preferred NATO and in Ireland and Finland national authority (Eurobarometer, no. 58).

As for international economic organizations, the same 2002 poll had prevailing support, with the exception of Germany, for strengthening the International Monetary Fund and the World Bank. All of the six publics strongly favored strengthening the WTO. This last finding may be of particular importance given the economic emphasis noted earlier and the widely held assessment that the European Commission was a good choice to negotiate trade matters on behalf of the member states (European Opinion Research Group 2001). While in 2001 many publics had reservations about the democracy and the transparency of the WTO, their judgments on other grounds were for the most part favorable. Majorities found the EU well represented and held the WTO to be "necessary," "an impartial arbiter," of "good reputation," capable of realizing the "benefits of globalization," and capable of defending the interests of others against the United States.

On balance, these data suggest that European politicians face incentives from public opinion for a multipronged international cooperation strategy: enhancing the EU's international role in civil power ways while containing direct budgetary costs to internal priorities; playing a second-to-none role in shaping the international system; and pursuing European and national interests through activism and enhancement of other major international institutions. Exclusive devotion to a single club is not a dominant agenda item, at least for the moment.

The final data on European opinion we consider deals with views of the United States. In other words, these data focus on the potential for a transatlantic international cooperation club. If such a club evolved, it could muster great economic and military resources on behalf of international order and progress. Some historical basis can be gained from polling on European public trust in Americans (1990 and 1996 in Eurobarometer, nos. 33, 46). Trust in Americans fell from 1990 to 1996 and changed from a higher to a lower degree of trust than was placed in peer EU populations. As table 3.2 shows, EU publics have had substantial reservations about U.S. approaches to foreign affairs.

More recent polling confirms attenuation of public views of a transatlantic club with shared policy goals and strategies (Chicago Council and Marshall Fund 2002; Eurobarometer, no. 58, 2002; Pew Research Center 2001, 2002a, 2003). EU-15 publics in 2002 had a positive majority for the U.S. role in the fight on terrorism and a plurality for contributions to world economic growth but not for world peace or reducing world poverty. A majority had a negative view of the U.S. role in protecting the environment. Polling of major European country publics (United Kingdom, France, Germany, and Italy) in 2001 and 2002 had large majorities believing that U.S. foreign policy did not take account of their interests in general or with respect to fighting terrorism. In 2003, majorities in those countries as well as Spain and Poland disapproved of American foreign policy in general and felt it had a negative effect on their countries (although the majorities were small in the United Kingdom). Large disapproving majorities were present for the Bush "Axis of Evil" formulation, steel tariffs, policies toward the Arab-Israeli conflict, rejections of the Kyoto agreement and of the antiballistic missile treaty. There were, however, large approving majorities for the Afghan campaign against the Taliban and al Qaeda, the pledged increase in foreign aid, support for free trade, and continued participation in peacekeeping in the former Yugoslavia. Whatever general negativism came to exist was not automatically applied to all areas of policy.

Yet from the 2001 situation where interests were not perceived as growing apart, major European publics moved to preferring a future marked by more European independence (majorities or pluralities in the United Kingdom, France, Germany, Spain, Italy, and Poland in 2003). When we combine these results with our previous observations, we have a picture of selective and perhaps contradictory permissions for selective, friction-laden cooperation. European publics seem to want strong U.S. international leadership and U.S. military specialization. At the same time, Europeans want to end America's sole superpower status and want no increase in U.S. defense spending but also want growth in U.S. foreign aid spending. They acknowledge the U.S. superiority in world influence while welcoming a check on some aspects of this influence in the WTO and perhaps in other international organizations as well. In sum, the preference is for cooperation when the United States in the European perspective is doing the right thing, but Europeans think that the United States often has not and increasingly is not doing that. The result is an interest in both cooperation with America and containment of it. European leaders may well conclude that they have public support to advocate cooperative provision of contributions to international order and progress but not to automatically follow what the United States prefers or even to pay a big bill for what European publics prefer.

A Variety of West Europeans

With regard to prospects of international cooperation within and outside of the EU, it seems useful to crudely categorize the various European publics relative to each other. In those relative terms, using many of the indicators discussed previously, we pay particular attention to instances when each public stands out from the general pattern of the EU-15. We define prominence as standing out on half or more of the indicators of special relevance.[37] We think two dimensions of opinion, and thus the indicators associated with aspects of each, are directly related to our interest in international cooperation and contributions to it. The first dimension is that of internationalism and the second is that of support for the European project.

On the first, we distinguish especially great public support or its absence into three categories. The indications of broad internationalism are especially strong support for EU enlargement followed by majority decision rules and a high degree of trust in the United Nations (indeed more in it than in the EU) and support for other global IGOs. We associate broad internationalism with especially strong tendencies to support international cooperation with nonmembers of the EU and broader international institutions (a larger public goods element). The indications of EU internationalism are especially strong support for common foreign and security policies for the EU and global assertion by it. If unaccompanied by broad internationalism, we associate EU internationalism with strong tendencies to support international activity that gives the EU an especially prominent role and advances direct European interests (i.e., a larger club element). If accompanied by broad internationalism, we associate EU internationalism with an emphasis on EU cooperation with a broader set of others in collective action with a less parochial emphasis (i.e., larger public and club relative to private elements). We view countries falling into neither category as having publics that prefer followership or abstention to leadership on international contribution matters.

A second dimension that we think matters for domestic constraints and incentives for international cooperation and contributions by the EU involves commitment to the EU and the "European project." We distinguish between prominence on EU intensification and on European identification. EU intensification features large perceived net benefits from membership, acceleration of integration within the EU, and jointness in policy management. We associate EU intensification with support for creating the institutional mechanisms that would enable the EU to play a greater role in international affairs in either of the ways mentioned in the previous paragraph. European identification especially involves European positive responses on identity, citizenship, attachment, dissolution regret, and trust. We associate it with strong support for EU international activity, which subordinates national to club goods. Publics manifesting high degrees of both the intensification and identification opinions are particularly likely to support initiatives that would raise the role and capabilities of the EU in international contributions. For us, a lack of prominence on either characteristic suggests that leaders will face more serious challenges in securing permission for such efforts and may well have incentives not to do so. If faced with a relatively less internationalist public, such leaders will have to justify contributions more on national grounds ("our" share of impure club goods). If faced with a broadly internationalist public, they will have to justify them more on extra-European spinoffs ("our" share of impure global goods).

Table 3.8 places the member publics of the EU in these categories. In terms of the EU as a broad and capable international contributor, a special role seems implied for Greece, Italy, Luxembourg, the Netherlands, Portugal, and Spain. Each of their publics stands out for European identification and intensification and European internationalism. The Netherlands and Italy are, however, also outstandingly supportive of broader internationalism and are thus relatively well disposed to contributions well beyond the EU. In contrast, France, Germany, and Belgium have publics less apparently supportive of the European project in general but unusually well disposed to European internationalism. Of those, only the German public was also especially well disposed toward

TABLE 3.8. Distinguishing among West European Publics

	European Internationalism	Broad Internationalism	Neither
European identification	Greece, Italy, Luxembourg, Portugal, Spain	Italy, Netherlands	Ireland
European intensification	France, Greece, Italy, Luxembourg, Portugal, Spain	Italy, Netherlands	Ireland
Neither	Belgium, Germany	Denmark, Germany, United Kingdom, Sweden	Austria, Finland

broad internationalism. We are somewhat more skeptical about the public or even club element for EU international action that will have especially strong support in Belgium, France, and Germany. Public support will hinge to a relatively large extent on perceived national (private goods) grounds. Finally, international contributions by Denmark, Sweden, and the United Kingdom seem especially likely to be supported by their publics, but that support will follow to an especially large extent from grounds other than European ones.

AMERICA IN THE WORLD

We now turn to American public and elite opinion. From the perspective of our interests in international cooperation and contributions to global order and progress, the central polling themes for EU publics involved desirable types of clubs and what those clubs should do throughout the world. When moving to U.S. surveys, the polling questions central to our interests are instead (1) what should the United States do to shape the world and to protect against threats from around the world? and (2) to what extent is that best done through military or nonmilitary means and unilateral versus multilateral methods? The answers involve combinations of beliefs about identity, self-realization, and the costs and benefits of particular policy emphases.

General Context: Activist, Selective Internationalism

Answers to the two previous questions help to structure some prominent typologies of American public and elite belief systems about foreign affairs. Four types of belief systems have been emphasized: hard-liners, who support militant internationalism (i.e., unilateral and military-power centered) and oppose cooperative internationalism (i.e., multilateral and non–military centered); accommodationists, who favor multilateral and nonmilitary tools and oppose unilateral and military emphases; internationalists, who favor those approaches preferred by both hard-liners and accommodationists; and isolationists, who favor none of those approaches (Chanley 1999; O. R. Holsti 1996; O. R. Holsti and Rosenau 1993; Wittkopf 1990, 1996).

A very large number of polls make it clear that the isolationist option has only modest minority support among publics and very little support among elites. This has been true since well before the end of the Cold War, be it for reasons of self-interest or shared identity. Approximately two-thirds of the public has persistently believed that "it is best for the future of the country if we take an active part in world affairs" rather than if we "stay out of world affairs. " The 71 percent taking the activist view in 2002 was the largest since the 1950s. Elites have been and remain nearly unanimous on that score (Chicago Council and Marshall Fund 2002; Gallup Poll Releases, June 24, 1999; Kull and Destler 1999; Richman 1994d). In 1999, 78 percent of respondents agreed that U.S. participation "in efforts to maintain peace, protect human rights, and promote economic development [serves] U.S. interests because [it helps] to create a more stable world that is less apt to have wars and is better for the growth of trade and other U.S. goals." In the same poll, a smaller majority (58 percent) rejected the view that "the world is so big and complex that such efforts only make a minimal difference with little benefit to the U.S." (Americans and the World 2001a).

A less-than-narrow identity basis is suggested by polling in 1993 and 1999 asking whether Americans "regard themselves as citizens of the world as well as citizens of the U.S." (Kull 1995–96; Public Agenda Online 1999). Large majorities (77 percent and 72 percent) responded in the affirmative, although in the early 1990s only about 20 percent chose an exclusively "world citizen" response (Inglehart, Basañez, and Moreno 1998). We observe that the world aspect of identity may provide some receptivity to international contributions with a public element; the American aspect may provide contributions with a private element featuring protection against foreign threats (what we call defensive internationalism). We are left to pursue the matter of the extent that American public and elite opinion in favor of internationalism equates with support for international cooperation and contributions with a substantial public goods element.

The American domestic context, then, shows little support for a generally isolationist stance. This context does, however, have aspects indicating support for a great deal of selectiveness about international activity. Foreign policy matters were in decline among "the most important problems facing the country." The share was ascertained for both publics at four-year intervals from 1978 through 2002 and for elites from 1978 to 1998 (Chicago Council and Marshall Fund 2002). Foreign affairs matters always made up a much smaller share of those problems than domestic ones for both publics and elites, until a recent high in 1986 at 26 percent and 42 percent. The share for the public subsequently declined to a record low of 7 percent in 1998, when it stood at 20 percent for elites. While the public share reached a new high (34 percent) in 2002, more than half of that percentage resulted from mentions of terrorism. General support for international activism does not, for the most part, suffice to offer a large amount of agenda space for international affairs. Decision makers thus have domestic political reasons either to pursue a large number of international matters in ways below the public's radar screen or to concentrate on a few matters and emphasize their direct domestic relevance. The former may well work to limit international contributions but also may provide incentives for multilateralism to fill the resource pot—that is, burden sharing. The latter may well favor a focus on international matters that credibly threaten domestic well-being but can still allow for interpretations that action against such threats benefits not only the United States. Such an interpretation may reduce possible tensions between American and world citizenship.

Within the selectivity constraint, U.S. officials need to weigh the relative and absolute support that public and elite opinion provide for each of the three internationalist positions and the applications of these opinions to specific situations. In the following sections, we will explore the policy possibilities provided by American views on the international role conducive to national self-realization, the preferred issues for activism, inclinations about who are good global partners and who are not, what causes to contribute to and which to oppose, and attitudes toward vehicles for multilateral collective action. The particulars of opinions about foreign aid, UN peacekeeping, and environmental quality are left to later chapters on those topics.

The U.S. World Role: Elements of Self-Realization

We explore what world role would fit with American self-realization by looking at general opinions about (1) American status in the world, (2) American rights and obligations, and (3) unilateral versus joint global activity to realize American status, assert rights, and meet obligations.

As for national status in the world, an increasing share of the American public in the last decade has seen the U.S. world role as growing (55 percent in 2002); more than 70 percent of elite and public samples that year saw it growing further in the next decade (Gallup Poll Release, April 1, 1999; Chicago Council and Marshall Fund 2002). In 1998, 62 percent viewed the United States as "the greatest power of the next century" (Americans and the World 2001b), and in 2002 respondents thought the United States more influential than other countries by a wide margin.[38] Those results resonate with a sense of national pride. In the 1995 twenty-three-nation poll drawn on previously, Americans ranked first in pride in the pillars of world power—political influence, economic achievements, and national armed forces—and valued those more than other attributes (T. W. Smith and Jarkko 1998). In 2002, a higher share of the U.S. public viewed the military as a positive influence in national affairs than was the case in all but a few African countries.[39]

This suggests that the American public is and will be receptive to foreign policy activity that seems to be consistent with continued pursuit of American power and influence in the world. The same set of surveys (table 3.1) found Americans near the top in perceived national superiority, a possible justification for international actions to export American practices to others. The 2002 poll drawn on for table 3.2 shows very large American public majorities with positive views of the international diffusion of U.S. ideas and customs, a view consistent with positive evaluations of its political and economic ideas, and science and technology performance.

Similar to those findings, there is strong support for the United States remaining number 1 in the world militarily rather than being one of several leading military powers (2002, 2000, 1999, 1993) ("Gallup Poll Topics: A–Z Military and National Defense" 2001; Pew Research Center 2002c). Support for economic primacy was less pronounced with majorities (1999, 1993) content with being only one of several leading economic powers (Gallup Poll Release, May 19, 1999). That possible moderation of desired status should be viewed with some reservation as polls in 1998 and 2002 found that a majority of the American public thought that economic matters were more important than military strength "in determining a country's overall power and influence in the world," a position with which most elites agreed when polled in 1998 (Chicago Council and Marshall Fund 2002; Reilly 1999). In any event, the prevailing view (65 percent) in 2000 had the United States as "the leading economic power in the world today" (Americans and the World 2001b). As the twenty-first century began, desired status matched the perceived status quo. Approximately two-thirds of respondents were satisfied with the "position of the U.S. in the world today" according to two polls in 2000, and more than 70 percent believed that in effect others in the world generally were satisfied as well (i.e., viewed the United States favorably) (Gallup Poll Release, March 28, 2001). These results imply that at least prior to 9/11, there was domestic support for actions that would strive to continue an acceptable international system characterized by American military and economic superiority. Trends were favorable and only needed to be continued. The open question was what lines of policy would suffice to do that.

Perceptions of desired status do not reveal information about the rights, obligations, and interests thought to be associated with world status and leadership. It is on those particulars that hard-liners, internationalists, and accommodationists differ. One kind of right is for a state to place its claimed national interests above those of others. Table 3.1 shows that in 1995, the balance of American public opinion was in that direction, although not to an extent greater than for many other national publics. The American tendency was then, however, greater than in earlier years. Eight polls from 1986 to mid-1993 asked, "Which of the following statements best describes the way you think the U.S. should pursue its national security interests throughout the world?" and posed a choice essentially between unilateralist, multilateralist, and isolationist answers.[40] Multilateralism did come first, with an average of 49 percent, followed by isolationism, with an average of 27 percent, and unilateralism, with 22 percent. A unilateralist-isolationist coalition might well, then, have as much public support as multilateralist advocates.

Numerous polls since the late 1960s (Pew Research Center 2002b) never found more than 34 percent agreeing that "Since the U.S. is the most powerful nation in the world, we should go our own way in international matters, not worrying too much about whether other countries agree with the U.S. or not." Very large majorities persistently agreed that "In deciding on its foreign policies, the U.S. should take into account the view of its major allies" and, in 2002, that the United States did in fact consider the interests of others. Only minorities agreed that "The U.S. should mind its own business internationally and let other countries get along the best they can on their own." Yet persistently large majorities agreed that, "We should not think so much in international terms but concentrate more on our own national problems and building up our strength and prosperity here at home." Taken as a set, these persistent responses suggest an acceptance of multilateral adjustment and a rejection of isolationism. They also suggest a rejection of unilateralism but with an exception clause when there was some danger penetrating America's domestic space and thus threatening security and prosperity.

In 1996, substantial majorities of military and civilian elites rejected the view that "what we need is a new foreign policy that puts America first, second, and third as well" (O. R. Holsti 1998–99). Of course, a broad interpretation of self-interests matters a great deal for the implication of ostensibly favoring adjustment to the interests of others. Consider, for example, responses to two 1994 questions: 84 percent agreed that the United States should sometimes "make sacrifices to help the world as a whole"; 75 percent agreed that "whenever it can, the U.S. should look beyond its own self-interest and do what's best for the world as a whole because in the long run this will probably help make the kind of world that is best for the U.S." (Kull 1995–96).

With regard to matters of security and order, U.S. public world role conceptions make military preeminence a matter of right and obligation and thus make the adequacy of military capacity a matter of recurrent concern. In a change from satisfaction with adequacy going back to the perestroika mid-1980s, public opinion moved (as of early 2001) to near equality between those who believed that defense spending was too little and national defense not strong enough and those who believed that the current level was about right. Those believing defense spending to be excessive had shrunk to small minorities ("Gallup Poll Topics: A–Z Military and National Defense" 2001). In 2002, there still was not a substantial plurality for increases in military spending. Less than 1 percent of the public drew from 9/11 the lesson that U.S. military strength was inadequate. Neither the public nor elites had much appetite for increases in an established U.S. military presence abroad (foreign basing) or for termination of such a presence (Chicago Council and Marshall Fund 2002)

As for how the United States should actually use that military capacity in foreign situations, the nature of permissions is less than clear. Even after 9/11, substantial majorities rejected a blanket "world policeman" role and thought that role was being played to an excessive degree. Yet substantial public majorities in the same 2002 polling approved of using U.S. forces to "uphold international law" or to curb terrorist or Islamic fundamentalist organizations. Then and earlier, very large majorities favored use of American forces to provide humanitarian relief and to end atrocities. Yet majorities did not support such commitments to end civil wars and bring peace. Even for countering the classic violation of international law of direct aggression by one state against another, support depended on the specific states involved. Repeated polling, most recently in 2002, never found majority public support for using U.S. troops as a unilateral action to counter a North Korean invasion of South Korea, Arab invasion of Israel, or Chinese invasion of Taiwan. Even an Iraqi invasion of Saudi Arabia did not yield majority support after 1990 (Chicago Council and Marshall Fund 2002; PIPA 2000b; Reilly 1999; Richman 1994a, b).

As for elites, military and civilian majorities in 1996 embraced an obligation to "take all steps, including the use of force, to prevent aggression by any expansionist power" (O. R. Holsti 1998–99). A different elite sample agreed in 2002 with the public on the dispatch of U.S. forces to stop atrocities and to curb terrorist organizations and Islamic fundamentalism. The civilian elite differed repeatedly with the public in the willingness to take unilateral military action to counter the state invasion cases mentioned previously (Chicago Council and Marshall Fund 2002).

With respect to international economic rights and obligations, table 3.1 shows that the U.S. public in 1995 was one of those most attached to the privilege of imposing import restrictions to protect its national economy (i.e., self-interest over the interest of others). A protectionist privilege for domestic jobs and industry received majority public support in most of numerous polls from 1992 to 2000 (Americans and the World 2002a; PIPA 2000b).[41] While elite sympathizers with the necessity for tariffs constituted only a substantial minority in 1986, 1990, 1994, and 1998, public pluralities or small majorities "sympathized" with that view on each occasion and in 2002 (Chicago Council and Marshall Fund 2002). And in 1996, large majorities of military and civilian elites agreed that the United States should use "threats of protectionism" to open Japanese and European markets to U.S. goods (O. R. Holsti 1998–99). This claim to unilateral foreign economic policy privilege cohabits in the American public with a positive view of free trade in general (an open world economy) and its benefits to the United States as a whole. In numerous polls between 1992 and 2002, majorities were usually positive (Americans and the World 2002a; Chicago Council and Marshall Fund 2002; PIPA 2000b).[42]

The apparent contradiction between self-realization through protectionism and through free trade is softened by the American public's view of foreigners' abuse of American economic openness and lack of reciprocity. Economic unilateralism becomes a sort of second-best self-defense. In 1999, 81 percent of the public saw the United States as "more open to imports than most other countries," and 45 percent of respondents saw other countries as benefiting more. In 1998, the United States was viewed as more open than Europeans in general (74 percent), in agriculture (71 percent), and in manufactured products (86 percent) (PIPA 2000b). In less comparative terms, Europeans have been viewed as inclined to free trade and Asians as not (in 1994 and 1998). And China has come to be viewed by large majorities as an unfair trader (Americans and the World 2002a, d; Richman 1994c). More recently, public majorities or pluralities have come to see the EU countries, Japan, and Mexico as free traders, with China still negatively viewed in that respect (Chicago Council and Marshall Fund 2002).

Other survey results underline the idea that the public has viewed protectionist unilateralism as a second-best defense and not as an unconditional national right. In 1999, reciprocity as a condition of U.S. openness was accepted by 64 percent of the public and rejected by only 28 percent. Even with low-wage countries, reciprocity was still accepted by 50 percent in 1999, as contrasted with plurality opposition to reciprocating in 1998 (Americans and the World 2002a; PIPA 2000b).[43] Even with that cautionary note, the claimed right to a protectionist option seems constrained since it is accompanied by acceptance by more than two-thirds of the public in 1999 and 1995 of the view that "As one of the world's rich nations, the U.S. has a moral responsibility toward poor nations to help them develop economically and to improve their people's lives" (PIPA 2000b). In short, trade opinions suggest that the American public holds a conflicting general principle of good international practice and perception of unfairness and abuse by some others.

In principle, one can imagine a reconciliation of rights and obligations through assertion of American-chosen rules binding both the United States and others. The public seems to take a position making the United States both a maker of and complier with rules. For example, in 1999 there was strong support for the United States entering into free-trade areas and agreements only if they would require the other parties to "maintain minimum working conditions" (93 percent); in a 1997 poll, strong majorities supported free trade only if other parties were required to maintain "workplace health and safety" (94 percent), to "prohibit child labor" (93 percent), to "protect human rights" (92 percent), to provide an adequate "minimum wage" (81 percent), and to guarantee the "right to unionize" (78 percent). While there is some recognition of the economic competitiveness advantages for the United States of such requirements, they also seem to be viewed as matters of normative obligation by very large majorities. In 1999, the conditions were held to be ones the United States should require even if they might mean foregoing a trade-liberalizing agreement because it would be immoral for the United States not to do so. In 2002, elites and the public were almost unanimous on including working conditions and environmental protection standards in international trade agreements (Chicago Council and Marshall Fund 2002). Such standard setting has been supported in general for linking human rights to American economic involvement (73 percent) and requiring U.S. firms operating elsewhere to abide by American environmental (88 percent) and labor health and safety (86 percent) standards. The predominantly avowed basis for those positions was a moral one (Americans and the World 2002a). Such standards preserve (and arguably expand) U.S. practices while intruding on those of other countries. This might be interpreted as a continuation of the theme of exceptionalism in American foreign policy that pervades much of the scholarship in the field.

There would be some relinquishment of unilateral rights if notions of American world role allowed for acceptance of common rules set by international organizations, especially if those IGOs were provided with enforcement powers. The American public seems disposed to both. Table 3.1 shows predominant agreement that international institutions should have enforcement powers. In 1999 and 2002, almost two-thirds of the public favored U.S. compliance with adverse WTO rulings, a clear supportive shift from a 1996 position. In 2002, a modest majority favored strengthening the International Court of Justice, as did majorities in earlier surveys.[44] A very large majority in recent years favored strengthening the World Health Organization and acceding to a comprehensive nuclear test ban treaty. A large majority then and earlier favored signing an international treaty banning land mines. That majority appeared even under conditions when it was not in America's strategic interest (1997). More weight was given to the risks land mines posed to civilians than any benefit in weakening an enemy (1999) (Americans and the World 2002a; Chicago Council and Marshall Fund 2002; PIPA 2000b).

As for war crimes, a battery of questions in 1993 had very substantial majorities favoring general provisions to bring leaders of countries before an international court if they were accused of seriously damaging the environment; invading and occupying neighboring countries; violating human rights, including large-scale violence against groups in the leaders' own countries; preventing democratic elections; or acquiring nuclear weapons. In 1999, 78 percent of those polled agreed that there were "rules or laws so important that if broken during war the person who breaks them should be punished," although only 40 percent favored having that punishment administered by an International Criminal Court (ICC). In 2000, 66 percent agreed that an ICC was needed as a "better way to prosecute war criminals," with only 29 percent more concerned that it might bring with it "trumped up charges ... brought against Americans, such as U.S. soldiers who use force in peacekeeping operations." A large majority was still in place in 2002 for U.S. support of an ICC, even with the risks it might bring for U.S. policy (Chicago Council and Marshall Fund 2002; PIPA 2000b).

American elites have increasingly shared the U.S. public's apparent willingness to be subject to rules. In 1996, only 13 percent of military and 35 percent of civilian elites agreed that "the time is ripe for the United States and other countries to cede some of their sovereignty to strengthen the powers of the United Nations and other international organizations" (O. R. Holsti 1998–99). As of 2002, civilian elites resembled the public, with large majority support for the ICC and treaties banning land mines and nuclear weapons tests (Chicago Council and Marshall Fund 2002).

This stew of role, obligations, and rights is accompanied by little appetite for the sort of preeminence central to hard-liner, unilateralist internationalism. Regarding solutions to international problems in general, large to very large public majorities (1995–2003) repeatedly rejected a "preeminent world leader" role in solving international problems in favor of doing "its share ... together with other countries." In 2002, the public by a very large margin favored "strong leadership" by the United States but also favored leadership being supplied by the EU and, to a lesser but still large extent, Japan. The balance of opinion on a number of troop-commitment scenarios turned positive when such actions were placed within a multilateral endeavor. The public has rejected and continues to reject any automatic and general "responsibility" to deal with "violations of international law and aggression wherever they may occur" (1999), to "settle international disputes" (1993) in general (Richman 1994a), or to "overthrow dictatorships" (2003). In 2000, 74 percent favored defense spending sufficient only "so that [the United States] can protect itself and to join in efforts to protect other countries together with allies or through the United Nations." In 1998 and 2002, large (if declining) majorities opposed responses to international crises without the support of allies. From 2001 on, numerous polls about the war on terrorism, Afghanistan, and Iraq repeatedly revealed a preference for use of force by the United States as part of a multilateral effort rather than on its own (Americans and the World 2002b, e).

While elites were more evenly divided in 1998 and 2002 on America responding without others, 1996 polling of military and civilian elites left little doubt about their preferences. At that time, 90 percent of each agreed that "increasingly countries will have to act together to deter and resist aggression." And 74 percent and 84 percent, respectively, felt that if "interests compel the U.S. to intervene militarily, it should be undertaken as part of a multilateral operation" (Center on Policy Attitudes 2000; Chicago Council and Marshall Fund 2002; Gallup Poll Release, March 8, 2001; O. R. Holsti 1998–99; Kull 1995–96; Kull and Destler 1999; PIPA 2003b; Richman 1994a).

The less-than-full similarity between these views and some of those noted earlier suggests that public permission for major international efforts, including but not limited to military interventions, will benefit from a multilateral aspect. A situation centering on unilateral action will have to pose a very compelling threat to self-realization if it is to garner public support. Neither accommodationists or unilateral asserters are holders across the board of reliably stable public majorities. Internationalists, with their broader portfolio of possible multilateral to unilateral options to be mixed for particular situations, are advantaged by public beliefs.

International Activism about What?

Given our earlier discussion, we expect that robust support for international cooperation and contributions will be selective and prevalent only for a few matters at any one time. What those will be is suggested by opinion on very important foreign policy goals (cooperation and contributions to achieve) and threats to "vital interests" (cooperation and contributions to forestall).

Publics and elites have often been asked about "very important foreign policy goals" for the United States. In this form of question, the items do not compete against each other, as multiple selections are allowed. Civilian elite and public results for 1986–2002 are displayed in table 3.9; the results for a different list of policy goals and samples of military and civilian elites from 1984 to 1996 are shown in table 3.10.

Even on casual inspection, it is striking how many of the most strongly supported goals contain a significant private benefit for the United States, particularly benefits of threat reduction and security enhancement. Most of the verbs in table 3.9 tell such a tale: *prevent* the spread of nuclear weapons; *control* arms; *protect* the jobs of U.S. workers; *stop* the flow of illegal drugs; *secure* energy supplies; *combat* international terrorism; *maintain* worldwide military supremacy; *match* Soviet military power; *contain* communism; *defend* the security of allies; *control* illegal immigration; *reduce* the U.S. trade deficit; *protect* the interests of U.S. business abroad. Whatever else, those verbs tell us a lot about the survey designers' and sponsors' view of the American international affairs culture.

With the exception of the goals for the global environment, reducing hunger, and (barely) strengthening the UN, only the items just mentioned were held to be "very important" by public majorities on more than two of the five polls. That is, most of the goals with less obvious private elements did not have broad public support. We infer that, except for the environment and hunger alleviation, the American public will be more easily mobilized for international activism (including cooperation and contributions) when private benefits are apparent and the focus is on reducing direct threats (Jentleson 1992; Jentleson and Britton 1998).

Elite opinions in table 3.9 emphasized fewer goals, but they were, for the most part, the same ones recognized by the public—arms proliferation, drug traffic, terrorism, military superiority, defending allies, and world hunger. Elites did not differ from the public by providing majorities for the other goals, including for almost a decade the environment. In both the elite and public samples, only minority support existed for a host of other goals that many people would consider central to international order and progress (promoting human rights, marketization, democratization, protecting weaker nations against aggression, and development). Elite responses from different samples (table 3.10)

TABLE 3.9. U.S. Foreign Policy Goals: Comparing Publics and Elites (in percentages)

Goal	2002	1998	1994	1990	1986
Prevent the spread of nuclear weapons	90	82	82	84	
	E89	E85	E90	E59	
Worldwide arms control				53	69
				E80	E83
Protect the jobs of U.S. workers	85	80	83	84	78
	E35	E45	E50	E39	E43
Stop the flow of illegal drugs into the U.S.	81	81	85		
	E45	E57	E57		
Combat international terrorism	91	79			
	E87	E74			
Secure energy supplies	75	64	62	76	69
	E51	E45	E67	E60	E72
Maintain worldwide military superiority	68	59	50		
	E52	E58	E54		
Match Soviet military power				56	53
				E20	E59
Contain communism				56	57
				E10	E43
Defend the security of allies	57	44	41	43	56
	E55	E58	E60	E56	E78
Control illegal immigration	79	55	72		
	E22	E21	E28		
Reduce the U.S. trade deficit	51	50	59	70	62
	E21	E34	E49	E62	
Protect the interests of U.S. business abroad	49		52	46	43
	E23		E38	E27	E32
Improve the global environment	66	53	58	73	
	E43	E46	E49	E72	
Strengthen the UN	57	45	51	52	46
	E28	E32	E33	E39	E22
Promote human rights in other countries	47	39	34	40	42
	E46	E41	E26	E45	E44
Promote market economies abroad	36	34			
	E27	E36			
Protect weaker nations against aggression	41	32	24	32	32
	E27	E29	E21	E28	E29
Combat world hunger	61	62	56		63
	E59	E56	E41		E61
Help bring democracy to other nations	34	29	25	28	30
	E33	E29	E21	E26	E29
Help improve the standard of living of less developed countries	30	29	22	33	
	E42	E36	E28	E42	
Strengthening international laws and institutions	43				
	E49				
Safeguarding against global financial instability	54				
	E49				

Source: Data from Chicago Council on Foreign Relations and Marshall Fund 2002.
Note: Elite responses are indicated by an "E." The question was, "I'm going to read a list of possible foreign policy goals that the U.S. might have. For each one, please say whether it should be a very important foreign policy goal of the U.S., a somewhat important foreign policy goal, or not an important goal at all." Percentages shown are for the "very important" response.

gave more standing than the public did to nonmilitary international cooperation but less to strengthening the UN. The percentages for nonmilitary matters tended to decline by 1996 and always were smaller for military than for civilian respondents.

Publics and elites have also had opportunities between 1994 and 2002 to express opinions on lists of possible "critical threats to the vital interests of the U.S. in the next ten years" (Chicago Council and Marshall Fund 2002).[45] The questions did not have the possibilities competing with each other, and the responses appear in figure 3.10.

The public seems in general more fearful than elites, with the possible exception of the fear of Islamic fundamentalism. The most pronounced fears pertain to violence and destructive weaponry—terrorism and WMD. As of 2002, public majorities treated two clearly nonmilitary matters as critical—AIDS (and other viral public health threats) and immigration—while elites were less impressed with both. Economic competition not only was less fearsome for elites but even for publics did not break through 50 percent by 1998, although very substantial minorities were concerned about it and about global warming. We will say more later about specific actors as threat sources; for now, we observe that among the specifically named foreign actors, both elite and public majorities identified only China. This picture suggests substantial public support for international activism, including cooperation to deal with terrorism, WMD, China, infectious-disease threats, and immigration.[46] Elite opinion, however, appears demanding only in the first three areas. As was the case for goals, the less identified possibilities included ones directly relevant to the issue areas discussed in later chapters.

Other data confirm the prevalence of anticipated threats of violent

TABLE 3.10. U.S. Foreign Policy Goals: Comparing Elites (in percentages)

Goal	1996	1992	1988	1984
Worldwide arms control	M59	M64	M39	M48
	C60	C73	C70	C72
Contain communism	M9	M13	M65	M60
	C15	C13	C34	C37
Strengthen the UN	M10	M35	M13	M5
	C27	C45	C28	C28
Combat world hunger	M10	M32	M30	M32
	C37	C56	C59	C57
Foster international cooperation to solve common	M40	M57	M48	M46
problems such as food, inflation, energy	C57	C72	C71	C67

Source: Data from O. R. Holsti 1998–99.

Note: "M" refers to military and "C" refers to civilian elites. They were asked of each possible goal whether they thought it should be a very important U.S. foreign policy goal.

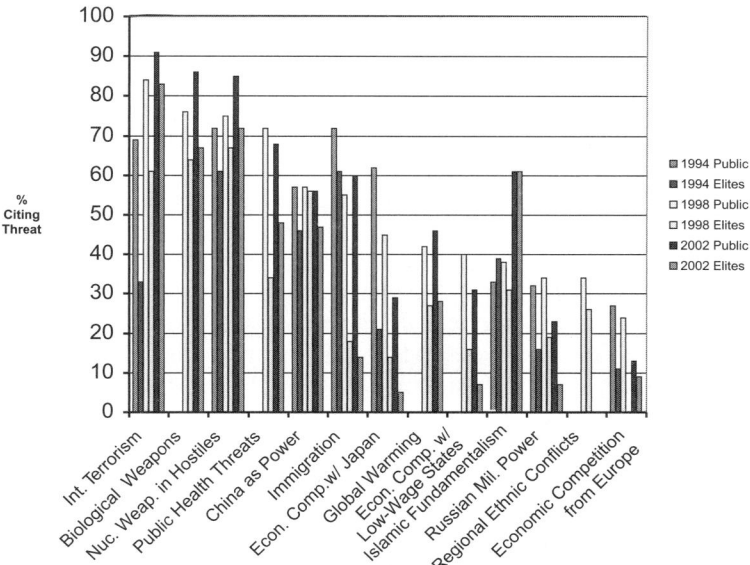

Fig. 3.10. Critical threats to the United States. (Data from Reilly 1995, 1999.)

destruction as the millennium came to a close and the twenty-first century began. In 1999, a majority thought it very or somewhat likely "that there will be another world war in the next ten years" ("Global Finance" 1999). That same year, only 50 percent of the public felt that the United States was more secure than at the end of the Cold War, and only 45 percent believed that international security had improved since that time. In 1998, when asked if particular nuclear weapons uses were very or fairly likely in the next ten years, 71 percent agreed when asked about other countries using nuclear weapons against each other; 60 percent agreed when asked about the possibility of a nuclear terrorist bomb against the United States. Substantial minorities thought it likely that the United States would be in a nuclear war in the coming decade (37 percent), about the same as those who thought that the United States would be attacked with nuclear weapons by another country in that period (Herron, Smith, and Hughes 2000). When elites and publics were asked in 1998 whether there would be more, less, or the same amount of bloodshed in the twenty-first century as in the twentieth, public pessimism was pronounced, with 53 percent expecting more and only 19 percent less. Even among the elites who were more optimistic, 57 percent foresaw more or the same (Reilly 1999). Fears of terrorist attacks were widespread prior to 9/11, although the majority expecting an increase in 1998 had shrunk to a split with the same level by 2000. Worry has remained a substantial minority sentiment about such attacks in the United States since 9/11, with a particularly prominent expectation involving the use of chemical and/or biological weapons (Americans and the World 2002b; Pew Research Center 2002b).

Clubs and Anticlubs in American Perceptions

International activism, cooperation, and contributions not only depend on the various ideas discussed to this point (e.g., importance of foreign policy matters in general, world role conceptions, generalized beliefs about rights and obligations, preferences for multilateralism, and recognized generic types of goals and threats) but also are affected by views of the specific others (i.e., nations, regional groupings, and nonstate actors) with whom and on whose behalf the United States might be active or against whom it would operate. From this perspective, international exertions can have a positive or a negative intent—to help or to hurt someone else. Foreign policy choice situations do involve specific others; preexisting views of those others thus enter into public support, indifference, or opposition to particular policy options. Established views of particular others then can help legitimate or delegitimate cooperation with or against them. Cooperation by and contributions from some others can help validate American policy in the eyes of the public, with the opposite consequences if that cooperation or contribution comes from different others. International activism pro or con can be constructed to have public and/or private elements depending on the characterization of the others in question, but each can be dominated by a private element.

Data are available for some nations, movements, and national groupings on three evaluative dimensions: affinity (as favorable and as threat posing), as a critical threat source, and importance (i.e., whether a particular state is a "vital interest"). We shall discuss these dimensions in turn.

Affinity opinions can be garnered from several types of queries about positive or negative affect. These probe the extent that particular others are viewed in "favorable," "warm," or "friendly" terms. As with trust, we reason that the predominance of such views implies a prima facie favorability toward joint actions; a predominance of negative views implies the opposite. The former implies that opponents of joint action face a greater burden of justification, as will proponents of collective action against well-regarded others. The latter implies that a greater burden of justification rests on proponents of cooperation with the negatively regarded, as it will for opponents of collective action to inflict damage on the negatively regarded.

A broad comparative picture appears in table 3.11 for the period 1989–2002 using several different measures. The first two columns (1989 and 2001) report net favorability response; the subsequent thermometer columns (1994, 1998, 2002) provide readings on a scale from the most positive of one hundred to the most negative of zero. The last two columns report net scores on an ally-to-enemy set of judgments in general (1993) and for reliability as a partner with respect to the war on terrorism (2002). The form of the questions does not place the political entities in explicit competition with each other, but opinions are limited to the entities posed to respondents. The results suggest that American public consideration of particular international affairs situations and options starts with the following groupings:

- an affinity core (Canada, Australia, and Great Britain);
- an inner circle (Japan, France, Germany, Italy, Mexico, and Israel);[47]
- a less close but positively regarded set (Brazil, Taiwan, the Philippines);
- those with no persistently preponderant positive or negative sentiment where a situational judgment might prevail (Argentina, China, South Korea, Poland, Russia, Turkey, Egypt, South Africa);
- those viewed somewhat negatively (Saudi Arabia [recently], Pakistan, Afghanistan, Nigeria);
- a set viewed very negatively (Colombia, Cuba, North Korea, Libya, Iran, Iraq, the Palestinian Authority).

We suggest that the EU has a generally positive evaluation, if only because of those for a number of its members. China by the measure in this table is on the edge between the situational and negative sets.[48] The relative affinity placements of the countries mentioned previously were generally supported by other surveys taken throughout the 1990s on favorability ratings, trust, and perceptions of countries as allies.[49] It is noteworthy that the publics of many of the countries in the three positive groupings have had reservations about U.S. approaches to international matters (table 3.2).

Critical threat sources as identified in table 3.12 enrich the perceptual picture painted by the results from table 3.11 with readings on Americans' perceptions of particular countries as the greatest current threat, a critical future threat, and the greatest future threat. Questions of the first and last types place the countries in competition with each other, but questions of the second type do not. For the second group,

TABLE 3.11. Americans' Evaluation of Others

	Favorability (net %)		Thermometer (0–100 scale)			Ally (net %)	Partner (net %)
	1989	2001	1994	1998	2002	1993	2002
Canada	91	83	73	72	77	80	
Mexico	43	41	57	57	60	34	
Brazil		52	54	54	55		
Argentina			47	49	47		
Colombia		−29			36		
Cuba		−41	38	38	35	−66	
Australia		77			77	66[a]	
Japan	46	52	53	55	60	15	48
China	−4	−3	46	47	48	−22	−3[b]
Vietnam		2			2		
Philippines		38			38	26[a]	
Taiwan		41	48	51	50	27[a]	
South Korea			48	50	46		
North Korea		−28	34	36	34		
European Union							62
United Kingdom	86	76	69	69	76	77	83
France	67	60	5	5	55	39	
Germany	64	59	57	56	61	33	
Italy		66	58	62	65	35	
Poland			52	50	50		
Russia	17	10	54	49	55	12	51[b]
Israel	37	33	54	55	55	24	40
Turkey				45	45		
Saudi Arabia	23	1	48	46	33		−18[b]
Egypt	43	32	34		45	14	
Iran	−62	−71	28	28	28	−74	
Libya		−64					
Iraq	−79	−76	24	25	23	−86	
Palestinian Authority		−38			−38	17[a]	
Pakistan				42	31		
Afghanistan					29		
India		28	48	46	46		
South Africa	−20	24	52	54	50		
Nigeria				46	42		

Source: Data from Gallup Poll Release, February 16, 2001; Americans and the World 2001b, 2002d, f, g; Richman 1994b; Chicago Council and Marshall Fund 2002.

Note: The first two columns provide net favorability percentages based on whether the respondent generally had a favorable opinion of a given country. Net favorability scores subtracted the sum of mainly unfavorable and very unfavorable from that of very and mainly favorable responses. Entries for China in 1991 are the average of responses to two questions; for Russia, of six; and for Israel, of five. The 2001 entry for the Palestinian Authority is the average of two. The thermometer columns (1994, 1998, 2002) present the mean response in a range where 100 is the most positive and zero the most negative. The Ally 1993 column reports the net response to a question asking the respondent to indicate whether a given country "is a close ally of the U.S.: is friendly but not a close ally; is not friendly but not an enemy, or is an enemy of the U.S." The net score subtracts the sum of the last two responses from that of the first two. The last column provides the net percentage viewing a country as a reliable partner in the war on terrorism.

[a] Indicates 1999 data.
[b] Indicates that the entry is the average of a question asked in 2001 and 2002.

TABLE 3.12. Country/Region Threats to United States (in percentages)

	Greatest Threat (current)			Critical Threat (future)				Greatest Threat (future)		
	1990	1996	2002	1990	1994	1998	2002	1991	1999 Mil.	1999 Econ.
Iraq	<1	36	23				wmd 72 E86		9	<1
Japan	8			Econ: 60 E63	Econ: 62 E21	Econ: 45 E14	Econ: 29 E5	11	<1	21
China	8	25	28	40 E16	57 E46	57 E56	56 E47	6	39	21
Russia/USSR	32	11	6	Mil: 33 E20	Mil: 32 E16	Mil: 34 E19	Mil: 23 E7 Pol. Turmoil: 27 E26	29	20	2
Iran	6	11	7					8	2	<1
Libya	2							1		
North Korea	<1	7								
Saudi Arabia										
Middle East							Conflict: 67 E73			1
Israel							Conflict 67 E73			
Pakistan			3				Conflict: 54 E61			
India			1				Conflict: 54 E61			
Germany								2	1	1
United Kingdom										2
Europe				Econ: 30 E41	Econ: 27 E11	Econ: 24 E16	Econ: 13 E9			
Cuba		5								
Serbia									1	
Mexico										2
Africa							Civil Wars: 24 E9			

Source: Data for Greatest current threat for 1990 from Richman 1994b; for 1996 from Americans and the World, 2000b; and for 2002 from Americans and the World, 2000e. Critical threat entries are from Chicago Council and Marshall Fund 2002. Future greatest threat entries on military are from Americans and the World 2000b, 2002d, g. Economic entries are from an Opinion Dynamics/Fox News poll in Public Agenda Online.

Note: Elite responses are indicated by an "E."

elite as well as public responses were available. Not surprisingly, the entries fit rather well with those in the previous table.

European states have little standing as a threat for now or the future, and the potential threat posed by EU economic competition has fallen to a very modest level for both the public and elites.[50] Japan's perceived threat clearly has become limited to the economic area and has declined to a low level for both the public and elites. A large decline, especially among elites, has occurred for Russian military power as well, with a shift to greater concerns with dangers posed by political instability there. Russia lost its primary enemy status of the Cold War period, moving to a point of neutral sentiment by 2000 ("Gallup Poll Topics: A–Z Russia" 2000). From 1988 to 1996, among both civilian and military U.S. elites, those viewing Russia as "generally expansionist rather than defensive in its foreign policy goals" shifted from substantial majorities to minorities (O. R. Holsti 1998–99). As for Iran, the threat has generally been relatively low but has experienced sporadic surges.

China clearly looms large as a continuing and future threat, although surpassed by Iraq in 2001 as a current national security threat and massively so in 2002 for elites and publics, with special reference to WMD. Yet perceptions of China as a current threat or as one among a number of critical future threats have stabilized in recent years rather than continuing to rise. Moreover, about 40 percent of the public in 1996 and 2001 admitted to more than a little concern or worry about the possibility of a military conflict with China (Americans and the World 2002d). Even among a cluster of Middle Eastern actors thought to be threatening, Iraq has stood out over the years. This may reflect an association in American thinking between Iraq and the threats of terrorism, Islamic fundamentalism, and arms proliferation. Concerns about proliferation probably also explain the mentions of North Korea. When posed in 2002, very high prominence among critical future threats was given to two conflicts with potential WMD use: India-Pakistan, and Israel-Arab. In contrast, the American public and especially U.S. elites give little standing to civil wars in Africa, where there is, of course, little in the way of WMD issues.

Opinions demanding action on sentiments toward particular foreign countries are likely to be influenced by judging the country to be one in which the United States has a "vital interest." These types of public and elite assessments appear in table 3.13, which shows the results of questions asked directly about each country with respect to vital interests from 1986 through 2002.

We estimate that countries always or almost always viewed as vital

TABLE 3.13. Countries in Which United States Has Vital Interest (in percentages)

	1986		1990		1994		1998		2002
	Public	Elites	Public	Elites	Public	Elites	Public	Elites	Public
Canada	78	96	77	90	71	93	69	89	79
Mexico	74	96	63	94	76	98	66	93	72
Brazil	44	63	39	51	34	49	33	75	36
Cuba					67		50		60
Haiti					56 (43a)		31		
El Salvador			50						
Japan	77	98	79	95	85	96	87	94	83
China	60	89	47	73	68	95	74	95	83
South Korea	58	80	49		65	90	54	82	69
Taiwan	53	48	46	47	49		52		65
Philippines	74	81	62	51					62
Indonesia							33	50	33
United Kingdom	83	94	79	86	69	82	66	84	78
France	56	82	45	63	39	59	37	57	53
Germany	76	98	73	95	66	91	60	83	68
Russia			83	93	79	98	77	95	81
Poland	35		45		31	46	31	42	
Ukraine					35	66			
Baltic					29	34	27	30	
Bosnia					44 (53a)		51	48	43
Turkey			41				33		52
Israel	76	86	67	78	64	86	69	86	79
Saudi Arabia	77	88	83	89	83	94	77	88	83
Egypt	61		53	76	45	78	46	66	53
Iran	51		56				61	72	75
Kuwait			77	69	76		68		
Afghanistan							45		73
India	36	55			31		36		65
South Africa	58	63	53	50	57	52	52	52	49
Nigeria	31		29						31
Rwanda					35				
North Koreaa					(62a)				62
Somalia					(39b)				
Argentina									39
Colombia									62
Iraq									76
Pakistan									76
Sudan									52

Source: Data from Chicago Council and Marshall Fund 2002; Richman 1994b.

Note: The council elicitation took the form, "Many people believe that the U.S. has a vital interest in certain areas of the world and not in others. That is, certain countries of the world are important to the U.S. for political, economic, or security reasons. I am going to read a list of countries. For each, tell me whether you feel the U.S. does or does not have a vital interest in that country."

aIndicates percentage who felt that the United States has "a great deal at stake."
bThe Somalia query was asked in 1993.

interests by a solid majority (66 percent or more) of elites and publics are ones for which policymakers are expected on a continuing basis to show that they are paying attention and being effective. For the period covered, Canada, Mexico, Japan, the United Kingdom, Germany, Russia, Israel, and Saudi Arabia have consistently been rated as vital. In recent years, that cluster has been joined by China. South Africa falls somewhat short of that standing, as do Taiwan and Cuba, although their evaluation is less clear because of the absence of elite data. Another set of countries have been viewed as highly important by elites but less so by publics. For these countries, we see incentives for active engagement unless policy costs trigger public opposition. Countries in this category include Brazil, South Korea, France, and Egypt. Poland and Indonesia have the same pattern of greater elite than public importance, but to a lesser degree. Finally, there are countries whose appearance seems situational (at least to the poll designers), as prominence is associated with current events salient for the United States. These include Haiti, El Salvador, the Philippines, Ukraine, Bosnia, Turkey, Kuwait, Afghanistan, Rwanda, North Korea, Somalia, Iraq, Pakistan, and Sudan. For those countries, we expect demand on policymakers for active policy to be episodic rather than continuing. That demand will be less a function of the continuing existence of those states than of their relevance to more general issues of current salience, such as (for now) terrorism and WMD.

Attributions of importance are also indicated by responses to questions asking for more comparative judgments. In 2002, attributions of world influence by the American public gave Great Britain higher standing than (in declining order) China, the EU, Russia, Germany, and France. The EU was thought by 50 percent of the respondents to have increased in that respect, but only a narrow plurality had that view of Japan. Whereas in 1998 a plurality saw Japan as more important for the United States than China, the two countries had slipped into a tie four years later. A majority saw Europe as more important than Asia, a margin wider than in earlier polls. Elite views, however, differed in important respects. Substantial majorities saw increases in the world leadership importance of the EU and declines in that respect for Japan. China had surpassed Japan in relative importance by a large margin, and the gap in the relative importance of Asia and Europe shrank. Numerous other polls suggest a public anticipation of growth in China's importance. For example, a large public majority in 1997 expected China to be a superpower, and in 1999 50 percent expected China "to pose the biggest challenge to America's world power status in the next one hundred years" (Americans and the World 2002d).

To summarize, we reason that active cooperation and contribution efforts will be most readily supported with core political entities—that is, those with both affinity and importance. Our general interpretation of the previously reported data is that only a few meet that test and cluster in the following order:

First Tier: Canada, Mexico, Great Britain, Germany, Japan, Israel, and the EU;
Second Tier: France;
Third Tier: Brazil, Egypt, South Africa, South Korea, Taiwan, Russia.

For states viewed in very negative terms but also as vital (such as Iran), support will exist for international cooperation and contributions that are perceived as working against those countries' current systems and international policy approaches. For countries lodged in less extreme positions on one or another of these dimensions (or not firmly placed at all), public support for active cooperation with or against will have to be generated by the situational context and framing in terms of more general issues. China is a prominent case in point. The more favorably the country is viewed, the less the resistance to cooperation with it and contributions to it and the more welcome contributions by it (e.g., Australia and Italy); the less favorably a country is viewed, the less resistance there will be to multilateral and unilateral contributions made against it and the more suspicion of contributions by it (e.g., North Korea and Cuba). We suggest that support for U.S. policy by first- and second-tier countries provides a sort of certification to Americans of policy merit. Opposition by these countries to contribution stances that American policymakers prefer may well work against permissions from a broader set of U.S. elites or even the public. Policymakers in such circumstances will have incentives either to modify policy accordingly or to counter such developments by playing up notions of foreign treachery. These propensities are particularly valuable for our understanding of the prospects for contributions to international order as many of the core countries listed earlier play large roles in the policy areas we discuss in our four subsequent policy chapters.

Multilateralism and Particular International Institutions in American Perceptions

In the contemporary world system, it is difficult to assess prospects for international cooperation without taking into account the role of multilateral forums and formal international institutions. Understanding the place of such institutions for U.S. policy is especially important given recurrent charges by allies and adversaries alike that American policy tends toward unilateralism and rejects international institutionalism. Our research on American internationalism has established that public and elite support for full-blown unilateralism is more an exception than a general tendency. Both, however, seem far more internationalist than accommodationist and thus have not so much rejected unilateral and military options as placed them in a larger portfolio. That finding leaves open the state of preferences about working with specific multilateral institutions. We shall examine views about the United Nations, NATO, the European Union, NAFTA, and the WTO.

Cooperating fully with the UN has been a substantial majority preference in repeated polls undertaken between 1980 and 2001. Payment of dues to the UN with no purpose specified and with no linkage to UN reforms has been a substantial majority preference when asked many times from 1994 to 2002. On questions linking dues payment to reforms (in the 1997–98 period), smaller majorities or pluralities rejected such linkage. When queried thirteen times (1990–99) about "overall" or "general" opinion of the UN, substantial majorities were favorable on all but one occasion. Substantial majorities rejected concerns about loss of sovereignty to the UN (1995–98) (Americans and the World 2001a, 2002c; Center on Policy Attitudes 2000; Chin and Marsh 1999; Pew Research Center 2002b; PIPA 2000b).

This rather stunning public support for the UN is even more striking in response to questions about strengthening the organization (Americans and the World 2002c; Chicago Council and Marshall Fund 2002; Chin and Marsh 1999). Strengthening was favored (in itself or as a very important or important foreign policy goal) by usually more and never less than a majority in the seven polls of the public conducted from 1986 to 2002. As shown in table 3.9, the portion of the public viewing strengthening the UN as a very important U.S. foreign policy goal was essentially stable, in the 46–57 percent range. And in fourteen questions about UN performance (1991–2001), majorities provided a positive evaluation in all but three, and a 50 percent negative verdict was reached in only one.

Public support for maintaining and strengthening the UN held up in spite of convictions by majorities and pluralities that the United States was assigned responsibility for an unfairly large share of the UN budget (1990, 1995, 1996). Substantial segments of the public (54 percent and 39 percent in 1995) also believed that the UN worked more for the benefit of others than of the United States (Americans and the World 2001a; Chin and Marsh 1999). Yet a substantial majority in 1995 agreed that there was "no special reason to distrust the U.N. more than other institutions" (Americans and the World 2001a). When the UN funding obligation formula was explained (as share of the world economy), a small majority still thought that the U.S. share was "too much" (1997). A majority did, however, find the share reasonable ("fair" or "about right") when it was placed in the context of the slightly higher EU total share and slightly lower Japanese one (1998) or in the context of the permanent Security Council member veto power over peacekeeping operations (1994) (Americans and the World 2000a). This picture clearly argues for continuing and growing cooperation with and contributions to the UN as a collective action body, at least in the public's view.

More recently, 2003 polling about the Iraq war found large public majorities convinced of the desirability of seeking UN authorization for American use of force (and for having sought UN authorization for that war) (Americans and the World 2002e; PIPA 2003b). A majority rejected the view that the UN was losing importance (Pew Research Center 2003). The UN was desired to be a major actor in the war on terrorism and in counterproliferation efforts directed at North Korea and Iran. Indeed the large majority that felt that the Security Council had the right to block proliferation by authorizing a preventive use of force far exceeded the split opinion on a national right to engage in unauthorized use of force (PIPA 2003c). As for the war on terrorism, there was near unanimity that the UN should play a major role, and very large majorities favored the Security Council having the power to require possible host states to accept a "UN sponsored police force, . . . freeze assets of suspected terrorist groups, . . . provide intelligence" on and arrest them, and send an "international military force" absent host government compliance (Americans and the World 2002b).

Those opinions should not be read, however, as blanket public support for a qualitative increase in UN power. Only a minority, albeit a large one (1995), expressed trust in the UN to do what is right "just about always" or "most of the time" (Americans and the World 2001a). Nor has there been much support for a general transfer of sovereignty to it. In 2001, the American public was asked to consider three roles for the "UN to play in world affairs today—a leading role where all countries are required to follow UN policies, a major role where the UN establishes policies but where individual countries still act separately when they disagree with the UN, or a minor role with the UN serving mostly as a forum for communication between nations, but with no policymaking role." A near majority opted for the second statement (49 percent), and only a modest minority chose the first option (19 percent), somewhat less than those preferring the minor role (28 percent) (Gallup Poll Release, March 8, 2001).

In addition, the American public has not been equally supportive of all areas of possible UN activity (Americans and the World 2001a).[51] Thirteen areas of activity were posed in 1995.[52] The ranking and distribution of responses suggests that the American public views the most appropriate role for the UN as that of a humanitarian welfare organization rather than a political, economic, or military one. In light of the hierarchy of "very important foreign policy goals" and critical threats for the United States, there seems to be a preference for a division of labor between those areas to be pursued in other ways and those where the UN should play a more prominent role. With respect to the issues discussed in later chapters, the latter is far stronger for the environment than for peacekeeping, foreign aid, or debt management and relief.

As for American elites, table 3.9 shows that strengthening the UN was advocated by a smaller share than the public and was in continuing decline after 1990. Table 3.10 showed that an early post–Cold War surge among both civilian and military elites was followed by a reduction to previous low levels. The coolness these results convey was not accompanied, however, by majority support for unilateral reduction of America's budget share (1996) but by the emergence of very substantial majorities among military and civilian elites agreeing that it was "vital to enlist the cooperation of the UN in settling international disputes" (O. R. Holsti 1998–99). Perhaps what elites have in mind amounts to wanting a follower (or source of blessings) with respect to collective action but not a world organization that presses for U.S. accommodation to group preferences. If anything, these polls show an accurate reading of the chances for permissions and support from the American public. With regard to invading Iraq, for example, the public clearly favored seeking UN support for military action and providing some time for inspections (even though the public was skeptical about their effectiveness).

Moving to perceptions of NATO, only single-digit minorities have favored withdrawal when polled between 1974 and 2002; public and elite majorities (except in 1990) have always favored U.S. commitment to that institutionalized club. In polls in 1998 and 1999, almost 90 percent viewed NATO as important or fairly important for U.S. interests. In 2002, 56 percent said the organization was essential (Americans and the World 2001a; Chicago Council and Marshall Fund 2002; Gallup Poll Release, April 1, 1999; Richman 1994a). NATO is, then, something to retain, as indicated in 1999 by the positive assessment by two-thirds of the public of NATO and substantial net opposition to replacement by a European Union force ("Global Finance" 1999). The public also seems to support expansion of NATO, especially with regard to Russia, although much thinner majorities favored the admission of some other states who were still candidates in 2002 (Chicago Council and Marshall Fund 2002). These findings clearly support cooperation and maintaining contributions.

The views of NATO are accompanied by rather positive ones toward the EU and about cooperation with that organization. We have already noted public support for strong international leadership by the EU, albeit with a preference that it not become a superpower. A substantial majority would prefer the retention of close ties over an increase in European independence. That desire may have at least something of a burden-sharing element. Large elite and public majorities reject specialized world roles with the United States focused on military instruments and the EU on development tasks. That same desire for burden sharing may underlie predominant public support for the EU to become more active in the Israel-Arab conflict and pay more of the costs of dealing with it. The EU is thus a wanted partner, and both the U.S. public and U.S. elites have recently been willing to accept some compromise of U.S. preferences in the interest of cooperation (Chicago Council and Marshall Fund 2002; Pew Research Center 2002c).

The strongly positive picture for cooperation with the UN, NATO, and the EU is not matched for the most comprehensive regional economic club to which the United States belongs, NAFTA. In numerous questions asked of the public from 1991 into 1996, what positive pluralities for membership occurred were very small and were often negative. In general, benefits to the United States were queried on many occasions in the 1991–2000 period. Stable pluralities with a positive view did not develop until the late 1990s. When benefits were broken down between U.S. workers and firms or investors, a strong difference emerged. Majorities consistently saw them as benefiting firms and investors (1995–99). Majorities or large pluralities saw negative effects on U.S. jobs and wages in response to four relevant questions (1993–96). Also, the national benefits were largely perceived as accruing to NAFTA partners (especially Mexico) rather than the United States in 1996 and 1999 (Americans and the World 2002a). In contrast, elites have expressed massively positive views on NAFTA (O. R. Holsti 1998–99; Reilly 1999). Although favorable views of NAFTA remain tenuous and highly controversial, there seems to be no massive swell of domestic opposition to maintenance of the cooperation the agreement involves. The distribution of public opinion was stable from 1998 to 2000, with a plurality supporting continuation with the proviso of changes. That hardly

Defensive Internationalism

suggests support for simply admitting more members to NAFTA to transform it into a Free Trade Area of the Americas or for emulating NAFTA in other trade arrangements.

The final institution for discussion here is the WTO. After an initial lack of public opinion about the organization,[53] a generally favorable assessment appeared in recent years. Majority support for strengthening was present in 1999 and 2002, and in 2000 respondees provided a positive evaluation in terms of benefits to the United States (Chicago Council and Marshall Fund 2002; PIPA 2000b). While hardly conclusive, these findings suggest support, at least in principle, for a global economic arrangement with what may be perceived to be equal, fully reciprocal requirements of all its members.[54]

American Contributions: Internationalist, Selective, Reactive, and Impure

Our story about American public opinion bearing on international cooperation and contributions has been lengthy and complicated. It is a thoroughly mixed bag posing difficult interpretive problems to policy establishments at home and abroad. Nevertheless, some major features can readily be summarized. The first is that opinion is internationalist in the sense of supporting military and nonmilitary action, both collective and unilateral. Those self-conceptions have foundations of widely viewed rights to preeminence and obligations about its use. Rights and obligations are seen less as contradictory than as mutually reinforcing. What those are tends to be both a reflection and a cause of selection of goals, threats, and others for attention. The public and elites tend to select goals and threats clearly linked to domestic damage or well-being, most obviously matters with a coercive, military focus.

Possibly as a result of a loss-avoiding rather than gain-achieving emphasis, there is a reactive tendency with two aspects that are important to us. The first is that desire for collective action follows rather than leads the emergence of major loss prospects. The second is that given the conceptions of rights and obligations, there is a tendency to react to possible signs of losing preeminence by more active internationalism. That internationalism gets applied to a map of the world on which a relatively few, mostly northern countries are stable, large features. Others appear and vanish only with crises. Crises are perceived deficits in the United States for sustaining its rights and meeting its obligations. Faced with crises or foreign drift away from followership, U.S. contributions may be motivated by the possibility of losing special status through inaction or excessive tolerance of others' differing agendas. Yet in responding, it will be important to limit costs that can waste or drain American resources for meeting future challenges to widely held rights and obligations.

These features surely suggest the necessary condition of a perceived private benefit to induce American international activity. Very importantly, domestic support does not preclude but can be buttressed by a credibly public element as well—that is, impurity. In effect, much of the opinion we have discussed rejects that the two elements are in a zero-sum relationship, instead supporting the notion of the United States doing good by doing well and, to a somewhat lesser but still significant degree, doing well by doing good. Given that prospect, it seems reasonable to support collective institutions perceived as conducive to those thrusts and to expect other countries to lend their support and bear some of the provision burden since they will get some of the eventual benefit. Within such a belief system, it also makes it reasonable to emphasize support from others in dealing with those who seem inclined to impose private bads on the United States. After all, such private bads are predominantly viewed in American opinion to produce jointly public bads for the affinity club and others around the globe.

JAPAN

We have argued that the underlying general polling themes for international cooperation and contributions for Europeans center on the nature of the EU as a club and for Americans center on the extent that the United States can and should shape the world around it. For the Japanese, the content of polls in the latter part of the twentieth century suggests a different fundamental question: How can Japan preserve its valued characteristics while avoiding international isolation and shocks endangering those values and Japan itself? The bases and prospects for international cooperation and contributions in terms of public support and opposition rest on a foundation provided by general views of the character of Japan, how others regard it, and threats and challenges posed by foreigners' views and international developments. Opinion on those matters yields preferences for certain types of actions and relationships as well as suspicion of others.[55]

Conceptions of Japan: Domestic and Foreign

Among the twenty-three publics polled in 1995 (table 3.1), Japan is second to none in perceived national superiority. But this finding leads to the following question: What are the key components of that sense of superiority? Surveys from 1990 through 2000 give a clear answer and appear

Defensive Internationalism

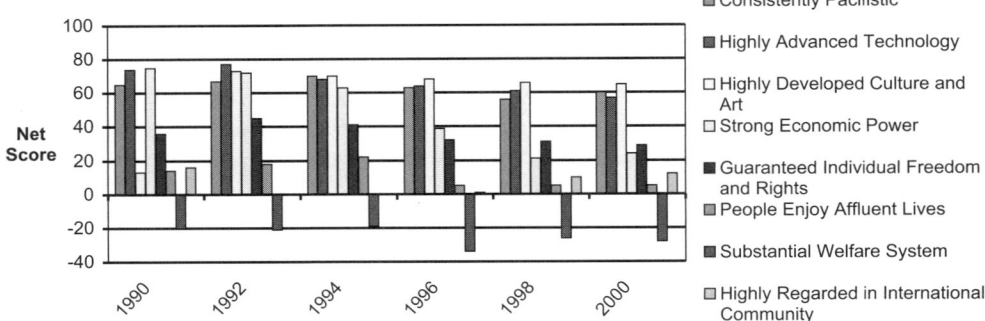

Fig. 3.11. What kind of country is Japan? (Data from Prime Minister's Information Office Surveys, JPOLL.)

in figure 3.11.[56] A sense of superiority has been based on being consistently pacifistic, technologically highly advanced, having a highly developed art and culture, and, to a declining degree in more recent years, being a strong economic power. It is not rooted in the "Japanese people leading affluent lives" or in Japan having a "substantial welfare system." The challenge is how to maintain and advance the central positive features without penalizing an economically unindulged population.

In meeting that challenge, Japanese leaders must cope with the Japanese public's perception that the country is not highly regarded internationally. This perception is confirmed by other polling results and likely colors the public's international policy inclinations. Trust in Japan attributed to other countries polled on six occasions 1991–97 was negative in three, including 1997, and, when positive, was lower than the net 26 percent of 1990.[57] When asked about Asian countries specifically (in 1994), the perception of Japan was a net negative 20 percent, and perceived Asian net dislike of Japan was even greater. These sentiments matter for a public with strong net feelings of closeness to its continental neighbors (table 3.1).

The Japanese public may indeed feel that foreign doubts are warranted. When asked about "confidence in Japan to deal responsibly with world problems" (on six occasions from 1990 to 1993), less than a net 10 percent expressed a great deal or a fair amount of confidence. With respect to Asia, there has been a continuing majority view that compensation for the damage caused by the World War II in the Pacific has been inadequate (in seven polls between 1994 and 1997). In 1995, large majorities recognized that Japan's past conduct posed ongoing obstacles to good relations with China and Korea.

The sensed Asian resentment has accompanied a lack of confidence about membership in other clubs of First World countries in particular.[58] Recognition of Japanese imperfection (at least relative to that in some other publics' perceptions of their own countries) includes trade matters. In 1995, a majority held Japanese trade policy to be unfair to other nations; in 1994, a large majority believed that national economic problems resulted from internal rather than external conditions; and in nine polls between 1991 and 1995 on trade frictions with the United States, six showed majorities assigning primary or shared blame to Japan. The three polls that found only attribution primarily to either the United States or Japan never had a margin blaming the United States of more than 9 percent.

Those who perceived Asian trust or non-Asian club memberships mostly attributed them to Japan's economic strength. Economic decline may then work to increase fears of isolation and support for countering it by additional efforts at international cooperation and contributions—as long as they do not clearly impose additional economic burdens on Japan's unindulged citizens. The possibility of isolation and a sense of limited influence were prominent even during the period of greatest economic strength. A large majority agreed in 1990 that in the world of the 1990s, "Japan will lose its credit in the international community and become isolated." Large majorities were concerned that "Japan will become isolated in the world if its economic frictions with other countries continue" (1990–93). Large majorities in 1990–91 also rejected pro-unilateralist possibilities such as "The world cannot get along without Japanese money" and technology or "If Japan's economic and technological power continue to grow, Japan cannot be beaten by foreign countries."

One possible way to improve Japan's situation might be self-transformation through internationalization. In annual polls undertaken between 1990 and 1997, only small minorities saw that course as damaging, and the bulk of opinions (40–48 percent) viewed it as "necessary," agreeing that Japan "has to become more international." Another path to improvement could be through a general increase in international activism and contributions in world affairs (1991–93, 1995), despite majority fears of the risks to "our way of life" from "being involved with other nations" (1991, 1993). Anything less was widely thought to risk the possibility of growing isolation because increased contributions were and would continue to be expected of Japan by "other countries" (1992, 1993). Heightened activism would best be accompanied, according to the Japanese public at levels rarely expressed elsewhere (table 3.1), by refraining from import limitations and abjuring the pursuit of self-interest in ways that might exacerbate the chances of conflicts with other countries. The latter finding of course fits with the prominence of a pacific posture in citizens' views of the nature of contemporary Japan.

The conception of that pacific posture is, however, complex and has been a matter of continuing reinterpretation. A 1994 question asking "What brought Japan peace for the past fifty years?" found respondents giving special emphasis to internal sources—the constitutional self-restraint provisions (Article 9), the "experience of a cruel war," and the "efforts of the Japanese people." Each was more identified than Japan's principal international alignment (the United States–Japan Security Treaty) and was far more so than such structural features as geography and the balance of power. While the public has not been predominantly convinced that Article 9 "appeals to the rest of the world" (1991), massive public majorities have believed that it will contribute to attaining world peace in the future and does contribute to the peace and safety of Japan (1992, 1997).

In both the early and mid-1990s, the public was convinced that Japan was not, should not, and will not become a greater military power than it was already—that is, not much of one, in their view (polls in 1990, 1991, 1994, 1995). In twenty polls taken from 1990 to 2000, the combination of those in favor of maintaining or reducing the current strength of the Japanese military exceeded that of those in favor of increasing it by a large majority except in one (*Government Poll Yearbook* 2001, 98, 505). The Japanese public has not tended to accept an obligation to "fight for their country" in event of war. Only an international low of 20 percent accepted that obligation in multination polling in the early 1990s (Inglehart, Basañez, and Moreno 1998). In 1999 only one-third agreed that "a person who is able should be willing to fight to defend his country." In 1997, only 8 percent indicated that they would respond to an invasion of Japan by joining the national military or engaging in guerrilla warfare. Nuclear weapons ownership has continually been massively rejected (1991,1994, 1995, and a Tokyo metropolitan sample in 1998 [Gallup Poll Release, June 5, 1999]).

The pacific self-conception should not be confused, however, with pacifism in the Western sense. The Japanese public has predominantly claimed the right of self-defense, enabling Japan to use military force to defend itself if attacked (large majorities in 1991, 1995, 1996, 1998). Understanding the significance of this result, though, depends on how self-defense is defined. In recent years (1998, 1999), public majorities have accepted expanding what falls under that right to include responses with arms including the dispatch of warships to "protect civilians, when on a mission to rescue [Japanese] civilians [abroad], . . . and to attack a foreign vessel invading Japanese territorial waters." That reinterpretation has not extended to granting to the military the national status associated with ministerial cabinet-level membership. In three 1997 questions, support for elevating the military post never exceeded 25 percent.

World Role Preferences and Expectations

In the post–Cold War period, the Japanese public has not viewed the external world as a benign place or expected it to evolve into one. The external world has posed a continuing and perhaps increasingly dangerous environment as measured by survey questions across a variety of issues ranging from world health concerns to military security and the prospects for lessening inequality between the North and the South. Asia was predominantly thought to be unstable, dynamic, and poor. By the late 1990s, substantial majorities agreed that "in the near future, countries around Japan will be involved in a war or conflict that may affect Japan's security" or worried about an event occurring "in which the U.S. needs to use its military power because military conflicts in areas surrounding Japan affect Japan's peace and security."

These opinions would raise the salience of choices about how Japan could deal with a dangerous and volatile world with minimum risk to the self-conception discussed previously and in light of others' negative views of the country. We shall summarize extensive polling results for attitudes about the following aspects of Japan's world role: (1) leadership and world influence; (2) association or alignment versus independence and neutrality; (3) the issues where cooperation and contributions should focus; (4) the currencies of contributions; and (5) the role of military instruments.

With respect to leadership, a large majority in 1991 and 1993 surveys supported taking such a role in Asia in the future when that was posed independent of alternative possibilities. Yet when that possibility was posed relative to other options (on four occasions in 1990–93), it was never chosen by more than 30 percent. Expectations that Japan would increasingly play an Asian leadership role were not held by a majority in 1991, and in 1993 the majority preference was for the status quo. When considering involvement in the world as a whole, in 1991 a small majority said that Japanese political leadership should be strengthened and chose the preferred future role as "an economic and political leader." By 1994, a large majority expected Japanese leadership in the twenty-first century to be no stronger than it already was. In 1999, less than 5 percent thought that Japan would be a "global leader" in the twenty-first century (*Government Poll Yearbook* 2001, 499).

While not tantamount to leadership, permanent membership in the United Nations Security Council may be considered as a role indicative of world influence and accepted contribution obligations in a small, high-status-club way. Preferences about Japan attaining permanent member status in fourteen polls (1991–2000) were consistently net positive, reaching net majorities in the more recent years. When asked in 1993 and 1994, however, about membership preferences if playing a military role came with it, opinion turned negative. In sum, the preferred world role sought status through membership while trying to minimize the military commitment that status might involve.

As evidenced by the UN Security Council possibility, the broad and continually preferred alternative to leadership has been alignment or associated membership in some sort of club—in other words, avoidance of isolation. The same 1990–93 questions where Asian leadership was a preferred role option showed only small minorities opting for an independent position and showed a large majority favoring partnerships with the United States and Western Europe (preferably and increasingly with both). An "Asia only" option to build an analogue to the European Community had much less support in 1993 (5 percent) than an Asia-Pacific one including the United States (61 percent) or a global one with no "particular emphasis on Asia" (24 percent). In 1995, a plurality favored an isolation-avoiding tack of getting closer to APEC, even though the Japanese public had formed no clear views of whether the organization was more or less beneficial to Japan. The isolation-avoiding desire may explain the massive majority in the multinational 1995 poll discussed earlier that selected unification with APEC in spite of the small minority that saw it as benefiting Japan. In questions asked monthly in 1990–94, alignment with the "liberal states camp" never received less than 61 percent, with a repeated ratio to a neutrality option of about 3 to 1.

A prime instance of this preference has been the United States–Japan Security Treaty. In twenty-six polls (1990–2000), opinion has always been more in favor of the treaty than against it in terms of maintenance and benefit to or usefulness for Japan compared to one or another way of going without it. The net positive score topped 50 percent in more recent years. Yet as of 1999, only a small minority saw the United States–Japan security alliance as the best focus for preventing conflicts in Asia (*Government Poll Yearbook* 2000, 448).

The treaty commitment could entail acceptance of the international military role often associated with major powers allied with America. The Japanese public certainly had little desire in 2002 to see a military superpower emerge to balance the United States (Chicago Council and

Marshall Fund 2002). Yet when polled in the context of the revision in recent years of the "United States–Japan Defense Guidelines" that regulate bilateral military cooperation, the Japanese public has instead favored constraining Japan's commitment in ways that fit with the pacific stance noted earlier and the perceptions of a conflict-prone world. That is, the public has tended to accept the need for isolation avoidance, even if doing so means increased contributions for conflicts "in the neighborhood" short of direct attack on Japan. At the same time, the Japanese public has drawn the line at commitments involving fighting war other than in defense of an attack on Japan—that is, contributions minus combat. Majorities have not favored automatic cooperative involvement with or without combat whenever the United States or the Japanese government requests it (1999) or fighting alongside U.S. troops (1997). The public has strongly preferred to limit cooperation to Japan's "territorial land, waters, and airspace," to nonmilitary support of the United States (1997), or to noncombat tasks for the Japanese military. In case of foreign military attack on Japan, the predominant choice has been not to meet defense needs unilaterally (9 percent) but through cooperative alignment (with the United States, 46 percent) and membership in a broader community (the United Nations, 36 percent) (1999).

With regard to the issues of most interest in our later chapters, repeated polling in the past decade shows high and quite stable support for efforts related to world peace and conflict mitigation, and to preserving the global environment.[59] When, over the same time period, the questions dealt with policy approaches pursued through the United Nations, the chosen emphases remained the same.[60] These emphases are compatible with the focus on the dangers of nuclear weapons and environmental degradation in table 3.3. The poll results appear in figure 3.12 and table 3.14.

The data suggest a continuing decline in support for contributions with a potential economic cost. That is true for the world economy items and is consistent with the very low support for the UN financial item in table 3.14. As early as 1991, a majority stood against increasing Japan's economic contributions "to the international community." Even shortly after the Gulf War (1993), the public was at best split on doing so. Even for the Gulf War, financial support pledges were viewed much less as the right thing to do than as an unavoidable price for avoiding isolation (1991). Human-resource contributions as distinct from financial ones in that time period also had far more support as being "inevitable" rather than appropriate in principle. We will return to public support for financial contributions in our later discussion of foreign aid.

Defensive Internationalism

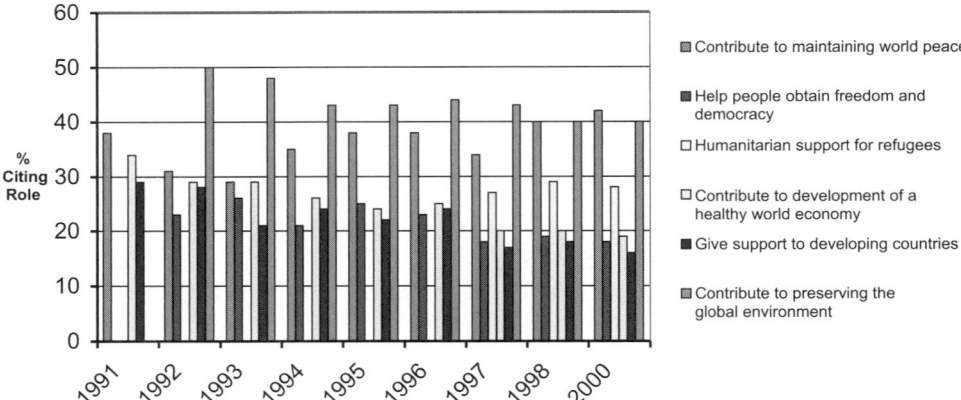

Fig. 3.12. Japan's role in the world. (Data from JPOLL and Japan Information Network, various years.) *Note:* Up to two responses permitted from list provided.

As measured by other poll questions, these patterns are compatible with preferences (in 1992, 1995, and 1999) for diplomatic contributions and exchange of technology and culture over financial ones. Military contributions were dead last. As we shall see in our chapter on peacekeeping, great efforts have been made to keep them there.

Country and Regional Appraisals

As with the United States, surveys of the Japanese public allow the drawing of some linkages between views of particular others and their implications for attitudes toward some broad lines of foreign and security policy. We begin with feelings of affinity and then turn to threat and importance (general and economic). Substantial polling has also occurred on evaluations of current, expected, and past relationships. Those responses might confirm policy success and necessity, thus arguing for support for continuity. If, however, those evaluations are inconsistent with affinities, importance, and threats, they suggest some public receptivity to policy modifications.

Net affinity data (1990–2000) are reported in table 3.15 for the countries and regions posed to the Japanese respondents. Japanese public affinity appears strong only with distant developed-world entities—most strikingly the United States, recently Australia and New Zealand (Oceania), and then what we choose to call the European Union/European Community ("nations such as France, Germany, and the U.K."). This is compatible with the mostly positive reactions to the aspects of

TABLE 3.14. Japan's International Relation Cooperation through the UN (in percentages)

	2000	1999	1998	1997	1996	1995	1994	1993	1992	1991
Maintaining world peace and safety	68	69	67	61	65	69	67	66	69	76
Developing science and technology including space	16	17	17	16	18	15	15	17	19	18
Human rights	29	27	24	23	27	28				
Rescuing refugees	29	33	32	28	25	27	26	26	33	38
Disarmament and prevention of weapons diffusion	40	42	31	28	29	33	28	28	29	32
Land mines	17	20	20							
Illegal drugs	23	27	22	29	22	19	18	22	23	22
Environmental protection	46	56	50	54	50	53	56	59	62	63
Population	12	11	11	12	12					
Gender equality for women	14	12	11	10	13	14				
Crime prevention including illegal gun trade	27	31	23	26	24	22				
Fight against terrorism	19	23	21	24						
Caring for children, handicapped, and elderly	29	35	29	25	32	26				
Financial contribution to UN	8	10	8	7	9	9				
Reform of UN	7	7	6							
Support for developing countries	29	33	36	31	36	37	35	34	40	44

Source: Data from JPOLL; Japan Information Network.
Note: Multiple responses were permitted from list provided.

TABLE 3.15. Japanese Affinities: Feelings of Closeness (net %)

	2000	1998	1997	1996	1995	1994	1993	1992	1991	1990
United States	48	58	50	54	44	50	56	52	61	53
EU/EC	10	20	8	5	−5	3	7	3	3	7
China	−2	1	−4	−6	1	7	11	15	6	10
South Korea	3	−4	−19	−24	−11	−11	−8	−9	−9	−7
ASEAN	22	−25	−15	−11	−12	−21	−18	−21	−23	−19
South Asia	−52	−48	−42	−34	−33	−39	−41	−39	−38	−48
Oceania	18	9								
Middle East	−67	−56								

Source: Data for 1990–98 are from Prime Minister's Information Office, commissioned polls in JPOLL; data for 2000 is from a poll commissioned by that office in *Government Poll Yearbook* 2002.
Note: The question was "How close do you feel toward [each country or region]?" The sum of not very close and not close at all is subtracted from the sum of very close and somewhat close.

Defensive Internationalism

U.S. soft power demonstrated in table 3.2. Net affinity with China has worsened and with South Korea has improved, bringing both to around a neutral point. Affinity toward the Association of Southeast Asian Nations (ASEAN) was strongly negative until recently and that with South Asia ("countries such as India and Pakistan") and the Middle East was extremely negative. Other polling found exceptionally negative feelings toward Russia/the USSR, especially as the end of the Cold War recedes into the past.

Table 3.16 presents responses to two types of questions about trust. The results resemble those for the possibilities presented in table 3.15. Note the high standing of the United States and other countries of the non-Asian First World. After a period of improvement, China seems to have fallen back to a neutral point similar to the one where South Korea was lodged.[61] Negative views of Russia strongly predominate. These opinions suggest a possible propensity to cooperate with and contribute to ventures involving collective action with OECD countries as well as a self-interest, situational scrutiny for joint action with China or South Korea. Given the Japanese public's professed closeness to Asia we saw in table 3.1, these views suggest a basic tension in Japanese opinions regarding its neighbors.

Perceptions of particular countries or regions as potential military threats to Japan have been posed in a variety of questions. Those questions providing comparative information about threat sources are summarized in table 3.17. The current and future threat responses convey the decline but not the elimination, of a perceived Russian threat. The Russian threat was increasingly matched or exceeded by one from

TABLE 3.16. Japanese Affinities: Trustworthiness (in percentages)

	1997 Trusted	1992 Trustworthy	1987 Trustworthy
United States	41	52	51
United Kingdom	26	40	42
Germany	18	24	31
Canada	19	25	30
Australia	19	31	38
France	14	26	32
Mexico	1	3	2
South Korea	8	9	8
China	9	32	19
Russia/USSR	1	2	1

Source: Data for 1997 from *Government Poll Yearbook* 1999, 534; for 1992 and 1987 from Richman 1993.

Note: The questions for 1987 and 1992 asked respondents to pick five countries as especially trustworthy from the lists given of ten; that for 1997, from a list of twenty-five.

China, and the rise of a North Korean one outdistanced the others. These results also suggest the decline though continuing residual presence of a perceived U.S. threat. Conflict on the Korean peninsula is of more concern than the conflict between China and Taiwan.

The early perception of the United States as a threat may have been rooted in concern over potential entanglement in Cold War and post–Cold War conflicts.[62] An entanglement fear, perhaps related to the valuation placed on relations with Asia, was also still pronounced in 1999. When asked why the United States had troops in Japan, only 31 percent said it was to protect Japan from foreign invasion, while 38 percent thought it was to "fulfill U.S. worldwide military strategies" and 19 percent thought it was to "prevent Japan from becoming a military nation." That seems compatible with the reservations about U.S. responsibility in Asia and international role, such as about excessive activism, in some of the items in table 3.2. Yet during the 1990s, possibly because of threat concerns with North Korea, China, and the Middle East, respondents showed a continuing desire for the maintenance of current security relationships with the United States. That fits with large majorities in polling from 1991 to 1999 that viewed the United States as a "reliable ally" that could be counted on to "help Japan militarily if Japan was attacked."

Opinions about country and region importance have been explored in several ways.[63] Relevant data appear in table 3.18. In terms of both general and economic importance, the United States and China have been the priority countries for the Japanese public, with a second grouping of

TABLE 3.17. Military Threats to Japan (in percentages)

	Current		Could Become			Most Likely	
	1990 (MRs)	1994 (MRs)	1994 (MRs)	1997 (MRs)	1999 (MRs)	1997 (1)	2000 (1)
Russia	47	35	36	23	19	7	9
United States	37	16	27	15	7	19	13
China	12	7	21	32[a]	25[a]	18	9
North Korea	16	60	66	69[b]	79[b]	29	44
South Korea	6	2	7	69[b]	79[b]	2	1
Middle East			6	15	11		

Source: Data from JPOLL and *Government Poll Yearbook* 2001, 500; 2002, 463.
Note: The first two columns present answers to "What countries pose military threats to Japan?" The next three columns to "What countries could become a military threat to Japan?" The last two columns to "What country is most likely to pose a military threat to Japan?" All except the last two allowed for multiple responses.
[a]Indicates that the response involved a China/Taiwan conflict.
[b]Indicates that the response involved a Korean peninsula conflict.

the ASEAN states and South Korea. Others register substantial importance for respondents only at particular times but even then do not seem to match the importance of the United States or China. This sort of mapping of the world may underlie a majority view that relations with the West and with Asia are equally important (1994).

Narrower questions confirm the emphasis on the general and economic importance of the United States. Majorities in 1991 and 1994 agreed that relationships with the United States were the priority for Japan. Moreover, few respondents expected the importance of security relationships with the United States to decline with the end of the Cold War (1991), and more than two-thirds in 1997 and 2000 wanted to continue the alliance in the twenty-first century (*Government Poll Yearbook* 1999, 535; 2001, 100). Three polls in 1990–91 had strong net majorities agreeing that "Japan depends on the U.S. for economic prosperity,"

TABLE 3.18. Country/Region Importance (in percentages)

	General					Economic			
	2000 (3)	1997 (3)	1996 (3)	1993 (MRs)	1993 (1)	1993—1 (1)	1993—2 (1)	1994 (3)	1995 (1)
United States	62	60	59	81	68	68	11	82	63
Canada	2	3	3					9	
Europe/EC	14	13	12	47	3	2	16	20	1
China	55	60	58	65	11	13	26	48	14
Taiwan	7	7	9			0	2		0
South Korea	25	18	22	47	3	2	7		2
ASEAN/SEA	23	36	36	30	5	3	13		10**
Central and South America	1	3	2	13	0			4	
Australia and New Zealand	1	1	2	25	0	1	3	10	
Africa	1	1	1	14	2			1	
Russia	12	8	8	37	2	1	5	4	0
North Korea	13	5	6	22	1				
Former Soviet Republics	2	1	1						
Eastern Europe				19	3			2	
Middle East	4	5	5	23	1	3*	0	7	1

Source: Data from JPOLL; for 2000 from *Government Poll Yearbook* 2001, 532–45; 2002, 515–35.

Note: Numbers in parentheses indicate the number of responses permitted, where 'MRs' indicates no limitations. Entries for 1996 and 1997 are the average of nine and five polls, respectively, and those for 2000 of twelve polls. In those years, respondents were asked, "In five years, which of the following countries or regions will become more important for Japan to form closer relationships?" The MR general question asked, "What countries would it be important for Japan to maintain friendly relations and influence with?" The single-response 1993 question asked them to select one possibility as most important.

In the 1993 economic importance questions, the first column shows responses to the actor most important for "Japan's economic well-being"; the second column, the second most important; the third column, the three most important; the last column, the single most important.

*Middle East oil companies.
**ASEAN plus Vietnam.

DOMESTIC SUPPORT FOR CONTRIBUTIONS

with only a 10 percent edge in 1990 for those agreeing with a similar statement about Western Europe. When asked in various ways in seven different polling questions (1997–99) whether the United States or China was of more or equal importance, the United States always came ahead of China. In terms of general importance, the U.S. margin over China was a net 40 percent or more; in politics, it was narrower (25 percent); and in economic matters it was narrower still (single digits). As of 1999, most Japanese saw no rival to U.S. great-power status in the twenty-first century (*Government Poll Yearbook* 2001, 499).

The perceived adequacy of current policy also may well depend on the fit between opinions about current relations and those about affinity, threat, and importance. Public conclusions are summarized in table 3.19.[64]

Only current relations with Western Europe have been viewed on a regular basis as largely positive. Those with the United States had, however, recovered from the trough of the 1990s economic-friction period. The recent readings on Australia and New Zealand are strongly positive. Those with China seem to have worsened, while those with South Korea have returned to the mildly positive point of 1994, and those with ASEAN have turned positive. Relations with Russia remain the province of negative perceptions. With regard to the United States, respondents were asked on numerous occasions to indicate if they expected relations

TABLE 3.19. Views of Current Relations (net %)

	2000	1998	1996	1994	1992	1990
United States (A)	60	55	10	−23	−5	53
United States (B)		42		11	5	25
EU/EC	33	29	33	34	22	30
China	−3	−6	−12	19	39	16
South Korea	15	−3	−19	15	6	
Russia	−52	−48	−51	−54	−64	
ASEAN	7	−6				
Southwest Asia	−18	−27				
Australia, New Zealand	38	23				
Middle East	−26	−27				

Source: Data from JPOLL; *Government Poll Yearbook* 2000, 99, 436, 444, 476; 2002, 89–90.

Note: The United States (A) row and those for the other entities present net responses when the sum of not very good and not good is subtracted from that of good and somewhat good. The United States (B) row contains the results when the percentage for not good is subtracted from good and when respondents had a third choice of neither. The third choice was always chosen by more than a third of respondents. When several polls were available for an entity in a particular year, the entries are the average of their responses. For Russia, two polls were available in 1998; for China, two in 1992; for the United States (A), three in 1996; four in 1994; and two in 1992; and for the United States (B), three in 1998.

to improve, worsen, or stay the same.[65] Results are reported in table 3.20. The negative or weakly positive values for improvement versus worsening in general terms and for economic relations are cautionary since they are accompanied, especially in more recent years, by a majority view of likely continuity. That continuity will, for the Japanese, require continuing attentive management, given that the public views foreign policy differences with the United States as based in differing values rather than divergent policies. In this sense, Japan is relatively unique among the forty-four nations polled in 2002 (Pew Research Center 2002c).

Continuity in Japan–United States relations would be less stressful for Japan if the United States would act in a less unilateral and military focused way while remaining internationally activist (1990). The Japanese public clearly does not want the United States to claim the role of "sole keeper of world peace" (1991) and did not see a continuing American claim to "leadership role in international politics" as particularly beneficial for bilateral relations (1995). After all, a narrow plurality (1994) lacked confidence that the United States "deals responsibly with world problems" (see table 3.2). Perhaps for those reasons, in the 1990s the Japanese public by only thin and declining margins thought Asia-Pacific peace and stability required a U.S. military presence and influence there; the Japanese public also consistently supported reducing the U.S. military's role in Japan.

In sum, public opinion presents Japan's leaders with an ambivalent and contradictory domestic constraint with respect to international contributions and cooperation. Isolation-avoiding views provide sup-

TABLE 3.20. Expected Future Relations with the United States (in percentages)

	Economic		General	
	Improve Less Worsen	Same	Improve Less Worsen	Same
1997	−12	56	12	69
1996	−12	56	13	69
1995	−14	45		
1994	0	36	−2	57
1993	−5		−2	56
1992	−20	39	55	22
1991	−2	40	−1	57

Source: Data from JPOLL.
Note: Entries for the Economic columns are averages of two questions in 1991 and 1995 and of three questions in 1992 and 1993. Entries for the General columns are averages of two questions in 1991 and 1996 and of three questions in 1993 and 1994.

port; other aspects of opinion provide wariness and resistance. If public views are determinative, we would expect policies of guarded cooperation and carefully conditional contributions. Each would be more likely in the wake of related efforts by the United States and EU and unlikely to be pathbreaking leadership moves. There would be public acceptance but hardly enthusiasm for contributions seemingly necessary to avoid severe U.S. displeasure. There may also be a disparity between the contributions showing strong public support and those aimed at avoiding isolation. Within this general pattern, Japan's contributions would be larger in nonmilitary than in military areas and larger in response to Asian requests than in their absence.

THE FIT WITH MUTED OPTIMISM

The opinions we have discussed generally suggest that most governments of the global North operate in the context of a domestic constraint that is neither fully supportive nor fully opposed to national contributions to global public goods production or public bads reduction. The comparative section and those on Western Europeans, Americans, and the Japanese did not confirm a simply optimistic expectation based on the evolution of collective identities or broad, inclusive interpretations of self-interest. Yet none of those sections confirmed the pessimistic, opposite view that would feature blanket rejection of club memberships or denial of the relevance to national fate of global goods or bads. Instead, we found substantial public and elite majorities in most countries supporting collective action of contribution and restraint on at least some issues. In short, domestic public and elite opinion in the countries surveyed suggests incentives to stay in what we call the muted zone.

The question of the incentives and permissions domestic opinion provides to operate more in the optimistic or the pessimistic part of that zone does not have a simple answer. The comparative section suggests national variation on that score, as does the section on Western Europeans. The sections on the United States and Japan suggest issue variation (the type of good or bad, and the pertinent production and contribution activities). Those two sections also suggest a significant degree of conditionality for the American and Japanese publics. That is, their stance on international contributions is likely to depend on perceptions of what other northern countries are contributing and what will ensue from large or niggardly contributions from Washington or Tokyo.

The comparative section suggests that domestic support for contribution postures closer to muted optimism's expectations are particularly likely in Japan, Canada, Italy, Germany, Spain, the Netherlands, Sweden, Norway, the Czech Republic, Hungary, Poland, Slovenia, and Slovakia. Our findings also suggest reservations about automatic following of "Made in America" doctrines about contributions and, by implication, Washington's preferences for contribution strategies, levels, or issue and geographic emphasis. The European section affirms a tendency for mutedly optimistic postures to have particularly high levels of public support in regional club or broader international terms in the countries just mentioned that are EU members and in Luxembourg, Denmark, Finland, and the United Kingdom. Less clearly, France, Greece, and Belgium might also join that grouping.

The section on Japan suggests the importance of self-realization and defensive internationalism as bases for public support of contributions. That is also true for the United States. The domestic constraint operating in the United States has elements conducive to both providing and limiting contributions, as either can be interpreted in self-realization and defensive internationalism terms. The U.S. section suggests less in the way of tolerance for a generally low or high level of contributions than it does demand for selectivity favoring the reactive use of the military instrument and leveraging contributions out of a small club of ostensibly like-minded states (many of which have publics closer to the optimistic end of the muted zone). Our findings also suggest a self-conception arguing against being marginal players in major international developments involving contributions and international club and institution formation. Post-9/11 polling does not suggest a preference for unilateral activism. Company is desired, if not always required.

Looking across the European, U.S., and Japanese sections, we find large areas of agreement on which others are likely to be important partners in international collective action and less than full (but still some) agreement on what are major future international problems. We also find clues that suggest some difference in the geographic focus of contributions more and less likely to have domestic support.

Less optimistically, we also found in domestic opinion serious limits in many countries on support for international contributions, including doubts about reciprocity and club membership payoffs, limited affinities across national lines, and priority for other concerns that could compete for resources. The balance between these and more conducive domestic opinion remains to be explored, particularly for matters clearly involving resource flows to the South from the North and accepting serious commitments that may clash with widely held views of what self-realization and defense against external threats involve.

The remaining chapters will explore that balance in several ways.

One way will be to understand better whether domestic opinion about specific types of contributions (foreign aid, peacekeeping, and environmental quality) fits with the general views reported in this chapter and their implications for levels and coordination of contribution efforts. A second will be to examine actual contribution efforts in these three policy areas and that of debt management and relief. That examination of actual giving behavior will look at its fit both with domestic opinion and with our muted optimism perspective. A third will be to gauge the giving behavior of a broader set of countries than major EU members, the United States, and Japan. What those others have been doing and are likely to do, after all, bears directly on the long-run prospects for contributions toward global order and progress.

4 INTERNATIONAL DEVELOPMENT ASSISTANCE

None of us . . . can afford to ignore the condition of our fellow passengers on this little boat. If they are sick, all of us risk infection. And if they are angry, all of us can easily get hurt.
—UN Secretary-General Kofi Annan

Compassion requires that we be hard-minded and insist that we measure the impact our assistance is having, so that we can constantly improve our effectiveness and participate in the development of human potential in Africa.
—U.S. Treasury Secretary Paul O'Neill

Of any foreign policy tool used during the Cold War, international development assistance (most commonly called foreign aid) was widely viewed as one of the most politicized within that struggle. Geographic patterns of aid paralleled quite closely the split between pro-American and pro-Soviet states, and the highest-profile aid recipients received their allotments in return for playing roles that fit into the strategic agenda of one of the two dominant states in the bipolar system. With the passing of the Cold War, however, that geostrategic rationale for donor policy lost punch as a compelling motive for giving and withholding aid. Continued development assistance funding from the United States and others has come to depend on justifications other than those derived from Cold War rivalry.

International development assistance is the first of several policy areas that we examine in this book. For each area, we will explore the extent that aid provision after the Cold War conforms with the general arguments introduced in chapters 1 and 2 and the implications of the domestic public opinion patterns discussed in chapter 3.

Our analysis of each specific policy area involves four broad tasks. The first is to establish the relevance of the policy area for our argument about the pursuit of global order and progress. That is, we provide a justification for our claim that the policy area has public and club goods elements and that the particular substantive area is treated in the policy debate in that way. The second task is to establish relevance in practice, an empirical demonstration that the policy area is one of continuing activity with ongoing implications for our conceptual arguments rather than largely a historical matter. With both forms of relevance established, the third task involves understanding the shares of public and club elements that exist in actual policy outputs. And the fourth task focuses on examining the division of labor that has (or has not) developed among the relevant contributors. In addition, for foreign aid, peacekeeping, and environmental quality we examine the pertinent public opinion polling to clarify the degree and nature of domestic support for efforts in those areas aimed at pursuing global order.

The second, third, and fourth tasks involve using indicators specific to the policy areas under examination. The possibilities of imperfection and the need for compromise on operationalized measures and systematic sets of data points are of course substantial and should be kept in mind in assessing our findings. When possible, we have used data for each area that are consistent across years, sources, and reporting structures. In this chapter, this means relying as much as possible on data published by the Development Assistance Committee (DAC) of the Organization of Economic Cooperation and Development (OECD).

Analysts of development assistance often distinguish between the quantity and quality of aid as a contribution to global order and progress. Later sections of this chapter consider both quantity and quality of aid contributions in an evolving international system. Given our conceptual arguments, the appropriate criteria for each are not those of a normative standard of enlightened, long-range aid in terms of absolute quantity (O'Hanlon and Graham 1997), one of public and club goods purity (Kanbur and Sandler 1999), or even one of an abstractly based optimal division of labor. Instead, in relativist fashion, we focus our attention on the magnitude and sign of changes over time in the quantity and quality of net development assistance contributions.

Accordingly, we examine the performance of the United States, Japan, and Western Europe (the bulk of the members of the DAC) since the Plaza Accord of 1985, an often-recognized switching point in hegemonic stature. Our tracking then extends into the last part of the twentieth century, a period marked by the end of the Cold War and by fashionable ideas rejecting the welfare state and its implications for policy approaches in many sectors domestic and international. For purposes of comparison, we shall on occasion include a pre-1985 benchmark.

We treat governmental foreign aid as consisting of both official development assistance (ODA) and official aid (OA), adopting DAC terminology. ODA is a governmental contribution to states that fall below a specified economic level of development. ODA ostensibly has as its main objective "economic development or welfare" of the recipient and is "provided on concessional terms." OA, a category "created after the collapse of the Soviet Union," encompasses "ODA-like flows" to transitional economies (World Bank 2001b, 339).[1] Given our interest in domestic support for contributions to global order and progress, we shall supplement consideration of ODA and OA with that of another DAC category introduced in recent years dealing with nongovernmental organizational aid (NGOA). NGOA consists of "private grants by nongovernmental organizations net of subsidies from the official sector" (World Bank 2001b, 339). The next chapter will deal with another major and overlapping aspect of financing to the developing nations, that of debt management and relief.

FOREIGN AID: AN IMPURE PUBLIC GOOD?

If foreign aid were a purely private good for the donor, it would lack relevance for our project. There certainly have been and are those who see it as such—as in Hans Morgenthau's (1962) analogy to the bribes of historic diplomacy. For foreign aid to have relevance for us, it must have at least some public or club goods element, but it need not be purely public by any means. Our purposes do not require defeating, however, the argument that foreign aid involves private benefits to the donor (an argument advanced by Meernik, Krueger, and Poe 1998; Patterson 1997; Schraeder, Hook, and Taylor 1998; Wang 1999). Nor do they require of us a manifesto about how unselfish or philanthropic foreign aid ought to be (e.g., Riddell 1999). For us, it suffices that the ongoing arguments about contributions to international development assistance and international cooperation for its provision are in large measure about the mix of private, public, and club benefits that have been and will likely continue to be emphasized (Center for Strategic and International Studies 1998; Ruttan 1996).

A prima facie case for foreign aid as a club good can be made by recognizing the existence of a club for the policy area—the DAC—and the continuing growth in its membership (Portugal and Spain in 1991, Luxembourg in 1992, Greece in 1999).[2] The Cold War pattern where Soviet and American foreign aid were directed to security allies or at least cooperator states is also compatible with a club interpretation. So too is the frequent presence of foreign aid and debt relief on the summit agenda of the G-7 (now G-8), and discussions within the more intimate world economic policy coordination clubs of what have been called the G-3 (Germany, Japan, and the United States) and the G-2 (Japan and the United States) (Funabashi 1989). And, as we shall see, public opinion in the European Union (EU) sees foreign aid as a policy area for jointness—that is, aid for EU recipients should be treated as a club matter. Finally, important aid functions and, as we shall see, a nontrivial share of national aid budgets, have been given to formal international institutions—in particular, the World Bank, the regional development banks, and the United Nations.

A prima facie case that foreign aid has a public element also appears in the definitions of ODA, OA, and NGOA. These types of aid emphasize contributions engendering less economic gain than would be available from those funds if used in other ways. In other words, ODA, OA, and NGOA provide a return that is below market rates. Moreover, the claim that development assistance contains a public goods element of some sort has a long tradition, going back at least as far President Truman's depiction of aid as a globally important contribution. We agree with this assessment and view aid as a potentially important contribution to the provision of public goods and to the limitation if not elimination of public bads for a collective that includes both donors and recipients. That, of course, was the thrust of calls for aid action over the past decades by statesmen such as Lester Pearson of Canada and Willy Brandt of Germany and by the United Nations beginning in 1970. These calls for aid, then, fall in line with the words of UN Secretary-General Annan at the beginning of this chapter and urge the formulation of policies for the twenty-first century that can stem the potential contagion through globalization of impoverishment, ill-health, and rage that development failures pose. Thus, aid is certainly conceptualized as something more than charity, a payoff for tolerating the status quo, or a cover for donor objectives other than human betterment in recipient locales.

In his analysis of the Cold War period, 1949–89, Lumsdaine (1993) showed that foreign aid can best be explained with substantial emphasis on donor national beliefs about the public interest in alleviating poverty and enabling less-developed nations to benefit from opportunities for economic growth and improvements in social welfare: "The essential causes lay in the humanitarian and egalitarian principles of the donor countries, and in their implicit belief that only on the basis of a just international order in which all states have a chance to do well was peace and prosperity possible" (30). For the Cold War period, he concluded that such a view provided a far better, though incomplete, explanation of differences in contributions by OECD members than did such explanations as (1) selfish motives of economic gain from trade and investment, (2) competition with the Soviet Union, (3) donor pursuit of prestige, or (4) the pure public goods and hegemonic-stability theories focusing on American leadership and its implications for the policies of others. In line with this view and our recognition of the importance of domestic factors of self-realization and identity, Noël and Thérien (1995, 552) examined the relationship between the presence of a domestic welfare state and foreign aid contributions and found that such "principles institutionalized at the domestic level shape the participation of developed countries in the international aid regime." In short, foreign aid contributions are significantly motivated by at least an impure public goods vision where benefits to others accrue benefits to the donor.[3]

In recent years, severe attacks from four different directions can also be interpreted as demonstrating the foreign aid/impure public goods debate. The first is from those who advocate greater priority for what are, from an international point of view, national private goods. They have called for more "aid" to at-home issues such as unemployment, social safety nets, urban decay, crime, and drug use (Grant and Nijman 1998). For them, the public element in foreign aid is too large. A second attack asserts that private sector involvement across developed and developing economies is a more effective way to accelerate development—and thus international order and progress—than is official aid. In this argument, the public goods aspects of foreign aid are viewed as less than those produced by private sector activities such as foreign direct investment. A third attack does not so much challenge the public good contributions that foreign aid could make in principle but contends that in practice, bad policies in both developed and developing countries deny that possibility. For them, foreign aid becomes captured by small international networks of elites who consider it a private good for themselves (Wedel 1998). The final attack calls attention to bad management, as in a 1999 Japanese government report that found such problems in about 40 percent of Japan's projects (Castellano 2000c) and excessive bureaucratization in American projects (Lancaster 2000b). Partisans of each thrust agree that aid should be changed but do not necessarily agree that it should be cut or ended.

Much of the argument about the balance between the public and private elements of aid has centered on the United States and Japan. This is partly because these two states have been for many years the two largest foreign aid donors and have provided a very large share of total DAC ODA provision (44 percent of net disbursements in 2000).[4] The empirical validity of such pessimistic interpretations of the American and Japanese policies will be discussed later in this chapter. At a more conceptual level, those specific characterizations should not be treated as necessarily running counter to our impure-public and club goods argument.

Our claim for public and club goods elements in foreign aid is not undercut and may eventually be bolstered by current debates in the United States and elsewhere about the proper functional emphases of foreign aid. For example, Carol Lancaster (2000a, b), a former U.S. State Department and U.S. Agency for International Development official, calls for shifting allocations toward humanitarian crisis relief, programs aimed at improving the quality of life abroad, and support for democracy and human rights. Contributions of those functional types are largely public-goods centered. Also in an impure public goods vein, J. Brian Atwood (1998), a former director of the U.S. Agency for International Development, argues that foreign aid both serves to prevent the breakdown of international order and, by promoting progress, increases American competitiveness in the world economy.

At a declaratory level, Japan's official statements about foreign aid have in the years of interest to us gone through three stages. From about 1987 to 1991, the emphasis was on fund recycling (related to Japan's large trade surpluses); from the early 1990s until 1999, the emphasis was on "aid as international public goods"; and more recently, the emphasis has been on aid as an instrument to advance national interests (Castellano 1999d; Maruoka 1999). Meanwhile, unofficial observers, both foreign and domestic, have emphasized benefits to the Japanese private sector (e.g., aid-funded contracts, a better business climate for Japanese foreign investment and banks, internationalization of the yen, and improved relations with the United States) (Arase 1994, 1995; Castellano 2000c; Ensign 1992; Hook 1995; Orr 1988, 1989–90).

We suggest that the more recent characterizations suffice to establish impurity but not the absence of a public element in Japanese aid. Followership of American wishes for foreign aid provision by Tokyo (Inoguchi 1986; Miyashita 1999; Rosecrance and Taw 1990) are partly based in perceptions of a G-2 club good element and may involve compliance with U.S. wishes for provision with some type of public goods element.[5] Further, Japan's foreign aid behavior may in significant part be not so much hostile to a public goods element as following from a different view of how provision enhances international order and progress (Pharr 1994). Based on that different approach, Wan (1995) arrives at a positive verdict on the extent to which Japan's contributions have been intended to support international order and progress rather than simply serving narrow national interests. If those interests lie in an open world economy, world peace and stability, Asian growth, Third World development, and even a decline in drug trafficking, they allow for the simultaneous presence of private and public elements (Castellano 1999d). Arguably, a shift toward private goods rhetoric may imply more a defense of aid with a public element in the face of domestic hard times than a rejection of it. Aid then becomes a way to avoid negative "direct spillovers of the lack of development in poor countries on to the well being of rich countries" (Jayaraman and Kanbur 1999, 419). That rationale is particularly persuasive if one views reducing those spillovers as centered on the "weakest-link" supply dynamic discussed in chapter 2.[6]

At a more inclusive level of international governance, explicit references to public goods motivations for and consequences of aid giving (and for our other policy categories, for that matter) are becoming increasingly prominent. One example is the UN Development Program's sponsorship of the *Global Public Goods* volume discussed in chapter 1 (Kaul, Grunberg, and Stern 1999). The World Bank's *Global Development Finance* (2001a) addresses the public goods consequences that development assistance can have as well as ways that aid can be better designed by donors and used by recipients to maximize public and private benefits. The bank (2001a, 110) identifies three main requirements for aid to fulfill its role as a producer of publicly consumable goods, in part by not denying the impurity of aid.

The first requirement focuses on coordination and integration of various nationally based aid programs and those of global or regional organizations. This would allow for complimentary donor specialization and the associated efficiency benefits. Such coordination also would enhance the role of multilateral forums and institutions that the bank (and we) think are more likely to generate higher levels of public outputs from aid than nationally based programs. While not emphasized by the bank, cooperation between bilateral, national donors can also help curb excesses in the pursuit of private benefits and increase the chances of burden sharing rather than burden shirking (Bobrow and Boyer 1996).

The second requirement pertains directly to the relationship between aid giving and debt management and relief for developing countries, the topic of chapter 5. The World Bank embraces the view that publicly and philanthropically funded aid programs must be leveraged with additional private monies to provide development finance of the quality and quantity that will lift countries and their citizens out of impoverishment. That of course partly accepts one of the criticisms of official aid noted earlier. While only partly determined by them, private sector flows are seriously affected by failures in debt management and relief. Thus, readers should relate our analysis and conclusions about aid in this chapter to the implications generated by our findings in chapter 5. It is essential to grasp the aid–debt relief interaction and the degree of contribution specialization that takes place among donor-creditors to fully understand the implications of aid for the future of the developing world. And as chapter 1 discussed, the future of the developing world will be a critical factor for the prospects of international order and progress.

The third issue raised by the World Bank in the public goods context is that existing global political frameworks must be enhanced to raise standards for and cooperation among donor and recipient NGOs, states, and regional and global organizations. While recognizing the limits of supranational governance at least in the near term, the bank argues strongly for the adoption and implementation of consistent incentives for donors and recipient nations to emphasize the public element of contributions and uses made of those contributions. This aspect of multilateral coordination goes beyond traditional "good stewardship" issues to the design of development finance systems that build on existing specialized competencies and inclinations of donor states, NGOs and IGOs. It also implies safeguards against the possible reduction of the public element through the cronyism and bad management emphasized in the third and fourth strands of recent critiques of foreign aid.

Important actors in the international community, whether considering state-level policy or regional and global organization programs, are surely paying increasing lip service to framing development in ways that produce publicly consumable outputs for both the underdeveloped and developed worlds. At least some actors are trying to do much more than that. The essence of the "rethinking of aid" recognizes that it does not have a single, built-in ratio of private to public goods and that "[f]oreign aid at different times and different places has . . . been highly effective [for development], totally ineffective, and everything in between" (World Bank 1998, 2). Similar themes were recounted in the press during the May 2002 trip through Africa made by U2 lead vocalist Bono and U.S. Treasury Secretary Paul O'Neill. Recognition of such variety and the critical nature of recipient policy systems has two implications. The first is that the global foreign aid portfolio will have to be diverse and nuanced and will have to take into account the strengths and weaknesses of recipients—the status and prospects of the "institution gaps" and "policy gaps" that exist across levels of development (World Bank 1998, 33).[7] The second implication is that foreign aid, including the debt management and relief discussed in the next chapter, offers no universal or quick cure for underdevelopment. Along lines argued earlier, we think that the chances of donors contributing to an instrument with such characteristics depends importantly on the zone of permissiveness home public opinion provides for governments to avoid throwing out the baby with the bathwater. We turn to those opinions in the next section of this chapter. Later sections will analyze actual foreign aid provision.

PUBLIC OPINION ON INTERNATIONAL DEVELOPMENT ASSISTANCE: WHO CARES? . . . AND WHO SHOULD BE CARED ABOUT?

The linkage between domestic practice along welfare state lines and foreign aid contributions during the Cold War period implies that publics tend to project onto foreign aid their interpretation of aid to domestic populations. This can make foreign aid a handout or a hand up, a governmental obligation and an acknowledged right of recipients or a matter of voluntary, humanitarian giving. Whatever the prevailing views in donor public opinion, foreign recipients always differ from domestic welfare recipients in one politically crucial respect: they do not vote in donor-state elections. Donor political elites thus need other reasons to believe that their publics will either support or at least not decisively punish leaders for providing foreign aid.[8]

We think such reasons for aid giving or the lack thereof are based to a substantial extent on the general opinions discussed in chapter 3 as specified and applied to the particulars of foreign aid. Thus, we expect overall consistency between opinions about foreign aid and the following conceptions discussed in chapter 3: (1) general notions of national roles in international affairs (rights, obligations, and values); (2) widely recognized goals and threats; (3) judgments about affinity, favorability, and importance of others in the international system who may be aid donors or recipients; and (4) support for formal and ad hoc multilateral clubs and institutions. Since the end of the Cold War, some of those general- and attentive-public opinions have been relatively stable, while others have changed. We then expect public opinion about foreign aid to have elements of stability and of change. In addition, foreign aid has its own interpreted history and connections with prevailing stable and changing beliefs about welfare provision that also enter into how publics view foreign aid.

Along those lines, we now turn to a summary treatment of OECD donor nation opinion on foreign development assistance, including what the Japanese refer to as "economic cooperation." Our discussion begins with self-reported activism in this area and then considers views on spending, importance and priority, national values and self-image conceptions, and the benefits and costs of foreign aid. We conclude by considering critical foreign aid cases that pose conflicts between images of particular recipients and generally declared justifications for providing foreign aid.

Activism

We previously recognized that activist minorities can have domestic support implications much greater than their numbers. Multinational polls in the early and mid-1990s asked about "voluntary activity" with respect to "Third World development and human rights" and support for "developing countries" (Hastings and Hastings 1995–96, 653; Inglehart, Basañez, and Moreno 1998, V25, V43). While only very small percentages reported themselves as activists in one or another of those respects, they were somewhat higher in some West European countries (Belgium, Finland, France, Germany, the Netherlands, Norway, and Sweden) and in Canada than in the United States or Japan. These minorities in Western European and Canadian publics may provide a pro-aid multiplier on the general sentiments of their publics not present in the larger economies of either the United States or Japan.

Support for Spending

Publics in Western Europe, the United States, and Japan have responded to a variety of questions about their preference for more, less, or the same foreign aid spending.[9] Data appear in tables 4.1 and 4.2. In 2002 (table 4.1), publics in France and Italy favored increases in economic aid and pluralities in Great Britain, Germany, and the Netherlands wished to maintain current levels. Yet in Great Britain, Germany, the Netherlands, and Poland, reductions were preferred to increases. West European publics (table 4.2) were asked in 1996 about spending by both their national governments and the European Union for aid to the developing countries. The publics in Greece, Ireland, Italy, Luxembourg, the Netherlands, the United Kingdom, Portugal, and Finland clearly favored increases in both. Only in Germany and Austria was there as much or more support for national reductions as for increases. Only Austria, Belgium, and Denmark lacked majorities for increases in EU multilateral giving. When asked earlier about humanitarian aid to non-EU countries, majorities were always in favor of increasing or maintaining it. In sum, the balance of West European public opinion

Defensive Internationalism

suggests prevailing support for maintaining and, in a number of cases, increasing assistance contributions.

In contrast, the U.S. public, (1986–2002) has strongly favored reductions in foreign aid spending, although to a lesser degree in recent years. In National Opinion Research Center surveys conducted annually from 1973 through 2000, foreign aid ranked last among twenty policy areas in terms of net support for governmental spending.[10] The predominant preference for cuts was, however, less in 2000 than previously (T. W. Smith 2001). Elite opinion has been somewhat more supportive, but only intermittently so. In 1998 it returned to its 1990 position, where more respondents favored increases than supported cuts (Reilly, various years), and by 2002 a majority of elites supported an increase of funds for economic aid. Public negativism may, however, have reflected massive overestimates of the share of American government foreign aid spending in the federal budget, in the aid contributions of the DAC as a whole, and in relation to the U.S. gross national product (GNP) (Chicago Council and Marshall Fund 2002; Kull and Destler 1999; PIPA 2001). When given more accurate information about what

TABLE 4.1. Support for Foreign Aid Spending

	U.S. Current Level	U.S. Net Increase Less Decrease	Japan Current Level	Japan Net Increase Less Decrease	Europe Current Level	Europe Net Increase Less Decrease
2002	35 (E 27)	−34 (E +44)			9	43
2001	32	−44				
2000	33[a]	−48[a]	41	−4		
1998	34[a] (E 43)	−43[a] (E +21)	42	5		
1997			45	15		
1996	22[b]	−64[b]	47	18		
1995	22[a]	−69[a]	43	21		
1994	24[b] (E 45)	−58[b] (E −11)	33	18		
1993	21	−64	46	19		
1992			45	22		
1991	19	−68	42	32		
1990	27 (E 34)	−54 (E +22)	43	23		
1986	35	−37 (E −39)		30		

Source: Data from Chicago Council and Marshall Fund 2002; Gallup Poll Releases, March 8, 2001; *Government Poll Yearbook* 2002, 90; Hastings and Hastings various years; JPOLL; Kull and Destler 1999; PIPA 2001; Reilly various years.

Note: E denotes elites. Europe refers to Great Britain, France, Germany, the Netherlands, Italy, and Poland.

[a]Average of three questions.
[b]Average of two questions.

is actually spent, pluralities favored maintaining the current level of spending and the minorities in favor of increases exceeded that for decreases. On the one hand, there may be a body of potential support based on conducive values and self-image waiting to be tapped. On the other hand, there may be a rather firmly rooted self-image of America as prone to naive generosity and free riding by others. We saw similar overestimates of U.S. contribution shares and generous behavior in chapter 3, and we will see them again in later chapters.

The Japanese public presents a pattern of opinion on levels of foreign aid spending that differs from that of both the West European and American publics. The most common Japanese opinion has been for maintaining current spending levels. An initially larger minority in favor of increases rather than decreases evaporated recently.

In much of Western Europe, we think the hard sell for politicians will be to reduce foreign aid and the easier sell will be to increase it. In Japan, the easiest course will be to maintain foreign aid. In the United States, the easiest course in terms of public support will be to cut foreign aid and the hardest will be to increase it. Elite views balance this preference. When presidential leadership entered the picture in 2003 with the Bush proposal to increase foreign aid, the opinion of the general public

TABLE 4.2. Support for Foreign Aid Spending: Western Europe

	National Government (1996)			European Union (1996)			Humanitarian Aid (1994)	
	Increase	Reduce	Net	Increase	Reduce	Net	Increase	Maintain
Belgium	41	40	1	45	32	13	15	38
Denmark	44	38	6	47	20	27		
France	47	38	9	60	20	40	32	30
Germany	40	43	−3	57	20	37	40	39
Greece	71	8	63	81	1	80	79	7
Ireland	68	10	58	72	3	69	55	27
Italy	64	14	50	71	6	65	60	23
Luxembourg	66	14	52	67	12	55	60	24
Netherlands	56	32	24	63	13	50	23	46
United Kingdom	60	21	39	61	12	49	24	42
Portugal	72	19	53	79	3	76	65	14
Spain	79	8	71	80	3	77	61	22
Austria	35	35	0	42	23	19		
Finland	65	24	41	66	11	55		
Sweden	45	39	6	52	12	40		
EU-15	55	27	28	63	13	50		
EC-12							42	32

Source: Data from Eurobarometers, nos. 42, 46.

became evenly split, suggesting the possibility of elite opinion carrying the day (PIPA 2003a).

Importance and Priority

For EU publics, foreign aid is overwhelmingly seen as a club policy issue. Few other policy areas received such extensive support by large majorities (1989–2002) for treatment by joint national and EU policy processes (Eurobarometer, nos. 39–58; Sinnott 1995b, 265–66).[11] A similar view appeared in the publics of EU accession countries in 2002 (European Commission, "Candidate Countries Eurobarometer" 2002). Of course, involving the EU may indicate either that foreign aid is too important and has too much of a club good element to be left to national efforts or that is so unimportant and privately unrewarding that it should be handed off to Brussels. There are indications that the latter is more likely than the former for European publics and elites. When offered as a choice to respondents, development aid was never seen by even 10 percent of any member publics as the "most important problem" for the EU in polls in 1998, 1993, and 1974 (Eurobarometer, nos. 39, 50). In 1998, only in Denmark did as much as 11 percent of the public think that "cooperation with countries in the Third World" was one of the three priority areas for the European Parliament (Eurobarometer, no. 50). Several years earlier, that focus got almost no mention among elites in any of the EU-15 as one of the "most serious problems or issues facing the EU for the next ten years" (Spence 1996).

EU publics were, however, far more positive in response to less demanding questions about the importance of helping "people in poor countries in Africa, South America, and Asia to develop" (1996, 1991, 1989) (Eurobarometer, nos. 46, 36; Hastings and Hastings 1988–89, 630).[12] Every public polled in each year had substantial majorities acknowledging importance. While those majorities were always greater in 1996 than at the end of the Cold War, that upward momentum was more pronounced right after the Cold War (1989–91). Contrasts were clear between the continuing increasers (Denmark, Greece, France, Ireland, Luxembourg, the Netherlands, Spain) and the recent decliners (Belgium, Germany). In 2002, when offered the opportunity to designate a global gap between the rich and poor as one of the two greatest threats to the world, only majorities in Germany and Poland did so (Chicago Council and Marshall Fund 2002).[13]

For the American public, foreign aid as a priority in its own right has increasingly little standing, although "too much" aid has ceased to be mentioned by a noticeable minority as a major foreign policy problem (Chicago Council and Marshall Fund 2002). The lack of priority for development of the global South as a foreign policy goal (i.e., "helping to improve the standard of living of less developed nations") seems to have been a constant since 1974 and in 2002 was last among twenty foreign policy goals in terms of those viewing it as very important. Among elites, the goal fared somewhat better, ranking twelfth, but had that status only for 42 percent of respondents (as it did in 1990) (Chicago Council and Marshall Fund 2002; Hastings and Hastings 1987–88, 580; 1994–95, 628; 1995–96, 652).

Whatever importance and priority various types and recipients of foreign aid may have could follow from perceived relationships—as cure, palliative, or bribe—to the "very important [American] goals" and "critical threats" discussed in chapter 3. There tends to be more importance and priority for foreign aid viewed as a means to combat international terrorism (especially), to counter the proliferation of weapons of mass destruction, to fight Islamic fundamentalism, to reduce drug imports and immigration, and to secure energy supplies.[14] There tends to be less importance and priority attached to it as a means for promoting human rights, marketization, democratization, and improving living standards. An intermediate degree of importance and priority would go to foreign aid to combat world hunger and infectious disease threats and to improve the environment.[15] Some similar possibilities might exist for American elites.

These surmises have some support from questions about priority within the generally low-priority area of foreign aid. From 1986 to 1992 to 2000, the types of countries getting priority shifted to those with the poorest economies obtaining the highest priority for a majority of respondents, while those based on U.S. security interests fell from a plurality to a small minority (PIPA 2001). Preferred functional emphases in U.S. foreign aid (1995 and 1998) were children's health, humanitarian disaster relief, and environmental protection more than political-military relationships (Adamson et al. 2000; PIPA 2001).[16] These results suggest that the public tends to view foreign aid as appropriately having a public goods element. They also, however, are compatible with the American public viewing it in welfare terms.

Importance and priority judgments could also be a function of the assessments people make about particular recipients, even if those assessments are made within the bounds of a generally negative view of the foreign aid instrument. Leaving aside for now the cases of aid to Russia and Africa from 1986 on, the American public was asked numerous times about increasing aid to specific national or regional recipients. In only one case was there more than a single-digit margin for increases ("South Americans fighting the drug problem"). For the most part, decreases were favored more than increases, especially in the cases of aid to Israel, Egypt, and the Palestinians. Elites felt differently and were predominantly positive about far more cases (e.g., Eastern Europe, developing countries in Asia and Africa, the newly independent states of the former Soviet Union, and the Palestinians) (Americans and the World 2003b; Chicago Council and Marshall Fund 2002; O. R. Holsti 1998–99; Reilly, various years).

Japanese respondents' views of importance and priority were higher than those of the United States and were perhaps more narrowly focused than those of West Europeans. In 1991 and 1997, the Japanese public was almost evenly split on giving priority to "support to developing countries" or to "domestic issues" (JPOLL, various years). Yet as we saw in chapter 3 regarding the role in the international community and the UN, help to developing countries was never in first place and has slipped in the past decade. As a result, we reason that granting priority to foreign aid will depend on perceived linkages between aid and the more generally favored roles—that is, with world peace and stability and environmental protection. A strong perceived link with the former would make foreign aid an arena in which Japan could play a major global role reaffirming rather than compromising its "pacific" character. As for the priority of various recipients, many polls in the past decade have emphasized Asia far more than any other region, with a balanced global program a distant second (*Government Poll Yearbook* 2000, 2001; Japan Information Network, various years; JPOLL, various years). That too fits well with the concerns reported in chapter 3.

To summarize, West European publics and elites do not seem to provide a mandate for the EU to treat foreign aid as a matter of great importance and priority, but the publics also do not seem to support the topic being ignored or downplayed by their national governments. The U.S. public generally rejects development assistance as a major policy instrument but would emphasize a human welfare rather than an economic or political development focus or even a political-military one. American elites are less negative and open to case specific recognition of the importance of the foreign aid instrument in ways compatible with emphases on a political-military rationale. The Japanese public gives the instrument more priority in general but does so perhaps more as a means to pursue world role priorities and to manage Asian and developed country relations than anything else.

INTERNATIONAL DEVELOPMENT ASSISTANCE

Values and National Self-Conceptions

For Western Europeans, support for foreign aid contributions is well based in values and national self-conceptions. Along these lines, we note the previously mentioned data illustrating the importance of a particular nation extending help to others, Lumsdaine's (1993) analysis of the values underlying historic aid patterns, and surveys showing at least 75 percent support for helping the developing world in each of the EC-12 in earlier polling (Hastings and Hastings 1987–88, 554).

The American public's declared values and national self-conception seem to clash with the same group's opposition to an overall increase in foreign aid spending. Repeated questioning over the past twenty years has never produced a public majority opposed to the United States providing economic aid, and elite support has never fallen below 86 percent (Chicago Council and Marshall Fund 2002). The apparent discrepancy may be explained by priorities for what foreign aid should be spent on and the views of benefits and costs discussed in the subsequent section.

Two-thirds agreed (in 1999 and 1995) that, "as one of the world's rich nations, the U.S. has a moral responsibility towards poor countries to help them develop economically and improve their people's lives" (PIPA 2000b). In 1998, many were "troubled" when hearing about "hungry children . . . in some part of the world outside of the U.S."; in 1995 and 2000, majorities supported taking part in a collective OECD effort to reduce world hunger (PIPA 2001). After 9/11, a massive majority supported "food and humanitarian aid to the people of Afghanistan" (*New York Times*/CBS News 2001). Similar support was manifested for countering terrorism "by providing food and medical assistance to people in poor countries" (Americans and the World 2002b). A majority rejected the view that food aid to "starving people" in North Korea should be withheld to put pressure on that country's nuclear program (PIPA 2003c). Reducing hunger was of course a prominent goal noted in chapter 3. These feelings and the justifications for aid contributions related to these sentiments suggest values in the espoused collective American identity that could motivate contributions. Other values and self-image elements, including expectations that the United States would be more generous than other rich countries, could have the opposite implication for aid provision.[17] As we move into the twenty-first century, American values do not in themselves support major increases in U.S. aid spending, with most of the public believing that U.S. foreign policy is doing well at promoting poor countries' economic development and democratization and at alleviating world hunger and the AIDS epidemic (PIPA 2003e). In combination, pro-contribution professed values pose a harmonization puzzle with negative views of foreign aid spending.

Some insight into possible harmonization can be gained from polling starting in 2000 that focused on public feelings about the different kinds of aid and the merits of different reasons for giving foreign aid (Chicago Council and Marshall Fund 2002; PIPA 2001).[18] The most positive feelings were expressed in response to foreign aid in the forms of food and medical assistance aimed at helping the "needy" or those in less of a position to help themselves—for example, "children" and "women and girls."[19] Political-military security possibilities (including fighting drugs) received much less support and were subordinated to relieving hunger. Less pro-foreign-aid sentiment was expressed about long-term political transformation (e.g., "democracy promotion"). Strongly anti-foreign-aid feelings were expressed about aid going to human-rights-violating regimes. The public's overwhelming rationale for giving aid was alleviating hunger and disease, with small majorities for poor country economic development and nuclear nonproliferation. There was less of a positive response to the reasons of democracy promotion, access to strategic regions, or increasing U.S. international influence. These value judgments also occur in numerous other polls taken earlier in the 1990s and in the 1980s (Kull and Destler 1999; PIPA 2000c; Reilly, various years). American elites, however, were more positive on those possibilities and reflected the public's support for the most popular foci.

While there was no predominant hostility to U.S. government contributions through standard aid bureaucracies, feelings were much more positive about contributions through NGOs and other voluntary organizations (including private charities, religious organizations, and the Peace Corps). In short, aid is good if it is designed to help people in need and delivered through voluntary organizations but is less appealing if it goes to recipients who are bad or is a cover for selfish, power-seeking ends. Our "welfare" or charitable giving interpretation is compatible with majority support in 2000 for multilateralism in aid contributions, even if it meant foregoing more "control, . . . credit and influence" in receiving countries (PIPA 2001).

For the Japanese public, the role of aid provider to developing countries was not one of the two world roles most preferred at the beginning or end of the 1990s, and the aid-provider minority declined (as reported in chapter 3). Nevertheless, large majorities have continued to favor maintaining or increasing Japan's efforts toward the South. On which reasons did those majorities most look with favor? In annual responses from 1990 to 2000, only three even got as much as one-third support

(*Government Poll Yearbook* 2001, 83; 2002, 90; JPOLL, various years).[20] These answers were, in declining order, (1) stabilizing developing countries as a contribution to world peace; (2) meeting a human obligation of developed countries; and (3) safeguarding environmental quality. Reasons focused on economic or international status benefits to Japan were used as justifications only by smaller minorities.

Whatever elites may think, publics seem to view foreign aid provision less as a core national interest matter and more as an obligation to provide a public good. Their support for it would then be significantly affected by opinions about whether foreign aid was being provided and used in that spirit. Therefore, missions such as the May 2002 Bono/O'Neill trek through Africa to assess the impact of aid programs might have a surprisingly large impact on public sentiments in either direction.

Benefits and Costs

Our data on the likely benefits and costs of foreign aid as assessed in public opinion are limited to the United States and Japan for the post–Cold War period. For benefits to the United States as a donor in polls between 1978 and 2000, the perceived effects on the American economy from economic development in the Third World moved from a substantial negative majority to a positive one by 1995 (Kull and Destler 1999; PIPA 2001; Reilly, various years). Political democratization was also viewed positively in terms of stability and friendly relations with the United States (PIPA 2001). Earlier years saw benefits of strengthening foreign friends, thus substituting their troops for American ones in international hot spots, and a cost of excessive foreign involvement (Hastings and Hastings 1986–87, 221; 1989–90, 189). These possible private goods and bads were not possibilities that loomed large in our previous discussion of the public's feelings about and reasons for foreign aid.

In contrast, the American public has long been doubtful about likely benefits to recipients, and that skepticism has grown stronger over time. In 1986, 88 percent identified misuse and corruption by recipient countries and their officials as a major problem. Almost the same percentage of respondents was seen on this issue in 2000. The average estimates of how much aid through government channels was skimmed off before reaching the needy were about 50 percent in 1986 and 60 percent in 2002; the question of aid through nongovernmental channels produced only somewhat better averages of about 30 percent (Kull and Destler 1999; PIPA 2001, 2003a). What did change were judgments about any offsetting benefits to recipient populations. Those went from positive majorities in 1986 and 1990 to doubts about much aid reaching the needy in 1992 and 1996 to average public estimates in 2000 and 2002 that less than a quarter of U.S. aid to poor countries "actually helps people who need it" (Hastings and Hastings 1989–90, 189–90; Kull and Destler 1999; PIPA 2001, 2003a). If little aid was used to further the relief of human misery (the most prevalent feelings and reasons for aid contributions), there was a "principled," unselfish reason for not giving it. Those opinions are also common in the U.S. welfare debate. In this view, giving conventional aid is not so much generous as gullible.

For the Japanese public, very large majorities in 1996, as in 1986, saw aid as helping recipients (Hastings and Hastings 1987–88, 196; 1996–97, 606). By 1998, about 30 percent had doubts on that score (*Government Poll Yearbook* 2000, 480). While not polled directly on the subject, there may also have been awareness that aid would benefit Japan as donor. Japanese-sponsored polling of other Asian publics clearly indicated that further aid giving would be good for Japan's relations with much of Asia and that cutbacks might worsen such relationships.[21] Polling in the late 1980s and early 1990s (the period of high trade friction), suggested that aid giving would also be good for Tokyo's relations with other developed-world donors.[22] Giving foreign aid could thus be viewed as a win-win situation for the Japanese and the recipients.

Critical Cases

Much of our discussion of public opinion about aid giving has emphasized obligations and a public element in contributions, aid as something that ought to be done versus something that promises a payback for the donor. The robustness of the former view among donor publics can be tested by looking at opinion about countries generally viewed in less than positive terms, as reported in chapter 3. Put bluntly, do humanitarian rationales dominate aid giving to countries that otherwise rank low on affinity and importance? Russia and Africa are arguably relevant test cases for the United States, and North Korea and Russia constitute such examples for Japan.

In U.S. public and elite opinion, Russia from the mid-1980s onward declined in importance parallel to the country's declining image as a threat source. Its human needs surely did not shrink, however, and, indeed, growing basic human-needs deficits were widely reported. Public majorities, however, opposed increasing aid to Russia on ten of eleven occasions between 1990 and 2002 (although majorities supported some emergency aid in 1992) (Chicago Council and Marshall Fund 2002; Gallup Poll Topics: A–Z Russia 2000; Hastings and Hastings 1991–92, 186, 589; 1993–94, 670; 1994–95, 622). The public's preference in 1994 was to let Russia solve its own problems. The second choice was to let the Europeans take the lead in assistance. Elites were less opposed to providing aid but wanted Europe to take the lead (Chicago Council and Marshall Fund 2002; Reilly 1995). The Russian case shows the serious limits on humanitarian obligations yielding public support for increased foreign aid provision.

Support for aid to Africa has increased in recent years, although African countries remained largely invisible in the affinity, importance, and threat data we reviewed. A 1994–95 public plurality preference for cutting aid to Africa shifted by 1999 to a majority for maintaining or increasing it, with a larger minority for increasing it that continued into 2003 (Chicago Council and Marshall Fund 2002; PIPA 2000b, 2003a). By then, substantial majorities appeared to accept arguments citing hunger, terrorism, and market potential for the United States and were less convinced by arguments giving Africa a low aid priority because of lack of vital U.S. interests. In line with chapter 3, as of 2000, AIDS alleviation joined the list of arguments accepted by a majority in support of aid (PIPA 2000b). Elites were already more positively disposed by 1994 and offered a large majority for increases in 2002 (Chicago Council and Marshall Fund 2002). These opinions are in line with our impure-public-goods perspective. Yet in the same period, the skepticism noted earlier about the likely results of aid persisted—corruption in African governments would keep contributions from achieving their potential benefits. The African case suggests both the strength of humanitarian motives and the reservations about foreign aid as an effective way of acting on such motives.

In chapter 3 we saw the negative views of North Korea and Russia held by the Japanese public. Several polls in 1997 on food aid to North Korea suggest that majority support would come only after demonstrated private-benefit conditions—policy changes by Pyongyang or isolation-avoiding donor club participation (JPOLL, various years). While opinion on aid to Russia fluctuated in the 1990s, the first half of that decade saw the public viewing aid as a carrot to be withheld until Russia accommodated Japanese preferences on the northern islands. Stability-enhancement rationales were more persuasive than ones of advanced countries' obligation, and aid provision was viewed as a donor club matter (JPOLL, various years). The two cases suggest the continuing importance of negative affinity for the Japanese public.

Aid reluctance associated with it could be countered, if at all, only if provision was perceived as useful for relations with donors who themselves were of substantial affinity and importance.

To summarize, our review of public opinion on foreign aid shows many Western European publics as the most broadly supportive of aid programs, the U.S. public as the least supportive, and the Japanese in an intermediate position. Few publics, if any, gave foreign aid general priority. Both Western Europeans and Americans may well think about foreign aid as they do about welfare programs, but their different positions on such programs lead to far more negativism in the United States. Nevertheless, humanitarian motives associated with charitable giving have relatively high American acceptance, as do the mechanisms of NGOs. So too does a self-image of responsiveness to human suffering, but acting on it is checked by suspicion of cheating by receiving governments. Political-military private-benefit rationales have more support among elites than the public. The Japanese public seems to see aid as a development and stability enhancer and thus of special merit for the region where development and stability matter most—Asia. They may also see it as helpful for good standing—that is, isolation avoidance—with Europe and the United States. The general implications are for stronger domestic permissiveness for aid giving in Western Europe and substantial permissiveness in Japan when the aid goes to Asia. In the United States, permissiveness is most likely to be present only for crisis commitments that are reactions to prevent human suffering rather than proactive approaches to aid policy. Overall, these domestic climates suggest some differences in the share of national means allocated to aid. They argue against any sustained major increase in the quantity of aid given by the members of the DAC club relative to their means. They also suggest that aid giving will not end. The subsequent examination of aid spending will see if those expectations based on public opinion match with what donor nations have done.

IS FOREIGN AID VANISHING?

If foreign aid is moving toward a trivial level, questions about the public goods provided by aid giving or the degree of cooperation among donors are of little import. In other words, if aid is falling away as a potent policy area both in terms of quantity and quality, why study its contributions to global order and progress? More concretely, why expect the first decade of the twenty-first century to be any less a "lost decade" for development assistance than the 1990s allegedly were? The answer to these questions is that aid continues to be important in both volume and type but is so in relatively complex ways. While aid has declined as a share of the finance available to the developing world, the surge in recent decades in private capital flows has been concentrated on only a few developing countries and, as we shall see in chapter 5, has major problems of volatility.

The continuing relevance of aid is hard to question when we account for the fact that many poor countries would undoubtedly be worse off without it. A crude measure of who aid recipients are and an indication of continuing relevance to global order and progress considers ODA receipts in relation to GNP. We suggest that sensitivity to aid reductions increases with the share of a recipient's GDP accounted for by aid. Along these lines, table 4.3 calls attention to countries and regions where that share is 5 percent or more. By our reasoning, aid cuts would have especially massive impacts where the share is 10 percent or more and could be even worse where it is 20 percent or more. The list does not fully convey those in need of aid because it omits countries with great needs for development assistance not already recognized in donor programs. If anything, this list understates aid dependency because this measure does not reflect NGOA shares of GNP.

TABLE 4.3. The Aid Dependent: ODA + OA as a percentage of GNP, 1997

	20% or More	10% or More	5% or More
Sub-Saharan Africa	Cape Verde, Guinea-Bissau, Madagascar, Mauritania, Mozambique, Sao Tome and Principe	Benin, Burkina Faso, Chad, Comoros, Congo, Djibouti, Eritrea, Guinea, Malawi, Mali, Niger, Rwanda, Sierra Leone, Tanzania, Uganda, Zambia, Zimbabwe	Angola, Burundi, Cameroon, Central African Republic, Ethiopia, Gambia, Ghana, Lesotho, Senegal, Togo, Namibia[a]
The Americas	Nicaragua, Guyana	Haiti, Suriname	Dominica, Honduras, Bolivia
Middle East			Jordan, Yemen
South and Central Asia	Bhutan	Kyrgyz Republic	Armenia, Maldives, Nepal, Tajikistan[a]
Far East Asia	Mongolia	Cambodia, Laos	
Europe			Albania, Macedonia[a]
Oceania	Micronesia, Marshall Islands	Kiribati, Samoa, Solomon Islands, Tonga, Vanuatu	Papua New Guinea

Source: Data from OECD, *Development Cooperation* 1999, statistical annex tables 25, 42; UNDP, "Human Development Report," 1999, 49–52.

Note: Entries reflect total net ODA and OA flows from DAC countries, multilateral organizations, and Arab countries.

[a]Entries were so placed by the UNDP for the same year but not by the DAC.

Defensive Internationalism

If the places listed matter for international order and progress, then aid still matters for those goals. Put simply, greater misery, turbulence, and state failure throughout the developing world has implications for the rest of the world (public bads) and also more narrowly for the donors (club bads). That denial would have to apply in general to sub-Saharan Africa and Oceania and to particular countries often viewed as important for threat containment in Central Asia, the Middle East, the Balkans, and Latin America.

The importance of aid for recipients, however, and their role in the global future need not equate with what donors do. Three sets of expectations merit consideration in this chapter. A more pessimistic school would expect aid to decline in importance for donors if we believe the hegemonic stability (both economic and political military) variants of public goods theory. In the wake of cuts by the hegemon, the development assistance contributions of others and the public goods elements of those contributions would shrink. The driver for these expectations is an alleged continuing pattern of U.S. decline and withdrawal from hegemonic provision, including foreign aid.

A more completely optimistic school would emphasize the increasing importance of aid based on convictions of emerging transnationally shared identities. Foreign aid contributions would increase in importance at least partly because of the higher public and club goods elements implied by merging identities. In this world, U.S. contributions would not appreciably decrease and those of others would possibly exceed and certainly match those of the United States.

But there is a third and more complex possibility with several phases characterizing the post–Cold War period. This scenario is compatible with our muted optimism view. The first phase, roughly beginning with the Plaza Accord and Gorbachev's perestroika in 1985 and running into the early 1990s, sees OECD foreign aid contributions increasing in the context of credibility for the prospects of global order and progress (i.e., a global security community) with a more inclusive identity. During that period, the American hegemon combined hegemonic political-military confidence with economic anxiety, resulting in demands for greater burden sharing. We would expect to see increases in development assistance contributions by others that are larger than those for the United States, but we would also not expect to see sharp U.S. cuts. The second phase, roughly beginning in the mid-1990s, would show the pessimistic vision marked by American cuts and hegemonic withdrawal and a combination of cuts and lessened momentum by other donors as common identity hopes eroded in the face of parochial assertiveness, primarily in the American political arena. U.S. cuts would be particularly severe and not fully matched by others. The third phase, roughly the late-1990s, would show at least a leveling off in the rate of reduction of development assistance and an increase in the public or club goods share. While U.S. aid levels would stop falling, they would not increase to the levels of the first phase and would not match the levels and increases of most others (especially those others with long-standing supportive domestic norms).

Perhaps the simplest indicator of the extent to which foreign aid is vanishing is that of net current-year dollars.[23] By this crudest of measures, DAC ODA in the 1990s substantially increased from 1990 to 1992 (and also from its mid-1980s levels), fell (with some ups and downs) to below the 1990 level in 1997, and then moved upward to about the 1990 level by 1999 and remained there in 2000 (Abrego and Ross 2001, 34). DAC OA, however, persistently increased into the mid-1990s only to fall and then rebound by 1998 to above its 1992 level. NGOA aid to the set of ODA-eligible countries fell from 1994, with a partial rebound in 1998 from its 1997 low; NGOA to the transitional (OA) economies increased very substantially after 1994. DAC NGOA 1998 provision to ODA- and OA-eligible national recipients combined exceeded that provided in 1994. In current-year dollars, the sum of net ODA and OA was substantially higher in 1994 than 1990, and the 1998 total of ODA, OA, and NGOA fell by only about 11 percent from that of 1994.

A more demanding measure of assistance contributions is that of real growth rates for DAC member countries, and this measure appears in table 4.4 for ODA and OA. The DAC aggregate data only crudely fit the phases mentioned previously. ODA increased as the Cold War wound down (1985–86 to 1990–91) and was followed by a very small decline between 1989–90 and 1994–95 that was offset by growth in OA (the values in parentheses). The subsequent decline in both ODA and OA between 1991–92 and 1996–97 continued but did so with a decrease in the rate of decline from 1992–93 to 1997–98. The more recent years showed an increase in both ODA (1997–98, 1998–99, 2000–2001) and OA (1997–98). With the exception of 1997–98, a majority of other countries either cut ODA less or increased it more in constant terms than did the United States. These countries' OA growth rates seem to have become less tied to those of the United States. The available observations show continuing growth in American OA contributions (largely to the transitional economies), unlike that for ODA. Few countries (only Denmark and Norway) increased their ODA contributions throughout the period, although they were joined for the last decade by Ireland, Luxembourg, the Netherlands, and New Zealand. No national contributor

TABLE 4.4. Growth Rates of ODA and OA (in percentages)

	1985–86 to 1990–91	1989–90 to 1994–95	1991–92 to 1996–97	1992–93 to 1997–98	1997–98	1998–99	2000–2001
Australia	−3.2	2.5 (−6.1)	−1.2 (−10.7)	−0.3 (−39.2)	6.3 (100)	−1.6	−4.0
Austria	2.8	9.3 (22)	−2.8 (−13.4)	−2.6 (−13.2)	−13.3 (5.5)	9.6	27.3
Belgium	0	−3.9 (29.7)	−2.7 (−27.6)	−0.8 (−10.3)	15.1 (15.3)	−11.6	6.9
Canada	1.2	−0.6 (47.9)	−4.0 (−2.6)	−3.9 (.2)	−11 (0)	0.2	−9.4
Denmark	3.7	3.3 (18.8)	3.7 (12.1)	3.8 (−1.0)	4.1 (−11.2)	2.7	−1.6
Finland	13.2	−14.5 (30.9)	−11.9 (−2.5)	−5.6 (12.8)	5.2 (15.4)	4.9	5.7
France	4.2	0.8 (51.6)	−4.2 (2.7)	−5.7 (7.5)	−8.7 (167)	−0.5	3.6
Germany	2.2	−0.9 (17)	−3.9 (−26.6)	−4.7 (−25.6)	−4.2 (−.9)	1.4	0.8
Ireland	−3.6	17.4 (27.5)	20.1 (−48.6)	19.8 (−49)	8.6 (0)	22.8	20.4
Italy	1.4	−9.7 (11.1)	−12.3 (−5.7)	−12.7 (−2.9)	78.4 (.8)	−20.8	18.6
Japan	7.1	0.2 (1.8)	−5.8 (−9.6)	−0.8 (−20.7)	22.6 (57.1)	26.2	−16.6
Luxembourg		14.4 (51.3)	15 (−19.8)	18.2 (−16.7)	18.1 (50)	5.9	16.1
Netherlands	1.8	−0.8 (11.7)	1.4 (−50.5)	2.3 (−20.5)	3.2 (1757.1)	6.1	−0.5
New Zealand	−2.4	2.7[a]	0.9 (−60.9)	3.9 (−47.1)	2.6 (0)	4.1	1.6
Norway	2.8	1.1 (32)	0.5 (3.6)	2.7 (−5.2)	8.4 (−7.1)	0.5	6.8
Portugal		8.3 (44.5)	−2.6 (−4.6)	−1.2 (5.3)	2.7 (22.2)	8.1	−2.5
Spain		10.1 (47.2)	−0.7 (−21.3)	0.3 (−46.2)	11.2 (66.6)	−0.8	43.9
Sweden	2.9	−1.8 (112.3)	−2.5 (−1.9)	−3.7 (−5.1)	−6.2 (−29.1)	8.1	2.4
Switzerland	4.6	3.0 (64.4)	−3.1 (1.0)	−2.1 (−4.6)	−2.6 (1.3)	11.9	0.1
United Kingdom	−0.1	1.8 (2.4)	−0.3 (.3)	0.6 (1.6)	8.6 (29.1)	−15.6	4.4
United States	0	−4.4 (45.4)	−8.9 (10.2)	−8.3 (15.4)	26.5 (8.3)	2.5	12.4
DAC total	4.0	−0.9 (24.4)	−4.6 (−9.2)	−3.6 (−4.5)	9.6 (19.1)	4.9	0.5

Source: Data from World Bank, *World Development Indicators,* various years; *Development Cooperation,* various years; www.oecd.org.

Note: Growth rates take into account changes in prices and exchange rates. Data for 1999 are preliminary. Entries for multiyear periods are annual averages. Entries are rounded to the near .1 percent. OA values in parentheses.

[a] No OA value was reported for New Zealand for this period.

cut expenditures throughout the period under examination, although France may have adopted that course for ODA. France, like the United States, was far more generous in OA, while a number of the countries marked by ODA increases were negative in OA real growth.

The data on real growth rates suggests that muted optimism seems more warranted than either hegemonic pessimism or shared-identity and domestic-norm optimism. Indications include the pattern of decline and then partial reversal in growth rates; the lack of emulation by others of the specific changes in U.S. growth rates; the presence of a core but only a small core of states committed to growth in ODA contributions; the absence of sustained defectors from contributions; and the increases in OA provided by the two major donors less forthcoming with ODA.

Neither current-year amounts nor real growth rates controls for the size of a contributor's national economy (or for the total DAC economy). As is customary in evaluating relative burdens, we use net flows as a percentage of donor GDP to assess the degree of donor effort. Table 4.5 reports such data for ODA. The sum of ODA and OA is in parentheses for the period after the OA category was established.

In the most aggregated terms—the DAC row in the table—we note that the decline in ODA began with little momentum in the 1980s, accelerated in the 1990s to a 1997 low, and then showed a modest increase in both 1998 and 1999. Until the mid-1990s, the reduction in ODA effort was largely offset by an increase in OA effort as a share of GNP, but less so subsequently. The three phases discussed earlier seem to have been present on this measure as well. The average ODA and combined ODA and OA percentages for most members of the DAC did not show the sharp declines of the United States or the decline and rise of Japan. The United States was never a particularly generous governmental contributor and from 1990 on almost always had the lowest level of effort of any DAC member for ODA and for ODA plus OA. Modest American increases after 1997 did not even remotely regain the levels of a decade earlier and were largely accounted for by monies for Kosovo relief efforts (World Bank 2001a, 88). Japan in contrast, had returned from earlier declines to surpass its previous level of effort by 1999 (largely in response to the East Asian financial crisis).[24] But the most recent Japanese government figures reveal that the Japanese ODA budget has declined significantly since 2000 in yen terms.[25] Declining Japanese ODA allocations also meant that the United States reclaimed the place of largest donor by volume in 2001 (Ohno 2003, 4). The expectations of the hegemonic-stability variant of public goods theory are thus not met by what we see in this data. Neither are those of total U.S. abandonment of the governmental development assistance instrument, especially when OA is included with its stable share of GNP from 1994 on. Given the more recent increases, table 4.5 fits best with our muted optimism perspective.

The data in that table also allow us to place DAC members in level-of-effort categories as development assistance providers. Supercontributors (.70 percent of GNP or above) were stable throughout the two decades and consisted of Denmark, the Netherlands, Norway, and Sweden. Major contributors (.40 percent of GNP or above) were not stable for the period covered. Early members (Belgium, Canada, France, and Germany) moved down to the next category, and only Luxembourg moved up to this grouping. A third category of modest contributors (.25 percent of GNP or above) had only the United Kingdom as a stable member. Many others lodged there momentarily, shifting, on occasion, upward to major contributor status (Finland, Switzerland) or

TABLE 4.5. ODA and (ODA + OA) as a Percentage of GNP

	1980–84	1985–89	1990	1994	1997	1998	1999	2000	2001
Australia	.48	.43	.34 (.34)	.34 (.34)	.28 (.28)	.27 (.27)	.26	.27	.25
Austria	.29	.25	.25 (.30)	.33 (.46)	.26 (.35)	.22 (.31)	.24	.23	.29
Belgium	.56	.47	.46 (.47)	.32 (.36)	.31 (.33)	.35 (.38)	.30	.36	.37
Canada	.44	.47	.44 (.44)	.43 (.44)	.34 (.37)	.29 (.32)	.28	.25	.22
Denmark	.76	.88	.94 (.95)	1.03 (1.06)	.97 (1.05)	.99 (1.06)	1.00	1.06	1.03
Finland	.29	.51	.65 (.66)	.31 (.36)	.33 (.39)	.32 (.39)	.32	.31	.32
France	.47	.54	.60 (.61)	.64 (.69)	.45 (.47)	.40 (.46)	.38	.32	.32
Germany	.46	.42	.42 (.49)	.34 (.46)	.28 (.31)	.26 (.29)	.26	.27	.27
Ireland		.22	.16 (.17)	.25 (.29)	.31 (.31)	.30 (.30)	.31	.30	.33
Italy	.23	.36	.31 (.32)	.27 (.29)	.11 (.13)	.20 (.22)	.15	.13	.15
Japan	.31	.31	.31 (.32)	.29 (.30)	.22 (.22)	.28 (.28)	.35	.28	.23
Luxembourg			.21 (.22)	.40 (.45)	.55 (.56)	.65 (.67)	.64	.71	.82
Netherlands	1.01	.96	.92 (.94)	.76 (.80)	.81 (.81)	.80 (.83)	.79	.84	.82
New Zealand	.28	.26	.23 (.23)	.24 (.24)	.26 (.26)	.27 (.27)	.27	.25	.25
Norway	.97	1.09	1.17 (1.19)	1.05 (1.12)	.86 (.90)	.91 (.95)	.91	.80	.83
Portugal			.25 (.26)	.35 (.38)	.25 (.27)	.24 (.26)	.25	.26	.25
Spain			.20 (.20)	.28 (.31)	.23 (.23)	.24 (.24)	.23	.22	.30
Sweden	.85	.88	.91 (.91)	.96 (1.01)	.79 (.86)	.72 (.77)	.70	.80	.81
Switzerland	.27	.31	.32 (.32)	.36 (.41)	.34 (.37)	.32 (.35)	.35	.34	.34
United Kingdom	.37	.31	.27 (.30)	.31 (.34)	.26 (.29)	.27 (.35)	.23	.32	.32
United States	.24	.21	.21 (.22)	.14 (.17)	.09 (.12)	.10 (.13)	.10	.10	.11
DAC total	.36	.35	.33 (.34)	.30 (.34)	.22 (.24)	.23 (.27)	.24	.22	.22

Source: Data from World Development Indicators (various years); Development Cooperation (various years); DAC web site www.oecd.org.

Note: 1999 data are preliminary. Entries are rounded to the nearest 1/100 of a percentage point. The sums of ODA and OA are in parentheses for the period after the OA category was established.

downward to lesser status (Japan, New Zealand, Portugal). Ireland moved up into the modest contributor category. The minor contributor category (less than .25 percent of GNP) had only one member throughout, the United States, which was joined frequently by Spain and Italy. Throughout, the larger economies of the G-7 made substantially less effort than did many of the smaller members, most notably the Nordic countries and the Netherlands (Abrego and Ross 2001, 33).

Observed differences in the level of effort suggest the possible importance of domestic norms and self-conceptions pertinent to development assistance. Here, the relatively high level of governmental contributions by Denmark, the Netherlands, Norway, and Sweden stands out along welfare state lines, as does the low level of the non-welfare-state-oriented United States. NGOA contributions also shed some light on domestically rooted national differences relevant to muted optimism about development assistance contributions to international order and progress. They bear on the possible presence of norms conducive to contributions but less so to the government as the primary contributor. Pertinent data appear in table 4.6.

NGOA contributions for 1994, 1997, 1998, and 2000 generally show increases in national contribution levels, most notably placing Switzerland in the major contributor category for all three points and Canada, Finland, Ireland, and the United Kingdom at or near it for two of them. The U.S. share (as well as the absolute amount) of development assistance provided through NGOA is strikingly high. Perhaps the low level of U.S. governmental contributions does not fully indicate a turning away from a national sense of contribution obligations. That national sense and the NGOA funding suggestive of it may provide a floor that prevents further decline in U.S. governmental development assistance. While the total percentage effort of American national development assistance remained low, even including NGOA, it is important to note that in absolute volume, U.S. aid exceeded the total of that from sixteen of the twenty-one DAC members in both 1998 and 2000.

WHAT OF THE PUBLIC AND CLUB ELEMENTS?

Our muted optimism perspective about contributions to global order and progress calls, however, for the public element of contributions to at least be maintained and preferably to increase over time. We use several measures of ODA contributions to arrive at judgments on these issues:[26] (1) grants and the grant element in ODA; (2) the share of ODA not tied to spending in the donor economy; (3) the share of ODA allotted to the poorest countries (LLDCs); and (4) the share of ODA and

Defensive Internationalism

OA contributed to multilateral institutions. We do not contend that such shares amount to pure public goods contributions, only that these shares have a larger public element than other forms of ODA and, in the case of the last measure, OA.

Grants and the Grant Element

Grants are exactly that—no repayment obligation is involved. Grants have become the largest part of ODA from the DAC as a whole, on the order of 70 percent in the second half of the 1990s (World Bank 2001b, 87). The grant element in ODA measures the concessionality of donor behavior (and thus parochial financial benefits foregone). More precisely, concessionality focuses on the interest rate of aid loans relative to market interest rates and the length of the repayment term. The

TABLE 4.6. Adding Aid from Nongovernmental Organizations (NGOAs)

	NGOA as a Percentage of ODA + OA				NGOA + ODA + OA (% GDP)				
	1994	1997	1998	2000	1986–87	1994	1997	1998	2000
Australia	.07	.14	.12	.15	.42	.36	.32	.30	.30
Austria	.04	.05	.08	.12	.21	.48	.37	.33	.36
Belgium	.06	.05	.04	.09	.49	.38	.35	.40	.43
Canada	.12	.08	.08	.09	.53	.49	.40	.35	.30
Denmark	.03	.02	.02	.02	.90	1.09	1.07	1.08	1.17
Finland	.01	.02	.01	.01	.52	.36	.40	.39	.36
France	.03	0.00			.59	.71	.47		.45
Germany	.11	.16	.02	.16	.47	.51	.36	.30	.35
Ireland	.42	.30	.23	.38	.33	.54	.40	.37	.35
Italy	.02	.03	.02	.02	.37	.30	.13	.22	.17
Japan	.02	.02	.02	.02	.30	.31	.22	.29	.28
Luxembourg	.07	.06	.05	.05	.17	.48	.59	.70	.72
Netherlands	.10	−.09	.05	.09	1.07	.88	.74	.87	1.03
New Zealand	.14	.10	.09	.11	.30	.27	.29	.29	.25
Norway	.10	.09	.09	.14	1.21	1.23	.98	1.04	.91
Portugal	0.00	.01	.02	0	.10	.38	.27	.27	.28
Spain	.09	.10	.10	0	.08	.34	.25	.26	.22
Sweden	.07	.01	.02	.01	.94	1.08	.87	.79	.86
Switzerland	.16	.07	.19	.18	.35	.48	.40	.42	.5
United Kingdom	.16	.09	.10	.11	.32	.39	.32	.39	.39
United States	.23	.38	.36	.52	.25	.21	.17	.18	.19
DAC total	.10	.11	.12	.16	.36	.37	.27	.30	.29

Source: Data from UNDP, *Human Development Report* 1999; *World Development Indicators*, various years.

Note: Figures for 1986–87 do not include OA figures, as they were not recorded at that time. Entries are rounded to the nearest .01 percent.

larger the grant element, the more ODA appears aimed at contributing to the welfare of others rather than at private benefits for the donor. Funds that are purely grants clearly have a 100 percent grant element; for ODA loans, if the interest rate charged is higher than the available market rate, the grant element may not exist regardless of official claims, and the public element is a mirage.[27]

Even with this in mind, we can safely say that for the DAC as a whole, the grants share of ODA and the decline in nonconcessional loans do not support strongly pessimistic appraisals of the "publicness" of aggregate aid giving. That does not deny the variation across states on grant elements and the extent that a different and lower assumed market interest rate could increase the actual public element in foreign aid. Given the large share of ODA coming from the United States and Japan, their grant elements are of particular importance, and Japan's surge in ODA in the late 1990s was accounted for much more in ostensibly concessional loans than in grants (Castellano 1999c).

Untied Aid

Aid tying refers to the requirement that bilateral aid received must be recycled and spent in the donor country, thus providing a private benefit to the donor. The World Bank believes that tying reduces the value of such aid by about 25 percent (World Bank 1998, 6). ODA may be fully tied, partly tied, or fully untied. The last has the possibility of the largest public good element and is reported in table 4.7.

For the DAC as a whole, the percentage of total untied ODA has fluctuated since the early 1970s. This fluctuation also marked the 1990s. Available data offer indications of several phases. The untied share increased for most donor governments from 1980 to 1994, declined through 1997, and finally reached a new high for most donors and the DAC as a whole between 1998 and 2000. If the 1998–2000 pattern continues, that would imply acceptance of a substantial public element with the marked exceptions of Canada, Spain, and the United States. Across our observations from 1994 on, Japan and Portugal (and to a lesser extent Norway) are the only donors with a continuing commitment to predominantly untied ODA. The recent predominance of untying occurred without U.S. leadership; indeed, the United States never stood out for untying behavior. This aspect of contributions to international order and progress through development assistance has seen others outperforming the American record. More recently, however, at the 2000 G-8 Okinawa summit, the United States, Japan, France, and Denmark blocked a deal for full untying that would have

Defensive Internationalism

included technical and food aid. Moreover, the share of untied aid in Japan's ODA has also reversed its long-term decline (Castellano 2000d; "Gifts" 2000). Untying behavior does not warrant even muted optimism about the growth of the public element in future ODA.[28]

ODA to the Least Developed Countries (LLDCs)

Given the low political-economic levels of development of the poorest of the poor (the LLDCs), this class of aid recipients offers less possibility of private economic benefits for donors. Accordingly, ODA to LLDCs has more of a public goods element than allocations to better-off countries. Data on allocations directed to LLDCs bilaterally and as an imputed share of aid through multilateral organizations appear in table 4.8.

ODA share to the LLDCs for the DAC as a whole peaked in the late

TABLE 4.7. Untied ODA (% of all ODA)

	1980	1991	1994	1995	1997	1998	2000
Australia	45	45	36		28	93	77
Austria				12		69	59
Belgium	15	15				50	86
Canada	6	6	27	15	15	35	25
Denmark	30	30		48	35	81	81
Finland	13	13	25	26	18	79	90
France	51	51	41	26		67	68
Germany	46	46	30	23	25	87	93
Ireland							
Italy	2	2	36	22		64	38
Japan	13	13	65	60	81	94	86
Luxembourg						94	97
Netherlands	34	34	80	43	21	86	95
New Zealand	32	32					
Norway	42	42	57	42	48	90	98
Portugal			64	55	73	83	98
Spain						26	47
Sweden	66	66	19	58		79	85
Switzerland	55	55	71	48		72	94
United Kingdom	15	15	23	19	24	80	92
United States	21	21				28	
DAC total		30	47	32	31	72	81

Source: Data from *World Development Indicators*, various years.
Note: All entries are rounded to the nearest percentage. In addition, the figures for 1980 and 1991 were actually identical as reported in the *World Development Indicators* when rounded to nearest whole percentage point.

1980s, fell to a low in 1998, and increased somewhat by 2000. Also noteworthy are the small shares devoted to these recipients by the United States and Japan. For Japan, recipient poverty mattered only after a higher level of recipient country wealth, a level well above that of the LLDCs (Alesina and Dollar 1998). Of the data on development assistance provided thus far, these are the most supportive of the expectations of hegemonic pessimists about the prospects for continuing contributions to global order and progress by major actors in the system. Nevertheless, and contrary to those expectations, several smaller countries often devoted a third or more of their ODA to recipients associated with a relatively high public goods element. Some were previously identified as supercontributors in terms of ODA share of GNP (Denmark, Norway, and Sweden); they were joined by Ireland, Portugal, and Switzerland on this measure. For those governments, ODA seems particularly motivated by public or club goods rationales, providing an op-

TABLE 4.8. Share of ODA Allocated to the Least Developed Countries (in percentages)

	1980–81	1986–87	1991	1993	1997	1998	2000
Australia	19	19	21	20	18	16	21
Austria	12	19	17	20	18	19	23
Belgium	56	50	30	23	27	28	25
Canada	32	32	27	23	23	20	17
Denmark	47	38	36	35	30	33	32
Finland	45	44	33	26	24	26	29
France	21	27	26	23	22	17	24
Germany	34	28	25	27	20	21	23
Ireland	21	36	30	40	48	46	48
Italy	42	50	20	24	26	36	27
Japan	31	27	15	17	19	15	15
Netherlands	34	34	25	27	27	26	25
New Zealand	16	20	17	20	23	21	24
Norway	44	41	46	43	40	37	33
Portugal			72	67	66	55	43
Spain		15	13	11	16	9	12
Sweden	41	39	39	33	30	28	29
Switzerland	40	39	30	33	33	29	30
United Kingdom	37	31	28	27	24	26	31
United States	21	18	14	23	19	15	20
DAC total	29	28	23	24	23	21	27

Source: Data from *Development Cooperation,* various years; "Japan: Comparative Aid Performance" 1993; UNDP, *Human Development Report,* various years.

Defensive Internationalism

timistic appraisal of the degree that some smaller states are willing (and able) to contribute where the larger donors are not.

Multilateral Contributions

We view ODA and OA given to multilateral institutions as having a smaller private goods component than bilateral aid (Bobrow and Boyer 1996). The size of that private element, however, has been the subject of considerable controversy (Sanford 2000, 10). Multilateral aid provides the donor with an inherently smaller degree of control over the distribution and use of funds. The recipient is more likely to give credit for the aid to the multilateral organization than to a particular donor government. Data appear in table 4.9 for shares of government development assistance provided through multilateral institutions. Those for

TABLE 4.9. Share of ODA and (ODA + OA) Provided to Multilateral Institutions (in percentages)

	1980–81	1990–91	1994	1997	1998	2000
Australia	27	37	24 (25)	27 (27)	22 (22)	23 (23)
Austria	12	35	18 (16)	42 (28)	36 (33)	39 (27)
Belgium	40	36	40 (45)	43 (46)	39 (43)	42 (48)
Canada	63	65	37 (37)	41 (38)	29 (26)	33 (31)
Denmark	57	63	44 (47)	38 (38)	40 (38)	39 (35)
Finland	53	59	27 (28)	47 (44)	47 (46)	42 (36)
France	45	49	22 (24)	24 (23)	27 (29)	31 (22)
Germany	50	48	39 (12)	58 (58)	36 (40)	47 (41)
Ireland	77	73	51 (54)	36 (36)	38 (38)	34 (34)
Italy	84	60	32 (36)	66 (69)	69 (72)	72 (56)
Japan	40	37	28 (25)	30 (30)	20 (20)	28 (28)
Luxembourg			32 (36)	29 (29)	31 (30)	26 (26)
Netherlands	41	55	32 (35)	28 (28)	30 (29)	28 (26)
New Zealand	45	46	23 (23)	27 (27)	25 (25)	25 (25)
Norway	56	56	27 (27)	30 (29)	28 (27)	26 (26)
Portugal		27	30 (36)	35 (39)	32 (37)	34 (31)
Spain		53	34 (42)	38 (38)	39 (39)	40 (39)
Sweden	47	58	25 (24)	30 (30)	34 (32)	31 (29)
Switzerland	60	58	26 (26)	37 (34)	30 (28)	30 (28)
United Kingdom	51	64	35 (47)	42 (44)	45 (48)	40 (36)
United States	50	35	27 (22)	28 (21)	32 (24)	26 (20)
DAC total	59	57	30 (30)	33 (32)	32 (32)	33 (29)

Source: Data from *Development Cooperation,* various years; World Bank, *World Development Indicators,* various years.

Note: The sums of ODA and OA are in parentheses for the period after the OA category was established.

ODA cover the past two decades and those for ODA plus OA cover 1994–2000.

Regarding the public goods elements, hegemonic pessimists will take heart from (1) the sharp decline from 1990 in the multilateral share of ODA; (2) the relatively low historical U.S. shares of ODA and the sum of ODA and OA; (3) the low share for Japan; and (4) the low and/or declining shares of some other DAC members (Australia, Canada, the Netherlands, New Zealand, Norway, and Switzerland). Muted optimists, however, will take heart from the stable share in more recent years, calling attention to the fact that some countries have a continuing larger multilateral share than the United States and Japan and that these countries tended to increase or hold steady in the 1990s (most obviously Belgium, Denmark, Finland, Germany, Ireland, Italy, Portugal, Spain, and the United Kingdom).

In sum, the various measures used to gauge changes in public and club goods elements of development assistance taken together do not suggest that the public or club goods element is in continuing decline, that it is smoothly responsive to a hegemon's preferences, or even that it is uniformly stable and established in donor country domestic politics. These measures also do not suggest a regularly rising share of those elements or a stable and large group of donors committed to growth. Particularly forthcoming providers change from facet to facet, with the United States outside their ranks for the last decade.

A FOREIGN AID SCORECARD

Table 4.10 displays the results of a crude summary index measuring both the quantity and quality of DAC aid behavior. As explained in the notes to the table, scores for quantity of aid as a percentage of GDP and for quality (evaluated in terms of whether a government has a public goods conducive emphasis [PGCE] in its approach to aid) run from a high of 4 to a low of 1. The table spans most of the last two decades. The results in this table run counter to an expectation that aid contributions are a function of hegemonic leadership. The persistently low scores of the United States both in quantity and public goods conducive emphasis are noteworthy. Most DAC members were more forthcoming in one or both of those senses. In both quantity and quality of aid, outstanding contributions were provided by Denmark, the Netherlands, Norway, and Sweden. A second band of contributors in both aspects arguably included Belgium, France, Germany, and Switzerland. Even for some DAC members (e.g., Italy, Portugal, and the United Kingdom) who do not do as well on quantity of contribution, quality had as of

TABLE 4.10. Foreign Aid Scorecard: Quantity and Public Goods Conducive Emphasis

	Early 1980s		Early 1990s		1998	
	Quantity (% of GNP)	PGCE	Quantity (% of GNP)	PGCE	Quantity (% of GNP)	PGCE
Australia	3	2	2	2	2 (2)	3
Austria	2	1	2	3	1 (2)	3
Belgium	3	3	3	3	2 (3)	3
Canada	3	3	3	3	2 (2)	2
Denmark	4	3	4	3	4 (4)	4
Finland	1	3	3	3	2 (2)	3
France	3	3	3	3	3	2
Germany	3	3	3	3	2 (2)	3
Ireland			1	3	2 (2)	
Italy	1	3	2	3	1 (1)	4
Japan	2	3	2	2	2 (2)	3
Luxembourg			1		3 (4)	
Netherlands	4	3	4	3	4 (4)	3
New Zealand	2	2	1	3	2 (2)	
Norway	4	4	4	4	4 (4)	3
Portugal			2	3	1 (2)	4
Spain			1	2	1 (2)	2
Sweden	4	4	4	4	4 (4)	3
Switzerland	2	4	2	3	2 (3)	3
United Kingdom	2	3	2	3	2 (2)	4
United States	1	3	1	2	1 (1)	2

Source: Scores are based on entries in previous tables.

Note: Quantity measures are for 1980–81 (early 1980s), 1990 (early 1990s), and 1998. Scores run from a maximum of 4 to a minimum of 1. A 4 signifies contributions equal to or greater than .70% of GNP; a 3, equal to or greater than .40%; a 2, equal to or greater than .25%; and a 1, less then .25%. Scores for the early 1980s are for ODA only. Those for the early 1990s are the same for ODA alone and for the sum of ODA and OA. The 1998 quantity entries are in the first instance for ODA only. Those in parentheses are for the sum of ODA, OA, and NGOA. Public goods conducive emphasis (PGCE) is also scored from a maximum of 4 to a minimum of 1. The scores aggregate those assigned to share of ODA untied, share of ODA going to the LLDCs, and share of ODA allocated to multilateral institutions. Each of those aspects was scored on a four-point scale with a maximum possible cumulative score of 12 and a minimum of 3. Those who receive across the three elements a total score of 10–12 receive a 4; those 7–9, a 3; those 4–6, a 2, and those a 3, a 1. Untied ODA scores are based on data for 1980, 1992, and 1998. Those whose untied share was greater than or equal to 80% receive a 4; those greater than or equal to 60%, a 3; those greater than or equal to 40%, a 2; and those less than 40%, a 1. LLDC scores are based on data for 1980–81, 1991, and 1998. Those whose share was equal to or greater than 40% receive a 4; those greater than or equal to 30%, a 3; those equal to or greater than 20%, a 2; and those less than 20%, a 1. Multilateral share scores are based on data for 1980–81, 1990–91, and 1998. Those whose share was equal to or greater than 40% receive a 4; those equal to or greater than 30%, a 3; those equal to or greater than 20%, a 2; and those less than 20%, a 1.

1998 reached the level most indicative of a PGCE. Overall, then, these findings present more reason for optimism for the longer term than pessimists would lead us to expect.

Division of Labor among Contributors

The degree of specialization represented by division of labor in functions and the geographical distribution of development assistance can also affect the significance of declines or increases in aggregate contributions. If there is an established division of labor, a decline or increase in effort by the hegemon or others tends primarily to affect only a subset of functionally or geographically focused contributions. If a new division of labor emerges, aggregate increases or declines may not be felt with full force across functions and recipients because of some degree of substitution of supply among donors. In short, the shifts in quality and quantity reported previously in this chapter need to be appraised in light of specialization in development assistance contributions.

Comparable information on the functional allocation of foreign aid sheds light on the extent that (1) overall DAC functional priorities have changed; (2) the United States, Japan, and the other DAC donors have engaged in functional specialization; and (3) their respective specializations changed following shifts in emphasis by one or another of them. Data for 1975–76 through 2000–2001 appear in table 4.11.

For the DAC as a whole, changes in functional emphases have favored social and administrative infrastructure and nonfood emergency aid. Shares allocated to industry and other production, to food aid, and to program assistance have shrunk. In relative terms, the "Other DAC" donors appear to have placed more emphasis on development assistance to social and administrative infrastructure and nonfood emergency assistance, Japan appears to have emphasized economic infrastructure, and the United States seems to have focused on social and administrative infrastructure, food aid, and program assistance. The United States has been the least concerned with economic infrastructure, agriculture, and industry and production aid; Japan, by contrast, has been the least concerned with food aid and nonfood emergency contributions.

The overall DAC shifts are not readily interpreted in public or club good terms but suggest that some aspects of development have been differentially affected by the changing shares of ODA provided. Also, from the public goods perspective, specialization and division of labor in contributions can be more effective and efficient among a club of states and for aid recipients (Boyer 1993; World Bank 2001a). Increased effectiveness, or a bigger bang for the buck, thus could have a

TABLE 4.11. Purposes of ODA (% of commitments)

	U.S.	Japan	Average Other DAC	DAC Total
Social and Administrative Infrastructure				
1975–76	8.1	3.3	17.1	19.9
1985–86	26.8	18.5	29.3	24.4
1990	12.0	20.1	27.9	22.0
1991–92	15.2	14.7	28.8	20.9
1998	35.4	19.6	33.9	30.4
2000–2001	42.2	20.6	38.3	32.1
Economic Infrastructure				
1975–76	2.6	37.7	17.8	14.4
1985–86	3.2	37.3	18.3	16.5
1990	2.8	32.0	12.0	14.6
1991–92	3.5	34.5	14.7	19.4
1998	7.3	37.8	8.3	17.7
2000–2001	8.8	32.9	6.8	15.7
Agriculture				
1975–76	8.1	6.0	9.6	8.2
1985–86	11.2	14.2	14.3	12.5
1990	2.3	12.1	11.2	7.5
1991–92	2.9	11.4	8.1	7.8
1998	4.1	9.3	6.6	7.3
2000–2001	3.9	9.0	4.9	5.9
Industry and Other Production				
1975–76	4.5	20.6	17.6	11.5
1985–86	5.4	14.1	13.0	11.3
1990	2.5	6.0	12.3	7.9
1991–92	2.8	10.6	6.1	6.9
1998	0.1	2.7	9.0	1.7
2000–2001	1.7	2.1	2.1	2.0
Food Aid				
1975–76	29.5	0.5	4.6	12.7
1985–86	12.9	1.4	3.6	6.4
1990	6.3	0.4	2.2	3.3
1991–92	7.3	0.4	3.5	2.7
1998	11.4	0.4	2.2	3.0
2000–2001	11.1	0.4	2.1	3.8
Program Assistance				
1985–86	41.7	8.3	7.8	18.2
1990	12.3	17.7	5.0	10.9
1992	15.5	10.8	7.3	10.4
1998	18.0	11.9	4.2	8.4
2000–2001	19.3	0.4	4.2	6.8
Debt Relief				
1985–86	0.5	3.2	1.6	2.8
1990	57.1	4.3	3.2	23.3
1992	30.0	6.2	15.6	14.7

TABLE 4.11—*Continued*

	U.S.	Japan	Average Other DAC	DAC Total
1998	0.6	3.0	15.0	8.6
2000–2001	1.3	15.2	8.4	9.8
Nonfood Emergency				
1985–86	2.3	0.1	3.5	2.2
1990	0.6	2.4	6.0	2.0
1992	4.0	1.9	9.4	5.1
1998	14.1	3.0	10.0	6.2
2000–2001	11.4	0.5	10.3	7.4

Source: Data from *Development Cooperation*, various years.

Note: Social and administrative infrastructure includes education, health and population, planning and public administration, and other (including water supply); economic infrastructure includes transportation and communication, energy, and other; industry and other production includes industry, mining, construction, trade, banking, tourism, other, and multisector. Columns do not add to 100 because of omission of allocations to administrative expenses, unspecified, and support to private voluntary agencies.

positive impact on prospects for order and progress in the South, even absent increases in absolute donor giving.

The substantial differences in donor emphases provide evidence that a significant division of labor has existed among DAC members. In particular, specialization differences would tend to reduce any general effects of U.S. reductions as long as Japan and other DAC members are increasing their aggregate contributions. Signs of at least tacit consensus across donors on functional areas for increase or reduction were more pronounced in the 1975–76 through 1985–86 period than subsequently. The waning of simultaneous changes in emphases suggests growing differences in donor philosophies of development assistance, a decline in leadership from any particular donor, and a more rooted and varied development assistance agenda among donors. Signs of substitution, where other donors step up to fill gaps in the wake of American reductions, are present in the more recent years for the Other DAC category with respect to debt relief. Of course, a consensus may emerge as part of rethinking aid that would diminish funding for large economic infrastructure projects in favor of other emphases, a shift stressed in Japan's 1999 major guidelines for its future ODA (Castellano 1999d).

Additional indications about the American role are provided by the volatility of functions emphasized at different times and instances of hyperspecialization. Instances of the former are the 1991–92 to 1998 shifts in social and administrative infrastructure, food aid, debt relief, and

TABLE 4.12. Receiving Regions' Sources of Foreign Aid (in percentages)

	U.S.		Japan		Other DAC	
	ODA	ODA + OA	ODA	ODA + OA	ODA	ODA + OA
Sub-Saharan Africa						
1980–81	15		7		78	
1990–91	11		9		80	
1994		13		11		76
1997		15		9		77
1998		12		10		78
1997–98	34		18		48	
2000		17		11		72
Middle East and North Africa						
1980–81	50		6		44	
1990–91	52		9		39	
1994		30		15		55
1997		21		18		61
1998		15		29		57
1997–98	25		8		67	
2000		32		20		48
Latin America and Caribbean						
1980–81	31		9		60	
1990–91	29		12		59	
1994		30		19		51
1997		24		19		57
1998		28		14		58
1997–98	17		11		72	
2000		35		20		45
Europe and Central Asia						
1994		36		3		61
1997		40		7		53
1998		43		7		50
2000		39		9		52
Other Asia and Oceania						
1980–81	14		30		56	
1990–91	7		43		50	
1997–98	11		40		49	
2000						
East Asia and Pacific						
1994		6		52		42
1997		4		45		51
1998		4		58		38
2000		7		59		34
South Asia and Central Asia						
1980–81	21		21		58	
1990–91	17		23		60	
1997–98	14		23		63	

TABLE 4.12—*Continued*

	U.S.		Japan		Other DAC	
	ODA	ODA + OA	ODA	ODA + OA	ODA	ODA + OA
South Asia						
1994		6		50		44
1997		2		43		55
1998		0		54		47
2000		8		48		44

Source: Data from *Development Cooperation*, various years; World Bank, *World Development Indicators*, various years.

Note: Data for the year pairs (1980–81, 1990–91, and 1997–98) use DAC definitions of regions and report only ODA. Data for the single years (1994, 1997, 1998, 2000) use World Bank definitions of region and report the shares received by a region from particular sources of the sum of net ODA and OA attributable to geographically specific sources.

nonfood emergency aid. A striking instance of the latter was U.S. debt relief for 1990. These characteristics indicate that U.S. reductions and relatively low levels of development assistance effort are less indicative of hegemonic withdrawal than of situational focusing of energy on immediate international and regional system management needs—crisis reaction and management, if you will. Longer-term development processes and economic growth needs requiring sustained and stable contributions are left more in the hands of other donors. In sum, functional specialization shares provide less evidence in support of either hegemonic pessimist or identity optimist views than in support of muted optimism about contribution adjustments to deal both with short-term crises and longer-run development challenges.

Turning to geographic specialization, we will examine three aspects: (1) the importance of different donors to recipient regions; (2) the importance of different regions for various donors; and (3) the extent that various donors have concentrated their development assistance contributions on a small number of countries. As with functional division of labor, we are interested in specialization and its changes over time, substitutions, and their implications. But in these data, we focus on geographic spaces in the global system rather than functional foci.

Information on the importance of different governmental donors to various aid-receiving regions includes imputed flows through multilateral organizations as well as bilateral flows. The data appear in table 4.12. Greater and lesser degrees of reliance by receiving regions on different donors provides a measure of how these regions will be affected by changes in the contributions by the donors. We use both DAC and World Bank categories, as explained in the notes to the table, so that some categories overlap geographically. World Bank data include both net ODA and OA flows together; DAC data is for ODA only.

Some donors clearly matter more to some regions than others on a sustained basis. That tends to be the case for both DAC and composite World Bank measures as well as regardless of differences in categories used by each organization and modified over time. For the consistent geographic categories, sub-Saharan Africa has clearly depended on aid contributions made primarily by DAC members other than the United States (aside from the apparently momentary 1998 upswing) and Japan; specifically, these African nations have relied on the Western Europeans. For the Middle East and North Africa, the largest role in provision has shifted from the United States to the other DAC members—again, the Western Europeans in particular. The European DAC members show signs of substitution for the U.S. role in more recent years. For Latin America and the Caribbean, the Other DAC category (mostly Western Europe) has been most important, followed by the United States.

With regard to regional categories whose definitions have changed, the share of contributions received by Other Asia and Oceania (in DAC terms) and by East Asia and the Pacific (in World Bank terms) show the relative unimportance of the United States compared with Japan and the Other DAC members. The rather recent Europe and Central Asia category shows the relative unimportance of Japan compared with the Other DAC countries and the United States. Interpretation is most difficult for the South Asia and Central Asia (DAC) and South Asia (World Bank) categories. Yet even here there are signs of division of labor with regard to the modest role of American contributions compared to those of the Other DAC grouping and Japan.

The data in table 4.12 suggest the relative insensitivity of receiving regions to changes in U.S. aid volumes (with the exceptions of Europe and Central Asia, Latin America and the Caribbean, and in earlier years the Middle East and North Africa). The various Asian groupings are the world's regions most sensitive to Japanese policy and expenditure changes and perhaps least sensitive to those of the United States.[29] Sensitivity to the changing aid contributions of the Other DAC members is widespread across regions, with sub-Saharan Africa sticking out as an extreme case. In general, the Other DAC states, especially Western Europe, have been relatively generous providers followed by Japan, as the data in tables 4.4, 4.5, and 4.6 show. That contribution tendency in combination with relatively low recipient-region dependence on U.S. aid bolsters our mutedly optimistic position.

Donor priority in regional terms provides some perspective about the extent of specialization in regional division of labor. Pertinent data are reported in table 4.13 for the largest contributors in absolute financial terms.[30] Donor regional specializations can be glimpsed even though the measurement used for the four pairs of years (1980–81, 1990–91, 1993–94, and 2000–2001) differs from that for 1994, 1997, and 1998. What that difference means for interpretation is relative confidence in over-time commonalities across the two sets of measurements, while judgments about changes in specialization over time should be limited within each set of measurements. Since observations at the same time period are based on the same measure, we can have confidence in comparisons of donor emphasis.

Overall, the entries suggest different and rather long lasting priorities among donor states. For the United States, the emphases suggest a "pivotal regions" approach to aid giving in terms of international tensions and strategic interests. Such an approach can be read as an extension of the argument of Chase, Hill, and Kennedy (1996). The pivotal regions reflected in American aid allocations are the Middle East/North Africa and Europe/Central Asia, a finding that sheds light on the otherwise hard to explain large historical allocations to Israel and Egypt and the more recent ones to the Balkans (Alesina and Dollar 1998). Japan's focus on East Asia is in line with foreign economic and security policy priorities and was strengthened in its 1999 ODA planning guidelines (Castellano 2000c). Much of the Western European emphasis on sub-Saharan Africa fits with old imperial ties and relationships, a "former colonies" bias. This approach seems validated for France and the United Kingdom and was found for them and for Australia, Belgium, Portugal, and Japan for the period 1970–94 (Alesina and Dollar 1998). For the same period, all the major DAC donors (the United States, Japan, France, Germany, and the United Kingdom) were prone to providing increased aid to states that voted with the donors in the UN regardless of the recipients' political economy needs and merits.

Yet much of the data in table 4.13 are also compatible with a more generalized commitment to global order and progress. In allocations to regions, those to sub-Saharan Africa and to the Middle East and North Africa are especially relevant. This is especially true when one focuses on donors such as Canada, the Netherlands, Sweden, Denmark, and Norway, which largely lack such obvious private goods relationships and imperial legacies.

But the world is, of course, composed of countries as well as of regions, and analysis at the country level may yield different results with regard to specialization, division of labor, and the underlying motivations at work. We know that the number of independent countries has increased in recent decades in many aid-receiving regions and that the

TABLE 4.13. Donor Regional Priorities (in percentages)

	Sub-Saharan Africa	Middle East and North Africa	Latin America and Caribbean	Europe and Central Asia	Other Asia and Oceania/East Asia and Pacific	South Asia and Central Asia/South Asia
United States						
1980–81	20	38	13		9	20
1990–91	19	48	16		6	11
1993–94	21	42	25		4	8
1994	15	16	14	26	4	2
1997	19	28	12	21	3	1
1998	13	34	13	25	3	0
2000–2001	29	15	19	8	10	19
Japan						
1980–81	15	8	7		36	34
1990–91	19	10	8		45	18
1993–94	14	20	12		31	23
1994	17	7	9	2	40	18
1997	12	26	11	4	34	15
1998	11	17	6	4	44	17
2000–2001	18	6	11	2	42	22
Canada						
1980–81	36	8	12		8	36
1990–91	43	9	13		14	21
1994	18	4	9	4	11	7
1997	19	41	11	13	9	8
1998	23	38	9	13	9	27
2000–2001	34	6	19	8	16	17
France						
1994	45	14	3	6	7	2
1997	45	29	4	1	4	1
1998	33	30	4	11	6	0
2000–2001	47	24	7	7	10	7
Germany						
1994	19	8	7	38	13	6
1997	24	30	12	14	18	3
1998	28	21	12	13	22	6
2000–2001	34	13	13	13	13	13
United Kingdom						
1994	35	4	5	13	10	14
1997	30	23	14	10	1	15
1998	35	23	10	8	7	17
2000–2001	49	6	10	8	8	20
Netherlands						
1994	31	4	16	7	0	10
1997	29	32	15	7	2	9
1998	29	29	15	12	2	7
2000–2001	43	7	13	11	13	14

TABLE 4.13—Continued

	Sub-Saharan Africa	Middle East and North Africa	Latin America and Caribbean	Europe and Central Asia	Other Asia and Oceania/East Asia and Pacific	South Asia and Central Asia/South Asia
Sweden						
1994	29	3	9	14	7	10
1997	31	28	8	16	1	6
1998	33	31	8	13	8	5
2000–2001	42	7	15	10	12	15
Denmark						
1994						
1997	34	29	6	12	10	9
1998	38	27	7	11	6	11
2000–2001	50	7	10	6	11	16
Norway						
1994	40	0	6	18	5	10
1997	42	21	7	13	7	9
1998	41	23	9	13	6	8
2000–2001	43	9	10	14	8	17
Italy						
1994	21	39	16	5	11	1
2000–2001	47	10	7	20	4	12
Other						
1994	25	6	13	12	24	6
1997	31	20	12	11	23	3
1998	32	21	14	10	19	3
2000–2001	38	5	12	10	25	10

Source: Data from *Development Cooperation,* various years; World Bank, *World Development Indicators,* various years.

Note: Data for the pairs of years use DAC regional definitions and include imputed multilateral as well as bilateral flows of ODA. Data for the single years use World Bank regional definitions and are for net bilateral ODA and OA with identifiable regional recipients.

fate of any single recipient country affects and is affected by the evolution of its neighbors. Any tendency by donors to concentrate their aid increasingly on a small number of countries may thus imply a growing de facto general shortage of aid contributions to global order and progress. To gauge such a tendency, we examine the degree to which DAC donors have concentrated ODA on their fifteen largest recipient countries in absolute current volume terms. These data appear in table 4.14.

The general pattern is for a decrease in concentration. This is true for DAC as a whole, the European Community and its successor European Union, and most donor states (albeit less so for Australia,

TABLE 4.14. Donor Country Concentration of ODA: Top Fifteen Bilateral Recipients as Percentage of Total ODA

	1977–78	1980–81	1987–88	1994–95	1997–98	2000–2001
Australia	72.7	67.9	54.3	56.1	54.9	55.9
	(22.1)	(21.3)	(33)	(23.4)	(24.3)	(23.7)
Austria	65	83.8[a]	50.4	62	41.5	46.7
	(23.9)	(23.8)	(32.2)	(21.5)	(35.8)	(31.3)
Belgium	53.4	54.8	40.3	22.8	25.9	22.2
	(36.8)	(29.4)	(33.8)	(44)	(39.5)	(41.0)
Canada	36.1	30.3	27.1	17.9	19.6	15.5
	(41)	(37.6)	(31.9)	(34)	(32.8)	(27.6)
Denmark	43.8	37.3	34.1	32.2	31.4	31.8
	(42.8)	(45.7)	(45.2)	(39.5)	(38.5)	(36.9)
Finland	45	44.2	44.8	38.4	29.5	26.8
	(51.2)	(41.2)	(38.2)	(33.4)	(46)	(41.1)
France	47.6	43.8	36.6	45	42.4	34.1
	(19.9)	(21.3)	(22.1)	(20.2)	(22.3)	(30.7)
Germany	36.9	42.7	32.7	34.2	31	24.9
	(31.4)	(25.9)	(27.4)	(32)	(31.9)	(38.5)
Ireland	10.5	21.9	27.8	37.5	44	42.9
	(79.6)	(65.5)	(54.4)	(44.9)	(36.8)	(35.0)
Italy	17.3	14.4	46.9	42.5	22.8	17.7
	(75.7)	(76.7)	(25.8)	(35.1)	(62)	(64.0)
Japan	55.2	54.2	53.7	48.9	50.1	48.9
	(30.1)	(31.5)	(26.4)	(23.4)	(19)	(21.2)
Luxembourg				60.4[b]	44.7	49.1
					(30.7)	(22.5)
Netherlands	53.4	50.6	40.5	28.5	26.5	26.7
	(25)	(23.6)	(29.7)	(28.6)	(27.2)	(28.0)
New Zealand	65	52.1	44.3	46.4	41	40.7
	(19.3)	(26.5)	(16.3)	(21.7)	(25.6)	(24.5)
Norway	42.3	39.9	39.2	36.5	31.7	28.0
	(44.8)	(42.4)	(41.2)	(27)	(28.9)	(28.1)
Portugal				59.9	58	67.2
				(31.9)	(33.1)	(25.9)
Spain			29.6	42.4	32.8	39.8
			(43.3)	(35.1)	(34.8)	(32.8)
Sweden	55.6	48.4	37.2	32	25.9	26.0
	(33.3)	(29.9)	(33.6)	(26.8)	(31.8)	(29.4)
Switzerland	45.8	32.3	32.3	26.5	21.7	23.9
	(34.4)	(30.4)	(28.2)	(27.1)	(32.9)	(29.1)
United Kingdom	35.2	42	29.3	27.1	29.9	32.0
	(42.4)	(31.2)	(43.2)	(45.1)	(41.3)	(40.7)
United States	42.7	43.6	41.4	38.1	24.8	26.3
	(34.5)	(30.4)	(26)	(22.7)	(27.1)	(24.7)
EU	51.7	47.9	44.8	28.8	31.1	36.5
	(0)	(0)	(0)	(0)	(1)	(8.1)

TABLE 4.14—Continued

	1977–78	1980–81	1987–88	1994–95	1997–98	2000–2001
DAC total	33.4	33.4	29.5	28.2	24.7	25.0
	(33.4)	(30)	(28.6)	(27.3)	(28.8)	(29.8)

Source: Data from OECD, *Development Cooperation,* various years.
Note: Percentages of total ODA given multilaterally are in parentheses. Subtracting the sum of the two figures in any cell from 100% provides the amount of ODA that is given to other bilateral recipients (beyond the top 15) or listed as "unallocated."
[a]The two figures in this cell sum to more than 100 because of a reported negative value (e.g., loan repayment) in the unallocated category.
[b]No multilateral ODA figure was reported for Luxembourg for 1994–95.

France, Ireland, Japan, Portugal, and Spain). When taken together with persisting donor regional specializations, the implication is the existence of a turn toward attention to sets of proximate countries with stability implications for each other. This development is consistent with muted optimism.

FOREIGN AID IN AN EVOLVING GLOBAL CONTEXT

Our examination of various indicators of the quantity of aid, of its public and club goods emphases, and of the division of labor found in foreign aid in general supports muted optimism rather than various pessimistic or more decidedly optimistic assertions. While the results do not all point in the same direction, they predominantly suggest that we have not entered into a period of broad and accelerating collapse of contributions to global order and progress—at least with regard to the foreign aid instrument.

We arrive at our appraisal in part because we find unwarranted the image of the United States as a contributor historically characterized by extraordinary unselfishness as well as functionally and geographically disproportionately large and broad aid contributions. We also come to this conclusion for three more positive reasons. First, we observe a pattern of continuing U.S. contributions in many, though not all, functional and geographic areas, especially when OA and NGOA are considered alongside ODA. Second, there is a long-established division of labor among donors that has limited the effects of American cuts. And last, but surely not least, Japan and other members of the DAC have persistently implemented long-standing aid emphases while somewhat broadening their country coverage and increasing the public and club goods elements of their aid allocations. Such patterns may in part be the product of an American legacy of ideals and practices aimed at promoting long-term order and progress in the global system after World War II (Goldstein 1993; Ikenberry and Kupchan 1990; Nau 1990; Nye 1990; Russett 1985). Or perhaps these patterns have followed from other actors' historical legacies, national role conceptions, and domestic politics. In any event, there is a floor in place that helps maintain a commitment to foreign aid as a contribution to global order and progress on the part of the American and non-American members of the DAC.

Foreign aid is of course only one, imperfect form of contribution to global amelioration. Yet the foreign aid record does suffice to caution us against a quick embrace of either extreme optimist or extreme pessimist positions on the volume and public and club goods elements of future international contributions. The optimism of rhetorical calls for grand aid goals and vastly larger programs remains unmatched by the contributions such calls would require. That has been true for more than three decades and seems unlikely to change, as shown by recent experience with the UN's proposed global AIDS fund and Western European "promises" at the UN Millennium Summit in 2000 (Schafers 2002; Stolberg 2002). Yet the calls continue to be made and seem to suggest recognition of public elements. These calls also serve at least to hold back demands for eliminating aid or cutting it sharply. Indeed, pledges (if not actual appropriations or disbursements) are on the rise. World Trade Organization member governments have doubled the target for contributions to a trust fund to provide trade-related aid to developing countries (World Trade Organization 2002). The Millennium Summit call to cut world poverty in half by 2015 was signed by 171 nations at the Monterrey UN Conference on Financing for Development in early 2002. Related to that event, the European Union, Canada, and the United States pledged to increase their foreign aid giving. And the Bono/O'Neill trip through Africa in May 2002 went forward in a search for aid programs "that work" to help build a political base for future contributions in the developed world.

While these developments provide reason for optimism, we think they warrant no more than a muted version. The pledges made at Monterrey fell far short of the funding level the UN and the World Bank have estimated is needed to reach the poverty-reduction goal and the historic UN goal of aid amounting to 0.7 percent of donor countries' GNP (Devarajan, Miller, and Swanson 2002). The EU pledge amounts to .39 percent of GNP for the future, and that of the United States reaches .13 percent ("Bush Vows Aid" 2002). Among the Europeans, this level was the product of hard bargaining in which some of the countries whose pro-giving behavior was previously mentioned as outstanding (Denmark, the Netherlands, Sweden) called for greater pledges but faced opposition from the larger economies of Germany, Italy, and Spain, which only reluctantly accepted the eventually pledged level (Beattie 2002; Dempsey and Beattie 2002). For those countries that would have to increase giving to meet such pledges, such as Germany, there was no consensus support among the major political parties ("Development Minister" 2002). Fulfillment of the U.S. pledge also depends on congressional approval, which had not yet been fully requested or provided at the time of this writing. The U.S. pledge was accompanied by demanding criteria for recipient "reform conditions" reminiscent of the "deserving poor" theme in domestic welfare policy (Bumiller 2002; Dao 2003). Further, the Bush administration proposals allow only a very small role for multilateral institutions. Massive European public majorities approved of the U.S. pledge, but, as discussed earlier, similar support is lacking among the American public. Whatever increase actually takes place in foreign aid to the world's poorest countries will have to be allocated to them in the context of fierce competition for "reconstruction" aid directed to places of geopolitical salience (such as the former Yugoslavia, Afghanistan, and Iraq).

For now, the bottom line of a more complex, impure public-goods-provision perspective is bolstered. Much of the aid-justification rhetoric at Monterrey focused on undermining conditions conducive to terrorism against the North, and some potential recipients have been quick to stress their relevance to the "war on terrorism." That motivation may be with us for a while; even before its recent salience, the quality of foreign aid contributions in impure public goods terms has shown some signs of improvement. Yet widespread trends in domestic politics and other demands on donor government finances may further call into question the welfare convictions associated with the political feasibility of foreign aid. These trends may also push aid to become increasingly private in terms of donor payoffs. There has been and probably will continue to be heated bargaining between the United States and other potential donors about the distribution of burden sharing for reconstruction aid, which in turn may delay and diminish its volume. For now, pending our consideration of three other policy areas in subsequent chapters, we can conclude only that muted optimism seems a serious competitor as a stance underlying policy forecasts and recommendations about international contributions in the recent past, present, and future.

5 INTERNATIONAL DEBT MANAGEMENT AND RELIEF

> *The wisest and most effective way to protect our national interest is through international cooperation . . . through united effort for the attainment of common goals.*
> —Henry Morgenthau

> *The world of economics and finance is full of mysteries. While many are genuine and arise from the complexity of human behavior, some appear artificially contrived by groups of players who find it convenient or advantageous to camouflage their activities from others.*
> —Alexis Rieffel

International development cooperation efforts are intertwined with the activities to which we now turn—the management and relief of international debt. In recent decades, debt problems have been on the global agenda in two distinct ways. The first pertains to extremely poor countries and the burden on their economic growth, public finances, and human welfare posed by large debts. Their problems were, for example, the focus of the international nongovernmental Jubilee 2000 campaign for debt relief that enlisted a range of support spanning from pop music stars to the Pope and unilateralist U.S. Senator Jesse Helms. For many of the poorest countries, there is a strong interaction between international debt management and official development assistance, our topic in the preceding chapter. As we noted in chapter 4, the budgeting practices of some creditors/donors place debt reduction inside foreign aid budgets, a practice that can pose "a trade-off between debt relief and other forms of development assistance" (Abrego and Ross 2001, 32).

The second variant centers on the difficulties of large, somewhat better off countries in meeting current debt obligations and retaining or attracting additional foreign capital. Countries such as Russia, Brazil, and Argentina fit squarely in this category. These problems have led to financial crises for the debtor nations, the creation of spillover effects on other developing countries (particularly for emerging markets), and implications for advanced industrialized creditors both public and private (as was the case in the Asian crisis of 1997–98). This aspect of international debt involves perceived risks not just to the debtor but also to the international financial system as a whole and has led to high-profile calls for an improved international financial architecture.

Both types of contemporary debt problem remain prominent in a changing context of global affairs (Dombrowski 1998). Part of that change has been the very rapid growth of capital flows across national borders accompanied by a surge in nongovernmental dealings, complex financial instruments such as derivatives, nearly instantaneous transactions, and volatile swings toward and away from developing countries and regions. This aspect of globalization has posed a rather unprecedented magnitude and complexity of policy challenges, even if the specifics of particular crises and responses to them have historical analogies (Eichengreen 1999). Another important change has been the growing role of multilateral institutions and clubs for dealing with international debt problems, most notably the international financial institutions (IFIs) of the International Monetary Fund (IMF) and the World Bank Group. Other, less formal clubs of creditor governments (such as the G-7 and the Paris club) and private creditors (the London club) have also played a role. A third change has been the emergence of a widely shared view that "responsible" developing countries can and will be attractive to foreign capital because of their "sound" macroeconomic policies, financial account liberalization, and disciplined banking systems. Yet international financial integration inherently brings vulnerabilities not under the sole control of either borrowers or creditors. The implications of these changes have for the most part come to be understood through post hoc analyses of severe debt cases. At any point in the past several decades, prevailing recipes have been heavily influenced by the "lessons learned" from the most recent, previous problem cases and policy strategies.

This chapter proceeds somewhat differently than those for our other issue areas. The next section presents a brief summary of key points in an effort to lessen some of the "mysteries" to which Rieffel refers and to help cut through the murkiness posed by bargaining ploys and limited candor witnessed in this issue area (see, e.g., Aggarwal 1996; Lee 1993). The rest of the chapter has three major parts. The first establishes the fit between international debt management and the themes emphasized in chapters 1 and 2—impure public goods, club theory, and multilateral institutionalism. The second provides a historical summary of the evolution of debt management practices and policy thinking since the Mexican crisis of 1982. The third part presents quantitative information on the contributions that were aimed at making developing countries' debt problems more manageable and at providing relief from debt burdens. The scarcity of public opinion data on debt management limits our assessment of its implications, though we expect some carryover from attitudes toward foreign aid and the general patterns discussed in chapter 3.

A PRIMER ON DEBT RELIEF

The formally declared goal of international debt management and relief has at its core achieving "external debt sustainability." That goal is met when debtors can meet their "current and future external debt-service obligations in full without recourse to debt relief, rescheduling of debts, or accumulation of arrears, and without compromising economic growth" (Abrego and Ross 2001, 39). What does that involve?

The total external debt stock of a country (owed to foreign creditors) includes its short-term debt (maturities of less than a year), long-term debt, and use of IMF credits. For the debtor, the credits may be privately held and not guaranteed by the receiving country's government or may be held and/or guaranteed by that government (sovereign debt). Creditors may be official (either a particular lending government or the multilateral IFIs) or private (commercial banks, bond purchasers). Standard ways of measuring the indebtedness of a country relate its debt stock and the bill for servicing it (i.e., debt service) to the debtor nation's export earnings, gross national product (GNP), or central government budget. The higher the ratio of debt stock or service to those macroeconomic indicators, the more indebted the borrower.

International debt thus varies in its providers and receivers and carries with it differences in the costs and benefits for the affected parties. Debt also varies in the number of parties involved with a particular debtor and the availability to creditors of legal recourse. In general, the larger the number of creditors, the more difficult it is to arrive at and secure compliance with a course of concerted collective action. Concerted action is more likely when it involves a few governments and the IFIs they dominate, consensus on goals, shared recognition of potential gains, a common view of the relationship between policies and outcomes, established decision-making processes, and influence-wielding experts in the debtors and creditors who embody those characteristics (Herring and Litan 1995). That conducive profile is often associated with avoiding "common aversions" (e.g., bank failures, national defaults, systemic disruptions of international trade and economic stability) (B. J. Cohen 1996 cited by Dombrowski 1998, 16).

International debt also varies in a number of other important characteristics, including interest rates, repayment terms, length to maturity, liquidity, and currency of payment. Interest rates may be set by the market or below market rates (concessionality). Repayment terms may be more or less generous (e.g., there may be a grace period before payments begin, and there may be flexibility in the payment schedule). The term to maturity may be as short as several months or as long as several decades, with the former creating a special degree of debtor vulnerability. Some credits are highly liquid (market listed stocks, bonds), while others are less so, with the former a greater source of borrower vulnerability and the latter of creditor risk. The credit may be denominated in a foreign currency so that the borrower is vulnerable to weakening of its national currency relative to the currency of credit. In short, the specific composition of the debt matters a great deal for the severity of the problems it may pose and for the efficacy of particular management and relief options.

From the perspective of enhancing development, debt should be viewed in the context of net resource flows. Those are usually estimated as including a debt element (loans disbursed to a country minus principal repayments on past loans and debt service charges), net foreign direct investment, net transfers in capital markets (bank lending, equity, and bond flows), and grants (transfers from donors with no repayment provisions). Net capital flows may be reduced by legal or illegal capital flight and round-tripping (as has been the case with Russia, China, and some African countries) (World Bank 2001a, 35). Development is held to be enhanced by a larger net resource flow and impeded by a more negative one. The extent that new lending creates positive net resource flows depends on whether it produces a positive net debt flow (new credits greater than debt repayment and service charges) and whether it is exceeded by reductions in the other resource flows. Also, the more volatile net resource flows, the greater the difficulty for the borrowing country. It is widely recognized that volatility reflects both the performance of the debtor (i.e., pull factors) and forces outside its control (i.e., push factors), such as interest rates in industrialized markets (where lower rates are better), the vigor of creditor economies (which can be helpful or harmful), and world prices and demand for a debtor's major exports (high prices and demand are best). Unfortunately, debtor attempts to compensate for adverse push or pull factors—for example, by imposing higher interest rates on domestic credit or reduced government spending—may well weaken economic performance and perceived stability. That is, the steps it takes to sustain an inflow of capital may have repercussions that cause the opposite.

The international creditor community faced with borrower problems of debt management has developed several distinct types of debt relief that move beyond demanding repayment in full according to the original credit terms, a scenario the international financial community may come to view as unrealistic. One type of relief is rescheduling and restructuring, where maturity dates and grace periods are extended for principal and/or interest. In such arrangements, the external debt stock is not so much reduced as it is made more immediately manageable (flow relief) by extension of deadlines into the future. Another type of relief is debt forgiveness, where either principal or interest or both are written off, shrinking the debt stock and/or cutting the debt service charges. Yet a third type of relief is termed debt stock reduction—that is, conversion schemes (e.g., buybacks, equity swaps, discounted bonds in exchange for long-term debt). Forgiveness and reduction can reduce the debt burden for developing-country borrowers.

Details of each debt relief scheme matter, and it is important to keep in mind several characteristics of these tools: the limits on the set of debtor countries eligible to apply for such relief; what debtors must do before they actually receive it; the share and type of their (old) debt or debt service to which relief can apply (in terms of lender and the cutoff date of borrowing eligible for relief); the extent to which any relief offered is additional to that already provided; and how much the relief really amounts to given the difference between the face value of the initial debt and its present value.

Debtors facing trouble with their current debt burdens have the choice of securing one or more of forms of debt relief from their creditors, threatening to repudiate their payment obligations, or defaulting by implicitly or explicitly declaring that they will not pay their debts in part or full.[1] Debtor credibility in leveraging any of these options is largely a function of creditor acceptance of debtor promises of future good behavior, the interaction of creditor goals and debtor problems, and the probability that default will trigger a major international financial crisis.

Put more broadly, the context and consequences of debt are thus a function of the prevailing international financial system and how it is affected by financial crises.[2] The key sites for the origin of such crises are relatively large borrower nations and their banks and firms, whose performances are extrapolated by private market makers to other developing countries. One then gets procyclical private flows—a herd behavior leading to incautious lending in times of optimistic appraisal of debtor prospects or simultaneous withdrawal when appraisals turn pessimistic (Santiso 1999).

Borrower countries wishing for positive net resource flows in a world of limited development financing can thus make one or more of three major bets.[3] The first is that the financial cost of the obligations incurred will be less than the value of the growth the received capital stimulates. The keys here are that the foreign capital received leads to increased investment rather than being used for immediate consumption (e.g., imported personal goods) and that the borrowed funds are used in rather than escaping from the receiving country. The second bet is that with a growth deficit, creditors will provide some option that is more attractive than the original terms facing the debtors. The third is that the loss of the shields of economic isolation from creditors and external factors will not in a politically relevant future confront the borrower with the need for adjustments that destabilize its domestic political and financial systems.[4]

Creditors are also making one or more major bets in providing capital to developing countries. Private lenders are wagering that the recipient will pay off enough of its obligations to make the transaction profitable or to provide otherwise unavailable beneficial business. If neither of those materializes, lenders estimate that warnings to the contrary will be sufficiently timely and clear to allow the creditors to pull out before incurring major losses. If not, lenders are assuming that their home governments or the IFIs will directly or indirectly cover the losses.

Official creditors also make bets on debt management issues. They often claim to be betting that by lending on conditional terms they will be able to influence the country to follow a path of sustained, attractive development and thus repayment. If not, these creditors may be wagering that recipient performance will be sufficiently more positive to make the loan a reasonably good bargain even without repayment compared to what would happen otherwise. The more positive aspects may or may not principally involve economic development. At least, creditors may calculate that they will have enough warning to isolate the rest of the world from any financial crisis in a particular borrowing country. At a minimum, creditors are betting that they unilaterally or through the IFIs and the less formal multilateral clubs will be able to muster the resources to work out any local or regional crisis before it poses grave stresses to the international financial system or creditor domestic system—and to do so without severely weakening the IFIs.

INTERNATIONAL DEBT MANAGEMENT AND OUR THEMES

As the quotation from Henry Morgenthau at the beginning of the chapter suggests, matters of financial stability and credit provision have a long post–World War II history as meriting collective action (Kindleberger 1973). But going hand in hand with the collective action assumption are the incentives for underprovision associated with most public-goods-centered problems (Bryant 1987).

Debt management and capital availability are intertwined for the poorest countries in ways that bear directly on their ability to achieve economic growth, provide resources for the social and physical infrastructure crucial for human development, and avoid the chaos of failed states as breeding grounds for international disorder and regression. If development of the global South is a good for the global North as well, effective debt management and relief for the poorest countries has a public goods element. The second variant introduced earlier poses a classic "weakest link" collective goods problem where a financial crisis for one large borrower produces the negative externality of contagion to creditor economies and lynchpin international institutions (World Bank 2001a, 110–25). Avoiding international crises and enhancing the effectiveness of IFIs then becomes a good for both debtor and creditor countries and private financial sectors. Development failures and chronic financial crises are, by extension, public bads (Wyplosz 1999).

Yet any particular international debt management arrangement has some private element as well, one that differs in its nature and size among the affected parties. Debtor countries have an interest in maximizing the net flow of resources to themselves and minimizing foreign control. Other developing countries have an interest in insuring that special treatment for their heavily indebted counterparts does not cut into the net flow of resources. Debtor countries also prefer to minimize the loss of macroeconomic control (i.e., sovereignty reduction) that creditor-designed debt management relationships often impose.

Private sector creditors also have an interest in debt management but focus more on immunization from losses and shifting costs onto official creditors (e.g., Lissakers 1991). They also wish to avoid regulatory restraints by donor or borrower governments on creditors' ability to pursue profitable courses of action. Particular creditor governments have an interest in the health and support of their own financial sectors; preserving stakes on other grounds (economic, political, and security) in one or another developing country or region; avoiding domestic political flak for previous policies and new initiatives; and minimizing their share of the costs of any debt management or relief. The IFIs have an interest in maintaining or increasing flows of resources to themselves from rich countries, their reputation for effectiveness in use of those resources, and a position of centrality in the international financial and development systems.

The negative implication of these diverse private goods elements is that international collective action is limited or delayed as the various parties bargain for the approach that provides them with the largest private good or least private bad (Wellons 1987). The positive implication of these private interests is that the parties have an incentive not to ignore debt problems but to search for relatively rewarding courses of action. For rich-country creditor governments and IFIs, support for collective action stems in part from a desire to maintain and advance an international economy in which they do well (Corbridge 1993) and to avoid its breakdown. For the developing countries, there is the magnet of the benefits of growth and subsidization by the First World compared to the downside of international economic isolation.

With these diverse interests in mind, a number of considerations lead us to mutedly optimistic expectations. Leaders in the provision of credit to, direct investment in, and trade with developing countries have reason to beware of possibilities of contagion spreading from one troubled debtor to all members of the emerging-markets category. That concern can motivate creditors whose economic growth strategies feature those markets. The development of creditor clubs and IFIs suggests possibilities for spreading the costs of debt relief among the rich countries and a need for some degree of apparent consistency and general development rationale in their treatment of classes of debtors.

The varying prominence different debtor regions and states have for different creditors suggests that some will be especially sensitive to the needs of particular debtors. This can have two consequences. The first is that particular creditors will step forward to provide relief even if others do not do so for those key debtors. One need only consider the special involvement of the United States in Latin American debt and of West Europeans in East European and Russian debt to understand this potential division-of-labor dynamic.

A second is that creditors may lobby international financial institutions for policies that pick up much of any debt relief burden for particular debtors. Those campaigns are likely to fare better when couched in terms of widely held principles (e.g., helping highly indebted poor countries [HIPCs] or supporters of the war against terrorism) rather than ones of parochial national interests (e.g., former French colonies). The prospects of free riding by other creditors may then be restricted, as may be the domestic costs for creditor-country politicians of an appearance of debtor free riding.

Further, traditional concepts of club goods theory need to be modified to take into account the degree to which the boundaries between producers and consumers of club goods are blurred for international debt management. Some national members of creditor clubs are themselves heavily indebted. More generally, in a traditional conception, providers would be the national governments or private creditors offering relief to avoid or reduce shocks to the international financial system they value, while debtors would free ride. That overlooks debtors' stakes in crisis avoidance, which can lead debtors to contribute to relief efforts by changes in domestic policies and institutions that are often part and parcel of extensions of debt relief (i.e., conditionalities). Taking those steps may well have private benefits (e.g., future competitively superior credit and investment merit) but can also spill over in a public goods way by illustrating the positive consequences of debt relief programs.

In short, the diverse population of general and specific clubs is conducive to debt relief provision partly based on considerations of private goods consumed, possibly supplemented by considerations of creditor self-conception such as humanitarian obligations. For any given debt relief case, the possible consequences allow for some definitions that feature impure public goods for some providers and induce international financial institutions to respond to the need for debt management and relief.

Beyond the complications posed by diverse private elements, there has been less than expert consensus on the relative public good provision associated with different debt management and relief strategies. Among economists, it is important to distinguish between the "system stability" and "system correction" perspectives. Both put forward public goods arguments to buttress their differing debt relief policy recommendations and after-the-fact evaluations. Both views have been expressed for well over a decade and continue to shape treatment of each fresh debt crisis, including the recent problems of Argentina.

The system stability view (e.g., Cline 1995) emphasizes the public goods of a sound international financial system, including healthy commercial banks in creditor countries and universal or near-universal access by countries and their firms to the international financial markets on a nonpunitive basis (i.e., creditworthiness). A more recent but compatible extension treats the financial and reputational health of IFIs (the IMF, World Bank, and regional multilateral development banks) as a public good. The discipline of repayment and steps to foster it are more than selfish actions, and debt and debt service relief, especially through forgiveness, may in the long run have negative rather than positive public goods effects. It may foster a climate of moral hazard that compounds debt management problems by encouraging dubious lending and excessive borrowing.

The system correction perspective (e.g., Dornbusch 1993; Krugman 1988; Sachs 1986) emphasizes that amelioration of debt and debt service burdens will lessen a growth-inhibiting and investment-discouraging "debt overhang." Relief provides a public good that enhances the welfare of debtor and creditor countries and their populations by inducing investment-stimulating growth; increasing the value of debts held by foreign creditors, both private and public; stimulating creditor-country exports and imports; and inhibiting the sorts of political and social instabilities in debtor countries and regions that can cause negative spillover effects. Steps to reduce debt and debt service burdens are then correctives that enhance more general international system prospects. Amelioration is a necessary condition for win-win outcomes between creditors and debtors. Reliance on imposed austerity or primarily creditor-advantageous measures (such as traditional rescheduling) limits rather than increases the supply of some important public goods.

Yet there are by now some commonalities between the two prevalent economic schools. First, both recognize that the treatment of international debt between richer and poorer nations has a substantial public goods element, even if the two views disagree about the appropriate distribution of burden sharing. Second, as time has passed, both have increasingly recognized four facets of diversity: (1) viable options for the problems associated with debtors demonstrating very different political economy capabilities; (2) contextual international economic circumstances such as commodity prices, U.S. interest and dollar exchange rates, and advanced-country growth performance; (3) identity groups and clubs in the international system in most urgent need of maintenance from one time period to another; and (4) public goods elements associated with any particular debt relief instruments depending on their specific terms.[5]

What was a debate between alternative policy models has become a more complex pharmacy featuring alternative warranted diagnoses and prescriptions based on contested understandings of what constitutes "best practice" for different types of crisis cases (Berthélemy and Vourc'h 1994; Cline 1995). This in part reflects the sobering stubbornness of the problems of the poorest heavily indebted countries and the recurrent financial crises in better-off borrowers.

Among political analysts, several themes stand out with respect to debt relief as a contribution to international order and progress. The first is to lower the chances of political destabilization of particular countries that providers view as crucial for regions important to the evolution of the international system. The second is to enhance the prospects of success of "demonstration case" regimes following policy recipes that providers believe will contribute to future international well-being. The third is to divert domestic pressures in provider countries away from economic nationalism (e.g., job losses from low-wage-country exports) by stimulating debtor growth and thus imports, which convert future relations and open international economy commitments into a positive sum game. Each involves triggering debtor-country changes (governance and macroeconomic policies) conducive to debt sustainability (e.g., Snider 1996). Each theme claims a public goods intent and calls for less-than-universal application to the developing world. Each, for its central cases, calls for measures that do not inherently inhibit debtor-country growth but do provide debt relief.

Our task in the subsequent sections is to establish to what extent our mutedly optimistic expectations are supported by developments in international debt management. We do not seek to determine whether the problems of poorest-country debt burdens and better-off developing-country financial crises have been eliminated. Both remain with us. Entries on the optimistic side of our ledger feature evidence of (1) increasing steps to reduce poorest-country debt burdens without worsening net resource flows to them; and (2) more effective efforts to prevent, contain, and work through financial crises. Optimism would also be buttressed by an increasing role for multilateral institutions, especially inclusive ones, emphasizing at least club and ideally world interests rather than those of individual creditors or debtors. Our optimism would finally be buttressed by more nations responding to the debt management challenge on the creditor side through relief and on the debtor side through institutional and macroeconomic policy improvements.

Entries on the pessimistic side of the ledger would feature evidence of lethargy in anticipating and responding to debt problems; protracted and difficult implementation of relief commitments; pressure for courses of action increasing debtor vulnerabilities; responses fueling moral hazard; and responses too little and too late to avoid volatility in net resource flows to developing countries or the massive worsening of such resource flows.

We noted earlier that the nature of international capital flows has changed dramatically in recent decades, as have lessons drawn about what courses of action worsen and lessen debt management problems. Our assessment of support for muted optimism needs to take these changes and learning about them into account. What matters for our view is whether (1) provision to debt management has increased given what were thought at the time to be the most pressing threats to international order and progress; (2) the provision strategies have changed as the limits on the efficacy of previous strategies became clearer; and (3) multilateral institutional and club capacities have grown in place of reliance on ad hoc, crisis reactive mechanisms.

A HISTORICAL REVIEW

Our historical review begins with the years before the Latin American crises of the early 1980s and continues with the "relief through austerity" period of the early to mid-1980s, the "relief through growth" period (the Baker initiative and the mid-1980s), and the "relief through reduction" period (associated with the Brady Plan of 1989). We conclude with a discussion of how relief through reduction has evolved into relief through forgiveness for the poorest countries (associated with the various stages of the HIPC initiative of 1996) and the varied responses to the severe and continuing financial crises in the period beginning with the Mexican crisis of late 1994–early 1995. Those concluding sections bring us to the present and perhaps provide the best indication of what may be expected in the next few years. Actual history is, of course, never so periodically neat. Debt management policy repertoires were augmented more than discarded, and almost every policy has some precedents prior to its period of centrality.

Prelude

The years before 1982 were not devoid of public-goods-related developments. The IMF and the World Bank were set up as public good or at least club good endeavors where the distribution of policy-setting power gave the United States a predominant but hardly exclusive role. The 1970s saw the framing of issues along North-South lines (e.g., the G-77), with each emphasizing different club goods and preferences for the treatment of debt. The recycling of petrodollars was seen as a system-stability problem whose resolution would benefit both oil-importing and -exporting countries. The 1980 Brandt Commission argued that development-supporting measures amounted to a global public goods contribution to system order and progress.

The obstacles to development posed to poor countries by debt service were recognized by the United Nations Conference on Trade and Development (UNCTAD) in 1967, and in 1978 it called for official creditors to cancel—that is, forgive—much of their debt to the poorest countries.

The call to convert concessional official creditor debt to grants ("retroactive terms adjustment") did not get wide acceptance, and by the fall of 1980, the G-77 accepted Paris club approaches, which offered little in the way of debt forgiveness or reduction. In the late 1970s, senior officials of the U.S. Treasury Department and the money center banks assured the U.S. Congress that there was no serious danger to the banking system from excessive developing-country debt relative to capacity and bank exposure (Levinson 1994). The climate in the economy and for ideas in the years preceding the 1982 Mexican payment moratorium declaration induced northern banks to lend without due diligence about creditworthiness—and with inducements to do so in creditor-country tax and regulatory rules, particularly in the United States (Bouchet and Hay 1989; Huizinga 1989; Lissakers 1991; United Nations Centre on Transnational Corporations 1992).

Between 1974 and 1982, circumstances created debt volumes and debt difficulties of a very severe nature for non-oil-exporting developing countries and for some oil-exporting nations as well. The indebtedness of the former surged from $130 billion to $614 billion, and debt management difficulties were compounded by shortened maturities, floating interest rates, and a substantially increased role in lending by commercial banks. The joint effects of these developments—and of a U.S. recession in the early 1980s, high U.S. interest rates, and a sharp fall in non-oil commodity prices—led to the crises of the early 1980s (UNDP 1996).

Relief through Austerity

The major response was to tie IMF conditionality (in particular domestic austerity policies and export earning priorities) to the extension of new private credit and to World Bank cofinancing that linked loans through cross-default clauses across the banks (Lee 1993). This was done primarily when needed on a case-by-case basis (Dombrowski 1997).

While rescheduling surged after 1978, the cumulative effects of skeptical financial market judgments regarding borrower creditworthiness and the associated high interest rate spread over LIBOR (London Interbank Offered Rate), high discount rates in secondary markets, and low levels of commercial lending led to negative net transfers from debtors to creditors by 1984 (Cuddington 1989). Rescheduling by the Paris club increased rather than reduced debt service obligations since interest was charged on the debt being rescheduled. "Repeater" rescheduling debtor countries were caught in a worsening debt-management spiral. It became clear that, for many debtors, the crisis was more than one of liquidity—one they could grow out of through discipline and sacrifice—even when they were willing to bear the substantial domestic economic, social, and political costs of that course of action. Many debtors found themselves caught in a downward spiral with negative implications for growth in their import demand and for creditor repayment. For the major Latin American debtors, improvements in net trade earnings in the relief through austerity period largely went to meet debt service to creditors (O'Brien 1993). The Asian newly industrializing countries could for the most part manage the tough medicine during the period, but most other debtors could not.[6]

Yet justifications for the treatment regime of this period were not lacking in proclaimed and perceived public goods elements. First, debtor countries have a stake in improved credit reputation and access to financial markets that debt forgiveness or reduction would damage. That is, "debt relief . . . would hurt the debtors more than it would help them, because it would cut the debtors off from future borrowing from the world financial markets, and thereby hinder their economic growth" (Sachs 1989a, 5). Thus, precedents for greater relief from official creditors (like those the Paris club provided to Indonesia and Ghana in the early 1970s) and commercial banks (like those the London club provided to Zaire in the mid-1970s) were not generalized.

Second, urgency came to be attached to dealing with what was seen as a "systemic risk for the world economy, because of the possibility that defaults of a small number of countries would cause a chain of failures in the international banking system, especially in the United States" (Berthélemy and Vourc'h 1994, 32). After all, Mexico, Brazil, and Argentina's 1982 debts to American banks represented 135 percent of the banks' capital. The austerity strategy amounted to containment of that threat and by 1985 had largely eliminated it. At least for Latin America, the treatment regime sacrificed development "to secure the stability of the international banking system" (Corbridge 1993, 60; also see Sachs 1989a, 1). In this way, creditor efforts to maintain system stability can be interpreted as prompted partly by the threat to their domestic political and economic systems and thus the international financial system. To that extent, they were attempts to prevent a publicly and privately consumable bad.

Third, repayment of international financial institution claims would benefit both creditor and debtor countries by containing costs of funds to the IFIs. Otherwise, the IFIs would have to either divert funds from lending or increase costs to borrowers (Rieffel 1994). In sum, options of debt repudiation or debt forgiveness were seen, at least in the creditor world, as public bads per se and as unnecessary to boot, given the prevailing liquidity and the resultant temporary nature of the debt problem itself.

The United States was a strong proponent of relief through austerity, although dissenting voices were not absent. The U.S. position fit with the priorities of U.S. banks and the ideology of the Reagan administration. Other creditors did not coalesce around an alternative approach.

Relief through Growth

By the mid-1980s, it became clear that reliance on austerity to deal with international debt problems was not producing the favorable access to the financial markets that debtor growth and thus political stability would require, especially in Latin America and Africa. With regard to major Latin American debtors, relief through austerity also had clear negative implications for U.S. exports. As a result, the U.S.-led Baker Plan emerged in 1985. Baker emphasized new commercial bank lending to seventeen severely indebted middle-income countries (SIMICs) in conjunction with debtor-country structural reforms and increased loan disbursements from the IFIs. The plan combined austerity with growth-stimulating additional lending and debt-burden-easing swap arrangements. It did not envision substantial forgiveness.

The Baker Plan period did build on the developments of the austerity period to achieve a "considerable reduction in the extent of the possible shock to the international banking system" (Cline 1995, 77). The ratio of interest payments to exports of goods and services improved for the six largest Latin American debtors of the Baker Seventeen, and the ratio of their debt to exports of goods and services (deflated) declined from its 1986 peak (Cline 1989).

Yet the envisioned flow of new lending did not materialize, with a shortfall from targets of about a third by banks and much more by the multilateral lending institutions, although official bilateral creditors did more (Cline 1995). There was no mechanism to insure additionality of these flows, and, indeed, there were net outflows from the seventeen Baker Plan SIMICs relative to total new lending by IFIs and banks. Nor was creditworthiness generally regained, as indicated by the continued decline in the valuation of developing-country debts in secondary markets. Voluntary debt reductions and transformations did increase substantially from 1984 to 1988 to the benefit of private creditors, but the various forms of buybacks and swaps did not provide additional growth-fueling resources for debtor economies (Claessens and Diwan 1989; Sung and Troia 1992). Meanwhile, debtor fatigue grew, as did the perception that Baker's 1987 menu options of buybacks, debt-for-debt swaps, and debt-for-equity swaps were more costly than beneficial (Dornbusch, Makin, and Zlowe 1989; United Nations 1993). And the Baker approach did little for the economically smaller and more numerous low-income debtor states.

During the latter part of the Baker Plan period, a view emerged that the public good of a stable international financial banking system was relatively assured but that of growth of the developing countries, with the desired political and social corollaries, was not. Courses of action were advocated that arguably would produce win-win outcomes for creditors (official and private) and debtors through orderly cuts of debt and debt-service burdens.

One set of developments occurred in ideas about the nature of the debt burden/economic growth relationship—in Sachs' phrase, a "basic efficiency case for debt reduction" (Dornbusch, Makin, and Zlowe 1989; Husain and Diwan 1989; Krugman 1989b; Sachs 1989a, 1989b). Existing debt and debt-service burdens did not represent merely a passing liquidity problem but instead amounted to a powerful set of structural disincentives to growth-conducive policies by debtor countries and international private finance—the debt overhang view. Correction was needed to enable the invisible hand to allocate capital efficiently in the world, and correction meant reducing debt and debt-service burdens directly rather than relying on the austerity/export growth recipe. Debtors could not realistically achieve the public goods ostensibly associated with nonrepudiation or nondefault without greater investment. Investment would be discouraged unless something more was done to reduce debt-associated burdens. Austerity and new lending recipes by themselves might well worsen matters for many debtor countries. The "system correctors" provided an economic rationale for creditor benefits from debt-burden reduction. In addition, the system correctors invoked public goods arguments about free-rider difficulties that (when stemming from commercial banks) implied a greater role for official creditors and (when stemming from bilateral governmental creditors) a greater role for the IFIs (Claessens and Diwan 1994; Husain and Diwan 1989; Sachs 1989a; Vos 1994).

Political experts (e.g., the Kissinger Commission report on Latin America) chimed in with the view that creditors risked dangerous instabilities and communist penetration in important regions unless a progrowth recipe could be found. Finally, some of the Latin American debtors employed brinkmanship about default and repudiation unless a new recipe was offered (Lehman 1993).

In this changing context, some American political actors and major financial houses made moves with a greater emphasis on debt-burden reduction.[7] The IMF created the Structural Adjustment and Enhanced Structural Adjustment facilities, hardly possible without U.S. agreement. In 1987, the British announced debt reduction based on IMF concessionality; in the following months, Canada, the Scandinavian countries, Italy, West Germany, and France all offered debt reductions. In addition, Japan pledged to offer concessional interest rates for the poorest African countries and the United States actually did so. The Venice G-7 summit in June 1987 produced agreement to extend maturity and grace periods for official creditor loans. Rather than relying on a single recipe, a "menu of options" approach was experimented with for Argentine debt in 1987 and Brazilian debt in 1988 to enable commercial banks to participate in debt relief and lower their exposure.

In 1987, the Paris club agreed to reschedule Brazilian debt without any commitment to IMF conditionality. In 1987–88, Canada and Germany converted official development assistance (ODA) loans to grants, and Japan added eight low-income countries to its program to finance debt service on its ODA loans with additional grants.

The Toronto G-7 summit of 1988 went significantly further, at least for low-income countries and for those whose debt was mostly with the official national creditors of the Paris club. The "Toronto terms" marked a shift to debt-burden cuts for eligible countries and away from reliance on austerity and new lending.[8] The menu offered three options in descending order of debt-burden relief: (1) write off up to one-third of the debt (the choice of France and Finland); (2) provide lower interest rates (the choice of Denmark, Germany, Italy, the Netherlands, Norway, Switzerland, and the United Kingdom); and (3) just extend maturity and grace periods (the choice of Belgium, Spain, and the United States). Belgium, France, Germany, and the United States all announced some debt cancellation for low-income African countries after Toronto.

Japan opted for all three options and proposed the Miyazawa Plan several months later, going beyond Baker's voluntary, case-by-base approach.[9] Counter to the expressed American desire for greater debt-management burden sharing, Washington did not welcome the Japanese initiative (even though in the following year the Brady Plan echoed much of it) (Stallings 1990, 24–25).

Relief through debt-burden cuts was coming into fashion without clear leadership from the U.S. executive branch. Leadership was coming from other advanced industrialized country governments. At the same time (roughly 1984–89), IMF decisions to lend were clearly less than ideal for debt sustainability (favoring recipients for new loans with the greatest debt burden whatever their repayment record and countries showing signs of shifting their international political alignment toward the United States) (Thacker 1999). Those patterns were hardly conducive to graduation for the recipients and were conducive to moral hazard and an interpretation of the importance of a U.S. private-goods element in decision making or at most some narrow form of club goods provision.

Relief through Debt-Burden Reduction

U.S. government leadership became more prominent with the announcement of the Brady Plan in 1989, an announcement made with Japanese support and over some significant European opposition. Brady argued that the "path toward greater creditworthiness and a return to the markets for many debtor countries needs to involve debt reduction" (1989, 118).

Brady options for the reduction of debt and debt-service burdens involved exchanging old debt claims for less demanding new ones. The Brady strategy combined concerted efforts where all creditors of a particular type had to participate with voluntary elements (allowing each creditor to choose from a menu of types of new claims for which it would exchange its old claims) (Claessens and Diwan 1994). A key financial underwriting role was to be played by the IMF, World Bank, and Japan. With U.S. leadership, the World Bank IDA Debt Reduction Facility was soon established. The combination of those monies with Swiss, Dutch, French, and Swedish funds led to five agreements by early 1993. Unlike relief through austerity and Baker, Brady involved strong northern government pressures—in particular, U.S. government pressure—on commercial bank creditors. Brady in its major applications (Mexico 1989, Philippines 1989, Costa Rica 1989, Venezuela 1990, Uruguay 1991, and Argentina 1992) (Bradlow 1994, 553–71) effectively reduced the burden of commercial bank debt by a third and that of total debt by 15 percent.

A 1989 IMF decision to lend to countries in arrears on debt service to commercial creditors strengthened the hand of sovereign debtors vis-à-vis commercial bank creditors (Wells 1993). At the same time, the provision of credit enhancements (as for the Mexican deal by World Bank and IMF escrow accounts, a Japanese government loan, and Mexico's own resources) lowered bank risk (i.e., "risk-compensated forgiveness"). Brady deals used mechanisms that transferred benefits in the here-and-now to the debtors, not just commercial creditors (Claessens and van Wijnbergen 1993). The Brady approach was subsequently extended well beyond its initial Latin American emphasis to nations as diverse as Nigeria (1992), Poland (1994), and Bulgaria (1994).

What Brady was doing for commercial bank lending had a debt-burden reduction counterpart for official creditors in the application to low-income countries of the Toronto terms and their successive modifications and forgiveness by some creditor governments.[10] By the end of 1991, twenty countries had availed themselves of the Toronto terms. Several months after the Brady Plan announcement, France forgave public debt to thirty-five low-income African countries. In September 1990, Britain proposed the so-called Trinidad terms, expanding the debt write-off share embodied in Toronto from one-third to two-thirds of eligible debt, although the Paris club did not accept the proposal at that time. The Paris club did, however, ease conditions for eligibility for rescheduling, extend the repayment and grace periods for ODA and other loans, and allow for equity, nature, and development swaps. Ad hoc case exceptions emerged for Egypt and Poland in the spring of 1991 with Paris club forgiveness of up to 50 percent (Riley 1993). That was generalized in the "enhanced Toronto terms" (sometimes referred to as the London terms) accepted by the Paris club in December 1991. These newly established terms called for 50 percent reductions in the net present value of debt service on non-ODA debts, with several options for achieving that goal. For ODA credits, debt service was to be rescheduled over thirty years, with a grace period of twelve years (IMF 1994).

The shift to forgiveness that began in 1989 and continued over the next few years is clear if one compares the developments of that period with what was done from 1978 to 1988, following the UNCTAD proposal ($3 billion of official debt reduction through cancellation of ODA debts and new grants, with two-thirds of the relief going to countries in sub-Saharan Africa).[11] In 1989 and 1990 alone, reduction in terms of face value of debt amounted to almost $15 billion from the United States, France, Germany, Belgium, and Canada. Those reductions were spread among debtor countries in Africa, the Caribbean, Eastern Europe, and the Middle East (IMF 1994). IMF decisions to lend, often a precondition for Paris club and London club relief actions, became more concerned with the borrower's degree of poverty (low per capita income). Yet IMF decisions also seemed during this period (roughly the early 1990s) to respond to alignment with or shifts in alignment toward the United States (Thacker 1999).

There were substantial improvements by the major developing-country debtors in terms of the debt-service payments-to-exports ratio and creditworthiness over 1982 levels (Cline 1995), even though the absolute amount of forgiveness relative to total debt was quite modest. Countries graduating from Paris club reschedulings increased from five in the 1980s to twelve from 1990 through 1993. In terms of 1993 prices and exchange rates, total net flows to developing countries (official development finance, export credits, foreign direct investment, international bank and bond lending, grants by nongovernmental organizations, and other private flows) surged from 1988 to 1994 from $98 to 175 billion, even though the first component declined by about 10 percent.

Yet it is important to note that during this period the "traditional" developing countries were joined by the transitional economies of Central and Eastern Europe and those of the former Soviet Union (Russia and the newly independent states) as seekers of international capital (Claessens, Oks, and Polastri 1998; UNCTAD 1994). Inflows to these transitional economies were substantial in 1990–96, with official flows relative to recipient GDP in the early part of the period rivaling those of the Marshall Plan to Western Europe. From another perspective, total inflows were small (averaging about 5 percent of GDP) and in some cases (notably Russia) even negative because of capital flight. By the end of the period, the transitional economies had both debt-sustainability success stories and middle- and lower-income countries with major debt burdens and problems. And the worldwide low-income countries' debt tripled from 1980 to 1995, with new borrowing exceeding the amount forgiven or reduced.

Persistent Problems: The Poorest of the Poor

By the end of the Brady period (roughly 1995), it was widely recognized that what arguably was working to alleviate the debt-management problems of many middle-income developing countries (IMF 1992) did not suffice for the problems of severely indebted low-income countries, a group largely populated by countries in sub-Saharan Africa. There was evidence that debt relief (and even more grants) were of quite limited effectiveness for them (Hernandez and Katada 1996), but the response was a set of steps to increase forgiveness of remaining debt burdens: the 1994 Naples terms called for a 67 percent reduction, and the Lyon terms, adopted in 1996, raised that number to 80 percent. A key role in implementing the Lyon terms was to be played by the HIPCs initiative of the same year for twentysome countries unquestionably having unsustainable debt.[12]

Before the 1999 Cologne summit, very few of the targeted countries had received additional forgiveness, and only a few more were expected to get it in the next year. This phenomenon resulted in part from the qualifying process and in part from concern among the debtors that availing themselves of HIPC terms would reduce the possibility of future concessional loans. Without such new loans, debtors would be extremely dependent on the uncertain prospect of an increase in grants. Some bilateral donors did extend additional forgiveness, but donor pledges to the HIPC Trust Fund were much less than the total required to fulfill its goals. It became clear once again that the debt-sustainability problem remained.

As the 1999 summit approached, Canada and Britain espoused the most generous reductions, joined by Germany (with 15 percent of the G-7 loans in question) and the United States (with 10 percent) up to the perceived limits of congressional toleration. Japan and France, respectively holding 44 percent and 25 percent of the total, would have done the bulk of the forgiveness and were thus more reluctant (Lewis 1999) and more desirous of spreading the burden of adjustment around the G-7. The summit host, German Chancellor Schroeder, then issued a call for total forgiveness for the HIPCs by the end of 2000.[13] In the end, the Cologne summit pledged a 90 percent or more level of forgiveness to an expanded set of more than forty HIPCs with a less-demanding process (the Enhanced HIPC Initiative). Shortly thereafter, President Clinton proposed full forgiveness by official and multilateral creditors for the HIPCs if they would do more to meet basic human needs and implement IMF/World Bank–recommended reforms.

In the months between Cologne and the Okinawa G-7 summit in July 2000, Enhanced HIPC hit snags, not just from its initial opponents. Congress resisted providing the U.S. share of funding. Japan's initial position was that Cologne terms' recipients would forgo new concessional loans and be eligible only for grants (Castellano 1999a). Germany was the last of the G-7 to agree to 100 percent relief, doing so some nine months after the Cologne declaration. Others—France, Spain, and Italy—were more forthcoming in terms of policy statements. At least partly fueling growing reluctance was the revelation that the one debtor closest to receiving full forgiveness (Uganda) bought a presidential jet for an amount about equal to savings in annual debt payments. The HIPC Trust Fund had received pledges of less than 10 percent of what it was expected to need (Castellano 2000a). Once again, a summit, Okinawa 2000, had an inspirational effect, with Japan becoming an enthusiastic supporter. It was also an occasion for additional promises to expedite the Enhanced HIPC and to focus the next WTO round on development.

By the end of the summer of 2001, most members of the Paris club had promised, beyond Enhanced HIPC, forgiveness of 100 percent of pre–cut-off date ODA and non-ODA loans. That relief would come only when the HIPCs reached the "decision point" in the authorized process and then only on flows (debt service). It would only take effect on debt stocks when an HIPC reached the "completion point." Until HIPCs reached the decision point (an approved Poverty Reduction Strategy Paper [PRSP] for which the World Bank provides a thousand-page handbook), they would receive Paris club rescheduling on Naples terms and perhaps also more concessional loans. With a PRSP accepted by the IMF and World Bank and only with matching steps by the Paris club and commercial creditors, debtor countries would get additional flow help with debt service while they established a track record of implementing PRSP promises. After that, at no fixed time, they would be judged to have reached the completion point at which debt stock forgiveness sufficient for debt sustainability would kick in with no further conditionality (Abrego and Ross 2001).

If and when Enhanced HIPC is completed (only two countries had reached that point as of July 2001), IMF estimates are that the target countries will have altogether received $140–50 billion of debt relief and had their debts and debt service reduced to about half of their debt burden absent Enhanced HIPC. That would, however, involve only a 30 percent reduction from what they actually paid in 1998–99, and the forecasts are highly dependent on what donors do about new credits, world economic growth, and debtors' domestic policies (Abrego and Ross 2001).

Such forecasts are highly sensitive to debtor country GDP and export growth rates, and restraint in borrowing by debtors and lending by creditors (World Bank 2001a, 100–105). The record of fulfillment by debtors of IFI reform conditions is poor, and the PRSP conditions demanding (Easterly 2001). In early 2002, U.S. proposals that up to half of IDA World Bank new credits to the poorest countries primarily be in the form of grants rather than loans were opposed by the British, allegedly on grounds of moral hazard but perhaps because of fears that the United States was really trying to undermine the World Bank. Some months later, the G-7 did strike a compromise favoring grants to the poorest countries for health and education uses (Blustein 2002).

At the declaratory policy level, there seems to have been clear and continuing movement toward an increased public goods element by creditors. It would, however, be unduly optimistic to conclude that practice matched declarations, although they moved in the same direction. In particular, each policy shift involved

- limits on the set of eligible countries;
- failure of many of those countries to meet qualifying conditions;
- failure of many of those that did to fulfill qualifying conditions;
- delayed provision of funds;

- worsening terms of trade; and
- declining availability of new loans.

Beginning in the mid-1990s, private creditors withdrew from or stopped making much in the way of new commitments to non-oil low-income countries and wrote off much of their earlier activity. Capital provision was increasingly from creditor governments bilaterally or through the IFIs. Creditor governments had increasingly already written off a large share of their bilateral loans. The issue in net resource flow terms has now become whether reduction would be at the expense of new grants and new concessional loans bilaterally or from the IFIs.

A Wave of Financial Crises

By the mid-1990s, the debt problems of the poorest countries were viewed as chronic. In contrast, financial crises involving middle-income developing countries were thought to be episodic and temporary. Brady had worked. The 1994–95 Mexican crisis did not seem to undermine this view in the creditor world. Instead, the crisis was initially interpreted as demonstrating the merits of a liquidity diagnosis, the effectiveness of nonconcessionary crisis-relief measures, and the feasibility, albeit imperfect, of containing contagion.[14]

Mexico was followed by other crises, which have continued (Thailand, Indonesia, South Korea, Russia, Brazil, Ecuador, Turkey, Argentina). Each crisis has been followed by a flurry of finger-pointing (debtor banks; debtor governments; northern commercial financiers; northern governments, especially the United States; the IFIs; and especially the IMF). Each crisis has been followed by much discussion in multilateral forums about changing the rules of the debt game and its key institutions. Those discussions have largely dwelled on problems and remedies discussed before the Brady period but never substantially put into practice. Yet after each crisis passed, so did the apparent urgency of following a new approach. The recent crises did reduce the uniformity of creditor-world diagnostic and prescriptive views, and timely collective action thus became more difficult, as the primer section of this chapter pointed out. Bailouts were funded, as shown by the approximately $280 billion for Mexico through 2000 (World Bank 2001a). Yet these remedies were reactive more than preventive in relation to threats posed by crises under way, again along lines discussed in the primer. This has had three negative consequences: bigger rescue packages; greater damage to their recipients; and more chance for contagion to spread to other developing countries (Wyplosz 1999).[15]

In short, evidence has mounted that middle-income developing-country financial crises may be as much a chronic part of the current international financial system as the debt burdens of the poorest countries. There have been, after all, about one hundred such crises in the past two decades.[16] It may be that we are now on the brink of a major change in relevant international financial architecture, but such changes to this point have not taken place at a rate matching the growth of creditor fatigue and debtor disruption.

The apparent success of the Mexican arrangement initially gave rise to confidence of four kinds. The first was that financial crises in large middle-income developing countries were of a temporary liquidity nature and subject to its remedies. Those remedies put the costs of relief on debtors far more than on creditors. The second was that international learning from the crisis—including better understanding of the danger of short-term, foreign-currency-denominated obligations—would make it possible to avoid them in the future (as suggested in Kapstein 1996). The third was that countries important to Washington for foreign policy reasons would not be allowed to founder under financial distress. The fourth was that debtor governments were capable of meeting tough conditions for relief and resuming growth before long. There is little reason to believe that the IMF rejected any of these implications.

The Mexican episode did not move American officials away from their previously established push for developing-country financial-market opening as part of the development recipe known as the Washington consensus. Financial market integration, with its private element opportunities for the U.S. financial-services sector, supposedly had a public element for the openers far greater than any risks it posed to them. U.S. administrations held and continue to hold to this view in spite of analyses showing that increases in international capital mobility have not been accompanied by development progress but rather have been accompanied by, if anything, a general growth-rate slowdown and that such effects vary widely with developing-country conditions (Eatwell 1997; Rodrik 1997; World Bank 2001a). Financial opening was a U.S. condition for Korea's admission to the Organization for Economic Cooperation and Development (OECD), was a priority as late as 1997 for the G-7, constituted a condition of East Asian (1997–98) crisis relief, was required repeatedly by the Congress for contributions to IMF relief resources, and formed part of Bush administration enjoinders to Argentina in 2002 (Altbach 1998; "I.M.F." 2000; Kristof and Sanger 1999; Sanger 1998b).

The Argentine crisis of 2002 initially seemed to mark a new degree of unwillingness by the United States to provide debt relief. This apparently firm new stance allegedly followed from the unwillingness or inability of the Argentine government to pursue economic reforms that fit the then-current Washington consensus. One result of the absence of relief was widespread, a quickly felt reduction in the Argentine standard of living. Yet it soon became clear that no such general and fundamental change in American policy had taken place. In the following months, the U.S. government supported new funding for Brazil and Uruguay. Additional IMF help was also soon forthcoming to those countries. And by early 2003 additional IMF funds were provided to help Argentina cope with its current debt problems, even though its head of state warned that the expected reforms were unlikely to be implemented (Rohter 2003). On a related note, Brazil was far more politically and economically important to the United States than Argentina, at least partly because of larger U.S. commercial bank exposure. Moreover, concerns were growing about regional contagion from the Argentine collapse. The conditions favoring Brazil and to a lesser extent Uruguay were hardly new ones in the history of relief to middle-income debtor nations.

In sum, American, IMF, European, and Japanese rescue actions in recent years indicate an unwillingness to allow countries of foreign policy importance to fail. Those actions thus had a private element but also had a regional club element spanning creditors and debtors and in some cases had an even broader public goods element with regard to international order and progress. Thus, there is a consistency in the provision of several bailouts to Russia after 1996 (based on cooperation on the former Yugoslavia, nuclear weapons control, and the war on terrorism), East Asia in 1997–98 (where Washington desired influence in the region of fastest-growing world importance), Brazil in 1999 and 2002 (a major American trading partner and Latin American leader), Turkey in 2000 and 2001 (a major associate for policy in the Middle East and Central Asia), and Pakistan in 2002 (Afghanistan and the war on terrorism, nuclear weapons control). Iraq seems a likely addition to that list, given U.S. commitments there.[17] For the United States and the IMF, each of those countries was "too big to fail" given broader objectives; for at least some of those countries, this situation also held true for some Europeans and Japan.[18]

The combination of recipients too crucial for foreign policy and private financial exposure to fail, the IFIs' aversion to debt defaults, and orthodox views of moral hazard and austerity conditionality has nonetheless presented a set of paradoxes involving the extension of large bailouts to prevent or limit defaults based on reform promises. If honored, those promises would impose immediate economic and social damage on the debtor, whatever the eventual benefits. The prospects for some major recipients meeting those promises were overestimated. Bailouts could and in some instances did dampen domestic pressures for reform, unwarrantedly assume central executive branch control of legislatures and subnational governments, and foster removal from office of the indigenous political figures preferred by the "rescuers."

The confluence of recurring severe crises, apparent IMF compliance with American priorities for recipients and terms of relief, and moves by Washington to retain control of the international financial system have led to tensions with other members of the G-7, resentment among other middle-income debtors, and open disputes between the World Bank and the IMF.[19] Those frictions have not been eliminated by post hoc American acceptance of rescue strategies that had initially been rejected. Prominent examples can be found in the East Asian crises. The United States, the IMF, and the Europeans bluntly rejected Japan's initial proposal for an Asian facility, only to subsequently accept it in modified form. Conditions for relief to Indonesia, featuring tough austerity measures, were imposed and then softened in the face of mounting turbulence.

With recognition of the inadequacy of established rescue strategies and institutions, a variety of proposals were advocated. Some called for a more independent IMF, others supported a more limited and competitive one or even its abolition, and still others advocated strengthened international institutions and processes.[20] The first approach has encountered U.S. resistance, although Europeans and Japan have shown some attraction to changes that would increase their influence. The second strategy—for example, smaller bailout packages—clashes with the amounts of rescue required and overlooks the benefits of the lightning rod the IMF provides for the various parties. The third tends to require major sacrifices of sovereignty by official and private creditors and debtors and constraints on their financial sectors.

In effect, the major change proposals sought to break out of the impossible trinity's tension between globalization of capital markets and national financial regulation by shifting regulation to the international level. Prominent suggestions have included the equivalent of an international central bank as a lender of last resort (as proposed by Richard Cooper in 1984); a global regulator to establish, monitor, and enforce standards on relevant national institutions (including going beyond the existing Bank of International Settlements code and the warning measures discussed at the 1988 Halifax G-7 summit); national adoption of "collective action clauses" for private bondholders to relax the current requirements for near unanimity for them to be bound to debt relief agreements (as approved by the G-10 in 1996 but not put into practice);

and some sort of international bankruptcy court to oversee workouts of economies in distress (as proposed by Sachs in the late 1980s).[21] The last proposal achieved prominence and support in the IMF and for a while in the U.S. Treasury in the light of the most recent Argentine crisis, only to be subsequently rejected by the Bush administration. It was opposed by major American and European banks and viewed skeptically by major debtors as a hindrance to future borrowing (Blustein 2001). Even without the U.S. rejection, the proposals held little prospect of rapid help for debtors because these remedies would have required approval by the legislatures of the 183 IMF member countries (Kahn 2001).

Not surprisingly, none of these grand measures have become facts of the international financial architecture, although there have been modest steps to improve Bank of International Settlements adequacy standards, warning of crises, and requirements for domestic financial regulation and to speed up IMF lending, similar to the Clinton-favored Contingent Credit Facility.[22] What has not received widespread support in the creditor world is forgiveness for the severely indebted middle-income countries beyond Brady type debt reduction, even in light of defaults on the arrangements it provided (as by Ecuador in 1999). Indeed, one of the strongest critics of the current system, the World Bank, has opposed a broad extension of forgiveness to large debtors ("Ecuador" 1999). It has not been alone in that sentiment. While forgiveness might pose grave problems for the financial health of the IFIs, the most common reason given by its opponents is moral hazard.[23] If that was valid, the bailout record should have been followed by even larger amounts and shares of private international lending going to developing countries. Yet with few exceptions (most dramatically China), those flows and their share have shrunk in recent years (Eichengreen and Hausmann 1999; World Bank 2001a).

Summarizing the History of Debt Management

In sum, the post-1982 history of debt relief shows an evolutionary pattern of reaction to continuing problems and their recurrence or continuation. While creditors have shown an increasing declaratory willingness to forgo private goods elements, that phenomenon has been more marked for debtors where creditors' had small stakes (the HIPCs). Even in such cases, implementation requirements have remained high, in part because of changing and expanding creditor notions of what effective relief and long-term debt sustainability require.

For middle-income developing countries, the picture is less promising from a public goods perspective. Relief certainly has been forthcoming, but it has come tardily and on terms that place the greatest share of costs on the rescued. Relief has often emphasized the course offering the greatest private and club goods to one or more creditors. The United States has clearly had a veto role on relief but has only intermittently gotten ahead of other bilateral and multilateral creditors in providing it. Other creditors have not taken a consistent position across debtors and time, sometimes resisting and sometimes initiating lines of action that, with all their public goods impurities, involved greater forgiveness and reduction. Those initiatives have been particularly pronounced during periods of U.S. inattention or resistance to internationally provided relief. There has been growing recognition, if not enormous action, on giving debt management and relief a high place on the agenda for collective action and using international coalitions and the IFIs to deal with debt problems. These features do not suggest a decline in impure public goods contributions. They do mute optimism, however, because of demonstrated inadequacy to cope with changes in the international financial system, overcome domestic constraints in creditor and debtor nations, and sufficiently expand IFI mandates and resources.

EMPIRICAL CHARACTERIZATION

We now turn to more systematic data on debt vulnerabilities, management, and relief with respect to its overall character and the contributions of various creditor countries.[24]

Debt Burdens

Comparisons of debt sustainability from 1980 to 1990 to 2000 in relation to export earnings and GNP indicate the stubbornness of debt-management problems. As shown in figure 5.1, for developing countries as a set, external debt as a percentage of GNP increased from 1980 to 1990 and from 1990 to 2000, albeit at a slower rate in the more recent decade, as did total debt service to exports of goods and services. The ratio of total debt to exports surged from 1980 to 1990 but then was partially rolled back in the subsequent decade. In sum, the worsening of debt sustainability problems was either slowed or partially reversed. These results are compatible with muted optimism but not with particularly bright views.

Figure 5.1, however, masked the differences in the debt situations of different groups of developing-country debtors, which are shown more

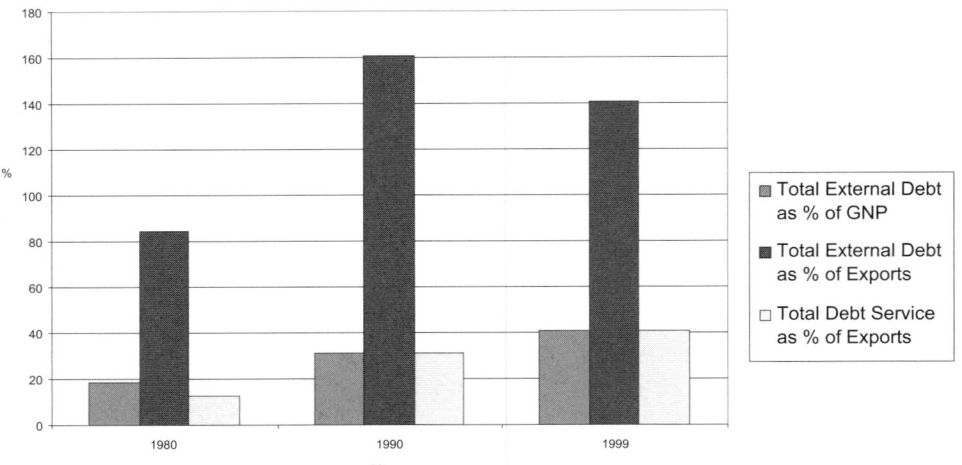

Fig. 5.1. Measures of debt sustainability (for all less-developed countries)

clearly in figures 5.2 and 5.3. For debt burden in relation to exports (figure 5.2), the situation of the severely indebted low-income countries improved only very slightly and that of the severely indebted middle-income countries worsened (although at a declining rate). The situation of moderately indebted low-income countries improved over the past two decades but did so at a declining rate, while their middle-income counterparts held steady in terms of debt sustainability during the past decade. Less-indebted developing countries faced a worsening situation from 1980 to 1990 before improving slightly over the next ten years. By this sustainability ratio, the groupings of developing countries with worsening debt problems were trimmed, but a core of troubled states surely remained.

Figure 5.3 reports for an extended set of developing-country categories three ratios for 1980, 1990, and 2000 indicative of debt sustainability: debt total to exports of goods and services (EDT/XGS); debt total to GNP (EDT/GNP); and total debt service to exports of goods and services (TDS/XGS).[25] The first measure, beyond repeating the patterns for those groups also represented in figures 5.1 and 5.2, shows that the Special Program of Assistance (SPA) countries somewhat improved their situation from 1990 to 2000 but that it was still much worse than in 1980. Debt relative to GNP tended to worsen for all groups, most dramatically for the severely indebted low-income countries, though the worsening was checked for the SPAs. The last meas-

INTERNATIONAL DEBT MANAGEMENT AND RELIEF

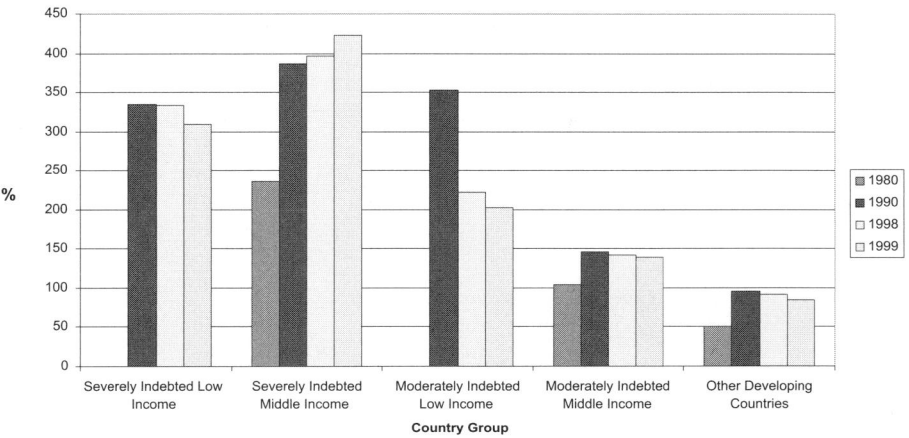

Fig. 5.2. Debt burden by country group

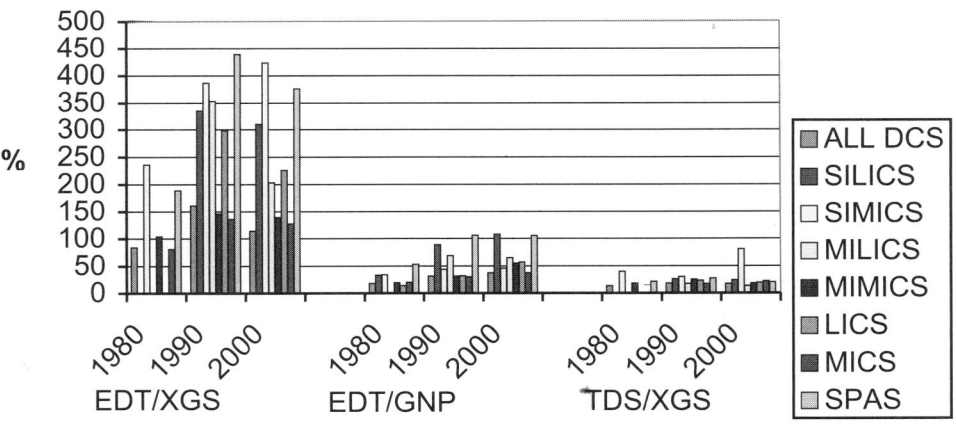

Fig. 5.3. Debt sustainability overview: All less-developed countries and income groups

ure, emphasizing debt service in general, shows modest improvements in the more recent decade with the exception of the severely indebted middle-income countries, whose improvement in the first decade was swamped by worsening in the second. Muted optimism is supported by the results of figures 5.2 and 5.3 in terms of the debt sustainability situation of the moderately indebted countries and the halt or slowing down of worsening in the ratios for most of the groups.

A crude sense of the risk to global order and progress posed by debt burdens and their location in the international system involves recognizing the countries and regions of special vulnerability, which represent sources of possible contagion and of the sorts of domestic poor performance conducive to negative externalities affecting the global North as well as the South. Table 5.1 groups countries by region and level of income and indebtedness using recent World Bank categories. The severely indebted low-income countries are most prevalent in sub-Saharan Africa, and the severely indebted middle-income countries cluster in Latin America, although neither class is without members in other regions. While the moderately indebted countries are less handicapped in development terms by debt and less prone to financial instability, their situations are in many cases vulnerable to contagion in emerging markets and adverse shifts in the terms of trade and demand for their exports. This table also shows just how wide a geographic spread exists for debt problems, meaning that virtually all creditor countries have widespread linkages to some debt-ridden countries through historical and commercial legacies.

Debt Management and Relief

The last few years of the 1990s were marked by substantial shifts in the shares of external debt provided by the multilateral IFIs, single national donor governments, and private sources. As shown in figure 5.4, the role of the IFIs increased for low-income countries in general and especially for the HIPCs. While declining, individual national donors still were the predominant source for those categories, with private sources least (especially for the HIPCs). In contrast, for middle-income countries, the predominance of private sources increased substantially, while that of individual-country official donors shrank and that of the IFIs was quite stable. In terms of the private element of debt extension, we reason that it would be greatest for private sources and least for the IFIs, with national government donors in an intermediate position.

As the various sets of terms discussed previously and summarized in table 5.2 indicate, declared creditor-government policies toward the low-income countries became substantially more forthcoming and differences in possible treatment of them compared to middle-income countries became greater. What that evolution actually means with regard to debt sustainability may be suggested by the frequency of "graduation" by countries rescheduling their debt with the Paris club. Between 1983 and the end of July 2001, thirty-five countries had graduated—nine low-income countries, twelve lower-middle-income countries, and fourteen

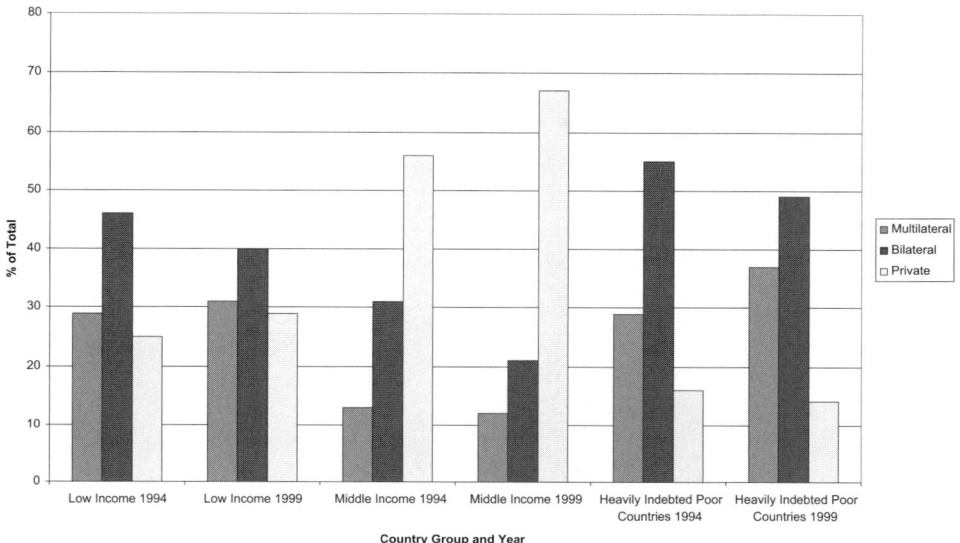

Fig. 5.4. Distribution of external debt

upper-middle-income countries (Abrego and Ross 2001, 11). All of the lower-income nations had taken advantage of London, Naples, Lyon, or Cologne terms. For the low-income countries, graduation has become increasingly frequent. For the middle-income countries, the high point was the early 1990s. Further, nineteen severely indebted low-income countries, mostly in sub-Saharan Africa, are currently operating under rescheduling agreements, usually on Cologne terms. Yet many of the graduates ostensibly no longer in need of debt relief through Paris club mechanisms appear in table 5.1, where they are underlined. Nine of them are still severely indebted, and fourteen remain moderately indebted. This picture supports a distinctly muted optimistic position on a shift toward debt burden sustainability but hardly supports blanket optimism with regard to alleviating that burden or elimination of middle-income country flashpoints prone to financial instability.

Other ways to view Paris club multilateral debt-relief agreements with official creditors involve the volume and terms of relief agreements as we move from the past to the present, their breakdown by different income groups of debtors, and the actual application of the successively more debt-burden-reducing sets of terms summarized in table 5.2. Data appear in tables 5.3 and 5.4.[26] Time periods were selected by the benchmarks they represent in the brief history presented earlier in this chapter:

TABLE 5.1. The Debt Burden, 2001

	SILICs	SILMICs	SIUMICs	MILICs	MILMICs	MIUMICs
North Africa					Algeria, Morocco, Tunisia	
Sub-Saharan Africa	Angola, Benin, Burundi, Cameroon, Central African Republic, Comoros, Congo, Democratic Republic of Congo, Ivory Coast, Ethiopia, Guinea, Guinea-Bissau, Liberia, Madagascar, Malawi, Mali, Mauritania, Niger, Nigeria, Rwanda, Sao Tome and Principe, Sierra Leone, Somalia, Sudan, Tanzania, Uganda, Zambia		Gabon	Burkina Faso, Chad, Gambia, Ghana, Kenya, Mozambique, Senegal, Togo, Zimbabwe		Mauritius

	SILICs	SILMICs	SIUMICs	MILICs	MILMICs	MIUMICs
The Americas	Nicaragua	Bolivia, Cuba, Guyana, Peru	Argentina, Brazil	Haiti	Belize, Colombia, Ecuador, Honduras, Jamaica, St. Vincent and Grenadines	Chile, Panama, Uruguay, Venezuela
Middle East		Iraq, Jordan, Syria				Lebanon
South and Central Asia	Afghanistan, Kyrgyz Republic, Pakistan			Yemen	Armenia, Bangladesh, Georgia, Turkmenistan	
East Asia	Indonesia, Laos, Myanmar			Cambodia, Mongolia, Vietnam	Philippines, Thailand	Malaysia
Europe		Bosnia and Herzegovina, Bulgaria		Moldova	Russian Federation, Turkey	Estonia, Hungary
Oceania					Papua New Guinea, Samoa	

Source: Data from World Bank 2001b, 150.

Note: SILICs = severely indebted low-income countries; SILMICs = severely indebted lower-middle-income countries; SIUMICs = severely indebted upper-middle-income countries; MILICs = moderately indebted low-income countries; MILMICs = moderately indebted lower-middle-income countries; and MIUMICs = moderately indebted upper-middle-income countries. Based on 1997 data, the per capita income category cutoffs are for low, $755; for lower-middle-income, $2,995; and for upper-middle-income, $9,265. Severe indebtedness means that the present value of total debt service to average GNP is higher than 80% or to exports of goods and services is higher than 220%. Moderate indebtedness means that the former is less than 80% but higher than 48% or the latter is less than 220% but higher than 132%.

TABLE 5.2. Evolution of Paris Club Rescheduling Terms

	Middle Income Countries	Lower Middle Income Countries, Houston Terms (since Sept. 1990)	Toronto Terms Options (Oct. 1988–June 1991)			London Terms Options (Dec. 1991–Dec. 1994)				Low Income Countries — Naples Terms Options (since Jan. 1995)				Lyon Terms Options (Dec. 1996–Oct. 1999)				Cologne Terms Options (since Nov. 1999)	
										DSR Maturing Flows	DSR Stocks	CMI	LM						
			DR	DSR	LM	DR	DSR	CMI	LM					DR	DSR	CMI	LM	LM	DR
Implemented																			
Grace (years)	5–6	up to 8	8	8	14	6	6	5	16	6	3	8	20	6	8	8	20	20	6
Maturity (years)	10	15	14	14	25	23	23	23	25	23	33	33	40	23	40	40	40	40	23
Repayment schedule	Flat/Grad.	Flat/Grad.	Flat	Flat	Flat	Grad.	Grad.	Grad.	Grad.	Grad.	Grad.	Grad.	Grad.	Grad.	Grad.	Grad.	Grad.	Grad.	Grad.
Interest rate	Mkt.	Mkt.	Mkt.	Redu.	Mkt.	Mkt.	Redu.	Redu.	Mkt.	Redu.	Redu.	Redu.	Mkt.	Mkt.	Redu.	Redu.	Mkt.	Mkt.	Mkt.
Reduction in NPV			33	20–30		50	50	50		67	67	67		80	80	80			90
Memo items ODA credits																			
Grace	5–6	up to 10	14	14	14	12	12	12	16	16	16	16	20	16	16	16	20	20	16
Maturity	10	20	25	25	25	30	30	30	25	40	40	40	40	40	40	40	40	40	40

Source: Data from Abrego and Ross 2001, 12; IMF, *Official Financing 1995*, 51.

Note: DR = debt reduction, DSR = debt service reduction, NPV = net present value, CMI = capitalization of moratorium interest, LM = nonconcessional option providing longer maturities, Mkt. = market, Grad. = graduated, Redu. = reduced.

1985 and the Baker Plan, 1989 and the Brady initiatives, and 1997 for the beginning of the latest wave of financial crises impacting world markets and the especially forgiving Lyon and Cologne terms.

The data in tables 5.3 and 5.4 show somewhat stronger reasons for optimism in the evolution of terms offered in debt renegotiations with official creditors. Most notable in this regard are three increases shown

TABLE 5.3. Agreements with Official Paris Club Creditors by Time Periods

	Number of Different Countries with Agreements during Period	Total Number of Agreements during Time Period	Average Share of Debt Consolidated (%)	Average Maturity of Consolidated Debt (months)	Average Grace Period of Consolidated Debt (months)
1980–85	30	71	89	107 (1 variable)	52 (1 variable)
1986–89	44	73	99 (1 variable)	126 (15 menu)	63 (15 menu)
1990–96	54	96	100	160 (51 menu)	72 (51 menu)
1997–2000	30	38	100	175 (27 menu) (1 variable)	79 (27 menu) (1 variable)

Source: Data from World Bank, *World Debt Tables*, various years.

TABLE 5.4. Agreements with Official Paris Club Creditors by Income Groups

	Number of Different Countries in Income Class with Agreements	Total Number of Agreements for Income Class	Average Share of Debt Consolidated (%)	Average Maturity of Consolidated Debt (months)	Average Grace Period of Consolidated Debt (months)
Severely indebted, low income	29	134 (4.6 per country)	98 (1 variable)	159 (65 menu)	66 (65 menu)
Severely indebted, middle income	15	68 (4.5 per country)	96	121 (10 menu, 1 MD)	61 (10 menu, 1 MD)
Moderately indebted, low income	9	27 (3 per country)	97	126 (1 variable, 14 menu)	59 (1 variable, 14 menu)
Moderately indebted, middle income	6	21 (3.5 per country)	96	140 (1 variable, 1 menu)	67 (1 variable, 1 menu)

Source: Data from World Bank, *World Debt Tables*, various years.
Note: MD = missing data.

in table 5.3: (1) in the average share of debt consolidated; (2) in the average length of the maturities of the consolidated debt and the use of menu options as a percentage of the total number of agreements negotiated; and (3) in the grace periods for payments on the consolidated debt. These three trends indicate a more debtor friendly approach to consolidation or at the very least an acknowledgment that creditors must work with debtors to increase the likelihood of obtaining repayment as well as the possibility that creditors are recognizing the interdependent nature of debt problems.

With regard to the income/debt burden group breakdowns in table 5.4, optimists would expect most debt sustainability activity for the severely indebted low-income countries, followed by the severely indebted middle-income countries. In terms of number of agreements per country, that expectation is met. Further, the severely indebted low-income countries have received the most forthcoming treatment in terms of maturity of any of the four groups. Yet in those respects, the moderately indebted middle-income countries received the second-best treatment of the group, treatment more conducive to debt sustainability than that offered to either their severely indebted middle-income counterparts or the moderately indebted low-income countries.

TABLE 5.5 Agreements with Official Paris Club Creditors: Use of Debt Relief Terms

	Number of Different Countries with Agreements	Terms				
		Toronto	London	Naples	Lyon	Cologne
1988	14	4				
1989	24	11				
1990	18	10				
1991	16	2				
1992	18		11			
1993	11		6			
1994	16		7			
1995	17			13		
1996	15			8		
1997	7		2	4		
1998	9			5	3	
1999	7			2	2	
2000	17			3	1	7

Source: Data from World Bank, *World Debt Tables,* 1996, 66–72; World Bank 2001a, 172, 175–82.

With respect to the sequence of increasingly debt reducing terms, pure optimists would expect that the adoption of each set would trigger a quick surge in agreements (relatively immediate use) and that over time fewer countries would need to avail themselves of the terms. Muted optimists would expect the new terms to be used but to be more strung out over time, with little sustained decline in the number of users for two reasons: first, the difficulties of qualification to take advantage of the new terms, and second, the inability of some eligible countries to achieve debt sustainability with previously offered terms. Table 5.5 conforms to those muted optimist expectations. While there is an initial surge in taking advantage of newly offered terms, we see some agreements using them in subsequent years. Further, the number of debtor-country users did not decline uniformly from 1988 to 2000.

Turning to multilateral debt-relief agreements with private creditors for the same time periods, table 5.6 shows a less distinct trend toward

TABLE 5.6. Agreements with Commercial Banks by Time Periods

	Number of Different Countries with Agreements During Period	Total Number of Agreements During Time Period	Average Maturity of Consolidated Debt (months)	Average Grace Period of Consolidated Debt (months)	Margin (%)
1980–85	31	75	91 (7 MD)	33 (7 MD)	1.68% (4 MD)
1986–89	34	53 (1 buyback; 1 debt exchange)	131 (8 MD)	46 (10 MD)	1.18% (9 MD)
1990–96	33	40 (14 DDSRs; 11 buybacks)	129 (3 MD)	35 (3 MD)	.91% (3 MD)
1997–2000	21	31		12 Voluntary Debt Swaps 7 Debt Buybacks 5 Debt Restructurings 4 Debt Reschedulings 2 DDSRs 1 Combination Voluntary Debt Swap and Buyback	

Source: Data from World Bank, *World Debt Tables*, 75–82.
Note: MD = missing data; DDSR = Brady-type government-supported debt renegotiations mostly for middle-income debtors.

longer maturities and grace periods than with official creditors, though treatment of debtors was more forthcoming after 1985. From the first to the third time periods, the lending premiums declined for renegotiated debt. More positively from a debt-sustainability and -relief point of view, the period from 1990 on was marked by the growing use of newer methods of debt-burden management and less emphasis on more traditional measures focused primarily on maturities and grace periods. This indicates some tendency toward greater flexibility and possibly creativity in the ways commercial creditors are working with debtors to find solutions to common problems.

Any optimism that these findings suggest about private creditor behavior is countered by the patterns in table 5.7. Here it is the middle-income countries (both severely and moderately indebted) that received the more forthcoming terms as measured by maturity and grace period lengths. This result may follow from commercial lenders' degree of exposure to their debt sustainability compared to that of the low-income countries and from creditor-government concerns with the stability of those middle-income debtors. With the rise of commercial lending into middle-income emerging markets in the late 1970s and

TABLE 5.7. Agreements with Commercial Banks by Income Groups

	Number of Different Countries in Income Class with Agreements	Total Number of Agreements for Income Class (average per country)	Average Maturity of Consolidated Debt (months)	Average Grace Period of Consolidated Debt (months)	Margin
Severely indebted, low income	18	59 (3.3) (8 buybacks; 1 DDSR)	87 (12 MD)	24 (12 MD)	1.2% (15 MD)
Severely indebted, middle income	14	59 (4.2) (2 buybacks; 7 DDSRs)	110 (4 MD)	39 (4 MD)	1.38% (4 MD)
Moderately indebted, low income	4	7 (1.75) (1 buyback)	89	33	1.54%
Moderately indebted, middle income	8	33 (4.1) (5 DDSRs)	151 (3 MD)	47 (3 MD)	1.4% (3 MD)

Source: Data from World Bank, *World Debt Tables*, 1996, 75–82.

Note: Table does not include data from table 5.6 (1997–2000) because none of the agreements entailed comparable quantifiable material to that for previous years. MD = missing data; DDSR = Brady type government-supported debt renegotiations mostly for middle-income debtors. One DDSR was undertaken with Costa Rica. Costa Rica is not included in any of these four income categories. Thus, the Costa Rican DDSR is included in table 5.6 but not table 5.7.

1980s, the middle-income groups posed heightened attractions and dangers for the commercial banks. In essence, private benefits (or potential large-scale private costs) may have been driving commercial bank action to default-avoiding adjustments. In any event, it is hard to argue that private creditors have moved their policies to provide a greater contribution to the development-financing needs of the low-income countries.

Relative Creditor Effort

Much of the argument in early chapters addressed the differences in the contribution efforts particular countries undertake. Chapter 3 suggested that some OECD countries, particularly some of the Europeans, would be more forthcoming than others. Chapter 4 sketched differences between OECD members in their foreign aid spending and its functional and regional emphases. Our historical review in this chapter showed little in the way of uniform leadership from the United States or Japan but revealed intermittent initiatives from some other Development Assistance Committee (DAC) members. We conclude our discussion of patterns of debt relief by considering its role in DAC members' total net ODA in 2000 in general and in the HIPC initiative. The patterns are defined in an inclusive way to embrace relevant contributions, but the donor countries differ in the extent to which debt-relief funds are located in their ODA budgets.[27] Donor behavior in 2000 appears in table 5.8.

Absolute amounts are indicative of the volume of debt relief provided to countries eligible to receive foreign aid. Here, France and Japan stand out, followed by Italy, Germany, the Netherlands, the United Kingdom, and then the United States. The size of these contributions does not fully conform to the size of ODA budgets, in which Japan and the United States are the largest. Shares of ODA for debt relief, a form of ODA with a particularly large public element, show a special degree of emphasis by Austria, France, Italy, and Portugal. If anything, debt relief for the HIPC initiative debtors has an even smaller private element. Here, the performance of France, Germany, Italy, Japan, and the United Kingdom is largest in quantity. In terms of emphasis, leadership is particularly pronounced by Italy, Portugal, Belgium, Canada, and France. U.S. debt relief to the HIPCs is one of the lowest in absolute and share terms. As with foreign aid in chapter 4, these aspects of debt relief tend to feature special efforts by some Europeans with respect to national priorities and by Japan in terms of quantity but not emphasis.

TABLE 5.8. Debt Relief Contributions in Net ODA, 2000

	Total ($ million)	Total (% of net ODA)	For HIPC Countries ($ million)	Bilateral Debt Relief for HIPC Countries (% of Net ODA)
Australia	13	1.3	4	.04
Austria	56	13.2		
Belgium	41	5.0	41	5.0
Canada	87	5.0	78	4.5
Denmark	27	1.6	20	1.2
France	498	12.1	175	4.3
Germany	235	4.7	150	3.0
Ireland	3	1.5	3	1.5
Italy	239	17.3	204	14.8
Japan	460	3.4	254	1.9
Netherlands	165	5.3	48	1.5
New Zealand	2	1.4	2	1.4
Norway	28	2.2	19	1.5
Portugal	26	9.6	19	7.0
Spain	17	1.4	8	.6
Sweden	38	2.1		
Switzerland	21	2.3	15	1.7
United Kingdom	155	3.4	113	2.5
United States	125	1.3	27	.3
DAC total	2,236	4.2	1,180	2.2

Source: Data from DAC Statistical Annex 2002, table 34, www.oecd.org/dac.

CONCLUSION

Our examination of the historical record and a variety of quantitative indicators of debt management and relief efforts surely does not warrant strong optimism about progress toward debt sustainability on the part of low-income or middle-income borrowers. Yet it does show growth in the recognition, particularly by creditor governments and the IFIs they control, that additional and innovative efforts are needed as well as some incremental steps to act on that recognition. The narrowly private element suggested by demands for full repayment on original terms has shrunk over time. Club activity through the Paris mechanism and the IFIs has grown. Terms have become less stringent, and large bailouts to avoid breakdown and continuing default by many large debtors have, if only reactively, grown over time. We think this phenomenon suggests movement toward recognizing a public element of shared consequence that links official debtors and creditors. At the same time, financial globalization has increased the challenges debt sustainability poses, especially with regard to heavily indebted middle-income countries.

With respect to national contributions to the debt-sustainability supply chain, we do not find a pattern of consistent leadership from any single creditor country or group of countries. What we find instead is shifting degrees of initiative, sometimes on the part of the United States and sometimes on the part of others. Whatever leadership America has provided does not seem to be a function of the country being in a period of hegemonic decline or ascension. Fluctuating creditor-country roles suggest that contributions are not on a smooth, increasing path and that they will be sensitive to changing patterns of politics and economics in creditor countries. Yet there clearly are stronger club mechanisms in place than had previously been the case, allowing for trading among creditors who see different degrees of impure payoffs from different modalities of debt relief for different debtors. There is little evidence that debt sustainability has worsened in the past decade as a general matter or that it has improved for all relevant classes and particular national debtors. This complex picture suggests that what was thought to be an episodic, passing part of the international political economy agenda has now become firmly placed on the list of problems that must be dealt with to move toward international order and progress. How to deal with the problems debt relief poses remains unsettled given the precedent-setting dilemmas posed by moral hazard and limited government control of private-sector financial actors.

Our conclusion is then one of muted optimism—a setting in which policy action follows severe problems and will many times be too little and too late but also in which problems are increasingly narrowed and eventually contained and their growth is reduced if not rolled back. Debt relief, like the other issues discussed in this book, is an unfinished story. It does not, however, show steady worsening since the 1982 Mexican crisis, especially when the changing understandings of development finance and vulnerabilities of more globally linked financial markets are taken into account.

6 UNITED NATIONS PEACEKEEPING OPERATIONS

In recent years, democratic peace theorists have spent much time heralding the end of the Cold War, the triumph of liberalism, and the emergence of a more peaceful international arena. But those more focused on regional conflicts, terrorism, failed states, and secessionist, independence-seeking movements have called into question such benign prospects of global order and progress. For the former, growth in international peacekeeping operations shows desirable commitments to advancing international order and progress. For the latter, the rise of peacekeeping operations is yet another indication of the disintegration of order in an increasingly discordant post–Cold War world, or what might be termed the "new world disorder."

Full-blown pessimists would try to wall the North off from the South, even if the contemporary version of the cavalry might sortie out occasionally to disrupt preparations for attack or disruptions aimed at the North. Muted pessimists recognize that international peacekeeping is one necessary way to deal with international disorder and regression but doubt that the quantity or quality will keep up with the growth and persistence of violent conflicts. Muted optimists view multilateral peacekeeping operations as increasing in quantity and effectiveness relative to the violent conflicts the world poses but not to the point of fully overcoming or preventing such conflicts. Full-blown optimists of the American primacy persuasion would suggest that the capability and will of the United States can achieve sufficient "situation dominance" to achieve peace in the world by vanquishing and replacing those who threaten it.

Like advocates of the soft hegemony, multilateralist position, we argue that multilateral peacekeeping is likely to produce public goods and reduce public bads for conflict cases "in which a measure of cooperation and collective international leadership exists" (Lake 1983, 523). Such action has been and will continue to be undertaken by the United

Nations, by other established international institutions such as the North Atlantic Treaty Organization (NATO), and by ad hoc clubs of countries with a common interest in involvement. We are less convinced that such endeavors will follow from zealous American leadership but believe that they will instead be rooted in defensive internationalism and self-realization motivations of non-American actors, even if the United States at times participates reluctantly. We think these motivations will grow as international trade and investment increase the developed world's stakes in a conducive climate for commerce (Moravcsik 1989) and as the global communications revolution quickly and dramatically conveys the human suffering associated with violent conflict to foreign publics. In effect, there will be substantial recognition that distant, initially localized conflicts and instances of "domestic implosion [can pose] a major threat to the stability of the international system" (Burley and Kaysen 1993, 9). That recognition will place a floor under contributions and, with ups and downs, feed demand for increased international efforts to lessen, contain, cool down, and resolve violent disputes whose negative effects can spill over state borders (e.g., Kegley 1996).

Muted pessimists, conversely, would emphasize offsetting groups of considerations. One example would be that the violent disputes that challenge peacekeeping have grown in variety and severity. Peacekeeping operations (PKOs) after World War II were largely thought of as confidence-building interventions to bolster truce and cease-fire arrangements already agreed to by the governments directly involved in conflicts. We have already indicated that the set of missions has expanded greatly to embrace conflicts within states and controlled territories, zones of turmoil with no functioning government, and transstate conflicts where a nonstate network attacks another state from a foreign sanctuary (e.g., K. J. Holsti 1995; Riggs 1995). In these intrastate, nonstate, and transstate conflicts, PKOs often do not have the consent of all the parties. They are "conducted during an ongoing conflict, in a country in the throes of a civil war, where serious violations of human rights are being committed and where force may need to be used to establish peace, using a mixture of persuasion and coercion, but not against a defined aggressor" (Stern 1998, 6). Such PKOs are intended to provide the physical security needed so that the UN, other international organizations and coalitions, and indigenous organizations can perform a host of other functions.[1] Finally, and more rarely, there will be "peace-enforcement operations" conducted against an identified and recalcitrant aggressor. Any given PKO may not be limited to one or more of these elements and can change its agenda after its activities are under way.

The resulting increases in the size, cost, and risk of PKOs make commitments a more serious and controversial matter today than at any other point in post–World War II history (Durch 2000). These additional types of conflicts and missions raise in acute form issues of humanitarian responsibility and the principle of Westphalian nonintervention in the internal affairs of states (Qin 1996; Wisnumurti 1996). Humanitarian issues have complex implications for intervening and how PKOs are conducted. Westphalian concerns may generate resistance to setting wide-ranging precedents for interventionist PKOs.

Further, the UN has never actually received the military commitments from its members that were envisioned in its charter (Article 43). Shifts to more difficult and coercive UNPKO missions have been accompanied by uncertainty, creating increased involvement of the legislatures of potential national contributors in the authorization process.[2] Other international and regional organizations, such as NATO, have faced complex problems of consent among their members as to engagement in and the conduct of particular PKOs. Concern about contribution prospects has been especially severe in relation to what the United States would do. Given the predominant and growing U.S. military capacity in the post–Cold War world, the prospects for multilateral PKOs may suffer in either of two ways. First, U.S. unwillingness to contribute to UNPKOs or other international peacekeeping operations (IRPKOs) may make others unable to make needed contributions. That could in turn feed into the historical lack of political will in the United States to be the sole or predominant contributor of money or personnel to UNPKOs or IRPKOS (Karns and Mingst 1995). Second, given its capacities, the United States may prefer unilateral action and not want to bother with the hindrances and transaction costs genuine multilateralism involves. Other possible contributors may in turn pull back from contributions that would subordinate their countries to the United States.

The analysis in the rest of this chapter does not attempt to provide an independent assessment of the much-argued question of what PKOs actually produce in terms of public goods. That question has been subjected to substantial analysis, especially for UNPKOs, in other forums. We think the findings generally support our muted optimist position. An especially rigorous and inclusive study has found that with regard to peace building in civil war situations, "multilateral, United Nations peace operations make a positive difference" (Doyle and Sambanis 2000, 779). Further, more modest and temporary effects that do not reach the level of full conflict resolution merit recognition. These possibilities include preventing escalation of conflicts in space and severity, tying down aggressive states and communal movements in low-level conflicts, maintaining established spheres of order and noncoercive relations, deterring third parties that might engage in unacceptable behavior, and setting precedents and conventions for international intolerance of gross barbarities (see Kerr and Mercer 1996). In addition, the contributions of UNPKOs should be evaluated relative to the investments made in them that recently amounted to about $1 for every $250 of global national military spending. They can also be evaluated relative to the less-than-comforting record of reliance on balance-of-power, unilateral imposition, or neglect approaches (Kegley 1996).

Recent analyses and experience also make clear that UNPKOs are not a magic drug for resolving conflicts. Yet even the most systematic of the analyses highlighting ineffectiveness (Diehl, Reifschneider, and Hensel 1996) fails to make the case that no positive consequences accrue from PKOs. In part, that is because the returns are not yet fully in for the post–Cold War world and for significant intrastate and transstate conflicts. It is also because counterfactual possibilities—what would have happened if there had not been UNPKOs—are not fully addressed and likely cannot be. Moreover, Neack (1997) correctly observes that UNPKO cases historically are characterized by an extreme degree of difficulty and very modest resource commitments.

What we will do in subsequent sections of this chapter is relate PKOs to public goods thinking, review support in northern contributor public opinion, examine UNPKO activity and contributions to it, and look in more detail at the U.S. role elsewhere.[3] We do not devote much attention to the activities and contributions associated with multilateral PKOs "blessed" by the UN but not financed through its institutions because of the limited availability of disaggregated data, although we acknowledge the importance of such actions.[4] We do include those PKOs and UNPKOs in our review of public opinion, in part because the questions asked often do not distinguish between the two types of PKOs. For the most part, we also exclude interventions where the primary conflict is between the intervener(s) and their targets. Prominent excluded cases are the post-9/11 U.S.-led invasions of Afghanistan and Iraq in the context of the declared American war on terrorism, although postinvasion international peacekeeping operations would still warrant inclusion by our rules.

PEACEKEEPING OPERATIONS AND PUBLIC GOODS

The pure public goods perspective on PKOs assumes that "preventing deadly conflict creates conditions that are indivisible and nonexcludable" and amounts to an "international public good" characterized by "security, well-being and justice" (Hamburg and Holl 1999, 367; Carnegie Commission 1997). For Mendez (1999, 389), "regional or local peace" is a "public good in that it is an element . . . of world order." A specific operation can provide "a regional public good . . . provided that it does not infringe on another region or country." Successful PKOs "provide an increased measure of world stability and security that benefits all nations—contributors and non-contributors—so that the benefits are non-excludable. Maintenance of world peace also yields nonrival benefits worldwide, because one nation's gains from world peace do not detract from other nations' available gains" (Khanna, Sandler, and Shimizu 1998, 181). As then UN Secretary-General Boutros-Ghali put it, "all states . . . have a strong interest in preventing a global pattern of violence, in checking the disease of conflict, and in deterring would be aggressors" (1996, 19). If we accept that a general human interest exists for the protection of "oppressed peoples and innocent bystanders" (Blechman 1995, 10), it follows that "humanitarian-based PKO also produces an output that possesses global nonexcludable and nonrival benefits" (Khanna, Sandler, and Shimizu 1998, 181). There is a clear supply chain from contributions to PKOs to production by those operations of a public good or reduction of a public bad.

Others agree with and amplify this interpretation. A U.S. Department of State publication asserts that

> Peacekeeping has the capacity, under the right circumstances, to separate adversaries, maintain ceasefires, facilitate the delivery of humanitarian relief, enable refugees and displaced persons to return home, demobilize combatants, and create conditions under which political reconciliation may occur and free elections may be held. In so doing, it can help nurture new democracies, lower the global tide of refugees, reduce the likelihood of unwelcome interventions by regional powers, and prevent small wars from growing into larger conflicts which would be far more costly in terms of lives and treasure. (1995, 377)

Diehl (1993a, 487) and the UN's review of PKOs (United Nations 1996, 3–5; 1990, 8) emphasize halting armed conflict and preventing its recurrence and secondarily creating a stable environment for negotiations that can lead to the resolution of the underlying issues of the conflict. Twelve more specific PKO activities identified by Diehl, Druckman, and Wall (1998) all seem to hold out more than private goods and bads.[5]

More specifically, it has been argued that UNPKOs have and are perceived as having more of a public goods character than other multilateral PKOs. "There is a clear advantage . . . to having neutral, impartial and universal auspices for resolving armed conflicts and potential conflicts" (Mendez 1999, 389, 397). UN-authorized PKOs will be more widely viewed as globally justified, impartial, and applied through some sort of universal criteria (Annan quoted in Crossette 1999a). On that basis, UNPKOs are to be preferred to other sorts of PKOs, and any particular PKO is conducive to the future provision of public goods because PKOs work "to enhance the effectiveness of the United Nations" (Boutros-Ghali 1995, 99).

These claims have several implications. First, UNPKOs that weaken rather than strengthen the effectiveness of the UN may reduce the prospects for public goods provision and bads reduction. Second, other forms of PKOs may be perceived as "hegemony by another name"—that is, schemes to benefit only a small club of contributors or even a single national contributor (Wren 1999a). For example, some Asian opponents of the Australian-led PKO intervention in East Timor conjured up images of "Caucasian troops imposing peace on Asia" ("'Howard Doctrine'" 1999). Australia might simply be acting as "deputy to the U.S. sheriff in the region" (*Australian Financial Review* 1999).

The pure public good conception of UNPKOs, then, carries with it several problems. UN auspices may meet but do not guarantee conditions conducive to publicness. Further, the pursuit of those auspices may come at a fearsome price: tardiness in acting to prevent or even to stop barbarities or the existence of inadequate capabilities for peace restoration or enforcement (Annan 1999; Crossette 1999b). Finally, if UNPKOs are held to be pure public goods, substantial free riding is expected, since the benefits will be available anyway. The result will be suboptimal amounts of provision, a situation that will worsen as "the size of the group benefiting from peacekeeping increases" (Khanna, Sandler, and Shimizu 1998, 182). Self-interest works against the interests of the collective. If UNPKOs are indeed a public good, then they will not be produced to the extent needed by the international system. The shortfall will increase if and when UNPKOs are mounted for additional regions and address a larger and more difficult set of conflicts. If contributions must come disproportionately from the larger powers, why not let them move directly to IRPKO actions and accelerate any public goods provision and bads reduction a particular peacekeeping action would provide?

The private goods view in its strongest form treats PKOs, including UN ones, as benefiting only each specific national contributor. A weaker form treats them as doing so for a small club of nations. In either case, the benefits are excludable and, for the most part, rival.

The most prevalent view of private benefits from PKOs focus on the benefits that accrue to a small club of actors—that is, the preservation of an advantageous and unequal status quo in a particular locale or around the globe. That argument has been made regarding PKO involvement for both middle and great powers (Mingst 1996; Neack 1995, 1997; Schnabel 1994). Thus, even the most humanitarian claims to a right of intervention through UNPKOs in intrastate disputes or in "state sponsors" of terrorism amount to depriving most nations of "sovereignty," their "last defense against the rules of an unequal world" (Crossette 1999b).

UNPKOs can also feature private benefits to a single national contributor or small contributor club. A French expert put it in unvarnished form:

> The policy is simple: encourage anything capable of strengthening the prestige and means of action of the Security Council, and, through it, France's own international influence. France's participation in peacekeeping operations is not part of some abstract logic of collective security. It serves material and immaterial aims of national interest such as security imperatives, self-image, and international prestige. (Smouts 1998, 8)

Along private goods lines, some states (and some individuals and military establishments) may actually make a profit from UNPKO or other PKO personnel contributions. Significant financial benefits may be garnered by governments and serving personnel. Finland, for example, provides special financial incentives to personnel in UNPKOs. Other countries may channel the reimbursements (generally about $1,000 per month) into central coffers while paying their troops much less (Bonner 1995). And some military establishments may take home UN-provided equipment and supplies (Morrison 1996), in addition to receiving the intangible benefits of experience and training. Even for the United States, per capita monthly payments from the UN have been more than twice the marginal cost of such an assignment (Holt 1996). While less calculable in monetary terms, sending military elements into UNPKOs may provide a private benefit for the contributing nation by helping to reorient its military away from interference in domestic politics. The private goods engine, however, provides no necessary match between motives for PKO contributions and the seriousness of the public or even club bads that a violent conflict may pose.

Taking all these arguments en masse, we think that there is some truth in both the public and private goods views. In the language of chapter 2,

UN and other multilateral PKOs involve joint products, highly impure public goods and bads, but not solely private ones. The implications for contributions to PKOs are, then, less bleak than either of the previous views imply. Self-interested pursuit of military security and defense private goods will stimulate higher production levels of the collectively beneficial security public goods (Russett 1970; Sandler 1977; Sandler and Hartley 1995). This logic calls into question Neack's (1995) notion that one can (or should) distinguish between self-interest and community interest for nation-state contributions to peacekeeping operations as mutually exclusive motivating factors. In the joint product model, an "increase in the size of the group [benefiting] does not necessarily worsen free-riding or suboptimality, provided that a sizeable portion of country-specific benefits is associated with peacekeeping" (Khanna, Sandler, and Shimizu 1998, 183). The benefits of PKOs as a general class of activity are, then, neither fully nonexcludable nor excludable, nonrival nor rival. Of course, the degree of publicness of the PKO goods contributed varies from case to case and between participants (Khanna, Sandler, and Shimizu 1999).

The joint products approach also does not hold that all members of the international system get the same degree of public or private benefits from PKOs. This approach does, however, hold that many countries get some of each. Those in or around the conflict locale consume the immediate and largely private benefits of peace or at the very least the lower levels of violence that PKOs can help produce. While these are privately consumed by states and populations in the geographic region, they are produced primarily by states outside the region that fund and staff any given PKO mission and the international organizations sponsoring the mission (such as the UN, NATO, the European Union, or the Organization of American States).

Those less proximate parties may, however, also gain a great deal. In terms of international public goods and contributor club goods, peacekeeping operations can reduce threats to international and regional peace and stability, improve the chances for governance along democratic peace lines, promote conducive conditions for foreign commercial and economic development interests in a region, and help achieve a number of humanitarian goals ranging from food distribution to the management of refugee problems. These benefits may fit well with contributor agendas for defensive internationalism and self-realization, including advancing contributor goals for international status and good relations with other contributors, whether they are nations or international organizations (Kammler 1997). Of course, the contributors may also gain one or more of the private benefits noted earlier.

The joint product formulation does not require that all members of a PKO-sponsoring international institution such as the UN or even an ad hoc club be in complete agreement about PKOs in general or a particular case as advancing international peace, order, and progress. For PKOs as for other international endeavors, divergent preferences about sites, modalities, and conditionalities—and thus about the when, where, and what of contributions—are not inherently signs of burden shirking. Instead, these differences may imply a cooperative and complementary division of labor, as with the provision of money, personnel, or equipment for UNPKOs or an emphasis on cases in a particular region of the world. Divergent preferences can follow from varying political and economic comparative advantages among states, a differentiation that can yield more efficient production of the public element of PKO activities at the collective level.

Even if we discount the significance of a private goods element in the provision of PKOs, they exhibit impurities in publicness because of the sometimes limited universe of potential consumers who benefit. Some violent conflict cases may get chosen for PKO treatment and get lots of resources, while others may be slighted in one or both ways (Lavrov 1996; Qin 1996). Most cases chosen for PKO treatment also carry with them what Sandler (1977) has called "thinning." That is, PKO resources committed to one violent conflict locale are inherently less available for simultaneous application beyond the immediate neighborhood. Whatever its declared intent, a particular PKO may evolve in ways that cast doubt on its impartiality and lead some of those immediately or indirectly affected by it to see it as a source of private and public bads (e.g., Ratner 1995). Finally, some PKOs from their birth may be framed in an effort to exclude some members of the international system from benefits because the powers that be view such actors as more committed to violence than peace. By analogy, fire departments try to contribute a public good to the general population but remain the bane of the minority of arsonists. Similar examples are evident internationally: the Bosnian Serbs were by most accounts the primary regional arsonists, and one or another of the groups espousing a violent settlement to territorial disputes in the Middle East may also play such a role.

Acceptance of the fact that some actors are excluded from consumption of public goods at various points in time and in various situations leads us to view PKOs in terms of club goods as well as joint products. Yet the membership of all the clubs involved can be quite large for the totality of recent and future PKOs. The relevant clubs are multiple and cross-cutting, fitting with our conceptual discussion in chapter 2. The greater the overlap in membership among the clubs and in club policy preferences for the pertinent region, the greater the likelihood for cooperative contributions to PKOs.

In sum, we recognize all the impurities of the public and club goods associated with international peacekeeping. Limits of supply, duration, coverage, and even impartiality do not make the activity simply about private goods for a tiny club. Benevolent motivations are not a necessary condition for contributions aimed at reducing violent conflicts. Violence reduction does not need to be achieved totally or permanently in all cases for PKO contributions to yield a condition more conducive to international order and progress than might otherwise occur.[6]

DOMESTIC SUPPORT FOR PKO

Peacekeeping operations tend to have a higher public profile than development assistance and a less arcane profile then debt management and relief. Domestic support for PKOs thus involves both general attitudes and judgments about particularly dramatic, hot-spot situations that appear and vanish from the view screen of policy officials, attentive publics, and mass publics.

We expect public opinion about PKOs to be broadly in line with the general patterns found in chapter 3. As we did for development aid, our review for PKOs considers general support for contributions, their importance and priority, related values and role conceptions about particular nations and intergovernmental organizations, and pertinent benefits and costs. For each, we will take note both of responses to general questions and of responses about specific situations. PKOs, like foreign aid, have a history of use and thus a legacy of interpretations bearing on support for current and future operations. We will recognize those legacies for different publics as data permit.

Support for Contributions: Money and People

American attitudes toward funding UNPKOs closely resembled opinions on the UN in general: predominant support for paying past-due bills, unwarranted beliefs in the large size of actual U.S. payments in both absolute and relative terms, and signs of some limited willingness to increase spending when informed about its actual level. The last two also apply to funding as a share of the U.S. defense budget (Americans and the World 2001a; Kull 1995–96; Kull and Destler 1999). In the early 1990s, a majority held that funds should be provided by all UN members and only a minority thought that funding should come only from the permanent members of the UN Security Council, Germany, and Japan (Hastings and Hastings 1992–93, 681).[7] Provision of personnel (i.e., troops) to UNPKOs as a general matter received sustained majority support in all but one of fourteen polls during the 1993–2002 period and trended upward, but blanket support was smaller when a "some of the time" option was available to respondents (Chicago Council and Marshall Fund 2002; Kull and Destler 1999; Reilly 1995, 1999).[8] U.S. troop participation was a substantial majority preference among elites polled in 1996 and 2002, with support even higher for NATO PKOs (Chicago Council and Marshall Fund 2002; O. R. Holsti 1998–99). By 2002, large public and elite majorities supported joint training by UN-member militaries and a small standing commitment of troops to a UN Security Council rapid deployment force (Chicago Council and Marshall Fund 2002).[9]

The American public did not present stable support or opposition to PKO participation even in those cases where the club affinity sketched in chapter 3 would presumably be relatively strong—for example, such as in the NATO cases of Bosnia and Kosovo. Historically, predominant support, if it developed at all, emerged only after each conflict had gone on for quite a while and faded when the participation situation became a prolonged one (Gallup Poll Releases, June 25, 1997). That may be changing somewhat, as indicated in 2002 by the large majorities for taking part in IRPKOs in Afghanistan and Bosnia. Conversely, also in 2002, the large public and elite majorities for participation in an IRPKO mission to enforce a future Israel-Palestinian peace agreement were not matched by similarly large majorities for such commitments prior to a peace agreement (Americans and the World 2003b; Chicago Council and Marshall Fund 2002).[10] When club affinity clearly was weak, as for Rwanda, Haiti, and East Timor, the American public did not provide majority support for personnel participation and indeed sometimes expressed majority opposition (Gallup Poll Release, October 4, 1999; Hastings and Hastings 1994–95, 293; PIPA 2000a).

Japanese public support for funding is suggested by the priority emphases for world role reported in chapter 3 but is seldom probed directly. In polls from 1991 to 2000 about the preferred level of participation in UNPKOs, the Japanese public has had a large and stable plurality opting for maintaining rather than increasing or reducing its participation. What has changed with the passage of time is a switch from a larger minority preferring reduction to one favoring increase (*Government Poll Yearbook* 2001, 84; 2002, 91; JPOLL, various years). Like the American public in the same year (1994), Japanese respondents wanted the financial and personnel burden shared by all UN members. As for Japanese personnel participation as a general matter, public opinion (in twenty-five polls from 1991 to 1997), moved from a close balance between support and opposition to sending the Self-Defense Forces to UNPKOs to clear majorities by 1995 and since (Hastings and Hastings, various years; JPOLL, various years; Richman 1993a, 1993b). Pluralities remained, however, for maintaining the current level of personnel involvement, not for increasing or reducing it. Majority support for participation was present for major cases with such Japanese involvement (Cambodia and Rwanda) (Hastings and Hastings 1992–93, 286; 1994–95, 273; 1995–96, 602; JPOLL, various years).

We lack comparable general data on Europeans. Data availability for comparisons between them and Americans improves when we turn to the cases of Bosnia and Kosovo (Hastings and Hastings 1993–94, 565; "NATO" 1999; Sinnott 1996). Those of course were cases for Europeans of special regional proximity and, given the public priorities noted in chapter 3, might well represent the maximum degree of public support for case-specific participation. For Bosnia (1993), majority support was present in all of the fifteen members of the European Union (EU) except Denmark, Germany, and Greece. Other polling in France, Italy, and the United Kingdom in the early and mid-1990s shows persistent support, and by 1996 a majority in Germany was favorable. When some of the EU-15 were polled on Kosovo (1999), German support for participation in IRPKOs (NATO) had come to predominate, as was the case in France and the United Kingdom. Unlike the Bosnian possibility, Kosovo received strong Danish support, while Italians moved in the opposite direction ("NATO" 1999; Sinnott 1996).[11] Any inferences about a positive trend should be guarded, given many European publics' preference for reducing Kosovo commitments and for a diplomatic emphasis.

Importance and Priority

The general public and elite opinion data in chapter 3 on goals, threats, and issue priorities could be read as providing a broad basis for PKO activity in at least some local conflict zones. In other words, that data could be taken as evidence that PKOs merit a high level of importance on governmental policy agendas in Western Europe, the United States, and Japan. Data for 1987–94 suggest that such a view was not in fact the situation for the publics of the four western permanent members of the Security Council as they considered PKOs by either their own countries or the UN (Hastings and Hastings 1987–88, 580–81; 1992–93, 680; 1994–95, 618, 621–22). The Japanese public took the same position on national priority but was more disposed than the others to support

UNPKOs. Of the Security Council four and Japan, as of 1994, only the United Kingdom came even close to majority support for treating UNPKO contributions as a national emphasis.[12] All, however, had larger minorities in support of doing so for UNPKOs than for other forms of multilateral PKOs. A UN mandate for PKOs apparently increased levels of public support but did not do so enough to give priority to the types of conflicts most relevant to such UN actions.

Importance and priority might arguably be much higher if probed in regard to particular, current situations rather than a more abstract international problem. A few bits of data suggest that this has not been true for West Europeans. Polling in 1994 of the publics of the EC-12 on whether Bosnia was the "main problem" facing that club never had Bosnia receiving even 20 percent of respondents in any country (Hastings and Hastings 1994–95, 526). More data are available for the U.S. public in terms of responses to "most important issue for the U.S. government" questions. Queries from 1993 to 1998 about such diverse PKO cases as the former Yugoslavia, Somalia, and Rwanda elicited support in the low single digits (Hastings and Hastings 1993–94, 136–38; 1994–95, 213; 1996–97, 392–94; 1997–98, 499). As noted in chapter 3, in 1998 only about a third of the public and a quarter of elites believed that regional conflicts were a critical threat to the United States. A less demanding probe into importance and priority asked for each of a number of conflict situations whether "development of a peaceful solution" was an important "foreign policy goal" for the United States. The breadth of the question suggests that it would be more likely to attract positive responses than a question focused only on PKOs. The situations were East Timor, Northern Ireland, Kosovo, Bosnia, and the Palestinian-Israeli conflict (Gallup Poll Releases, October 4, August 2, 1999). In none of those cases did a majority judge the matter very important, though all were thought to be important (i.e., those selecting "very important" plus those selecting "somewhat important") by majorities. Perhaps the American public would like to have the United States be an architect of world peace but falls short of accepting an emphasis on PKOs as a necessary major element of such solutions.

The 9/11 attacks and the ensuing military responses by the United States clearly differed in the nature of the bads posed by conflicts distant from the United States. The status of international terrorism as a major threat (i.e., a private bad) to the United States was, as we saw in chapter 3, already prominent in public opinion. As our joint product view would suggest, after the attacks, most of the public gave reducing such attacks against the United States the status of an absolute priority (a "must do"). Attaching a similarly imperative quality to reducing the "number of terrorist attacks against other countries" found less but still modest majority support (Americans and the World 2002b). The strong 2002 support for participation in IRPKO in Afghanistan and in case of an Israel-Palestinian peace agreement may well follow from the critical threat status attached at that time to terrorism and a possible war between Israel and Arab states.[13] There is no evidence that support was generalized for what was viewed by only a small minority as a critical threat from civil wars in Africa (Chicago Council and Marshall Fund 2002).

Values and Role Conceptions

As with foreign aid, opinions in this category are about normative evaluations of what should and ought to be done about specific issues or cases and about the rights, obligations, and responsibilities of actors in the global community. Polls in the United States, Europe, and Japan allow us to explore such role preferences for UNPKOs and IRPKOs.

Substantial majorities in the United States and Japan (1997) saw a role-fulfillment deficit for the UN in meeting its "international dispute resolution responsibility" (Hastings and Hastings 1996–97, 677). They have not agreed on what the UN should do differently about PKOs. Only minorities in Japan seemed to have supported militarized peace enforcement or preemptive deployments (JPOLL, various years). At about the same time (the early 1990s), U.S. public opinion was roughly similar in favoring a UN emphasis on peacekeeping and humanitarian relief (Hastings and Hastings 1992–93, 178; Richman 1994b). By the mid-1990s, the American public began to favor a more militarily forceful emphasis for the UN that focused on acquiring the military infrastructure and readiness to exert its will in a more compelling and timely way (Americans and the World 2001a; Kull 1995–96; PIPA 2000a). In general, the contrasting public positions in the United States and Japan on the appropriateness of using force to pursue "world justice and order" seemed increasingly applied to PKOs.[14] The British public's majorities (1993–96) for provision of "general peace enforcement" seem closer to the U.S. position (Hastings and Hastings 1995–96, 272–73; 1996–97, 286).[15]

As the twenty-first century began, the European Union had set for itself what are commonly referred to as the "Petersburg missions"—"humanitarian and evacuation missions, peacekeeping and restoring peace"—and had called for the establishment of a rapid reaction force (RRF) with such capacities. In 2000, the RRF was viewed positively by majorities in each of the EU-15 (an average of 73 percent) but with below-average public support in Germany, Spain, Austria, the United

Defensive Internationalism

Kingdom, and Ireland. Yet only 7 percent of the EU-15 public favored giving the authority for dispatching such a force to a majority vote in EU institutions. Still, 47 percent would have such authority reserved to the governments that were willing to send troops. At the same time, majorities in each of the EU-15 viewed provision of international disaster relief and peacekeeping and restoration as proper roles of their national military establishments (Manigart 2001).

Polling in 2002 in six European countries (and the United States) assessed approval of the dispatch of national military forces in a variety of situations. Two of those, "to help bring peace in a region where there is civil war" and "to assist a population struck by famine," have special relevance in their own right and when compared to other types of situations. Net scores appear in table 6.1. The polled European publics all massively support such commitments in famine situations. To a smaller extent, they also would make such commitments to end civil wars. German opinion is less supportive of such activities than public opinion in other European publics but still provides approving majorities. By ways of comparison, net support among the five EU publics polled was much lower for joining in U.S. counterterrorist military actions and was negative in the same 2001 poll in the other EU member states. Compared to the United States, the role conceptions of the European publics seem much more positively disposed to PKOs and even to famine relief.

U.S. and Japanese publics have long preferred a PKO role in a multilateral endeavor rather than as a unilateral national project. This multi-

TABLE 6.1. Net Approval for the Use of National Military Forces, 2002 (in percentages)

	Great Britain	France	Germany	Netherlands	Italy	Poland	United States
Ensure supply of oil	28	−4	−14	−1	7	17	35
Destroy terrorist camp	72	70	29	43	53	56	86
Bring peace to civil war region	55	54	21	49	72	48	5
Liberate hostages	69	68	42	63	69	63	62
Famine relief	81	79	69	87	83	87	65
Uphold international law	72	71	42	74	69	73	55
To fight terrorism, send troops to fight with U.S. forces	49	13	17	28	6		

Source: Data from Chicago Council and Marshall Fund 2002; European Commission, *Flash Eurobarometer* 114 2001.

Note: The question posed for all but the last row was "For each of the following reasons, would you approve or disapprove the use of [own country] military troops?" For the last row it was "Among the following measures, which ones seem appropriate to you: to send [nationality] troops to fight with the U.S. forces?"

lateral preference (the UN or NATO) has been strongly expressed repeatedly by the American public for the last decade (Americans and the World 2001a; Chin and Marsh 1999; Kull and Destler 1999). U.S. military and civilian elites have seemed no more attracted to unilateral PKOs and have substantially favored a multilateral approach (O. R. Holsti 1998–99).[16]

Post-9/11 American opinion has vastly favored a multilateral response. That was true with regard to preferring UN Security Council authorization for the American response. The public was split on attacking terrorists abroad without it. This also was the case for building the broadest possible coalition of other countries, well beyond current alliance partners, and having them join in the military actions in Afghanistan. Indeed, very large majorities favored the unprecedented exercise by the UN Security Council of powers to intervene in countries where terrorist groups were operating, even including "sending in an international military force to capture the suspected terrorist group if the country refuses to do so." As for international peacekeeping in postwar Afghanistan, the plurality preference was for the United States taking "a large role but not the lead" (Americans and the World 2002b). These preferences fit well with relevant findings in chapter 3.

Mixtures of support for international activism against dangers and the unwillingness to bear the whole burden of undertaking it also fit with chapter 3 findings. Since 9/11, very large majorities have favored military action against terrorists in locales other than Afghanistan, whether or not those groups were connected to the attacks. The support for a broader campaign, however, was very sensitive to other countries' willingness to participate. With it, support was massive; without it, only a narrow plurality was evident. When the focus went beyond terrorism to proliferation of weapons of mass destruction and attacking Iraq, support was for most of the post-9/11 period far stronger with than without cooperation from regional and European allies and UN endorsement (Americans and the World 2002e; PIPA 2002).

The American public's value base for participation can be garnered from tables 6.1–6.3. Table 6.1 shows that even the substantial support for the purpose of famine relief was less than that expressed by polled European publics, and American support was strikingly less than that of the Europeans for ending civil wars. A military response to attacks on the United States has long had near unanimous support, but that is usually not the trigger for most of what we treat as PKOs. Relevant pre- and post-9/11 data are summarized in tables 6.2 and 6.3. The most widely accepted justifications for current and hypothetical situations were those of strategic interest and reducing human suffering (civilian casualties, atrocities, starvation) and are displayed in table 6.2. That seems in line with opinions on America's proper place in the world and on alleviating global hunger reported in chapter 3. Justifications involving long-term "nation building" (ending civil wars, installing proper governments) had less although still substantial minority support, as would be expected from the goal information in chapter 3. With regard to specific past cases (table 6.3), U.S. strategic interests were not compelling for majorities, but responses to barbarism and human suffering were. Small majorities also accepted the justification of removing an evil leader. Other data do not suggest that the public sees even humanitarian justifications as obligations in all relevant cases, and of course those objectives are most readily invoked after suffering is demonstrable and publicized. The less-preferred justifications imply long-term sustained missions, while the more preferred may not (see also Jentleson 1992).

Afghanistan after 9/11 met the strategic-interest test for almost all Americans, with near universal support for the intervention. Those polled massively supported American leadership and supported military efforts to counter a strategic threat and remove an evil leader/regime from power there. Even before the end of 2001, however, public opinion preferred a far more modest U.S. role in terms of subsequent "peacekeeping forces," "providing food and economic aid," and "shaping a new government." In short, views of the desirable U.S. role became ones familiar in the recent decades of multilateral peacekeeping.

There is also a prima facie tension between two often-present opinions in the American public: support for forceful PKOs (e.g., bombing

TABLE 6.2. U.S. Public Acceptance of Use of Military Justifications and Objectives (in percentages)

	2002	1998–99	1994–95	1990–93
Civilian casualties		79	64 (avg. 3)	53 (avg. 2)
Atrocities/genocide	67 (avg. 3)	63 (avg. 5)	56 (avg. 3)	57
Humanitarian aid, starvation	68 (avg. 2)		72 (avg. 2)	74 (avg. 5)
Peace, end civil wars	35 (avg. 2)			15
Proper government			43 (avg. 2)	47
Fight, repel aggressors			41	49 (avg. 2)
Strategic and economic interests, defense of close ally, defense of U.S. citizens	62 (avg. 7)		67 (avg. 4)	66 (avg. 4)

Source: Data from Americans and the World 2001; Chicago Council and Marshall Fund 2002; Hastings and Hastings 1992–93, 178; Kull 1995–96; PIPA 2000a, c; Richman 1994a, b.

Note: Entries are for current and hypothetical cases.

campaigns) and humanitarian PKO rationales. In the aggregate, the tensions have been managed in one or both of two ways. The first is a sort of "lesser of two evils" approach in terms of harm to civilians (as with Serbia and Kosovo in 1999) (Gallup Poll Release, April 2, 1999). According to these views, coercive peace enforcement will in the long run serve the affected population better than the situation that is likely to develop without the use of force. The second is to view such destructive, collateral damage to civilians in the PKO locale as justifiable because the action is less peacekeeping than defense of the United States against critical threats. That is, coercive peace enforcement will in the long run serve the interests of civilians in the contributor countries to an extent overriding harms to those in the theater of operations. The American public had already embraced that view of force against terrorists before 9/11 in polling about Clinton-era missile attacks against "terrorists in Afghanistan and Sudan" (Gallup Poll Release, April 2, 1999). After 9/11, large majorities continued to support the use of force even when there were chances of death to "thousands of innocent civilians" in the wrong place at the wrong time (Americans and the World 2002b).

As seen in chapter 3, Japanese public opinion strongly favors a national role promoting world peace but does not emphasize the military instrument for doing so. Preferences for the national role in PKOs laboriously try to accommodate both themes by reconciling them with the general acceptance of contributions as being compatible with the spirit of the peace constitution and thus an appropriate way to help achieve "global peace and stability" (*Government Poll Yearbook* 1999,

TABLE 6.3. U.S. Public Acceptance of IRPKO Historical Case Justifications and Objectives (in percentages)

	Kosovo (1999)	Bosnia (1994–95)	Rwanda (1994–95)	Somalia (as shown)	Iraq/Kuwait (1998)
Civilian casualties	65	51 (avg. 2)	74		
Atrocities/genocide	69	64	71 (avg. 2)		
Humanitarian aid				82 (1995)	
	65 (avg. 3)	87	66 (avg. 2)	75 (1992)	
Peace, end civil wars	58 (avg. 3)	50 (avg. 3)		43 (1995)	
Proper government				56 (avg. 2) (1992)	
National interests	41 (avg. 3)	37 (avg. 5)	41 (avg. 2)	31 (avg. 2)	
Remove evil leader	56 (avg. 2)				51 (avg. 3)

Source: Data from Americans and the World 2001a; Gallup Poll Releases, March 26, April 2, 1999; "Gallup Poll Topics: Kosovo" 2000; Hastings and Hastings 1992–93, 287; 1995–96, 276; 1996–97, 276; 1997–98, 192–93; Kull 1995–96; PIPA 2000a, b; Richman 1994b.

506; 2002, 512). Among the Japanese public in the mid-1990s, a general "responsibility" to provide "troops to enforce peace plans" when asked to do so by the UN did not garner majority acceptance, although providing financial help narrowly did. A similar "responsibility" for "giving military assistance" to allies "in trouble spots" was strongly rejected (JPOLL, various years; Richman 1993a, 1993b). Even with growing acceptance of military personnel participation, such a role was to be played in an essentially nonmilitary way.[17]

Benefits and Costs

We conclude our summary of opinion data by discussing retrospective and prospective perceptions of PKO benefits and costs. In 1993–96, opinions on whether UNPKOs are a generally helpful activity fluctuated between a majority and more divided in the United States, Germany, and the United Kingdom. The Japanese public tended to have a more sustained positive view (Hastings and Hastings 1992–93, 681; 1994–95, 621; 1995–96, 209). Additional data suggest that there was less of a tendency to view UNPKOs as a burden than a benefit but that pessimism exists about the more traditional forms of PKO endeavors (i.e., peace monitoring and interposition after a cease-fire). The American and British publics, as we have seen, were more inclined to new forms (i.e., large-scale peace enforcement and peacemaking) and the Japanese public was not. In the same period, very large U.S. majorities viewed more muscular UN and IR PKOs as on balance beneficial in terms of burden sharing and containing defense spending requirements. Only a small minority felt that benefits were in effect precluded by the PKO situations being "of little concern to the U.S." (Americans and the World 2001a).

More militarily forceful PKOs of course raise the prospect of the potential cost of casualties. The publicly supported Japanese role in PKOs seems to exclude missions with that cost. The British public was not inclined to give that cost a decisive place in its evaluations of troop participation when polled about the Gulf War and Bosnia (Hastings and Hastings 1990–91, 216; 1995–96, 272–73). The U.S. public in repeated questioning in the past decade usually drew the line at more than a few American casualties but not at none or a handful (Iraq in the Gulf War and more recently Bosnia and Kosovo) (Gallup Poll Release, February 18, 1998; Gallup Poll Topics: A–Z Kosovo 2000; Hastings and Hastings 1990–91, 226, 229, 302; 1995–96, 276). The post-9/11 campaign differs sharply, perhaps because the triggering attacks already imposed civilian and military casualties on the United States. Majorities in repeated polls support the Afghan intervention even with expectations that it will involve "several thousand" or a "large number" of U.S. troop deaths (*New York Times*/CBS News 2001; Americans and the World 2002b). Casualty aversion is then reduced for cases clearly involving direct aggression against the United States (a private bad). Even for other circumstances, casualty aversion reduces public support only when the risk is seen as above a very low acceptable threshold and clear majorities expected it to be below that for Somalia (1992), Haiti (1994), and, in most relevant polls, Kosovo (1999) (Gallup Poll Topics: A–Z Kosovo 2000). Thus, optimism may be a necessary condition for initial participation, and a shock effect from unexpected casualties may have a large negative impact on public support for continued American personnel participation.

Of course, tolerance of even minimum casualties occurs in a context of net benefits attributed to PKOs with regard to particular cases or to setting helpful precedents for others to avoid the actions generating the need for future PKOs. Much data was available on relevant opinion only for the United States, and these data hardly suggest predominant perceptions of substantial benefits or even stable perceptions of modest benefits. This was true prospectively or concurrently for Haiti (1994), Somalia (1992), Iraq (1998), and Bosnia (1993) (Gallup Poll Topics: A–Z Kosovo 2000; Gallup Press Release, April 2, 1999; Hastings and Hastings 1993–94, 294).[18] Expectations for Kosovo were very volatile (Gallup Poll Topics: A–Z Kosovo 2000; Gallup Press Release, April 2, 1999). Those polls after 9/11 found gloomy majorities on whether military attacks on terrorists would reduce or increase chances for further terrorist attacks on the United States (Americans and the World 2002b).

Retrospective assessments were only slightly more positive. Large majorities saw both the Kosovar and Serbian populations as losers in that conflict, and only very small majorities thought the situation had been "worth going to war over" or that sending "military forces" had not been a "mistake." The public did not view the Kosovo outcome as a significant presidential achievement and was split on whether involvement in Kosovo increased international respect for the United States. Yet majorities thought the forceful measures against Serbia (1999) and Iraq (1998) had resulted in America appearing "stronger" to the "rest of the world" (Gallup Poll Topics: A–Z Kosovo 2000). While precedent-setting views about the Gulf War having a useful deterrent effect on others were largely positive ("serve notice [on] aggressors"), a majority in 1999 rejected that benefit of IRPKOs in the former Yugoslavia ("prevent other governments around the world from committing human rights atrocities") (Gallup Poll Release, June 24, 1999; Hastings and Hastings 1990–91, 302).

Japanese polls indicate another aspect of net benefits that relates to chapter 3's emphasis on avoiding isolation: avoiding costs of censure for not contributing to PKOs. Avoiding foreign negativism was a majority assessment in Japan itself (1992) and was well grounded in polls with Japanese involvement in key affinity and importance regions (i.e., North America, Western Europe, and East Asia) (JPOLL, various years; Hastings and Hastings 1990–91, 230; 1991–92, 631, 645; 1994–95, 273; 1995–96, 606; Richman 1993a, 1993b).

In sum, what we can determine about domestic support in the United States and Japan for PKOs suggests that such support is for the most part episodic or extremely conditional. What U.S. support exists has its foundation either in humanitarian obligation or perceived threats to core interests, not in confidence about the results or tolerance of American casualties. Japan's public support features avoiding costs of nonparticipation and minimizing those of participation. Scant European data suggest a special degree of support for PKOs close to home and a degree of British tolerance for the risks that forceful PKOs entail, but not special optimism about its results. These constraining attitudes coexist with a desire for UNPKOs as the preferred modality but at the same time pose serious questions about the contributions the major Organization for Economic Cooperation and Development countries will make to enable the UN to fulfill successfully that desired mission. The message to political elites seems to be an inconsistent one--proceed multilaterally, but do not commit us to very much for very long in very many places.

UNPKOS: CONTRIBUTION FACTS

We examine four aspects of contributions to UNPKOs: (1) general patterns of activity; (2) personnel contributions; (3) financial contributions; and (4) the role of the United States. The underlying issues in the first three sections are (1) whether and to what extent provision and providers have been increasing in amount, and (2) whether and to what extent the diversity of cases and providers suggest that UNPKOs are increasingly being treated broadly as an impure public good rather than only being such for a small and unrepresentative club of nations. The issues in the fourth section are narrower and deal with the historic U.S. role as a provider and with changes in that role.

Given our reasoning about PKOs as impure public goods with joint products for their contributors, we expect our examination of contributions to UNPKOs to find that:

UNITED NATIONS PEACEKEEPING OPERATIONS

1. Use of UNPKOs has increased in the post–Cold War period in a nonlinear fashion, with greater geographic diversity of cases and broadening participation in both financial and personnel terms.
2. Support for UNPKOs continues to be maintained in both financial and personnel terms.
3. U.S. contributions may show signs of fluctuation but not sustained and irreversible decline.
4. Evidence of fluctuating U.S. contributions has been accompanied by evidence of sustained and/or increased contributions by other countries that were not significant contributors in earlier periods.
5. Counter to hegemonic-stability and pure-public-goods interpretations of UNPKO provision, small countries have been contributors to UNPKOs (particularly in terms of personnel) at levels higher than expected, relative to economic size.
6. In support of the public goods element, UNPKOs continue to be provided to an extent greater than is proportionate to national economic wealth by a small fraction of the states in the international system.
7. In support of the public goods element, demand for UNPKOs increasingly involves assertions of a general human right to security, regardless of the importance of the conflict site for the interests of specific nations.
8. In support of the private goods element, member states of the United Nations continue to deny to it the mandate and capability to mount PKOs before a conflict situation has deteriorated to the point where the potential gains and losses for crucial nations (the UN Security Council permanent members) or a relatively small club become persuasive.

General Patterns

As shown in the appendix to this chapter, the number of peacekeeping operations increased sharply after 1987 in comparison to the record from 1945 to that date. The thirteen cases from 1948 through 1987 are almost evenly divided between observer missions (six cases) and peacekeeping forces (seven cases). Between 1987 and February 2003, forty-two new cases were undertaken, seventeen in the form of observer missions and twenty-five involving peacekeeping forces. In addition, the more recent period saw the continuation of five earlier efforts (UNTSO, UNMOGIP,

Defensive Internationalism

UNFICYP, UNDOF, and UNIFIL) of which two were observer missions and three involved peacekeeping forces. As of June 1998, the number of active operations (sixteen) exceeded the total for 1948 through 1987 (Browne 1994, 1995; Lewis 1997; Mendez 1999; Neack 1995; United Nations Military Adviser's Office 1991–95).

The number of relatively large scale cases (with authorized strengths of 1,000 or more personnel) also increased in recent years. In the earlier period, seven of the operations had that characteristic; in the latter period, at least sixteen of the initiated cases did, plus three of the continuations (Browne 1994; Mendez 1999; United Nations Military Adviser's Office 1991–95).[19] Although the number of participants involved in the summer of 1998 had fallen sharply from 1993, it was still substantially greater than for any single time in the earlier period except for the blip in the early 1960s for the former Belgian Congo operation. Further, central UNPKO staff in 1998 had reached four hundred up from nine persons in 1989, although that number had not further increased by 2000.[20] The financial burden involved in UNPKOs, while down from 1993–94 levels, was expected to amount to $826 million for the fiscal year July 1998–June 1999 (Mendez 1999) compared with approximately $364 million for 1986 and 1987 combined (Independent Advisory Group on UN Financing 1993; Lewis 1997). Like personnel, budgets rose.

With respect to location, UNPKOs have recently become a more global activity, as table 6.4 shows. Although North and South America saw no activity in either the pre-1988 period or thereafter, the early (and more recent) Middle East focus was joined in the later period by Africa and to a lesser but substantial extent by Europe (the former Yu-

TABLE 6.4. Location of UNPKO Cases (in percentages)

	Pre-1988 (N = 13)	Started on or after 1988 (N = 43)	Active as of 2003 (N = 14)
Central America, Caribbean	8	16	0
Europe	8	21	21
Middle East	54	5	29
South Asia	15	5	7
East Asia	0	5	0
Oceania	8	5	7
Africa	8	42	29

Source: Data from United Nations Department of Peacekeeping web site http://www.un.org/Depts/dpko/dpko/home.shtml.

Note: Entries are rounded to the nearest percentage point.

goslavia and the newly independent states of the former Soviet Union) and by Central America and the Caribbean (even if those commitments have ended).

The general patterns are compatible with increased contributions to the public goods associated with peacekeeping—increases in the number of operations, the rise in demand for large-scale peacekeeping force actions, and the increased geographical coverage of provision. Although declines in the numbers of operations and participants from the surge in 1993–94 did take place, there was another upswing of activity in new missions in 1997 (MINUGUA in Guatemala, MONUA in Angola, and UNTMIH in Haiti). Subsequent cutbacks were only a prelude to major new operations in Kosovo and East Timor. That, rather than linear growth, is what we expected.

Personnel Contributions

Personnel contributions, whatever their motives, are one major way to contribute to UNPKOs and thus the public good of systemic order. To examine those contributions, it seems wise to look further than the raw number of countries providing personnel and the total number of personnel referred to earlier. (From the end of 1993 to mid-1998, the number of countries providing personnel ranged from seventy to seventy-six, well above Cold War levels. The number of personnel did decline from the mid-1993 peak of 78,744 to 14,570 as of mid-1998 but had rebounded to almost 37,000 in early 2003 (Crossette 2000b; www.un.org 2003).

To begin that exploration, we look at the activists—those nations participating in a substantial share of the UNPKO cases in one or more periods. We use involvement in 20 percent or more of the cases in at least one period as our threshold, while we provide data enabling the use of a higher threshold.[21] The results appear in table 6.5.

By our rather conservative criterion, the earlier period had thirty-two activist nations. For those cases active in early 2003, there were forty-three activists. That is consistent with increased willingness to contribute repeatedly to UNPKOs and the public goods they can produce. Willingness has been more widespread for post–Cold War initiations than for the residue of previous decisions. The marked persistence in the activist category of most of the nations who qualified in the pre-1988 period suggests a degree of support in their polities that overrides shifts in domestic politics and international circumstances. In other words, UNPKO activism can become a habit.

TABLE 6.5. Frequent Participants (% of cases)

	Pre-1988 (N = 13)	Active as of 2003 (N = 14)
Canada	100	64
Sweden	85	79
Norway	77	50
Finland	69	50
Ireland	69	57
Italy	69	57
United States	69	43
Denmark	62	57
Australia	54	29
India	54	50
Netherlands	54	
Austria	46	50
Ghana	46	50
New Zealand	46	29
Brazil	38	
Indonesia	38	21
Japan	38	
Nigeria	38	36
Switzerland	38	36
Soviet Union/Russian Federation	38	64
Belgium	31	36
Burma	31	
Chile	31	29
Nepal	31	43
Sri Lanka	31	29
United Kingdom	31	64
Pakistan	23	50
Argentina	23	50
Germany	23	21
Peru	23	
Yugoslavia	23	
Ecuador	23	
Poland		57
France		57
Uruguay		57
Bangladesh		50
Jordan		50
China		50
Malaysia		43
Kenya		43
Slovak Republic		43
Turkey		43
Egypt		36
Hungary		36
Czech Republic		36

TABLE 6.5—*Continued*

	Pre-1988 (N = 13)	Active as of 2003 (N = 14)
Senegal		36
Tunisia		36
Spain		29
Zimbabwe		21
Fiji		21

Source: Data from Browne 1995; Neack 1995; United Nations Military Adviser's Office, 1991–95; www.un.org.

Note: Entries are rounded to the nearest percentage point.

The activists were never uniform in politics, levels of economic development, or home region, but the countries have become noticeably more diverse (especially in the last two respects) with the end of the Cold War. Let us turn to diversification of participation as shown by the home regions of those who sent personnel in the various cases.

If UNPKOs are primarily an impure club good for the advanced countries, we would expect the bulk of the personnel providers to be those in North America and Europe. If it offers goods (whatever their public and private mix) for a larger and more diverse club, we would expect nations situated elsewhere to provide the bulk of the country participants. What is clear for the pre-1988 period is that operations were staffed quite narrowly, with 62 percent of the cases having 50 percent or more of personnel provided by North American or European countries. This is particularly striking when we take into account the small number of Warsaw Pact member states that participated in such operations (Bobrow and Boyer 1997; www.un.org 2003). The percentage of cases with disproportionate Western European and North American country participation recently has shrunk, especially when we take into account the surge in participation by countries previously in the Warsaw Pact or the USSR for operations started from 1988 onward. This shift does not gainsay the fact that North American and European states remain more participatory than others in relation to their share of memberships in the UN.

Further light can be shed on the origin of participants by region if we look at the percentage of cases where a major geographic region was represented. When looking at participation this way, only Central America and the Caribbean states overall manifest predominant and sustained low levels of participation over time. Otherwise, participation has been quite diverse and widespread geographically and has

TABLE 6.6. Share of UNPKO Personnel (in percentages)

	12/31/93	12/31/95	4/30/97	3/31/03
Argentina	2.0	1.6	2.5	1.8
Australia			0.1	2.3
Austria	1.2	2.7	3.6	1.2
Bangladesh	4.9	6.5	4.8	7.1
Belgium	2.1	2.2	3.5	
Bolivia				0.6
Botswana	1.6			
Brazil	0.2	3.7	4.2	0.2
Bulgaria			0.3	0.3
Canada	3.0	3.6	4.5	0.7
China			0.2	0.3
Denmark	1.9	1.0	0.5	0.2
Egypt	3.1	0.5	0.4	0.3
Fiji	0.9	2.0	2.6	0.6
Finland	1.1	3.3	4.1	0.2
France	9.1	1.5	1.9	0.9
Germany	1.9	0.1	0.8	1.1
Ghana	1.2	3.4	3.2	5.9
Guinea				2.2
Hungary			0.4	0.4
India	8.4	6.7	3.6	7.4
Indonesia	0.1	2.4	0.8	0.1
Ireland	1.2	2.4	3.4	0.7
Italy	4.9	0.3	0.4	0.5
Japan			0.2	1.4
Jordan	2.8	0.4	4.7	4.4
Kenya	1.5	0.2	0.4	4.8
Korea, Republic of			0.3	1.3
Malawi				0.1
Malaysia	2.6	0.3	0.5	0.4
Morocco	2.1			1.8
Nepal	2.8	3.7	3.2	2.5
Netherlands	1.6	0.8	0.4	
Nigeria			0.3	8.9
Norway	2.5	3.4	2.5	0.2
Pakistan	7.3	4.7	7.2	11.4
Philippines				0.5
Poland	2.1	3.1	4.6	2.0
Portugal			1.7	1.9
Romania	0.3	2.9	3.3	0.6
Russian Federation	1.5	5.6	5.1	0.9
Saudi Arabia	1.1			
Senegal			0.3	1.4
Singapore				0.7
Slovak Republic	0.6	2.0	2.4	1.6
South Africa				0.4

TABLE 6.6—Continued

	12/31/93	12/31/95	4/30/97	3/31/03
Spain	1.9	0.1	0.4	0.4
Sweden	2.5	0.8	0.7	0.2
Thailand				1.5
Ukraine	0.5	2.1	1.7	2.9
United Kingdom	4.0	1.5	1.8	1.6
United States	3.7	9.2	3.3	1.6
Uruguay	1.3	3.0	0.5	4.3
Zambia	1.3	1.2	2.3	2.5
Zimbabwe	1.3	2.9	3.1	0.2
Share Provided	94.1	91.8	97	97.4
Top 10	54.2	50.7	46.4	59.6
N of Participating Countries	70	76	71	89
Total number of personnel	69,961 (incl. 25,747 in Somalia and 15,900 in Cambodia)	31,031	23,874	37,105

Source: Data from Browne 1994; United Nations Military Adviser's Office, 12/31/95, 4/30/97, www.un.org, 2003.

Note: Entries are rounded to the nearest .1 percent. Empty cells indicate situations where contributions were less than .1 or no information was available.

become even more so in recent years (Bobrow and Boyer 1997; www.un.org 2003).

Questions remain about the relative numbers of personnel provided and the share of provision associated with those numbers. Accordingly, we turn to concentration of provision at four recent points in time, the end of 1993, the end of 1995, the end of April 1997, and the end of March 2003. Many United Nations members were making no personnel contribution at those times (or indeed at any time). Table 6.6 reports which countries provided 0.1 percent or more of the personnel involved in all UNPKOs at any of the four times as well as some summary information.

As of the end of 1993, thirty-three countries provided 1 percent or more of UNPKO personnel, twenty-seven were doing so two years later, twenty-six were doing so as of April 1997, and in 2003. Only eleven countries were above the 1 percent threshold at all four snapshot times. The qualifying providers contributed about 94 percent of all personnel in 1993, 92 percent in 1995, and about 97 percent in both 1997 and 2003. The share provided by the top ten nations in each period declined, however, from about 54 percent in 1993 to about 46 percent in

1997 but climbed to nearly 60 percent in 2003. Bangladesh, India, and Pakistan were among the top ten providers at all four times. In 1993, they were joined by the United States and Nepal, which stayed in the top ten in 1995. Other members of the 1993 top ten (Egypt, France, Italy, and the United Kingdom) then left that group. The 1995 group included Ghana, Norway, Brazil, and the Russian Federation. The last two retained that status in 1997 and were joined by Finland, Jordan, Poland, and Austria, while Nepal and the United States left the top ten. In 2003, Jordan remained in the top ten and Ghana, Kenya, the Netherlands, Nigeria, Ukraine, Uruguay, and Zambia achieved that status. Canada was in the top ten for the first three times.

We see in table 6.6, then, a mixed picture in terms of our reasoning. Negatively, we note the decline in the number of providers above our 1 percent threshold from its 1993 high, the larger share of provisions from a small set of countries, and the relative withdrawal over time of some major providers. Yet there also is support for our reasoning in more participation in the top ten by countries outside the U.S. alliance system, and the number of providing countries in 2003. In sum, provision surely is significantly concentrated in absolute terms but is so among a diverse and changing set of states, suggesting that a diverse set of motivations is at work.

One of those motivations clearly is regional relevance, as evidenced by the role of neighboring member states in East Timor for peace enforcement and peace restoration. That case seems to show the impure-public-goods conception at work. Australia, New Zealand, Thailand, and the Philippines played a special role, and Malaysia, Singapore, and China provided contributions. A Thai officer was the deputy commander of the UN Security Council–authorized intervention force (INTERFET), and a Philippine general was designated to replace an Australian as head of the United Nations Transitional Administration in East Timor. The small club good in question in East Timor seems to be one that is increasingly relevant for the core members of ASEAN. Yet participation has not been limited to a regional club but also included the United Kingdom, Denmark, Sweden, the United States, and Portugal. The "coalition of the willing" arguably goes well beyond those with a substantial private goods element at stake (Chongkittavorn 1999; Crossette 1999a; Mydans 1999; Revise 1999).

From the perspective of provision of personnel, our findings fit predominantly with our expectations but with a clear note of moderation about their limits. Broader acceptance after the Cold War of rationales for provision is indicated by the increase in the number of activist states, their growing diversity in regional terms, and the decline in the incidence of abstention by whole regional sets of UN members. Some major providers were and are not in either the great-power or middle-power leagues. Personnel numbers remain above their prevailing Cold War levels. On the negative side, though, many member states refrained from personnel participation; Europeans and North Americans still loom large; many regions stand aside from a substantial share of UNPKO cases; the bulk of the provision comes from a small fraction of UN member states; and the number of serving personnel has fallen from the 1993–94 peak.[22] We will return to the overall balance of implications for our expectations after considering financial contributions and the U.S. role.

Financial Contributions

Public finances are seldom simple, straightforward, or uncontroversial. Those for the UN and UNPKO in particular are no exception (Coklas 1995; McDermott 1994; Scroggins 1996).[23] Understanding the financial end of PKO is clearest when the UN establishes a special assessment account for a given UNPKO operation. That has been by far the most common method in recent years. Historically, however, some operations have been funded out of the regular UN budget, by "voluntary contributions" (UNFICYP), or by a very small set of nations (UNSF and UNYOM) (Browne 1995). This rather lumpy, multiple-source accounting system makes understanding the financial contributions difficult, especially for earlier missions.

The UNPKO budget soared from $230 million in 1988 (and the 1980–88 average of slightly less than $300 million) to $3.6 billion in 1994. The budget fell in 1996, when NATO assumed Bosnia responsibilities, to $1.35 billion and held at that level for 1997 (Durch 1993; Hill and Malik 1996; Lewis 1997; United Nations General Assembly 1997). That decline was scheduled to continue in fiscal year 1999 (July 1, 1998–June 30, 1999) to $826 million, a figure that took no account of the United Nations Interim Mission in Kosovo. In fiscal year 2000, estimates are of $2.6–3 billion for UNPKOs.

Bills do not, of course, necessarily equal payments. By the end of 1995, the UN was owed $564 million for the regular budget and $1.7 billion for identifiable PKOs. As of the end of 1996, the regular budget's unpaid assessments had fallen to $511 million and those for UNPKOs had dropped to $1.6 billion, the first decline in the latter since 1991 (United Nations General Assembly 1997). Unpaid contributions remained at about that level through mid-1998.

Funding and assessment of equitable shares of funding for UNPKOs have long been difficult subjects (Independent Advisory Group on UN

Financing 1993; Mills 1989). The financial side of UNPKOs has resembled a "financial bungee jump, often undertaken in blind faith that timely appropriations will be forthcoming" (Richard Thornburgh quoted in McDermott 1994, 5). After all, the first UNPKO endeavor at peace enforcement and restoration (ONUC in the Belgian Congo) triggered a financial crisis for the UN in the 1960s, as did the surge in such operations in the first half of the 1990s.

To further complicate matters, the percentage assessments for individual countries for the UN regular budget and for identifiable UNPKOs can differ, and the assessment schedules in percentage terms have changed over time. Although the resulting murkiness is not completely impenetrable, it does deny us the degree of clarity available for personnel contributions.

The assessment shares levied on UN members for the regular budget provide the starting point for arriving at the assessments for UNPKOs. The former have been based on payment capacity derived from national income for multiyear prior periods with a ceiling maximum of 25 percent for any single member and a floor of .001 percent for any member with the exception (beginning in 1997) of an annual bill of $10,000 for the smallest and poorest members (Crossette 1997). Special allowances in this framework were made for below-average per capita income (national poverty) and debt burden. The historical nature of the national income statistics used placed historically rich countries (e.g., the United States) at a disadvantage relative to those with rapid recent economic growth (e.g., the Asian newly industrialized economies).

Assessments for UNPKOs have used an approach adopted in 1973 by the General Assembly. The basis of the regular budget assessment was modified as follows. Countries were placed into four groups: (1) the five permanent members of the Security Council (the United States, United Kingdom, France, Russia, and China); (2) twenty-two mostly advanced industrialized economies in Europe but also including Australia, Canada, Japan, and New Zealand; (3) about one hundred other members whose regular budget assessments were below 1 percent (with Brazil as an exception) and more than one quarter of which were at the general floor rate; and (4) the poorest and smallest countries, which basically incurred no assessment. Group 2 was assessed at its regular budget rate. Groups 3 and 4 were assessed at only 20 percent and 10 percent, respectively, of their regular budget obligations. Group 1 got the reverse treatment—80 percent of the aggregate assessment of group 3 countries and 90 percent of that for group 4 countries were added to the regular group 1 budget share. Each group's obligations were aggregated, and the rate for individual country members was calculated from the share that their rate on the regular budget scale constituted of the group aggregate.

As a consequence, group 1 was supposed to carry 60 percent of UNPKO costs, group 2 about 30 percent, and groups 3 and 4 very little (2 to 5 percent). The group 1 countries received a share of UNPKO assessments about 25 percent higher than their bill for the regular budget. The free-riding incentives were clear for the permanent members of the UN Security Council because shortfalls in payments were made up out of the regular UN budgets for which they were assigned a smaller share (Khann, Sandler, and Shimizu 1999).

We note these complications, especially the relationships between regular budget assessments and that for UNPKOs and between UNPKO assessments and Security Council membership, because of the issues about contributions inherent in those relationships. We shall discuss in the U.S.-role section the increasing political demands for and recent changes in these formulas. For our purposes, however, we take the historical assessments as the best available starting point for analyzing financial contributions in the past few decades. With all their flaws, the payment formulas reflected differentials in capacity to provide impure public goods and convictions that the ostensibly more powerful and better off have greater stakes in and responsibilities for systemic order and progress. We also note that the advantageously low assessments for UNPKOs for countries in groups 3 and 4 increased their chances of private financial benefits from personnel participation in UNPKOs.

A good starting point for analysis, however, is not always the same as a good ending point. Accordingly, after looking at the assessments, we examine payments made and the relationships between assessments and payments. For each—who is supposed to pay, who pays, and who pays and who owes—we consider explanations related to public goods theory.

WHO IS SUPPOSED TO PAY

The consequent extreme concentration of charges for provision is shown in table 6.7, which includes all states scheduled to contribute 1 percent or more of the general and/or identifiable UNPKO budgets in 1995, 1997, and 2002. With a UN membership of 188 states, the financing for whatever public goods the UN provides has, for practical purposes, been expected to come from 15 countries, especially for identifiable UNPKO special assessments. The list of countries in table 6.7 also clearly shows that budget bearing was heavily concentrated on the world's largest economies, even if some (like Russia) were not particularly the most

Defensive Internationalism

vibrant or stable ones. This finding is not surprising but emphasizes the fact that the assessment of payment burdens has been made primarily on a crude ability-to-pay to basis.

WHO DOES PAY

Khanna, Sandler, and Shimizu (1998, 1999) have done the most systematic work on payments made for UNPKOs, and we will begin by summarizing it. Their 1998 article deals with payments for the period 1976–96, focusing on countries that as a set provided 97 percent of UNPKO payments (for the special assessment accounts and the Cyprus operation). We use their data (1998, 185) to arrive at the percentages paid by each country as a percent of total UNPKO payments received for the 1990s and add data for 2002, as shown in table 6.8.

The findings repeat the message of table 6.7—a small percentage of UN member states has carried the financial burden for UNPKOs.

TABLE 6.7. Budgeting Concentration (in percentages)

	Regular Budget			Identifiable PKO		
	1995	1997	2002	1995	1997	2002
United States	25.0	25.0	22.0	31.2	30.9	27.2
Japan	14.0	15.7	19.7	14.0	15.6	19.7
Germany	8.9	9.1	9.8	9.0	9.1	9.8
France	6.3	6.4	6.5	7.9	7.9	8.1
United Kingdom	5.3	5.3	5.6	6.6	6.6	6.9
Italy	4.8	5.3	5.1	4.8	5.3	5.1
Russian Federation	5.7	4.3	1.2	7.1	5.3	1.5
Canada	3.1	3.1	2.6	3.1	3.1	2.6
Spain	2.2	2.4	2.5	2.3	2.4	2.5
Brazil	1.6	1.6	2.1	0.3	0.3	0.4
Netherlands	1.6	1.6	1.8	1.6	1.6	1.8
Australia	1.5	1.5	1.6	1.5	1.5	1.6
Sweden	1.2	1.2	1.0	1.2	1.2	1.0
Ukraine	1.5	1.1		1.5	1.0	
Belgium	1.0	1.0	1.1	1.0	1.0	1.1
Republic of Korea			1.9			0.9
Argentina			1.6			0.5
China			1.5			1.9
Mexico			1.1			0.2
10 Largest	77.9	78.2	77.8	87.6	87.8	85.6
All 1% or More	83.7	84.6	88.7	93.1	92.8	92.8

Source: Data from Bite, 1996; United Nations Secretariat, 1995; 1997; 2003.
Note: Entries are rounded to the nearest .1 percent.

TABLE 6.8. Payment for UNPKOs (in percentages)

	1980	1988	1992	1994	1996	2002
Australia	2.4	1.6	1.7	1.7	1.4	<.1
Austria	0.8	0.7	0.8	0.8	0.8	1.1
Belgium	1.8	1.3	1.3	1.3	1.8	0.5
Canada	4.7	2.9	3.7	3.4	2.9	NA
China	0	0.9	0.9	1.0	1.9	1.55
Czech Republic				0.2	0	<0.1
Czechoslovakia	0	0.7	0.5			
Denmark	0.9	0.7	0.7	0.7	0.7	<0.1
Finland	0.6	0.5	0.6	0.6	0.6	<0.1
France	7.0	7.8	9.0	5.4	8.2	10.5
Germany	8.6	8.0	10.3	9.4	9.3	0.7
Greece	0.5	0.6	0.2	0.1	0.1	0.7
Iceland	<0.1	<0.1	<0.1	<0.1	<0.1	<0.1
Ireland	0.2	0.2	0.2	0.2	0.2	<0.1
Italy	5.0	5.1	2.9	5.0	4.6	2.6
Japan	9.5	8.5	9.6	12.7	8.7	36.8
Luxembourg	0.1	<0.1	<0.1	0.1	0.1	<0.1
Netherlands	1.8	1.6	1.8	1.6	1.5	0.5
New Zealand	0.1	0.2	0.3	0.3	0.2	<0.1
Norway	1.0	0.8	0.7	0.6	0.5	<0.1
Poland	0.1	0.1	0.1	0.1	0.2	0.2
Portugal	<0.1	<0.1	<0.1	0.1	0.1	1.4
Russia/USSR	3.5	25.6	0	8.5	19.8	NA
Slovakia				0	<0.1	<0.1
Spain	NA	0.4	1.1	2.9	3.5	4.91
Sweden	1.5	1.2	1.3	1.2	1.1	<0.1
Turkey	<0.1	<0.1	<0.1	<0.1	0.3	0.3
United Kingdom	7.2	7.5	7.3	6.7	6.7	0.2
United States	40.2	18.4	42.6	34.0	20.8	29.5
NATO	78.9	55.2	81.8	71.2	60.9	52.0[a]
10 largest	89.9	87	90.2	89.7	86.4	89.7
13 largest	93.2	89.9	92.6	93.8	88.5	91.0
UN total	100.0	100.0	100.0	100.0	100.0	100.0

Source: Data from Khanna, Sandler, and Shimizu 1998; United Nations Secretariat 2003.

Note: Entries for 1980–96 are converted from the amounts of payments in constant U.S. dollars reported by Khanna, Sandler, and Shimizu 1998, 185. Germany entries are for West Germany in 1980 and 1988 and for unified Germany in 1992–2002. Russia entries are for the Soviet Union in 1980 and 1988 and for the Russian Federation in 1992–2002.

Entries include payments made as of January 1, 2002, on all current UN peacekeeping operations, with the exception of UNTSO, UNMOGIP, and UNAMA, due to a lack of information as reported by the United Nations Secretariat 2003.

[a]This entry reflects only eighteen members of NATO. It excludes Hungary.

Fourteen nations appear in both tables 6.7 and 6.8. For both the assessments and the actual payments, ten countries rack up close to 90 percent of the totals. The countries appearing in both tables are in the same quantitative ballpark. Concentration of payments, however, has not increased over time.

Khanna, Sandler, and Shimizu go on to apply a standard public goods approach to determining disproportionate burden sharing among the states in table 6.8 for UNPKOS (the correlation between UNPKO payments and gross domestic product (GDP) and between UNPKO payments and GDP per capita). The authors find no strong pattern of correlations for the sample as a whole or for the subset composed of current NATO member countries plus Australia, Japan, Sweden, and the Soviet Union/Russian Federation, either with GDP or GDP per capita. They do report strong relationships in several years (1993, 1994, 1995) for the NATO-members subset but recognize that such was not the case even in proximate years of the post–Cold War period (1990, 1991, 1993, 1996). After hedging carefully, they conclude that the strong relationships suggest that "purely public joint products of peacekeeping are, in part, behind NATO UNPKO payments in the 1990s" (1998, 188) and that the disproportionality would increase if other non-UN PKOs were included.

In sum, their findings do not support the pure-public-goods view in more than a weak fashion—that is, for several years for NATO members. The other major PKO contributors do not show evidence of free riding, as public goods theory would lead one to expect. What Khanna, Sandler, and Shimizu and our own 2002 data do suggest, with reference to the bottom rows of table 6.8, is that NATO shares of UNPKO payments declined after 1992. That decline reflects less a shift by NATO's European members than one by the United States. Since the decline appears to begin in 1994, the peak year for UNPKO payments, others must have been willing to bear a larger share of a larger pie and, in 1996, a larger share of a shrinking pie.

Probing further, Khanna, Sandler, and Shimizu (1999) pursue the search for explanations of payments in the 1976–96 period as a whole. They examine twenty-five countries that made about 96 percent of the payments for UNPKOs from 1986 through 1996 (the sixteen current NATO members plus Australia, Japan, Sweden, Austria, China, Finland, Ireland, New Zealand, and Russia as an assembly of the federation, Ukraine, and Belarus). Their analysis does not disaggregate by time periods, preventing discernment of trends and shifts, but does report country-specific results. Assessment-share rules basically remained constant during the period.

The authors posit that demand for UNPKO by those contributing states involves a combination of demand for a private benefit and a public benefit and examine the effects of GDP, "spill-ins" (i.e., responses to the payments of others), involvement in international trade, and, of course, assessment shares. The GDP relationships are weak, evidencing little free riding among the twenty-five. The trade relationships tend to be positive (for nineteen of the twenty-five countries). Spill-ins offer the strongest explanation—that is, as others involved pay more for PKO, most of the twenty-five pay more. Yet there are important national differences. Among the most heavily assessed countries (the permanent members of the Security Council), Russia and China respond negatively, while the United Kingdom and France almost match and the United States exceeds the spill-in. Among the group 2 countries, all except Greece and Spain respond at a level near or greater than the spill-in. Those who more than match it are Belgium, Italy, Luxembourg, Japan, Sweden, Austria, and Finland, thus showing an extra commitment to UNPKOs, as does the United States. Finally, Khanna, Sandler, and Shimizu report evidence contrary to the incentives mentioned earlier to shirk PKO assessments in favor of those for the regular budget. Instead, the former seem to more effectively overcome "free-riding incentives" (1999, 365).

WHO PAYS AND WHO OWES

The differences between assessment schedules and payments can shed light on national stances toward the provision of the public good of UNPKOs over time. Yet given the range of assessments, absolute amounts owed are a less satisfactory indicator than the gap between the share of payments scheduled for particular countries and the share of the uncollected payments owed by the same country. After all, the largest debtor can also be the largest payer. Given the concentration of scheduled payments to the identifiable UNPKO budgets, we need to pay special attention to those countries whose percentage contributions as a share of their scheduled assessment exceed their share of monies owed and those that manifest the opposite behavior. The former are for practical purposes making a larger impure-public-goods contribution than the share assigned by the assessment schedule benchmark, while the latter group is making a smaller contribution.

We examined financial contributions in these terms for UNPKO assessments and share of arrears for prior periods as of December 1995 and for the current period as of February 1997. We did so for all member nations whose scheduled percentage of UNPKO special assessments was equal to or greater than .1 percent after rounding in either period. Relevant information appears in table 6.9, in which the entries report the assessment share—arrears share gap remaining as of the end of 1995 for prior periods (column A) and for 1997 (column B). Entries in columns A and B were arrived at by subtracting the country percentage of pertinent arrears from the percentage assessed to that country. Positive numbers in A and B show a relatively forthcoming stance toward provisions for UNPKO compared to the de facto behavior of the members as a whole, and a minus sign indicates the opposite. An asterisk indicates that payment has been made in full.

Most of the thirty-eight states listed in table 6.9 fall into one of three categories based on columns A and B:

1. consistent supporters whose share of payments scheduled exceeded their share of payments owed for prior and current levies;
2. volatile states with positive scores for one and a negative for the other; and
3. consistently unsupportive countries with negative scores in both columns.

Consistent supporters were most common (Australia, Austria, Belgium, Canada, China, Denmark, Finland, France, Germany, Greece, India, Ireland, Italy, Japan, Luxembourg, Mexico, the Netherlands, New Zealand, Norway, Portugal, South Korea, Spain, Sweden, and the United Kingdom). The consistently unsupportive were few in number (Belarus, Kazakstan, the Russian Federation, Saudi Arabia, Ukraine, and Venezuela). The volatile states were Argentina, Brazil, Iran, Poland, South Africa, and the United States.

These results are roughly confirmed for later-year data. By late 2002, the United States owed $536 million for the PKO budget, though that amount had dropped from more than $800 million earlier in the same year. Japan, somewhat surprisingly, was also behind in its PKO dues. Other countries, including Germany, France, the United Kingdom, Canada, the Netherlands, Australia, and Russia had paid in full (see www.globalpolicy.org/finance/tables/pko/due2002.htm).

As these findings suggest, the UN relies heavily on advanced industrialized democracies to fund PKOs. Defection from that supportive cluster by the United States clearly has serious implications for provision if it continues, given the shares shown in tables 6.6 and 6.7. An adverse shift in the demand for UNPKOs by one or more permanent (veto-holding) members of the Security Council could also pose important other

TABLE 6.9. Paying and Owing for UNPKOs

	A 1995 (%)	B 1997 (%)
Argentina	0.1	0
Australia	1.5	1.5
Austria	0.9	0.8
Belarus	−5.2	−0.2
Belgium	1.0[a]	0.8
Brazil	0.3	−0.3
Canada	3.1[a]	3.1[a]
China	0.9[a]	0.8
Czech Republic		0.3[a]
Denmark	0.7[a]	0.7[a]
Finland	0.6[a]	0.6[a]
France	7.9[a]	7.8
Germany	8.7	9.1[a]
Greece	0.1[a]	0.2
India	0.1[a]	0.1[a]
Iran	−1.6	0.5
Ireland	0.2[a]	0.2[a]
Italy	4.8[a]	4.5
Japan	14.0	10.5
Kazakhstan	−0.6	−0.4
Korea, Republic of	0.2[a]	0.1
Luxembourg	0.1[a]	0.1
Mexico	0.2[a]	0.2
Netherlands	1.6[a]	1.5
New Zealand	0.2[a]	0.2[a]
Norway	0.6[a]	0.6
Poland	−1.9	0
Portugal	0.1	0.2
Russian Federation	−40.4	−9.3
Saudi Arabia	−1.2	−0.1
South Africa	−0.5	0.3
Spain	2.3[a]	2.3
Sweden	1.2[a]	1.2[a]
Turkey	−0.2	0
Ukraine	−19.8	−13.6
United Kingdom	6.6[a]	6.6[a]
United States	22.5	−33.5
Venezuela	−1.0	−0.2

Source: Data from United Nations Secretariat 1997.
Note: Entries are rounded to the nearest .1 percent.
[a]Paid in full.

sorts of obstacles. The persistent nonsupporters are a diverse lot, but there is an especially noticeable presence of states formerly in the USSR. To this point, then, we see a substantial stable positive core for provision, a smaller set of the more reluctant potential providers, and grounds for concern with defection from the discrepantly providing group.

Our review of financial contributions levied and provided has produced mixed results with respect to our expectations. In part this is because of the structural constraints established by the UN's funding formulas. These formulas in effect make fiscal provision for UNPKOs the province of a small fraction of UN member states. By 1995, there were clear signs of erosion among the members of the contributor club, especially for the United States, that were only partially counterbalanced by the more forthcoming stance of a number of former Soviet bloc countries. The obvious implications of the erosion are a chain of consequences that impede reimbursement to personnel providers and thus reduce the private goods element in what UNPKOs offer. That can compound problems with the amount of provision. It is also worth noting the impact of continued volatility and unpredictability in U.S. support. Although some progress has been made in recent years on the American commitment to UN programs across the board, U.S. arrears for PKOs still exist. This is especially worrisome given the volume of the U.S. contribution and its large percentage of the total budget (Global Policy Forum 2003; O'Hanlon 2003; United Nations General Assembly 1997; Wren 1999b).

Finally, it is pertinent to note that for the larger list of countries in table 6.9, the relationships between GDP and PKO assessments for the year calculated (1995) are modestly negative (.32).[24] With a different and more inclusive sample of financial contributors and for one year, our Spearman rank order correlations go even further than those of Khanna, Sandler, and Shimizu (1998, 1999) in pointing away from the association expected by pure public goods theory. Public goods expectations of hegemonic provision would have the economically larger nations bearing the larger UNPKO burden relative to GDP—that is, the correlation should be positive. Assessments for those who were asked to pay a noticeable amount do not follow the logic of larger economies bearing larger PKO burdens. This is an even more striking finding when taken in tandem with the results of tables 6.8 and 6.9, showing that several larger economies are also in arrears on UNPKO contributions or are behind the curve in terms of what others are doing financially to support UNPKOs. Free riding there may be, but it is by both the richest and poorest members of the UN system.

At face value, the denial of hegemonic stability expectations about public goods provision is positive from an order and progress perspective. It indicates that large hegemonic provision of UNPKO goods is not proportionally dominant and that some smaller states are bearing large PKO burdens. Conversely, it also means that the economically largest states—those with the potential to supply the largest amounts of funding—are not the ones bearing the heaviest relative burdens. Thus, even though there is evidence that supportership is indeed occurring along the lines of our expectations, our optimism is tempered by the financial magnitude of the UNPKO endeavor.

People and Money

We argued earlier that the provision of impure public goods can benefit from specialization in type of contribution. The benefits can include both reductions in the opportunity costs to the contributors and gains in efficiency of provision (and thus an aggregate increase in the supply of public goods provided). Let us look at the personnel and financial contributions from this perspective.

We limit our discussion to the minority of UN members who have made substantial contributions in at least one of the two forms discussed previously. Of those, states falling into the following not fully exclusive categories are particularly relevant to our interests.

> *Comprehensive supercontributors* provide substantial personnel across time in terms of operations participated in (table 6.5) and share of personnel provided (table 6.6). Members of this group also persistently pay for UNPKOs (table 6.8), and pay a share of payments assessed greater than their share of UNPKO bills unpaid (table 6.9). When it is known, they also either come close to matching or even exceed the spill-ins from the contributions of others. They are Austria, Canada, Denmark, Finland, Germany, India, Ireland, Italy, Norway, Sweden, and the United Kingdom. As we approach the present, they arguably have been joined by Australia, France, Japan, Poland, Slovakia, and Spain.[25]
>
> *Reliable comprehensive contributors* meet all the previous criteria except for only one of the share of cases or share of personnel scale. They are Belgium, the Netherlands, and New Zealand. As we approach the present, they arguably have been joined by China, the Czech Republic, Portugal, and Turkey.
>
> *Comprehensive personnel-specialized contributors* match the comprehensive contributors on personnel but not on financial

contributions. They are Argentina, Brazil, Ghana, Indonesia, Nepal, Pakistan, the Russian Federation, and the United States. As we approach the present, they have been joined by Bangladesh, Egypt, Fiji, Hungary, Jordan, Kenya, Malaysia, Romania, Senegal, Ukraine, Uruguay, Zambia, and Zimbabwe.

Regular personnel-specialized contributors provide personnel to a substantial share of operations, but provide only small shares and regularly do little for finances on a regular basis—and often not even on an occasional basis. They are Chile and Sri Lanka, and more recently Tunisia.

Personnel dropouts achieved our threshold of frequency of personnel provision or share (never both) before 1988 but did not subsequently sustain or retain those levels. They are Burma, Ecuador, Peru, Morocco, Saudi Arabia, and Yugoslavia.

Reliable financial contributors are those whose share of levies exceeds their share of debts for both pre-1995 and the 1997 current period assessment but who do not meet the personnel contribution criteria for inclusion in one of the first two groups. They are Greece, Luxembourg, Mexico, and South Korea.

Financial newcomers moved from a cumulative share of payments less than their levies for the period up to 1995 to a share greater than their levies for the 1997 current period. They are Iran and South Africa.

Financial defectors are those who pulled back from the previous standard in their current period contributions to the extent that their share of monies owed exceeded their share of the UNPKO assessment. They are Brazil and the United States.

The comprehensive group of UNPKO supporters with continuing apparent allegiance to such efforts remains a small but growing band of overwhelmingly politically and economically western and northern countries. Japan arguably should be in this set because of the size of its financial contributions and the policy shift in the early 1990s that allowed for personnel contributions to peacekeeping forces rather than just observer UNPKO missions (although not peace-restoration or peace-enforcement operations).[26] The "static small club" description is, however, modified by the diversity apparent historically in personnel providers and the substantial list of newcomer contributors. The particularly negative information for our expectations about the provision of the impure public good of UNPKOs involves the financial aspect that shows few newcomers, historical narrowness, and a shift away from support by the United States.

UNITED NATIONS PEACEKEEPING OPERATIONS

The American Role

Our initial discussion of hegemonic stability in relation to UNPKO goods provision emphasized the importance of the United States. The central questions are: (1) What role did the United States play historically in provision? (2) How has that role changed? (3) What is likely to happen in the next few years?

With regard to providing personnel, the pre-1988 role had the United States involved in about two-thirds of the cases. That fell in later years to about two-fifths. U.S. personnel involvement, then, was never a necessary condition for the UN to engage in PKOs. From 1988 on, the United States has participated in about the same number of cases, even though the percentage in which it participated fell substantially. The U.S. share of participants was always much less than its share of financial contributions and has declined sharply. More recently, in the Clinton and George W. Bush administrations, U.S. Department of Defense officials have launched a major push to reduce PKO troop commitments—and not just for UNPKOs (cutbacks in Haiti, Bosnia, and the Sinai) (Myers 1999).[27] Suggestions have been made that when PKOs become police operations to provide local inhabitants with security, the missions should be staffed by police rather than soldiers (Sciolino 2000). Candidate Bush rejected U.S. forces ever serving under UN command (Crossette 2000c). Our data do not take into account for either recent or earlier periods the substantial off-the-books support U.S. personnel and equipment not formally assigned to UNPKOs have provided to those operations.[28] What is clear is that in recent years, U.S. personnel contributions to IRPKOs not financed through the UN have vastly surpassed contributions to UNPKOs.[29] Those IRPKOS, through NATO or with core-affinity countries, may offer a particularly large club good.

On the financial side, the United States clearly has been expected to provide a very large share of PKO monies—an even larger share than for the regular UN budget (table 6.7)—and, whatever its shortfalls, has paid a very large share (table 6.8). The United States has not, however, been uniformly forthcoming. In addition, 1997 saw a massive gap between share paid and share billed. Increases in U.S. nonpayments seriously exacerbated the chronically tenuous state of UNPKO finances (65 percent of the global total of UNPKO assessment arrears as of October 1999). Further, massive American nonpayments of UN regular budget assessments reduced the capacity to pay for UNPKOs from that budget (Wren 1999b). By the fall of 1999, there were even very real prospects that the United States would lose its vote in the General Assembly as a result of this nonpayment.

With regard to future financial provision, one possibility is that the United States has embarked on a course of radical and rapid withdrawal that will trigger erosion by the other traditional supporters. There were two nonexclusive ways to avoid that possibility, at least for a while. One was to enlarge the membership of the UN Security Council, as Japan and the EU suggested as long ago as 1996 (Grimmett 1996; Wanner 1996). That idea eventually was abandoned in part because of U.S. insistence on retaining the full veto power over UNPKOs associated with Security Council membership (Crossette 2000a).

The second has perhaps been achieved through UN's general acceptance of a deal struck between the Clinton administration and the U.S. Congress in 1999 and largely accepted by the UN in 2001. The terms of the deal were that (1) the UN accept and the United States pay its massive arrears over several years as payment in full, although the UN claimed arrears of $1.6 billion; (2) the U.S. share of the regular budget be cut from 25 percent to 22 percent; (3) the U.S. share of UNPKOs be cut to 25 percent from 31 percent; and (4) the UN accept certain administrative reforms (Alvarez 2001). The deal has resulted in some phased payments of past due monies (note the upswing in share of payment in 2002 (table 6.8)), but has not prevented continued congressional delays and conditions on release of those payments, funding for new operations in situations of urgency (such as Sierra Leone), and cuts in budgets proposed by the White House (Crossette 2000e; Lacey 2001; Weiner 2000a, b). In addition, the demands of the post-9/11 war on terrorism have diverted attention to other budget issues and oversees priorities, making the U.S.-UN relationship and its budgetary implications at least initially less important (especially in the unilateral context with which the war in Iraq was pursued in 2003).

The future of U.S. contributions to UNPKOs will continue to be determined by the shifting sands of international events, UN financial and organizational reform, and U.S. domestic politics (disputes between the major parties and between the executive and the Congress). It is unwarranted to conclude that the United States is firmly and unswervingly set on a course that will undermine provision of the impure public goods of UNPKOs or on the opposite more forthcoming course. Devices, however, have been found to avoid prior congressional notification and approval of such involvement.[30] The vehicle of a UN Security Council–supported multinational force instead of a formal UNPKO skirts those obstacles, as in East Timor. The U.S. financial stake in UNPKOs amounts, after all, to less than 1 percent of the country's defense budget. Further, as we have discussed, public opinion has preponderantly supported U.S. contributions to UNPKOs and a general strengthening of the

UN. There is little reason to expect that the conflicting policy motivations of avoiding failed UNPKO missions (e.g., Somalia) and seeming responsive to humanitarian disasters (e.g., Rwanda) will lead either to consistent nonprovision or timely and generous provision.

CONCLUSIONS AND SPECULATIONS

While the final returns are hardly in, it is clear that most of the post–Cold War period saw an increase in the provision of the impure public goods of UNPKO, albeit with periodic declines, and in the diversity of contributors and beneficiaries. A core of supporting states has continued to behave in ways compatible with our expectations about the provision of impure public goods. Other countries have joined that group, especially, but not only, in terms of personnel contributions. For some of the newcomers—and, indeed, for the long-term continuing contributors—there is surely a substantial private goods element, including a monetary element. The most material form of the latter, net revenues from the dispatch of forces, does not, however, apply to all those who increased their participation.

According to hegemonic-stability views, these patterns should not have occurred in the context of sharp U.S. withdrawal consequent to its once-dominant provision. Here our conclusions are more mixed and speculative. Persistently strong correlations should have existed between national UNPKO/GDP burden and national GDP and substantial free riding. For noticeable contributors, that does not seem to have been or to be emerging as the norm. U.S. personnel provision was never a sine qua non for UNPKOs, and the evidence of its decline is open to counterinterpretation in light of contributions to UN-approved but otherwise-financed IRPKOs. Conversely, U.S. monies have been and remain crucial. As the critical financial supporter, the United States did go into the tank. It remains to be seen whether that withdrawal marked the beginning of the end of the needed degree of financial provision for substantial further UNPKOs or rather just served as a trigger for adjustments to enable future provision. There are substantial signs that it is only part of an adjustment process about the American share of financing and not the U.S. rank among financiers. Thus, we are left with a mutedly optimistic appraisal of the likelihood that UNPKOs as impure public goods will continue at levels substantially higher than those of the Cold War period, even without a guarantor power as a leader in rapid provision of people or money.

Several themes in the once-again active debate about the UN role in peacekeeping suggest that the contention over what types of goods

UNPKOs provide and thus what contributions are warranted is far from resolved. The renewed vigor of that debate follows from humanitarian disasters in Rwanda, Srebrenica in Bosnia, East Timor, Sierra Leone, and Congo. In each of those cases, the challenge has involved not the absence of any UN presence but instead one that was incapable of coping with uncooperative local leaders and their armed and violent supporters.

In response, there have been pleas to enable the UN to engage in quickly triggered and more militarily capable and thus preventive and decisive interventions. Advocates contend that these changes are appropriate because of a "developing international norm in favor of intervention to protect civilians from wholesale slaughter" (Annan quoted in Crossette 1999a). Just as governments are supposed to defend against public bads by providing citizens with the public good of safety, so too should the UN in cases of government failure. Carried to its logical conclusion, the UN would have a standing force (as proposed by some Nordic countries and Canada) and a quick authorization mechanism. It now has neither. It should have both and use them "based on legitimate and universal principles" (Annan 1999).[31] Instead, the UN still must rely on the hope that some member state will fill the gap, as the British and others did in Sierra Leone in 2000.

Other observers contend that such changes would go too far by denying to sovereign governments their obligation to pursue private goods and avoid private bads or because the UN cannot be relied on to apply "universal and legitimate" principles. That school is alive and well. Illustrations include China's veto of extending the UNPKO in Macedonia because it established diplomatic relations with Taiwan, the Congo government's resistance to allowing UN peacekeepers freedom of movement, bills in the U.S. Senate prohibiting a UN standing force, and legislation barring U.S. troop participation without an explicit exemption from possible international war crimes prosecution.

The fact that this debate is ongoing seems compatible with UNPKOs remaining in the middle zone of impure public goods. Reliance on non-UN PKOs for peace enforcement may also be tardy or unsustained in providing safety. But such activities are undertaken and demanded because of the recognition that they provide desired club goods with more than private elements. The members of such clubs are quick to seek UN approval and shift tasks to the UN (as in Kosovo). The vigor of the debate in itself implies that the demand for peacekeeping in its broadest sense will not go away, supporting our mutedly optimistic expectations that a changing set of countries eventually will find themselves persuaded to make provisions that at least partially meet that demand rather than ignoring it.

UNITED NATIONS PEACEKEEPING OPERATIONS

Appendix: Peacekeeping Missions (as of February 2003)

STARTED 1948–78

Observer Missions

UNTSO—UN Truce Supervision Organization in Palestine, 1948–; Middle East.
UNMOGIP—UN Military Observer Group in India and Pakistan, 1949–; Jammu, Kashmir, Pakistan, and India.
UNOGIL—UN Observer Group in Lebanon, June–Dec. 1958; Lebanon.
UNYOM—UN Yemen Observer Mission, July 1963–Sept. 1964; Yemen.
DOMREP—Mission of Representatives of the Secretary-General in the Dominican Republic, May 1965–Oct. 1966; Dominican Republic.
UNIPOM—UN India/Pakistan Observer Mission, Sept. 1965–Mar. 1966; India-Pakistan border.

Peacekeeping Forces

UNEF I—UN Emergency Sinai Force I, 1956–67; Gaza, Egyptian Sinai.
ONUC—UN Operation in the Congo, 1960–64; Congo.
UNSF—UN Security Force in West New Guinea, Oct. 1962–April 1963; West Irian.
UNFICYP—UN Force in Cyprus, 1964–; Cyprus.
UNEF II—UN Emergency Force II, 1973–79; Suez Canal, Sinai.
UNDOF—UN Disengagement Observer Force, 1974–; Israel-Syria, Golan Heights.
UNIFIL—UN Interim Force in Lebanon, 1978–; Southern Lebanon.

STARTED 1988–2002

Observer Missions

UNGOMAP—UN Good Offices Mission in Afghanistan and Pakistan, Apr. 1988–Mar. 1990; Afghanistan, Pakistan.
UNIIMOG—UN Iran-Iraq Military Observer Mission, Aug. 1988–Feb. 1991; Iran, Iraq.
UNAVEM I—UN Angola Verification Mission, Jan. 1989–May 1991; Angola.
ONUCA—UN Observer Group in Central America, Nov. 1989–Jan. 1992; Costa Rica, El Salvador, Guatemala, Honduras, Nicaragua.
ONUSAL—UN Observer Mission in El Salvador, May 1991–Apr. 1995; El Salvador.
UNAVEM II—UN Angola Verification Mission II, May 1991–Feb. 1995; Angola.

UNOMUR—UN Observer Mission Uganda-Rwanda, June 1993–Sept. 1994; Uganda.

UNOMIG—UN Observer Mission in Georgia, Aug. 1993–; Georgia.

UNOMIL—UN Observer Mission in Liberia, Sept. 1993–Sept. 1997; Liberia.

UNASOG—UN Aouzou Strip Observer Group, May–June 1994; Chad, Libya.

UNMOT—UN Mission of Observers in Tajikistan, Dec. 1994–May 2000; Tajikistan.

UNAVEM III—UN Angola Verification Mission III, Feb. 1995–June 1997; Angola.

UNMOP—UN Mission of Observers in Prevlaka, Jan. 1996–Dec. 2002; Croatia.

MINUGUA—UN Verification Mission in Guatamala, Jan.–May 1997; Guatemala.

MONUA—UN Observer Mission in Angola, July 1997–Feb. 1999; Angola.

UNOMSIL—United Nations Observer Mission in Sierra Leone, July 1998–Oct. 1999; Sierra Leone.

MONUC—UN Organization Mission in the Democratic Republic of the Congo, Nov. 1999–; Democratic Republic of the Congo.

Peacekeeping Forces

UNTAG—UN Transition Assistance Group, Apr. 1989–Mar. 1990; Namibia, Angola.

UNIKOM—UN Iraq-Kuwait Observer Mission, Apr. 1991–; Iraq-Kuwait border.

MINURSO—UN Mission for the Referendum in Western Sahara, Apr. 1991–; western Sahara.

UNAMIC—UN Advance Mission in Cambodia, Oct. 1991–Mar. 1992; Cambodia.

UNPROFOR—UN Protection Force, Feb. 1992–Mar. 1995; first stage, Croatia, Bosnia, and Herzegovina, Macedonia; second stage, Bosnia and Herzegovina.

UNTAC—UN Transitional Authority in Cambodia, Mar. 1992–Sept. 1993; Cambodia.

UNOSOM I—UN Operation in Somalia, Apr. 1992–Mar. 1993; Somalia.

ONUMOZ—UN Operation in Mozambique, Dec. 1992–Jan. 1995; Mozambique.

UNOSOM II—UN Operation in Somalia II, May 1993–Mar. 1995; Somalia.

UNMIH—UN Mission in Haiti, Sept. 1993–June 1996; Haiti.

UNAMIR—UN Assistance Mission for Rwanda. Oct. 1993–Mar. 1996; Rwanda.

UNITED NATIONS PEACEKEEPING OPERATIONS

UNCRO—UN Confidence Restoration Operation in Croatia, Mar. 1995–Jan. 1996; Croatia.

UNPREDEP—UN Preventive Deployment Force, Mar. 1995–Feb. 1999; Macedonia.

UNMIBH—UN Mission in Bosnia and Herzegovina, Dec. 1995–Dec. 2002; Bosnia and Herzegovina.

UNTAES—UN Transitional Administration for Eastern Slavonia, Baranja, and Western Sirmium, Jan. 1996–Jan. 1998; Croatia.

UNSMIH—UN Support Mission in Haiti, July 1996–July 1997; Haiti.

UNTMIH—UN Transition Mission in Haiti, Aug.–Nov. 1997; Haiti.

MIPONUH—United Nations Civilian Police Mission in Haiti, Dec. 1997–Mar. 2000; Haiti.

UNPSG—United Nations Civilian Police Support Group, Jan.–Oct. 1998; Danube region of Croatia.

MINURCA—United Nations Mission in the Central African Republic, Apr. 1998–Feb. 2000; Central African Republic.

UNMIK—UN Interim Administration Mission in Kosovo, July 1999–; Kosovo.

UNAMSIL—UN Mission in Sierra Leone, Oct. 1999–; Sierra Leone.

UNTAET—UN Transitional Administration in East Timor, Oct. 1999–Mar. 2002; East Timor.

UNMEE—UN Mission in Ethiopia and Eritrea, June 2000–; Ethiopia and Eritrea.

UNMISET—UN Mission in Support of East Timor, May 2002–; East Timor.

Source: Browne 1994, 1995; Mendez 1999; Neack 1995; United Nations Military Adviser's Office 1991–97; www.un.org.

7 PURSUING INTERNATIONAL ENVIRONMENTAL QUALITY

International environmental issues provide a wealth of vivid examples of the challenges for collective action in contemporary international relations. Almost any example features the frequently cited tension between the benefits of global and national environmental quality and the international and national interests that focus on avoiding the costs associated with proenvironmental policy. Globally, those costs may take the form of hampering the development of the global South and the competitiveness of the advanced industrialized countries (AICs) of the North.[1] Such tensions, evident in many media-hyped stories today, are prominent in the familiar "tragedy of the commons" imagery popularized some thirty years ago.

The twin imperatives of growth and environmental quality were embodied in Principle 21 of the UN-sponsored 1972 Stockholm conference. Put simply, Principle 21 concluded that no country should act in ways that would hurt others and that every country has a right to development. The priority given to each of these components remains controversial and unresolved to this day.

This relatively simple formulation of environmental collective action problems does not fully capture the range of issues involved in contributions to providing environmental public goods and reducing the associated public bads. It also stops short of answering the larger question of how the level of environmental collaboration among international actors fits within the overall prospects for global order in the coming years. In particular, it ignores (1) the conceptual complexity of the public goods problems presented by international environmental issues; (2) the ways that states have worked to achieve some level of international environmental cooperation—and the ways in which they have failed to do so—in such notable cases as the Montreal Protocol on the Ozone, the Framework Convention on Climate Change, the Biodiversity Convention, and the Kyoto Protocol; and (3) the leadership and obstruction shown by some states both in terms of multilateral negotiations and state policies and performance bearing on international environmental quality goals.

This chapter focuses on these topics by looking at the record of global environmental cooperation and state action in support of that record from the perspective of how these efforts reflect a potential orientation on the part of states to develop and maintain longer-term cooperative relationships in the international system. First, we lay out the underpinnings of our conceptual perspective as it relates to global environmental affairs, with reference to some major historical elements. Second, we discuss domestic support for international environmental cooperation as evidenced by public opinion data. Third, we provide a quantitative examination of the contributions made to the environmental quality supply chain, in particular by the AICs but also with some reference to those of the rest of the world. This section seeks directly to provide an understanding of the extent that particular countries are leaders or laggards in their attempts to reduce international environmental bads.

PUBLIC GOODS, PUBLIC BADS, AND THE GLOBAL ENVIRONMENT

In previous chapters, our discussion of public goods and their conceptual relationship to issues of international cooperation focused both on the collective provision of impure public goods and on the reduction of impure public bads. Consequently, for development assistance, we emphasized the internationally consumable benefits that can be derived from foreign aid flows to the developing world. For debt management, we focused largely on the ways creditors and debtors work together to produce stable economic relationships and to avoid potential economic and financial disasters. For peacekeeping, we focused on avoidance or reduction of bloodshed and human suffering and their negative spillovers through operations in conflict-torn regions of the world.

When considering environmental affairs, our focus turns more toward considering what has been and will be done by particular nations and international groupings to reduce the many local and transboundary public bads that exist and are being further produced in the contemporary world, a focus well illustrated for global climate change by Luterbacher and Sprinz (2001). We recognize that global economic development over the past 200 years has centered and continues to center on industrial and agricultural activities, with corollaries of extensive reliance on fossil fuel consumption, consumption of renewable and nonrenewable natural resources, and the use and production of commodities harmful to human health and to ecosystems. Substantial damage has occurred and continues to occur to the environment and poses challenges both of cleanups and bending down the curve of a growing generation of insults to the environment. Thus, when considering the global pursuit of environmental quality, we must focus on efforts to reduce such things as the production of carbon dioxide emissions because they contribute to global warming and on efforts to clean up toxic waste sites identified as threats to fragile ecosystems. We do so without denying the relevance of traditional conceptions of steps to enhance contributions to the production of public goods and reduction of public bads, such as signing onto environmental protection agreements.

We also recognize that the impacts of deterioration in environmental quality are broader and in many instances more indirect and thus more pervasive than one might think when first examining environmental issues. For example, much has been written in recent years about the ways that environmental problems can result in conflict between international actors (see Gleditsch 1998; Gleick 1993; Homer-Dixon 1991, 1994; Lipschutz 1989; Lowi 1993; Payne 1998). From the potential for water-based conflicts in the Middle East and elsewhere to the environmental problems caused by refugee flows to conflicts over control of oil and other strategic resources, lack of attention to environmental affairs has the potential to produce significant negative spillovers into political relationships around the world. As a result, failure to attend to environmental policy today in serious and straightforward ways that foster international cooperation may well lead to larger-scale public bads demanding more intensive policy treatment in the future. Even when dealing with the production of public goods in the environmental policy arena, the specter of public bads looms large.

Moreover, environmental affairs possess a more truly international and often indeed a global character than the other policy areas we have discussed thus far. The "shared fate" transboundary effects of acid rain, global warming, ozone layer depletion, and other icons of environmental degradation force environmental policy into international and global policy arenas whether states like it or not. Examples include the use of high-sulfur coal in the American industrial Midwest that results in acid rain falling on Canadian forests and illegal trafficking in Freon, a rival to cocaine in its yield of illegal profits (Blair 1998). Because of its continued illegal use in air conditioning and other cooling systems, Freon contributes to the depletion of the ozone layer. While development-assistance policies, for example, could be pursued with programs and funding devised and driven by individual states or small groups of states (albeit in less-than-optimal ways), environmental problems often demand multilateral and indeed global collective action for successful amelioration.

At first glance, that requirement, taken together with the conflicting interests introduced at the beginning of this chapter, suggests pessimism. Yet in the environmental realm, the work of Ostrom (1990, 1992a, b), McKean (1992) and others on the management of common pool resources (CPRs) provides a conditional basis for our mutedly optimistic perspective. Conceptually, CPRs resemble public goods, focusing on resources where "it is costly to exclude potential beneficiaries from gaining access to the resources and . . . each person's use subtracts resource units from those available to others" (Ostrom 1992a, 243). This definition suggests that CPRs are parallel in the public goods field to goods that exhibit some degree of rivalry in consumption and thus in an environmental context run the risk of overuse by those consuming the good.

Ostrom's approach nevertheless suggests that opportunities for cooperation in governing the use of such resources can exist but that successful governance depends on the presence of the following characteristics among the members of the pertinent group (1992b, 347).

> *Shared values*—in our case, this means that the major powers in the system share a commitment to supporting international cooperative efforts and that there exists some commonality of values—though not perfect—about how that should be achieved.
> *Stability in membership* among the relevant club members.
> *Extended time horizons*—a long-term set of relationships must exist among the group in question analogous to the logic of Axelrod's (1984) pathbreaking work on cooperation.
> *Multiplex relationships*—the specific issue is embedded in a more extensive series of relationships that exist among the members of the collective.
> *Capacity to directly communicate,* among relevant states, firms, nongovernmental organizations (NGOs), and international organizations.

Building on these ideas, Young (1997) further argues that governance of CPRs can arise when members of a group find that they are interdependent. But instead of interdependence necessarily producing conflict among members as they confront their interrelationships, it can emerge as the basis for cooperation:

When opportunities arise to enhance social welfare by acting to coordinate the activities of the individual members of the group . . . interdependence leads to interactive decision making and generates the potential for collective-action problems in the sense that individual actors, left to their own devices in an interdependent world, frequently suffer joint losses as a result of conflict or fail to reap joint gains due to the inability to cooperate." (4–5)

When Ostrom's characteristics of governance situations (as based in identity and interest) exist within an interdependent collective, the likelihood for joint gains is higher, though certainly not guaranteed or necessarily obtained to optimal levels.

The question these conditions raise is, of course, whether they are present or emerging in the international system. For several of them—most obviously multiplex relationships, the ability to communicate, and awareness of interdependence as suggested in chapter 2—the answer clearly is yes. Several others are more problematic but are hardly ruled out in contemporary international affairs. The conditions of extended time horizons and stability in membership seem to rest on the sort of identity and interest constructions discussed in chapter 3, and we found grounds for both optimism and pessimism. As for shared values, the next section of this chapter will examine to what extent they are present.

It is important to note a prominent body of opinion suggesting that, even if the Ostrom/Young conditions do not yet exist, they are in the process of being created through the actions of NGOs and international governmental organizations (Luterbacher and Sprinz 2001). At least since P. M. Haas (1992), the role of expert epistemic communities has been held to be responsible for greater steps to reduce environmental bads. Similarly, McCormick (1999) stresses NGOs' impact on the evolution of environmental policy, identifying the lack of authoritative international environmental law as a primary reason for the important role of NGOs. The past thirty years have seen NGOs playing significant roles in promoting environmental activism at a variety of governmental levels and through a variety of different political methods. The World Wildlife Fund, the Sierra Club, Greenpeace, Climate Network Europe, the European Environmental Bureau, and many other organizations have attracted extensive media attention to environmental issues, mobilized scientific communities for political action, and been involved in introducing environmental issues into electoral campaigns in countries around the globe.

Soroos (1999) argues that the evolution of international governmental environment organizations (most notably the United Nations Environmental Program [UNEP] and the Global Environment Facility [GEF]) has done much to maintain whatever effort exists for dealing with the serious environmental deterioration problems confronting the globe. Even though state sovereignty remains the primary roadblock to successful management of environmental problems, Soroos believes that the state of affairs would be worse without these groups' role in the evolution of global awareness and policy in the environmental realm. The positive impact on environmental affairs that can be obtained through effective institutions is echoed clearly by the work of Mitchell (2001) and Arce, Daniel, and Sandler (2001), as well as in Luterbacher and Sprinz (2001). There are, then, substantial arguments that international institutions, particularly in the transboundary policy arenas engendered by global environmental affairs, can have distinctly positive impacts on international cooperation and the propensity to contribute that such cooperation involves.

Even if one makes much of these developments, it is important to note continuing unresolved issues about the best approach to the environmental bads supply chain—that is, the relative emphasis on the best-shot, weakest-link, and summation approaches introduced in chapter 2. In the environmental issue area, all three approaches have merits and limitations and raise complex issues of equity, incentives, and management (Heal 1999; Patterson 2001; Wiegandt 2001).

In line with the best-shot conception, priority would go to increasing environmentally friendly scientific and technological contributions by the nation (and its research and development [R&D] community and firms) most equipped to invent, produce, and diffuse them. That nation is generally held to be the United States, although it could be Japan or the European Union (EU) collective. In terms of weakest-link conceptions, many environmental problems result from the careless actions of a few firms or states that in effect impose environmental bads on neighbors or even the whole international collective, either knowingly or through negligence. The appropriate strategy would then be to induce the single or few predominant negative contributor government(s) or industrial subsector(s) to change behavior. In national terms, that would often be the United States (or in the future China or India) and the motor vehicle and electric power generation industries. Otherwise, others might see little to be gained in the way of public bads reduction from more restraint on their part. For the summation conception, we note that success on many policy efforts in this issue area depends on the additive (and possibly multiplicative) efforts of most AICs and large, rapidly developing economies; manufacturing, production, and resource extraction industries; and even individuals. Especially when considering such problems as transboundary pollution, global warming, or ozone depletion, the efforts of a great many actors matter for reducing environmental public bads.[2]

The feasibility and specific content of any one of these approaches varies from environmental issue to issue. That is, different issues pose collective action problems that differ in their severity with the resulting variety of adopted ameliorative international measures. Of special importance, these approaches may differ greatly in the extent that they pose massive private net economic costs to particular nations and their major industries, the vulnerability of the proposed course of international action to free riding, and the inclusion of transfer payments to other countries from those expected at the same time to bear the greatest burdens of reduction in their own environmentally harmful behavior. These differences may in large measure account for the recent mixed history of international collective action for environmental quality. That history provides grounds for both optimism and pessimism and features the importance of the considerations central to impure public goods and club theories.

Perhaps the most prominent example supporting optimism about achieving the conducive conditions and thus about contributions to reducing environmental public bads is the 1987 Montreal Ozone Protocol cutting chlorofluorocarbon (CFC) emissions by 50 percent and the subsequent 100 percent reduction. Given the dynamics of a situation where the United States was the home state for the largest producer of CFCs (DuPont), and was also the largest consuming state, the likelihood of hegemonic leadership in the banning of the ozone deteriorating chemical was, at first glance, small. According to P. M. Haas (1992), the push from scientific evidence and the political mobilization of the international scientific community provided the impetus for the recognition of the need to solve the CFC problem. Even more striking is the argument made by Benedick (1991) regarding the Montreal Protocol. The Montreal agreement was not made in response to specific harmful developments but rather was preventive action taken without (at the time) measurable evidence of CFC impact on the ozone layer.

Yet others (Barrett 1999; Paarlberg 2001) argue for the importance of additional circumstances. These included the small size and labor force of the producer industry in the signatory economies; the few, tightly linked states that were the major producers; the ready availability of replacement chemicals; and a near equality between the benefits and costs of reduction to the United States (both of which were relatively small compared to some other pollutants). Further, the agreement contained substantial elements insuring that it would result in actual reductions, including measures to discourage others from CFC production, safeguards against free-rider exploitation of reductions by the current producers, subsidies for developing and transitional economy countries' reductions, and (at least in principle) trading of emission entitlements. In short, the protocol was relatively attractive in the prospects it offered for production in the sense of reduction of public bads from contributions and involved a minimal trade-off between bolstering environmental quality and bearing private net economic costs. Whatever the set of reasons, the Reagan and George H. W. Bush administrations ultimately adopted an approach that would limit further environmental damage and induced European and Japanese acceptance of that approach.[3]

A prominent and more pessimistic example focuses on efforts to reduce global warming emissions. Here the United States surely has not taken a leadership role but instead has worked to dilute or oppose reduction commitments (Balakrishnan 2002; Paarlberg 2002; Schreuers 2001; Sell 1996; Sprinz 2001). Evidence of this laggard approach is seen in several significant developments: (1) at the Rio 1992 Earth Summit that produced the United Nations Framework Convention on Climate Change; (2) in the 1997 U.S. Senate resolution opposing a global warming treaty with substantial costs to the U.S. economy or lack of provision for emission cuts by the global South; (3) in the U.S. reduction stance at the meeting later that year that resulted in the Kyoto Protocol; and (4) most extremely, in the 2002 formal withdrawal from the Kyoto Protocol. The relevant diplomacy for reductions has instead featured leadership from the EU, an intermediate position by Japan, and resistance from the United States and some others, such as Canada and Australia.

The global warming international agreement story has resembled that for ozone in featuring for a time increasing declaratory commitments to public bads reduction (from the Rio proposed goal of reducing carbon dioxide emissions to 1990 levels by 2000 to the Kyoto goals of cuts below 1990 levels by 2008–12). Yet those declarations have taken place in a far different setting: lack of developing-country reduction obligations by major current and potential emitters; massive impacts on and opposition from major industrial sectors and their labor force; and massive national economic costs often estimated to exceed the resulting benefits. In effect, the prospects for achieving the public goods of reductions were called into question by the lack of developing-country commitment and massive private bads to some major AIC polluters. Further, the private bads element was very different in its magnitude for various members of the developed-country club. It seemed particularly low for those who after the Cold War had already lowered their emissions (e.g., and most obviously, Germany's "wall fall" reductions and those from closing down dirty industrial facilities in Russia and East-Central Europe). In effect, the United States was being asked to bear particularly large, relatively immediate private costs, given its established emission practices, in exchange for uncertain future public benefits. Steps to increase confidence in long-term global reductions would call for possibly large subsidies to large developing economies—that is, the "undesirable" prospect of more foreign aid. Further, the passage of time has made it clear that barring rather unlikely developments, Japan and the EU (especially if enlarged) are unlikely to meet their Kyoto reduction agreements (European Commission, "Europeans and the International Crisis" 2001; Kameyama 2001).

Yet at this point, the global warming story does not warrant complete pessimism. Kyoto continues with non-American support, and the U.S. position may change with more evidence of the private bad of damage from climate change (Revkin 2002) and congressional–executive branch bargaining ("Crossroads" 2002). Further, the Kyoto process shows signs of acquiring features relatively attractive to U.S. interests, as in the 2001 Marrakech agreements, including emissions trading and the clean development mechanism. Indeed, the story may eventually bolster the case for muted optimism by demonstrating in clear terms the possibility of reductions in bads in the face of U.S. resistance. That is, progress in reducing the public bads posed by global warming may come to resemble that with protecting global biodiversity (the 1992 Convention on Biological Diversity) that progressed with the 2000 Biosafety Protocol over U.S. opposition.

Thus, we argue that the likelihood of steps in line with muted optimism will be affected by the degree of support for or tolerance of bads-reduction policies in the publics of the states involved in global environmental policy. Accordingly, we now turn to the constraints and opportunities domestic public opinion provides for contributions to environmental quality.

PUBLIC OPINION ABOUT THE ENVIRONMENT: AHEAD OF THE POLICY CURVE

Compared with the public opinion data on foreign aid and peacekeeping, those on environmental matters are much richer in types of questions asked, numbers of surveys, and countries polled. This may be because environmental goods and bads are matters of concern whose private, club, and public elements are far more sensitive to international factors and far more directly and widely intrusive into daily life in the global North than are foreign aid, peacekeeping operations, or debt relief. The consequences of environmental deterioration are hard to limit geographically, and decisions affecting the environment range from the individual level (e.g., whether to recycle) through systemwide forums (e.g., global conferences like those held in Rio in 1992 and Kyoto in 1997). Also, in their several decades of public salience, environmental policy matters have not until recently been as readily fit into an existing construct of international political economy or security (see, e.g., Matthews 1989; Ullman 1983). Interested portions of the establishment and counterestablishment may have felt a greater need to gain information about public opinion on this relatively new and complex set of issues. In addition, unlike foreign aid and peacekeeping operations, large and noticeable social movements have arisen in support of greater environmental protection. Such movements present political management challenges to politicians. That management process requires an understanding of the extent that such movements have wide or narrow, deep or shallow public support.

With these considerations in mind, we follow a structure similar to our analyses in chapters 4 and 6 by examining: (1) citizen activism; (2) spending, regulation, and cost bearing; (3) importance and priority; (4) values and role conceptions; and (5) a summary of impressions about the costs and benefits of environmental policy.

Citizen Activism

Several patterns emerge in the 1990s when we examine the degree of pressure placed on politicians to take a pro-environmental-contributions stance.[4] In many of the Organization for Economic Cooperation and Development (OECD) countries of Europe and North America, a substantial fraction of citizens clearly claimed active involvement in environmental affairs. In a number of those countries, that involvement extended to membership in organizations of 10 percent or more of those polled (the United States, Australia, New Zealand, the Philippines, Denmark, Sweden, Switzerland, and especially the Netherlands). In many of these countries, a third or more of respondents claimed to have contributed money and lent their names to the sort of policy demands that petitions convey to decision makers. Canada, Australia, and New Zealand stand out for both forms of activity, and the United States and the Netherlands cross that threshold for one or the other. In the United States and in the EU, environmental NGOs seem to have more credibility with the public than other institutions do.[5] It is reasonable to conclude that, for most of the OECD countries, environmental organizations had a breadth of funding and voice that would be hard to ignore in domestic politics.

Spending, Regulation, and Cost Bearing

Contributions to environmental amelioration and protection can be made through both spending and regulation. Each can be undertaken as a national, international, or transnational matter. Each can involve burden bearing by different elements of a society.

Opinions on central government spending were available to a useful extent only for the United States and several European countries. American polls from 1982 through 2000 persistently showed majorities in favor of increased government spending for the environment as a general matter: support peaked in 1988 and was subsequently limited to a stable small majority.[6] That stance seems significant since it regularly exceeded by a large margin support for increases in most other government spending (T. W. Smith 2001). For the United Kingdom, polls from 1989 through 1993 consistently showed only small minorities for reduction in spending. U.K. support for spending increases fluctuated between a majority and a plurality and thus appeared to outweigh those favoring reduction (Hastings and Hastings 1989–90, 481; 1992–93, 1077–08; 1993–94, 109). Polling in 1993–94 in five EU member states (Germany, Ireland, Italy, the Netherlands, and the United Kingdom) usually yielded majority support for government spending on behalf of the environment (ISSP 1995).

Public majorities (usually massive ones) supported their government "doing more" or being more concerned with environmental protection in general. That was true in the United States (1988–2000), United Kingdom (1989, 1992, 1997), Japan (2000), Canada (1989, 1990), and India (1992).[7] The U.S. majority, however, was substantially smaller in the 1999 and 2000 polls than in earlier surveys. As for West Europeans, the effectiveness of public-sector bodies (local, regional, national, EU, and worldwide) in protecting the environment found no positive majority verdict for any of them in 1992, 1995, or 1999, with particularly negative verdicts most recently (European Commission, *What Do Europeans Think* 1999).

Regulation offers a way for governments to do more other than through visibly higher spending. The American public supported increased governmental regulation when queried in 1995, 1997, 1998, 2001, and 2002 (Americans and the World 2003a; Gallup Poll Release, March 16, 2001; PIPA 2000c).[8] In the five-country European polling mentioned earlier, the passage of "stricter laws" not only was supported massively by each public but was more popular than a variety of possible spending, taxation, and rationing actions (ISSP 1995). Polling of the EU-15 publics in 1999 and 2002 showed the same relative preference (European Commission, *What Do Europeans Think* 1999; European Opinion Research Group 2001). While very substantial net majorities supported regulation of citizens with respect to the environment in eighteen of twenty countries polled in 1993–94 (ISSP 1995), more specific questions have revealed only minority support for energy-consumption restraints on citizens in the United States and the EU (Gallup Poll Release, March 16, 2001; ISSP 1995). In contrast, the twenty-country poll found near unanimity in all of its publics on regulation of businesses, large majorities in the United States supported such measures in 2001, and considerable support also existed in 1999 in the EU (the "polluter pays" principle) especially in France, Belgium, and the Netherlands (European Commission, *What Do Europeans Think* 1999; Gallup Poll Release, March 16, 2001; ISSP 1995).[9]

What about support for environmental protection spending and regulatory authority for international organizations? On financial outlays to an international environmental agency, a 1992 poll of twenty-four countries found supportive majorities in all but one (a plurality in India) (Dunlap 1994). Those majorities exceeded two-thirds in Canada, Korea, Finland, West Germany, Hungary, Ireland, the Netherlands, Poland, Portugal, Switzerland, the United Kingdom, Russia, and Nigeria. Results fell below that level in Mexico, the United States, Japan, Denmark, Norway, Turkey, Brazil, Chile, Uruguay, the Philippines, and India. When asked that same year about relinquishing autonomy to an international environmental agency, majorities were still present in every polled public but were always smaller (Dunlap 1994). Yet they still fell below 60 percent only in Denmark, Chile, Uruguay, and India.[10] Also in 1992, massive majorities in the United States, Japan, the United Kingdom, Germany, and France supported the Earth Summit's international regulation of carbon dioxide emissions (Hastings and Hastings 1991–92, 648).

Even with these relatively supportive findings, public opinion provides limited permissions to governments. The limits are indicated by responses that relate government environmental protection actions explicitly to economic costs to citizens. While large majorities in the early 1990s asserted their willingness to give up part of their income for environmental quality, substantial majorities at that time also usually rejected bearing a variety of types of personal financial costs. The notable exceptions were Denmark, the Netherlands, Sweden, and Iceland. Public opinion was effectively split in the United States, Canada, Japan,

South Korea, China, India, Germany, the United Kingdom, Finland, Norway, Spain, Czechoslovakia, and Russia. Higher prices were only relatively acceptable compared to tax increases, and net majorities were willing to accept cuts in their standard of living only in West Germany, Italy, Norway, and sometimes marginally in Japan. Blanket permission for imposing costs to protect the environment in terms of public majorities' net acceptant of higher prices, higher taxes, and cuts in standard of living was absent except in West Germany, Italy, the Netherlands, Spain, and Japan (Inglehart, Basañez, and Moreno 1998, V12–V14; ISSP 1995). The American public was notably missing from that set, although more recent American majorities have said that "environmental improvements must be made regardless of cost" in six polls in 1998–2002. Yet those majorities evaporated when probed about specific cost estimates (Americans and the World 2003a). Much other polling has confirmed the greater resistance to higher taxes than higher prices and the lack of widespread majority support for either as a possible corollary of protecting the environment. That has been true of American, Japanese, and West European publics, with the possible exceptions of West Germany and the Netherlands.[11]

In sum, the message seems to be "do more" while masking or minimizing directly associated economic costs. That preference probably does not differentiate between the efforts of national and international organizations to protect the environment and certainly sends a cautionary message to decision makers about exactly how far the public wants policies to go when costs will be perceived and felt by citizens.

Importance and Priority

Policymakers' judgments about public permissiveness for environmental contributions necessarily have to consider views about them in relation to other issues of public concern, especially given the limited mandate the opinions discussed previously suggest. We begin with public views about a trade-off between environmental quality and economic growth and then consider responses to decreasingly demanding types of questions about the importance and priority of environmental protection in general. As data permit, we will distinguish opinions about those matters as national or global issues. Finally, we will consider opinions about the importance and priority of particular environmental issues. The prospects of public permissions for international collective action to reduce environmental bads should in our view be more promising when there is little perceived clash with economic growth or jobs, a high degree of importance and priority for alleviating environmental problems outside as well as inside one's nation, and agreement on which particular environmental issues call for special emphasis.

We begin with a mid-1990s comparative perspective on the actual and desirable stance relating prosperity to environmental quality with the last four columns in table 7.1. Entries without parentheses are the actual percentages endorsing the pertinent view; those in parentheses are the net percentages, taking into account those who reject that view.

The notion that economic growth is inherently negatively associated with environmental protection was rejected by small majorities in a number of OECD countries (the United States, Canada, Australia, New Zealand, Ireland, Norway, and Israel). Substantial plurality rejections were found in the Netherlands and the United Kingdom. In contrast, the trade-off was widely seen in Japan, West Germany, Italy, Bulgaria, Hungary, Poland, Russia, and Slovenia. A need to choose between reducing unemployment and protecting the environment was a majority or large plurality view in South Korea, India, Italy, Portugal, Spain, the Czech Republic, Hungary, Slovenia, Turkey, Brazil, and Nigeria. That need was not widely accepted elsewhere. The view that growth was a requirement to have environmental protection had majority or large plurality support among most publics, with the Netherlands being the only robust exception.

More recently, Americans have thought that win-win alternatives are possible and are not just options that sacrifice one or another good. This was true in general and when emissions reductions were linked to "saving money in the long run" or to creating "new jobs through new technologies" (1997–99 polling in America and the World 2003a). A lose-lose linkage also seemed to receive large majority acceptance—for example, allowing American companies to move to countries with lower environmental standards would result in losses of U.S. jobs and "greater harm to the environment" (PIPA 2001). Such linkages might well work to reduce any tension in attitudes between environmental quality values and responsibilities, on the one hand, and the pursuit of personal or national private economic benefits, on the other.

Recent data suggest that EU publics, however, have come to see a lack of positive economic consequences from environmental protection efforts as they relate to helping the economy as a whole, job creation, and social benefits. In 2002 this was the view of majorities except in Ireland and Italy (European Commission 2002, "Sustainable Development"). This suggests serious reservations since there has been the widespread view that environmental policy should "take into account social and economic effects." These reservations are held somewhat at bay by the larger minority thinking that environmental protection creates rather

TABLE 7.1. Environmental Protection Emphasis: Excessive or Not (in percentages)

	Worry Excessive (1993–94)	Anxiety Excessive (1990–93)	Urgency Overstated (1990–93)	Growth Need Not Harm Environment (1993–94)	Employment Harmed by Environmental Protection (1990–93)	Economy Underemphasized (1993–94)	Growth Necessary for Environmental Protection (1993–94)
United States	33 (−17)	46	29	53 (32)	31	42 (−2)	51 (25)
Canada	21 (−45)	48	22	58 (38)	30	25 (−36)	45 (12)
Japan	27 (−21)	50	12	15 (−45)	22	27 (−21)	53 (36)
Australia	28 (−28)			52 (32)		26 (−32)	39 (7)
New Zealand	28 (−29)			59 (41)		30 (−28)	38 (−1)
South Korea		49	22		47		
China		33	32		26		
India		66	37		62		
Philippines	53 (31)			33 (−8)		49 (19)	74 (66)
Belgium		44	19		37		
Denmark		54	18		33		
France		59	19		38		
Germany							
West	27 (−32)	34	12	28 (−23)	21	33 (−20)	44 (13)
East	32 (−20)	43	11	39 (−1)	31	44 (5)	48 (17)
Ireland	42 (−7)	39	26	52 (20)	36	55 (17)	66 (45)
Italy	36 (−16)	53	18	23 (−33)	49	46 (5)	47 (11)
Netherlands	32 (−17)	31	17	42 (12)	22	29 (−23)	30 (−12)
United Kingdom	33 (−15)	54	22	42 (16)	32	40 (−7)	48 (22)
Portugal		66	24		53		
Spain	38 (−13)	61	25	33 (−9)	42	39 (−5)	60 (38)
Austria		51	19		33		
Finland		35	13		22		
Sweden		53	16		36		
Iceland		25	15		28		

Country						
Norway	26 (−29)	55	16	59 (41)	33	27 (−32)	46 (11)
Belarus		64	20		22		
Bulgaria	70 (54)	68	19	25 (−33)	26	45 (1)	82 (73)
Czech Republic	36 (−15)	58	17	45 (9)	44	40 (−4)	83 (76)
Estonia		49	9		18		
Hungary	65 (58)	78	39	24 (−16)	59	47 (20)	71 (60)
Latvia		61	9		11		
Lithuania		31	13		17		
Poland	40 (−5)		12	31 (−18)		50 (13)	81 (70)
Russia	56 (41)	26	12	25 (−16)	14	24 (−27)	67 (56)
Slovenia	49 (11)	84	31	29 (−19)	62	54 (28)	69 (53)
Israel	43 (21)			53 (28)		31 (−22)	61 (37)
Turkey		50	26		44		
Argentina		53	29		29		
Brazil		63	30		47		
Chile		71	40		57		
Mexico		62	30		30		
Nigeria		70	66		63		

Source: Data in 1993–94 columns are from ISSP 1993; data in 1990–93 columns from Inglehart, Basañez, and Moreno 1998; V15–V17.

Note: Parenthetical entries subtract those who thought that worry or anxiety were not excessive, thought that growth did harm the environment, thought that economic concerns were not being slighted, and thought that growth was not necessary for their country to protect the environment from those with the views described subsequently (the entries that are not in parentheses). Under worry, unparenthesized entries are for those who agreed that "People worry too much about human progress harming the environment." Under anxiety, they are for those who agreed that "all the talk about pollution makes people too anxious." Under urgency, they are for those who agreed that "Protecting the environment and fighting pollution is less urgent than often suggested." Under growth need not harm the environment, they are for those who disagreed with the statement that "Economic growth always harms the environment." Under employment harmed by environmental protection, they are for those who agreed that "If we want to combat unemployment in this country, we shall just have to accept environmental problems." Under economy underemphasized, they are for those agreeing that "We worry too much about the future of the environment and not enough about prices and jobs today" (in Japan, "and not enough about recession"). For the last column, entries are those agreeing that "To protect the environment, our country needs economic growth."

than costs jobs (European Commission, *What Do Europeans Think* 1999).

Of course, even citizens seeing a tension between increased prosperity and environmental quality could favor maintaining current degrees of emphasis on the latter. For the mid-1990s, the margin with that view is indicated by the parenthetical numbers in the "economy underemphasized" column of table 7.1. Views that the relative emphasis was sufficient predominated only in Canada, Japan, Australia, New Zealand, West Germany, the Netherlands, Norway, Russia, and Israel.[12] Perhaps more tellingly, responses to questions about whether growth in general should have priority over environmental quality (with no explicit reference to costs) have usually rejected that policy posture. That has been true in the United States, Japan, Western Europe, India, Thailand, Latin America, Australia, Korea, and urban China.[13] Yet all the EU publics in 2002 had massive majorities feeling that the environment was being shortchanged in policy decisions about "the economy and employment." To complicate the message drawn earlier, some but not all publics apparently tend to react negatively to a policy posture that explicitly subordinates environmental considerations to broad national economic ones. As a result, national policies that do so may not play well politically. Yet even those publics often do not want the opposite priority either—in effect, a desire to have one's cake and eat it too.

The limits on warranted expectations of what environmentally friendly contributions publics will permit also need to be seen relative to other problems competing for policy attention. Questions about what is "the most important problem" or several "most important problems" facing a respondent's nation can provide that perspective. When three or fewer responses were permitted, the environment was almost never ranked highly.[14] When the most serious national problem is placed in the future, as in a 1995 poll, majorities did pick the environment in the United Kingdom and Germany but did not do so in France, the United States, or Japan (Hastings and Hastings 1994–95, 654).

With regard to the most important problem for the EU, observations spanning several decades appear in the first three columns of table 7.2. For many of them, the percentages are in the same low range as those already mentioned. They were clearly higher throughout only for Denmark and the Netherlands and recently for Finland and Sweden, although those for Germany, Luxembourg, and the United Kingdom were marginally higher than those of most non-European publics.

A less demanding form of question checks if publics, in effect, think environmental protection needs substantial policy attention—is it for their country or international grouping a priority, urgent, critical, serious, or among the most important problems? Returning to table 7.1, we see that in the early 1990s only modest minorities in any country except Nigeria thought the urgency of environmental problems was overstated. Further, in 1996, polling of seventeen countries south of the United States found very large majorities in each believing that environmental problems were already urgent (Hastings and Hastings 1996–97, 638–39). This has also been a widely prevalent view among publics and elites in EU countries(as shown in the last three columns of table 7.2). Yet West European publics' view of urgency declined in the later 1990s, especially in Belgium, France, and Ireland. Further, only 5 percent of elites mentioned the environment when asked in 1996 "for the next few years, which are the most serious problems and issues facing the EU?" (Spence 1996). While absolute identification as a priority is massive in table 7.2, further examination of those and other polls refines that judgment.

TABLE 7.2. Environmental Protection and the EU

	Most Important Problem			A Priority		F Elites 1996, Score	Urgent Now		
	A 1974 %	B 1993 %	C 1998 %	D 1998 %	E 2001 %		G 1986 %	H 1992 %	I 1999 %
Belgium	5	8	5	73	83	8.0	62	85	55
Denmark	11	33	29	97	95	8.4	77	87	70
France	5	6	6	87	89	7.4	56	80	52
Germany			10	81	83	7.9		89	70
West Germany	3		12				89		70
Greece		8	3	98	95	9.2	84	97	91
Ireland	3	5	7	92	90	8.5	56	70	56
Italy	2	8	6	85	89	8.6	85	91	80
Luxembourg	6	14	11	89	93	8.1	83	83	68
Netherlands	11	28	18	87	88	8.0	63	84	70
United Kingdom	4	14	14	88	85	7.7	67	82	66
Portugal		5	5	86	92	8.3	71	73	82
Spain		3	5	86	88	8.4	72	82	73
Austria			9	79	83	8.1			67
Finland			19	87	86	8.1			74
Sweden			34	96	97	8.8			87

Source: Data for A, C, and D from Eurobarometer, no. 50 (1998); for B from Hastings and Hastings 1993–94, 580; for E from Eurobarometer, no. 56 (2001); for F from Spence 1996; for G and H from Hastings and Hastings 1986–87, 583; 1992–93, 596; for I from Eurobarometer, no. 51 (1999).

Note: Responses in columns A–C are those of the publics picking the environment as the most important common problem; D and E are those of the publics choosing the environment as one of a number of possible priorities for common activity; F presents the scale scores on degree of priority accorded by elites on a scale with 10 as the highest to one as the lowest; G–I, the percentages of publics viewing environmental protection as "an immediate and urgent problem."

First, only very few members of each European public would deny priority standing for the environment. Second, it ranks in the middle of a set of issues for priority, being at or near the top only in Denmark, Sweden, the Netherlands, Finland, and the United Kingdom (Eurobarometer, nos. 51 [1999], 56 [2001]). That finding argues against a surge beyond current support for EU environmental-protection actions, as do the smaller majorities giving it priority among the candidate countries (European Commission, "Candidate Countries Eurobarometer" 2002).

Overall, when asked only about the environment as a national problem, a wide range of publics provide majorities viewing it as serious, important, or a priority.[15] Yet those percentages either tended to decline when the environment was put in the context of other problems or were less than those accorded to other problems.[16] Recent illustrations appear in two multinational polls as shown in tables 7.3 and 7.4 for national water-quality problems and threats to national interests from global warming. Our surmised shift from higher priority in isolation than in competition with other issues fits with the predominant tendency of shifts for both national water quality and global warming threats to lower-priority rankings than the initial priority-according percentages might lead one to expect.

TABLE 7.3. National Seriousness of Environmental Problems, 2002: Poor Water Quality among Very Big Problems

	High Rank (1–2)	Medium Rank (4–6)	Low Rank (7–10)
50% or more		Angola, Bangladesh, Guatemala, Honduras, India, Ivory Coast, Mali, Mexico, Nigeria, Senegal, Uganda	Pakistan, South Africa
33–49%	South Korea	France, Japan, Kenya, Lebanon, Tanzania, Uzbekistan, Ukraine	Bolivia, Brazil, Ghana, Italy, Peru, Philippines, Russia, Turkey, Venezuela
Less than 33%	Jordan	Czech Republic	Bulgaria, Canada, Germany, United Kingdom, Indonesia, Poland, Slovak Republic, United States

Source: Data from Pew Research Center 2002.

Note: Entries are for percentages saying that water quality was for their country a very big problem, and ranks reflect that percentage in relation to the nine other possibilities asked of respondents: crime, ethnic conflict, corrupt political leaders, moral decline, terrorism, spread of HIV/AIDS, poor-quality schools, immigration, and people leaving the country for jobs. Queries used for environmental problems did not place the items in explicit competition with each other.

The entries in table 7.3 also suggest that publics in much of the South will be more supportive of water-quality improvement efforts than those in much of the North. The result is not encouraging in terms of a perceived private element of benefit from contributions for most northern politicians (with the possible exceptions of France and Japan). As for global warming, we see greater demand from West European publics than from the American public. Because American elites are much less likely to view global warming as a critical threat than the U.S. public, there may well be a special degree of friction between them and West European publics (and possibly elites) on that issue (Chicago Council and Marshall Fund 2002).

What about the importance and priority of the environment as an international rather than national problem?[17] In 1994, with several responses permitted, publics in the United States, Japan, Germany, and the United Kingdom chose the environment as among the "most serious current world problems" to only a very small extent: 2 percent in the United States, and in the 10–12 percent range in the other countries (Hastings and Hastings 1994–95, 619). When the question was about the future, the numbers jumped to majorities in Japan and Germany; the U.S. percentage remained the smallest (Hastings and Hastings 1992–93, 680). In 1999, only 6 percent of the American public chose the environment as the "most important problem facing the world in the 21st century" (PIPA 2001). A 2002 multinational poll provides more recent readings on a far larger set of countries, as noted in chapter 3. Results in terms of the percentage viewing "pollution and other environmental problems" as one of the two greatest threats to the

TABLE 7.4. National Seriousness of Environmental Problems, 2002: Global Warming as a Threat to Vital National Interests

	High Rank (1–3)	Medium Rank (4–6)	Low Rank (7–11)
50% or more	France, Italy	United Kingdom	
33–49%		Germany, Netherlands	United States
Less than 33%		Poland	

Source: Data from Chicago Council and Marshall Fund 2002.
Note: Entries are for the percentages saying that global warming was either a "critical" or "extremely important" threat to their country's vital interests in the next ten years. Ranks reflect that percentage in relation to the ten other possibilities asked of respondents: political turmoil in Russia, economic competition from Europe or the United States, the development of China as a world power, Islamic fundamentalism, international terrorism, large number of immigrants and incoming refugees, globalization, military conflict between Israel and its Arab neighbors, Iraq developing weapons of mass destruction, and tensions between India and Pakistan. The queries used for environmental problems did not place the items in explicit competition with each other.

world today and its rank among the five problems offered to respondents appear in table 7.5.

Of the countries polled in 1992 and 1994, the results a decade later suggest a more prevalent view of the importance of environmental problems. Also, a clear gap had opened between Japan in that respect (urgency) and Germany and the United Kingdom, with the United States still relatively indifferent. The entries in this table contrast with those in tables 7.3 and 7.4 in several respects, with implications for public demand for environmental contributions and international coalitions. First, most southern publics express less concern or priority for world environmental problems than they did for national water quality. Second, percentages seem, if anything, to show less priority than the rankings. Third, there is a larger potential support club across regions other than Africa and levels of national development and international significance.

As a practical policy matter, we expect politicians also to take into account the importance and priority given to or withheld from particular environmental issues. We suggest that international collective action is more likely for those topics granted particular importance and priority by many publics and by clubs whose publics resemble each other in those terms.

TABLE 7.5. The Dangerousness for the World of Environmental Problems, 2002

	High Rank (1–2)	Medium Rank (3)	Low Rank (4–5)
50% or more	China, Japan, South Korea, Ukraine		
33–49%	Bolivia, Canada, Czech Republic, Guatemala, Honduras, Philippines, Vietnam	Italy, Jordan, Mexico, Peru, Russia, Venezuela	Slovak Republic
Less than 33%		United Kingdom	Angola, Argentina, Bangladesh, Brazil, Bulgaria, France, Germany, Ghana, India, Indonesia, Ivory Coast, Kenya, Lebanon, Mali, Nigeria, Pakistan, Poland, Senegal, South Africa, Tanzania, Turkey, Uganda, United States, Uzbekistan

Source: Data from Pew Research Center 2002a.
Note: Percentages are those saying that pollution and other environmental problems pose either the first or second "greatest threat to the world." Ranks reflect those percentages relative to the four other "dangers in the world today" posed to respondents: nuclear weapons, religious and ethnic hatred, infectious diseases/AIDS, and the rich-poor gap. The items are in explicit competition with each other.

A 1992 poll in twenty-two countries diverse in location and level of economic development found more emphasis on air pollution followed by water quality than on waste disposal and natural resource loss (Hastings and Hastings 1992–93, 643). That same year, a poll asked for seriousness judgments in twenty-four countries about air pollution and global warming (Dunlap 1994). More publics provided majority (and large majority) support to the seriousness of air pollution than to that of global warming. The prominence given to air pollution relative to global warming has continued in the U.S. public in polls 1998–2000 (Americans and the World 2003a; Gallup Poll Releases, February 20, 2001; PIPA 2000c). The reason seems to be a perceived lack of urgency about global warming, the lack of felt need for major and costly steps to be taken now versus a less demanding gradualist approach in line with the public shifting the effects of global warming from the present toward the future between 1992 and 2001 (Americans and the World 2003a; Gallup Poll Archives 1997; PIPA 2000c). By contrast, two-thirds of the Japanese public in 2000 saw global warming as the most important world environmental problem (Government Poll Yearbook 2002, 552).

We conclude that most publics pose a complicated permissiveness problem for their political leaders. They do not want the environment ignored, but only minorities often seem to want it really to take priority over other matters. The demand for at least the appearance of action seems especially pronounced in a number of West European countries (most notably, the Nordics, the Netherlands, and the United Kingdom) and possibly Japan and South Korea, although not all to the same degree. Others in the North and the South—and in the East and the West—seem willing to accept some action on some environmental issues. There is, however, little sign of a mounting demand for international collective action (at least beyond the EU), and there are some signs that urgency is, if anything, declining among the Europeans. Finally, and compatibly with recent developments in U.S. policy, there is much less demand from the American public than from publics in the other countries mentioned for major, immediate action to curb global warming or indeed for environmental betterment more generally.

Values and Role Conceptions

Opinion data on values and role conceptions provide another angle of vision on public support for environmental quality. Opinion on these counts may or may not be compatible with views on the more explicit trade-offs and priorities discussed previously. When value concerns and role conceptions emphasize environmental quality more than acceptance of economic and other burdens did, we expect countries and clubs of countries to be particularly active in ways that call little attention to self-interested reasons to reject contribution options. One such possibility involves signing on to good-behavior codes that are more expressions of sentiment than a submission to penalties for noncompliance.

We view dissatisfaction with current levels of environmental quality as an indication of unmet values. Multicountry polling in 1992 suggests the degree that public judgments on national and global environmental quality might provide support for actions to reduce environmental bads. We reason that the more negative the verdict on current national quality, the larger the perceived private bad reduction element from ameliorative steps; by contrast, views that world environmental quality is worse than national quality will lead to perceptions of a relatively large public element. We group the publics into majorities of two-thirds or more, smaller majorities, and minorities based on whether respondents view the quality as bad or fairly bad. The data appear in table 7.6.

Impure-public-goods thinking would not find the 1992 results promising for international collective action given the high overlap between those publics who tended to think of their national situation as not bad and those who thought the world's situation was bad. That expectation would only be strengthened by the more recent large majority of Americans satisfied with the quality of their national environment and the lack of majorities in any of the EU-15 that feel that they have "reason to complain" about the environment where they live (European Commission, "Sustainable Development," 2002; Gallup Poll Release April

TABLE 7.6. Is Current Environmental Quality Bad, 1992?

	National	World
Two-thirds or more	Hungary, Poland, Turkey, Chile, Russia	Japan, United Kingdom, West Germany, Canada, Mexico, Denmark, Finland, Ireland, Netherlands, Norway, Portugal, Switzerland, Hungary, Poland, Chile, Uruguay
Smaller majorities	Mexico, Japan, Philppines, India	United States, Turkey, Brazil, Philppines, India, Russia, South Korea
Minorities	United States, Canada, United Kingdom, West Germany, Denmark, Finland, Ireland, Netherlands, Norway, Portugal, Switzerland, Brazil, Uruguay, Nigeria	Nigeria

Source: Dunlap 1994.

22, 1999). Nor would the lack of overlap in the higher-priority rankings of 2002 in tables 7.3–7.5 offer much in the way of encouragement. Publics' motivation for contributions to reducing environmental bads may have to rest on other value and role conceptions.

Value concerns in the present can also reflect views of national environmental quality trends with optimistic or pessimistic implications for the future, with the former implying a less substantial private-element incentive for increased contributions. Data are available for the United States, the United Kingdom, Germany, and Japan. The American public stands out for majorities seeing "progress" in "dealing with environmental problems in the past few decades" ("Gallup Poll Topics: A–Z Environment" 2000). In five surveys (1990, 1991, 1995, 1999, 2000), more than 75 percent of respondents saw "a great deal" or "some progress." Those seeing a "great deal" increased steadily.

The Japanese public was divided almost evenly in 1993 and 1996 on whether environmental quality in their country had improved or worsened (JPOLL, various years). When given the choice of whether environmental quality would improve, stay the same, or worsen in the future (1990, 1996, 1997), the percentage expecting it to worsen declined sharply, to about one-fourth (Hastings and Hastings 1991–92, 112–13; 1997–98, 112; JPOLL, various years). Other evidence suggests the prevalence of a pessimistic view. When given only a better/worse choice (1992, 1993, 1997), the pessimistic view predominated (Hastings and Hastings 1992–93, 102; 1997–98, 113; JPOLL, various years). Annual polls repeatedly show that, unlike most other aspects of Japanese life, the country is seen as headed in a worse rather than a better direction with respect to environmental quality (JPOLL, various years).[18]

German public opinion had a plurality (1997) that believed that the country had made "a little progress"; like the United States several years later, about a third of respondents saw a lot of progress. In Britain, the public in 1990 had substantial majorities seeing a worsening of air and water quality from the past to the survey but was divided on whether conditions would improve in the future. Pessimism about environmental quality in general was the majority view several years later (1993) (Hastings and Hastings 1991–92, 107–8; 1993–94, 102). We suggest that the U.S. public, compared to the others discussed, would provide less support for a sharp departure upward in environmental protection efforts.

A clear linkage between environmental bads and value concerns marks the extent to which factors widely thought hazardous to the environment are also thought dangerous for the respondent and his or her family. That linkage was very pronounced in the twenty-country

1993–94 polling (ISSP 1995). The environmental hazards posed were those of: "air pollution caused by cars," "nuclear power stations," "air pollution caused by industry," "pesticides and chemicals used in farming," "pollution of your country's rivers, lakes, and streams," and a "rise in the world's temperatures caused by the 'greenhouse gas effect.'" Near unanimity prevailed on each being an environmental hazard, and majorities always greater than 60 percent thought each threat more dangerous personally. These perceptions of negative effects were also found in numerous other polls.[19]

It is noteworthy that the U.S. public departed from the general pattern with respect to global warming and the greenhouse gas effect. Americans' acknowledgment of negative current health effects flipped from about a two-third majority (1993–95) to the opposite in 1997, although the shift for future health effects was less drastic (Gallup Poll Archives 1997; Hastings and Hastings 1993–94, 114; 1994–95, 125; 1997–98, 115).

Perhaps a weaker indication of value shortfall involving the environment may be an expression of feelings of "worry" about environmental quality in general or specific environmental problems. As reported in table 7.1, only minorities in the OECD countries thought general environmental worry to be excessive. Views on excessive anxiety, perhaps a stronger sentiment, were more diverse and, when the same national public was polled for both questions, those viewing anxiety as excessive were usually more numerous than the question about worry.[20]

Other polling finds that feelings of worry or concern predominate both for the environment in general and for at least some, if not all, particular environmental problems. This stance characterizes the publics of the EU-15 for a host of issues and has recently increased for many of them; it has been joined by majority opposition to food-related uses of biotechnology and genetic modification.[21] Large Canadian majorities expressed sustained concern for all problems posed to them in 1989, 1990, 1992, and 1994.[22] Majorities of Japanese respondents expressed concern for the environment in general (1990, 1992, 1997) and for numerous particular issues in 1992 and 2000.[23] Americans fit the same pattern ("Gallup Poll Topics: A–Z Environment" 2000). As recently as 2001, more than three-fourths admitted to a "great deal" or "fair amount' of worrying about environmental quality (Gallup Poll Release, March 16, 2001). For over a decade (1989–2000), such has also been the case for water and air pollution, toxic waste contamination, and loss of natural wildlife habitat. By 1999, worry had reached a similar level for damage to the ozone layer, loss of rain forests, radioactive contamination from nuclear facilities; as of 2000, worry about species loss also reached that level. Smaller majorities expressed such concern about acid rain and, by 2000, global warming though, with smaller shares worrying "a great deal."

There is clearly widespread concern that the environment is at risk. That, like earlier conclusions, suggests a lack of public permission for apparent governmental indifference to environmental concerns and indeed fits with the general support for governments doing more, as noted earlier.

Public permission for contributions to reduce environmental bads can, as we have suggested in earlier chapters, also stem from views of rights and obligations in the sense of responsibility for outcomes. Views on those matters imply an appropriate national or club role in working toward reductions. Publics who view their country or club as especially responsible for international bads are, we think, likely to be more accepting of the burden of contributions to reduce those bads. People who view the bads as primarily the fault of others are likely to view the contribution burden as appropriately falling on those others. Those who see bads as stemming equally from both their actions and those of others are likely to favor a shared burden of remediation. We explore these considerations beginning with multinational polling in 1991 and then turn to more fragmentary recent data.

When asked who was responsible for world environmental problems, majorities attributed primary responsibility to the AICs of the North only in Denmark, Finland, West Germany, the Netherlands, and Norway.[24] Only pluralities did so in Japan, Korea, Poland, and Turkey. The view of developing nations having equal responsibility was accepted by majorities in Canada, Mexico, the United States, Hungary, Portugal, the United Kingdom, Brazil, Chile, the Philippines, and Russia and by a substantial plurality in India (Hastings and Hastings 1992–93, 108–9). We suggest that publics in the first group would have been more likely to support contributions to environmental quality despite what the developing countries do. Those in the second group would have been inclined to want some effort by the South. Those in the third group might accept matching bads-reduction burdens for the North and the South but not especially heavy burdens on the North.

At least with respect to natural resource depletion, the American and Japanese publics do seem to largely acknowledge responsibility for reducing the environmental burden their nations generate (Adamson et al. 2000; Hastings and Hastings 1992–93, 90; 1997–98, 111). This suggests that resistance to a special responsibility position should not be confused with rejection of any responsibility by either the Japanese or the American public (Hastings and Hastings 1992–93, 103; 1993–94, 114; JPOLL, various years; PIPA 2000c, 2001).

Whether for reasons of perceived responsibility or for other reasons, publics may be more or less in favor of their nation or club playing a leading role in international environmental collective action. Preferred national activities for the twenty-first century were polled in 1995, with contributions to environmental protection being designated by a large majority in Germany, a near majority in the United Kingdom, and minorities of less than 40 percent in Japan, France, and the United States (Hastings and Hastings 1995–96, 123). Other data suggest Japanese public preferences for a much greater emphasis in their international role. Recalling chapter 3, the most preferred international role was contributing to "preserving the global environment" (1991–2000), and the second-most-preferred emphasis was UN activities (1991–2000). Many other polls (1990–97) show such preferences as well as one for an increase in such efforts.[25] In recent years, those preferences have been less for leadership than for a club approach (JPOLL, various years), a stance fitting with the general inclinations reported in chapter 3.

As with foreign aid, Japanese-sponsored polling abroad stands out for trying to ascertain what contributions would do for international relations with others. The stronger the desire attributed to others for environmental contributions from Japan, the greater the private benefit element the Japanese might attribute to making those contributions. In that sense, in the mid-1990s, substantial and growing minorities often encouraged Japanese contributions in China, Thailand, Indonesia, Vietnam, the Philippines, Korea, and Malaysia. The Japanese public (1994, 1996) placed environmental protection cooperation near the top of nine possibilities for what Japan should do "to improve relations with Asian countries" (Hastings and Hastings 1994–95, 572; 1995–96, 593, 601, 609; 1996–97, 608; 1997–98, 199).[26] International environmental protection contributions and cooperation may then have been seen as useful in pursuing several of the concerns attributed to the Japanese public in chapter 3: avoiding isolation and improving relations with both North Atlantic and Asian countries.

With regard to Europe, environmental protection has long been one of the issue areas most identified for internationalization (joint national and EU management).[27] In 1996, more than 75 percent of the public in each of the EU-15 thought it "really important" to have "common laws" for environmental protection within the EU (Eurobarometer, no. 46, 1996). In 2002, the EU level of governance was preferred to any other level in eight of the member publics (European Opinion Research Group 2001). The European publics seem to have desired to have the environment constitute a central piece of club business, to have the Germans stake some claim to particular leadership on the subject, and to be divided about whether national initiatives should be hostage to whatever zeal other European governments might manifest (European Commission, *What Do Europeans Think* 1999). We have already noted the stronger support for contributions on a variety of bases in a number of the EU countries than elsewhere.

How has U.S. public opinion on the American role with regard to environmental protection compared with that of Japanese and European publics? Part of the answer can be found by returning to chapter 3. "Improving the global environment" was from 1990 to 2002 a "very important foreign policy goal" for the American public. As of 2002 it had increased from the narrow majorities of much of the 1990s but had not returned to the level of support of 1990. For elites, a decline occurred after 1990 and continued through 2002, falling well below a majority level. Other aspects of American public opinion on an approach to international environmental protection are also consonant with themes developed in chapter 3. There was a predominant conviction that any solution must be multilateral and must get "all countries involved in addressing the problems" (1999 in PIPA 2000b). In line with the positive position about granting some authority for international organizations seen in chapter 3, only one-third (1999) accepted the view that "there should not be an international body that tells countries what to do" on environmental matters. A large majority (also in 1999) thought that the World Trade Organization should consider environmental matters when making trade decisions (PIPA 2001), and very large elite and public majorities thought it appropriate to make minimum environmental protection standards part of international trade agreements (Chicago Council and Marshall Fund 2002). Poll results were contradictory on leadership when distinguishing between unilateral initiatives as distinct from matching what others were willing to do. In some polls, preferred multilateralism takes the form of obligations on the part of the developing world as well, especially for such countries as "China, India, and Mexico" (polls in 1997, 1998, and 2001).[28] In other polls (1998 and 2001), majorities thought that the United States should reduce emissions either unilaterally or in a coalition of the willing (Americans and the World 2003a).

These results leave considerable ambiguity about what policy leeway on emission reductions associated with global warming the public is willing to provide to an American administration. Opinion on the Kyoto agreement and on pertinent George W. Bush administration policies may provide some clarification. The American public was queried on support for participation in the Kyoto agreement ten times from 1997 to 2002 with substantial favorable majorities in ten of those instances.[29] The public was asked to evaluate the U.S. rejection of the agreement in five instances in 2001–2, and in each case, small majorities or large pluralities opposed withdrawal. These results are compatible with the tendency, demonstrated in polls in 1997–98, for a preponderant plurality to think that the agreement did not go far enough toward emission reduction and with the preponderantly negative view of the 2001 American government decision not to impose a reduction unilaterally on carbon dioxide emissions (Americans and the World 2003a). In short, public permission for U.S. participation in the Kyoto process seems to be present and continuing.

The American public has recently shown some signs of awareness of the possibility that others were more environmentally proactive and of agreeing that those positions were acceptable. A public plurality thought that "the countries of the European Union . . . generate less pollution and greenhouse gases per person than the U.S." (PIPA 2001). And, in 2002, large elite and public majorities accepted the right of the EU and Japan to require genetic-modification labeling of U.S. products they might import even if doing so would cut into U.S. exports (Chicago Council and Marshall Fund 2002).

There are also signs that assumptions of independent, nationally determined moral responsibility about the environment were thought to provide appropriate grounds for unilateral proenvironment standard setting by the United States. In 1999, majorities supported trade sanctions on nations threatening sea life as well as the right of countries to "restrict the imports of products if they are produced in a way that damages the environment." As we see in our discussion of standards in chapter 3, this moralism can include American obligations as well as rights—here for environmental protection matters. A large majority agreed that it "just isn't right" for the United States to use international emission permit trading "to try to buy our way out of the responsibility to clean up our share" of greenhouses gases and agreed that it was "a bad idea because it would allow rich countries to pay for reducing emissions abroad while doing less to reduce them at home" (1998 polling in PIPA 2000c). In more general questioning on environmental conduct, a large majority said that "it would be wrong for American companies to do . . . in other countries . . . something to the environment which is wrong inside the U.S." (1999 polling in PIPA 2001).

Claims to the high ground of national right may be facilitated by the previously noted American public rejection of a necessity for choice between economic self-interest and environmental protection. That view may, of course, seem at best naive and at worst deceptive to those in the world who fail to see how they too can simultaneously have both environmental quality and economic growth.

The role conceptions we have reviewed seem to suggest an American public not so much hostile as erratic and conflicted in its support for international cooperation and contributions to environmental protection.[30] We also see a Japanese public more disposed toward both but not disposed to leadership. The public opinion base in domestic politics for consistent leadership seems stronger in several West European countries (Germany, the Netherlands, the Nordics, and the United Kingdom), although it may have reached its peak.

Summarizing the Perceived Benefits and Costs of Environmental Protection

In both the North and the South, contributions to environmental protection are widely viewed as desirable in light of the risks associated with environmental deterioration and of desires to reduce those current and potential bads. Accordingly, making contributions is declared as in principle worth foregoing economic gains but seems to lose that edge when associated with direct, large private economic losses. For general publics, the edge is more readily maintained when the protection measures are not directly linked to such private losses, thus favoring regulatory measures and especially ones impacting industry more directly than individuals.

In general, majorities have been aware of bads associated with environmental damage at home and abroad, now and in the future. Majorities, however, have not been convinced that those bads were or would become sufficiently great to warrant policies chosen solely to avoid adverse environmental consequences. Several European publics come closest to providing exceptions. Also, those most aware of bads were not always the same from environmental issue to issue, as shown in tables 7.3–7.6. This suggests evolving and continually realigning coalitions of initiative takers, relatively compliant followers, and reluctant others relating to protection measures for a continually changing set of issues and problems. For example, some national publics did not take consistent majority or plurality positions for initiative or delay on both air pollution (more a private element) and global warming (more a public element). The domestic politics of policy support and action may lend themselves less to across-the-board contributions than to a fluid, issue varying set of contributors who fade in and out of favoring tangible contributions to particular environmental protection measures.

While recognition of world environmental problems has been widely shared, there has been much less agreement between national publics on the locus of responsibility for those problems. Judgments in that respect suggest differing degrees of emphasis on free riding and the private element associated with contributions. Those most inclined to accept responsibility were often not those most concerned with the private national element of environmental quality—for example, a number of the European countries with particularly large environmental activist minorities. It remains to be seen if their views have or will overcome other public priorities for the EU. Even further, the lack of zeal for environmental policy on the part of some current and soon-to-be EU members with different domestic political pressures will also require some policy navigation. Our data review suggests the strength in many West European publics of attitudes supporting contributions for private, club, and public element reasons. The United States, if anything, showed a decline in such sentiments in recent years and seems at best to have reached a plateau in such support. This should not be confused, however, with support for rolling back promised environmental protection efforts. The Japanese public seems strongly supportive within the constraints of its general notions of Japan's character and might well be disposed to cooperate in an isolation-avoiding and relationship-facilitating fashion, especially if both the United States and the EU were to take the lead.

EXAMINING ACTUAL CONTRIBUTIONS

The previous discussion sets the stage for us to examine what has actually been done in terms of three broad types of contributions to environmental quality: (1) financial contributions; (2) international environmental policy action, including participation in relevant international agreements and programs to preserve existing ecosystems; and (3) restraint in the production of environmental hazards and depletion of nonrenewable resources. Our analysis is limited with regard to the universe of countries affecting the environment (because of our focus on countries where substantial comparable information over time is most available) and with regard to environmentally relevant indicators (because of our decision to select indicators that either provide broad rather than narrow measures of environmental contributions or illuminate key contributions to the reduction or exacerbation of global climate change). These compromises seem appropriate given our special interest in contributions from the North and the largely nonexcludable harms posed by global warming.

Financial Contributions

Financial contributions to environmental quality include both national efforts and contributions to international activities. For the former, we consider public-sector R&D spending on the environment and public-sector spending for pollution abatement and control.

R&D. Table 7.7 displays data on OECD-country public-sector environmental R&D spending. The shares of a country's spending allocated to environmental challenges appear in the first four columns, followed by percentage changes in those budgets. Germany and the United States lead in national public-sector R&D emphasis on the environment, followed by France in recent years. Canada, the United Kingdom, and Italy are in a second tier. The Japanese share was strikingly low before 1998, when the country joined the second tier. As for changes in absolute

TABLE 7.7. Public Sector Environmental R&D Spending

	National Environmental Share (%)				Change National Budget (%)		
	1985	1990	1995	1998	1985–90	1990–95	1995–98
Canada	4.8	3.3	3.7	6.6	3.7	29.8	−14.1
Mexico		0.7	0.3	1.0		51.2	129.5
United States	27.6	23.2	24.5	39.7	28.0	21.2	11.4
Japan		2.7	3.5	6.7		46.9	31.5
Australia	2.6	2.7	2.6		56.3	−15.1	
New Zealand		0.4					
Austria	0.5	0.8	1.1	1.5	159.3	65.0	−11.5
Belgium	1.9	0.5	0.8	1.6	57.3	83.9	27.5
Denmark	0.6	1.4	1.5	2.2	276.5	19.5	0.1
Finland	0.6	0.6	1.0	1.7	37.5	110.1	11.5
France	5.2	5.4	11.7	18.3	60.1	147.9	7.2
Germany	31.8	24.8	22.5		18.7	4.1	
Greece	0.5	0.4	0.4		−1.6	2.9	
Iceland			0.1	0.1			17.6
Ireland	0.1	0.1	0.1		40	57.1	
Italy	4.9	9.0	7.0		180.6	−10.0	
Netherlands	5.3	4.9	4.4	7.2	41.8	2.2	13.4
Norway	1.0	1.2	1.1	1.8	79.0	4.7	17.7
Portugal		0.7	0.4	2.5		−24.3	49.8
Spain	0.5	6.3	3.4	4.4	1970.4	−42.6	24.5
Sweden	2.1	3.2	2.0	0.8	93.0	−26.8	−72.6
Switzerland		1.1					
United Kingdom	10.1	6.6	7.3		0.5	33.7	

Source: Data from OECD, *Environmental Data* 1997, 1999.

effort, we note a general tendency for very substantial increases between 1985 and 1998 but a slackening rate of increase in more recent years for many countries. Sustained increasers over the three time periods were limited to the United States, Belgium, Finland, France, the Netherlands, and Norway, with Denmark in that category to a smaller degree. If missing data showed growth, possible additional states would be Japan, Germany, and the United Kingdom. Of course, national traditions about emphasis on R&D and on public-sector R&D differ, as do funding availabilities with shifting government revenues.

Pollution Abatement and Control. Partial data on public-sector spending on pollution abatement and control are available for OECD countries for the period 1985–98 (OECD, Environmental Data 1997, 1999). Generally, no clear trends are evident, though priority in this area of spending was particularly high throughout the period for Austria, France, and Germany. While the United States trended upward, it still attached less priority throughout than those countries and in 1994 even lagged behind such OECD newcomers as South Korea, the Czech Republic, and Slovakia.

We recognize that priority given to pollution abatement and control is imperfectly reflected in government spending and that a variety of nonbudgetary measures, such as tax incentives, can stimulate private-sector efforts. Very fragmentary data show the United States as a high and increasing contributor in these terms, with approximately matching degrees of priority by Germany and the Netherlands and, for 1994, Korea and in first place the Czech Republic.

Contributions to World Efforts. Table 7.8 contains data on financial contributions by OECD countries to three global environmental efforts: the Multilateral Fund for the Montreal Protocol (MLF), GEF, and the Environmental Fund (EF), which provides the bulk of support for UNEP's operations. None of these are funded on a user-fee basis (unlike the International Maritime Organization) or under general UN allocation formulas for national contributions. None have missions in addition to the environment (unlike the United Nations Development Program or its Fund for Population Activities). The EF data also enable some over-time comparisons.

All of the columns (the MLF for 1995, the GEF for 1996, 1998, and the EF for 1990, 1994, 1996, 2000) show most funding coming from the historical members of the OECD. For the MLF and GEF, the United States is the largest contributor, followed by Japan, Germany, France, the United Kingdom, and Italy. Those six states provided almost two-thirds of the MLF funds and three-quarters of those for the GEF.

The EF presents a more complicated picture. The last four columns show percentages of actual contributions to the EF in 1990, 1994, 1996, and 2000. OECD dominance is pronounced (only five nations outside the historic OECD contributed as much as .1 percent of the EF budget for even one year during the 1990s). Concentration in the six countries mentioned previously remained high but was less pronounced in 1990 and 1994, falling to less than 40 percent in 1996 before rebounding to almost 60 percent in 2000. What about individual contributing states? The 1990–96 period had declined greater than the aggregate by the United States, Canada, and the Netherlands, and total withdrawal by

TABLE 7.8. Contributions to World Efforts: Shares of Total Budget (in percentages)

	MLF95	GEF96	GEF98	EF90	EF94	EF96	EF00
Canada	3.65	4.28	4.43	1.83	2.44	.77	1.85
United States	22.52	21.26	21.59	22.28	31.87	14.66	17.71
Japan	14.62	20.50	20.72	13.35	13.86		11.12
Australia	1.78	1.47	1.62	0.67	1.13	1.23	0.73
New Zealand	0.28	0.28	0.28				0.13
Austria	0.88	1.00	1.01	0.87	0.76	1.16	0.91
Belgium	1.24		1.72	0.66	0.66		1.24
Denmark	0.77	1.76	1.44	1.11	3.00	4.93	3.96
Finland	0.67	1.09	1.11	4.12	4.91	4.07	6.23
France	7.04	7.08	7.27	3.42	3.04		2.01
Germany	10.48	11.87	11.05	11.30	8.61	13.11	11.99
Greece	0.41	0.25	0.28				0.06
Ireland	0.21	0.12	0.28	0.17	0.14	0.30	0.26
Italy	5.04	5.67	4.54	0.61	1.96		1.18
Netherlands	1.76	3.53	3.66	2.54	2.83	1.02	6.19
Norway	0.65	1.52	1.57	3.87	3.17	4.81	4.35
Portugal	0.23	0.3	0.28				
Spain	2.32	0.86	0.83	1.15	0.96		1.38
Sweden	1.30	2.88	2.90	5.47	4.00	6.14	3.61
Switzerland	1.30	2.25	2.20	2.32	4.04	6.66	5.11
United Kingdom	5.89	6.65	6.98	11.02	9.34	11.71	15.43
Subtotal	83.04	94.62	95.76	86.76	96.72	70.57	95.39
Russian Federation			0.28	11.6	0.16		0.86
Poland					0.15	0.21	0.24
Republic of Korea			0.28	0.05	0.15	0.17	0.37
China			0.41	0.21	0.19		0.44
Kuwait				0.40	0.30		
Total			96.73	99.02	97.67	70.95	97.3

Source: Data from Begerson and Parmann 1996, 1997, 2000; UNEP Communication, February 11, 1998.

Japan, Belgium, France, Italy, Spain, Russia, China, and Kuwait. It also had increases from Switzerland, Denmark, Australia, Ireland, Poland, and Korea and more modest declines by Germany, Sweden, Norway, and Austria. More recently, U.S. contributions moved upward but did so to a smaller degree than those of Japan, Belgium, Finland, France, Italy, the Netherlands, the United Kingdom, Russia, Korea, and China. Some others, however, declined. Many countries were apparently making their contributions on a basis other than emulating those of the United States (Bergerson and Parmann 1996, 1997, 2000; UNEP Communication, February 11, 1998).

International Environmental Policy Action

A different form of support for environmental quality involves participation in intergovernmental environmental agreements. We examine participation at the end of 2000 for the agreements shown in box 7.1.[31] Table 7.9 displays state scores for agreement participation. There is a pronounced fit between the states that were shown as especially forthcoming on the financial measures discussed previously and those with high levels of involvement in this form of international collective action. In a preliminary way, we can conclude that money and action go together on environmental issues. That is, the West Europeans stand out, while the United States is in a lower though still active category. The U.S. grouping also includes many former Soviet bloc states. Japan lags further behind the United States and other AICs. The lowest scores are predominantly held by developing countries, fitting with the widespread concern that exists about the potential environmental threats posed by such countries' inaction on environmental matters.

Unilateral Protections. Globally beneficial contributions may be made unilaterally as well as multilaterally. One aspect of those unilateral actions consists of national steps to protect particular portions of ecosystems under a state's control. This measure of unilateral action is shown in figure 7.1, focusing on that part of a state's total land area that is protected under the management categories defined by the International Union for Conservation of Nature and Natural Resources.[32]

Austria, Denmark, Germany, New Zealand, Switzerland, and the United Kingdom are the leaders by this measure of environmental contribution. A second group comprises France and the United States. Other countries lag a bit further behind. Of the first group, it is interesting to note that each country is relatively small in landmass, suggesting that the protection areas have greater significance given limited

BOX 7.1. Environmental Agreements Indexed in Table 7.9

General Environmental Concerns
- Convention on Access to Information, Public Participation in Decision Making, and Access to Justice in Environmental Matters
- Convention on Environmental Impact Assessment in a Transboundary Context

Atmosphere
- Aircraft Engine Emissions
- Convention on Long-Range Transboundary Air Pollution
  - 1994 Sulfur Protocol
  - 1988 Nitrous Oxides Protocol
  - 1991 Volatile Organic Compounds Protocol
  - 1998 Heavy Metals Protocol
  - 1998 Persistent Organic Pollutants Protocol
- Vienna Convention for the Protection of the Ozone Layer and three additions
  - Montreal Protocol
  - London Amendment
  - Copenhagen Amendment
- UN Framework Convention on Climate Change
  - Kyoto Protocol

Hazardous Substances
- Convention on Civil Liability for Damage Caused during Carriage of Dangerous Goods by Road, Rail, and Inland Navigation Vessels
- Convention on the Control of Transboundary Movements of Hazardous Wastes (Basel Convention)
- Food Agricultural Organization (FAO) International Code of Conduct on the Distribution and Use of Pesticides
- Convention on the Ban of the Import into Africa and the Control of Transboundary Movements and Management of Hazardous Wastes within Africa (Bamako Convention)
- Convention on the Prior Informed Consent Procedure for Certain Hazardous Chemicals and Pesticides in International Trade
- Convention to Ban the Importation into Forum Island Countries of Hazardous and Radioactive Wastes and to Control the Transboundary Movement and Management of Hazardous Wastes within the South Pacific Region (Waigani Convention)

(continues)

- Convention on the Transboundary Effects of Industrial Accidents
- European Agreement Concerning the International Carriage of Dangerous Goods by Road

Marine Environment
- Convention on the Prevention of Marine Pollution by Dumping (London Convention)
  - 1996 Protocol
- International Convention for the Prevention of Pollution from Ships
- International Convention on Civil Liability for Oil Pollution Damage
  - 1992 Protocol
- International Convention on Oil Pollution Preparedness, Response, and Cooperation
- International Fund for Compensation for Oil Pollution Damage
  - 1992 Fund Protocol
- International Convention Relating to Intervention on the High Seas in Cases of Oil Pollution Casualties
- United Nations Convention on the Law of the Sea
- International Convention on Liability and Compensation for Damage in Connection with the Carriage of Hazardous and Noxious Substances
- Convention for the Protection of the Marine Environment of the Northeast Atlantic
- Convention for the Protection of the Marine Environment of the Baltic Region (1992 Helsinki Convention)
- 1974 Helsinki Convention
- Conventions within the UNEP Regional Seas Programme
  - Black Sea
  - Wider Caribbean Region
  - Eastern African Region
  - Kuwait Region
  - Mediterranean Region
  - Red Sea and Gulf of Aden
  - South Pacific Region
  - Southeast Pacific
  - West and Central African Region

Marine Living Resources
- Convention on the Conservation of Antarctic Marine Living Resources

- International Convention for the Conservation of Atlantic Tunas
- International Convention for the Regulation of Whaling

Nature Conservation and Terrestrial Living Resources
- Antarctic Treaty
  - Madrid Protocol
- World Heritage Convention
- Convention on the Conservation of Migratory Species of Wild Animals
- Convention on International Trade in Endangered Species of Wild Fauna and Flora
- Convention on Wetlands of International Importance (Ramsar Convention)
- Food Agricultural Organization (FAO) International Undertaking on Plant Genetic Resources
- Convention on Biological Diversity
- Convention to Combat Desertification
- International Tropical Timber Agreement

Nuclear Safety
- Assistance in the Case of a Nuclear Accident or Radiological Emergency
- Convention on Early Notification of a Nuclear Accident
- Vienna Convention on Civil Liability for Nuclear Damage
- Convention on Nuclear Safety

Freshwater Resources
- Convention on the Protection and Use of Transboundary Watercourses and International Lakes

national territory. This is not meant to belittle the contributions made by such geographical giants as Canada and the United States, but it does show the value placed on preserving a significant portion of existing ecosystems by those northern countries with less landmass to devote to environmental preservation.

Comparable data from the World Bank (2001, World Development Indicators) for 1999 show the share of protected land for the high-income countries as greater than those for other income categories. The data also suggest the substantial contributions of this kind (at least on paper) by many other states not included in figure 7.1. The Dominican

TABLE 7.9. Participation in International Governmental Agreements (in percentages)

Most Active (70% or more)	Score	Very Active (60–69%)	Score	Active (50–60%)	Score	Active Tendency (40–50%)	Score
Italy	75.21	Norway	69.23	Poland	58.97	Hungary	49.57
France	74.36	Denmark	66.67	Belgium	58.12	New Zealand	49.57
Germany	73.50	Greece	62.39	Russian Federation	57.26	Chile	48.72
United Kingdom	73.50	Switzerland	62.39	Croatia	55.56	Japan	48.72
Finland	71.79			United States	54.70	Latvia	48.72
Netherlands	71.79			Bulgaria	52.14	Egypt	47.01
Sweden	71.79			Portugal	52.14	Australia	46.15
Spain	70.94			Ireland	51.28	Czech Republic	46.15
				Luxembourg	51.28	Iceland	46.15
				Austria	50.43	Romania	46.15
				Canada	50.43	European Union	46.15
				Slovenia	50.43	Korea	45.30

Less Active (30–40%)	Score			Active (50–60%)	Score	Active Tendency (40–50%)	Score
						South Africa	45.30
						Tunisia	45.30
						Uruguay	45.30
						Argentina	44.44
						China	44.44
						Mexico	44.44
						Peru	44.44
						Brazil	43.59
						Morocco	43.59
						Panama	43.59
						Slovakia	42.74
						India	41.88
						Ivory Coast	40.17

Less Active (30–40%)	Score					Least Active (0–30%)	Score
Monaco	39.32	Israel	34.19	Fiji	29.91	Marshall Islands	26.50
Ukraine	39.32	Kenya	34.19	Jordan	29.91	Mongolia	26.50
Estonia	38.46	Papua New Guinea	34.19	Togo	29.91	Paraguay	26.50
Sri Lanka	38.46	Antigua and Barbuda	33.33	United Arab Emirates	29.91	St Kitts and Nevis	26.50
Liechtenstein	37.61	Lebanon	33.33	Yugoslavia	29.91	Bolivia	25.64
Senegal	37.61	Turkey	33.33	Algeria	29.06	Honduras	25.64
Venezuela	37.61	Jamaica	32.48	Armenia	29.06	Tanzania (United Rep. of)	25.64
Cuba	36.75	Nigeria	32.48	Georgia	29.06	Sudan	25.64
Cyprus	36.75			Mauritania	29.06	Suriname	24.79
Philippines	36.75						

	Score
Nepal	23.08
Yemen	23.08
Zimbabwe	23.08
Comoros	22.22
Djibouti	22.22
Dominica	22.22
Malawi	22.22
Solomon Islands	22.22
Sudan	22.22
Suriname	22.22
Azerbaijan	22.22

Country	Score	Country	Score	Country	Score
Ecuador	35.90	Seychelles	32.48	St. Vincent and Grenadines	29.06
Lithuania	35.90	Vanuatu	32.48	Saudi Arabia	29.06
Pakistan	35.90	Cameroon (United Rep. of)		Barbados	28.21
Ghana	35.04		31.62	Benin	28.21
Malaysia	35.04	Guatemala	31.62	Gambia	28.21
Columbia	34.19	Iran (Islamic Rep. of)		Guinea	28.21
Costa Rica	34.19		31.62	Mali	28.21
Indonesia	34.19	Mauritius	31.62	Nicaragua	28.21
		Belarus	30.77	Niger	28.21
		Congo (Democratic Rep. of)		Singapore	28.21
			30.77	Syrian Arab Rep.	28.21
		Gabon	30.77	Trinidad and Tobago	
		Malta	30.77		28.21
		Moldova (Rep. of)		Vietnam	28.21
			30.77	Kuwait	27.35
				Macedonia (Rep. of)	
					27.35
				Liberia	26.50

Country	Score	Country	Score
Bangladesh	24.79	Zambia	22.22
Belize	24.79	Myanmar	21.37
Grenada	24.79	Namibia	21.37
Guyana	24.79	Uganda	21.37
Mozambique	24.79	Uzbekistan	21.37
Oman	24.79	Libyan Arab Jamah.	20.51
Qatar	24.79	Chad	19.66
Tonga	23.93	Maldives	19.66
Albania	23.93	Bosnia-Herzegovina	18.80
Bahamas	23.93	Botswana	18.80
St. Lucia	23.93	Equatorial Guinea	18.80
Thailand	23.08	Central African Rep.	17.95
Bahrain	23.08	Kazakhstan	17.95
Burkina Faso	23.08	Korea (People's Democratic Rep. of)	17.95
Congo	23.08	Microesia (Federated States of)	17.09
Dominican Republic	23.08	Samoa (Western)	17.09
El Salvador	23.08		
Madagascar	23.08		

Source: Begerson and Parmann 2001–2.

Note: See box 7.1 in the text for complete set of agreements. A score for each country was calculated as follows. With a few exceptions, participation scores for each of the possibilities were assigned on a three-point scale: 0 = not signed, ratified, accepted, or approved; 1 = only signed; 2 = signed and ratified, accepted or approved. The exceptions were Antarctic Treaty (2 = consultative party, 1 = non-consultative party, 0 = neither); Aircraft Engine Emissions, Distribution and Use of Pesticides, and ITTA (1 = member, 0 = nonmember); FAO Plant Genetic Resources (1 = adhered; 0 = not adhered). In our coding, states could obtain a maximum participation score of 117. Percentages in the table reflect the percentage of the 117 total possible score.

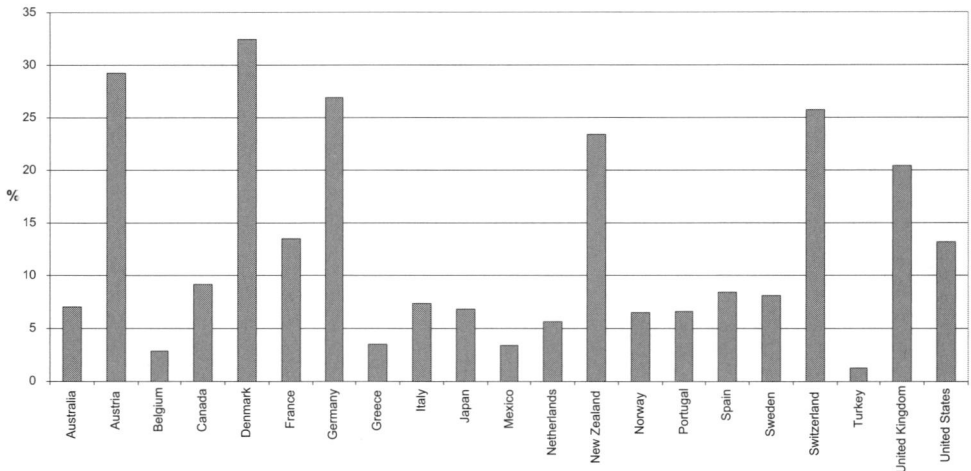

Fig. 7.1. Protected areas as percentage of total land areas, 1999. (Data from World Resources Institute 2001.)

Republic, Ecuador, Slovakia, and Venezuela exceeded the 20 percent level; Botswana, Cambodia, Chile, Cuba, the Czech Republic, Guatemala, Israel, Oman, Pakistan, and Tanzania surpassed 15 percent. Fourteen other countries met or exceeded the 10 percent level, and nineteen others topped the 5 percent level. In sum, there is widespread formal effort to make contributions to the environment by protecting natural areas. A similar pattern of widespread contributions marks shifts away from deforestation between 1990 and 2000.

Avoiding Public Bads

Our preceding measures indicated increasing contributions to or at least acknowledgment of the importance of environmental quality. We now turn to an examination of the generation of environmental bads with a substantial public element. We limit our attention to two broad types of public bads: (1) excessive consumption and resource depletion as measured by energy consumption and water use; and (2) generating water- and air-polluting emissions.

ENERGY CONSUMPTION EFFICIENCY

The energy consumption data in table 7.10 show gross domestic product (GDP) in purchasing-power-parity terms per unit of energy use in 1980 and 1997 for countries with available data for both time points.[33]

We view inefficiency on this measure (i.e., a low score) as indicative of a tendency to generate environmental bads through economic activity and high scores as showing more compatibility between protecting the environment and economic growth. For each time period, the data show national performance in these terms and thus allow us to compare performance by different states despite the different motives for policy

TABLE 7.10. GDP per Unit of Energy Use (purchasing power parity $ per kilogram oil equivalent)

	1980	1997
Seven or more	Latvia	Argentina, Bangladesh, Colombia, Costa Rica, Dominican Republic, El Salvador, Italy, Morocco, Peru, Philippines, Portugal, Switzerland, Sri Lanka, Uruguay
Six or more	Morocco	Austria, Brazil, Guatemala, Ireland, Japan, Panama, Tunisia
Five or more	Algeria, Costa Rica, Philippines, Portugal, Uruguay	Algeria, *Chile*, *France*, Greece, *Haiti*, Israel, *Mexico*, Paraguay, Spain, *Thailand*, Turkey
Four or more	Argentina, Bangladesh, Brazil, Colombia, El Salvador, Greece, Guatemala, Haiti, Paraguay, Peru, Switzerland, Tunisia, United Arab Emirates	Australia, Belgium, Bolivia, *China*, Ecuador, Egypt, *Gabon*, Ghana, Honduras, Hungary, India, Indonesia, South Korea, *Netherlands*, Nicaragua, *Norway*, Pakistan, Senegal
Three or more	Austria, Bolivia, Chile, Democratic Republic of Congo, Dominican Republic, Ecuador, Egypt, Haiti, Israel, Italy, Japan, Jordan, South Korea, Mexico, Nicaragua, Panama, Saudi Arabia, Spain, Sri Lanka, Thailand, Turkey	Cameroon, *Canada*, Finland, Iran, Jordan, <u>**Latvia**</u>, Malaysia, *Nepal*, *Romania*, Singapore, South Africa, Sweden, Syria, *United States*, Zimbabwe
Two or more	Australia, Belgium, Cameroon, France, Ghana, Honduras, Hungary, Indonesia, Iran, Ireland, Malaysia, Netherlands, Norway, Pakistan, Senegal, Singapore, South Africa, Sweden, Syria	Benin, *Bulgaria*, <u>**Democratic Republic of Congo**</u>, Ethiopia, Jamaica, Kenya, Kuwait, <u>**Saudi Arabia**</u>, Venezuela
One or more	Benin, Canada, Ethiopia, Finland, Gabon, India, Jamaica, Kenya, Kuwait, Nepal, Romania, Trinidad and Tobago, United States, Venezuela, Zimbabwe	Congo Republic, Nigeria, Trinidad and Tobago, <u>**United Arab Emirates**,</u> Zambia
Less than one	Bulgaria, China, Congo Republic, Mozambique, Nigeria, Zambia	

Source: Data from World Bank, *World Development Indicators*, 2001.
Note: Countries in bold italics increased their efficiency by two or more units, those in bold increased it by one unit, and those in underlined bold decreased it by one unit or more.

performance. Looking at changes from 1980 to 1997, increasing GDP per unit of energy used suggests improvements by particular states and illustrates which states have made the greatest progress in this regard. We emphasize that these data are not about absolute energy consumption but only about consumption relative to economic activity.

As the twentieth century ended, the data in table 7.10 provide grounds for muted optimism.[34] Most of the world's larger economies were in the more efficient categories, including most West Europeans, Japan, and many developing nations. Few countries—mostly small economies—were in the lowest three categories. Our optimism is muted, however, because of the presence of some high contributors on our other issue areas (e.g., Canada, Finland, Sweden) in a relatively inefficient category. The United States is also placed in a lower position.

As for changes in efficiency, the countries in the last column of table 7.10 who improved massively outnumber those whose efficiency performance either remained unchanged or worsened. The widespread improved performance included all the larger economies where data were reported for both time periods as well as many smaller economies in Europe, North America, Asia, and Latin America. Improvements were global in nature and not just limited to the OECD countries. Among the OECD countries, performance was especially impressive in Italy, Portugal, Switzerland, Austria, Ireland, Japan, France, Mexico, and Spain. Other data will help us put this relative optimism into a more comprehensive context.

WATER USE AND POLLUTION

Water issues are increasingly becoming the focal points for serious political and even military clashes around the world. Water issues generally focus on two sets of problems: resource depletion and emissions of water pollutants. In each case, lower amounts are more environmentally beneficial than higher ones. For water resource depletion, comparative time-series analysis becomes more problematic. We can, however, examine scattered snapshots of water use throughout the OECD countries, drawing data from various years.[35]

If we consider a 20 percent withdrawal a cause for environmental concern, most of the states shown lie well below it. Exceptions, however, include some countries important for collective action, such as Belgium, France, Germany, Italy, Japan, the Netherlands, and Spain. Hungary shows an extreme withdrawal level in the World Resources Institute data, although that country is much lower in the World Bank data. But when considering the potential water threats in developing countries,

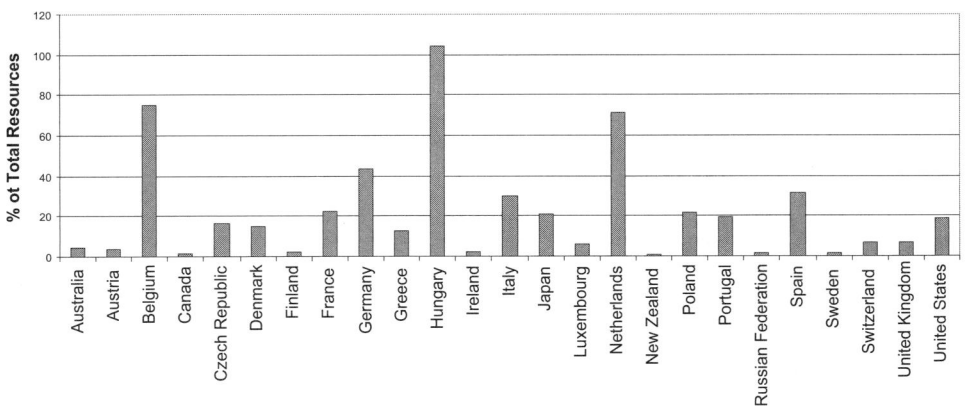

Fig. 7.2A. Total annual water withdrawals as percentage of total internal renewable water resources, various years. (Data from World Resources Institute 2001.)

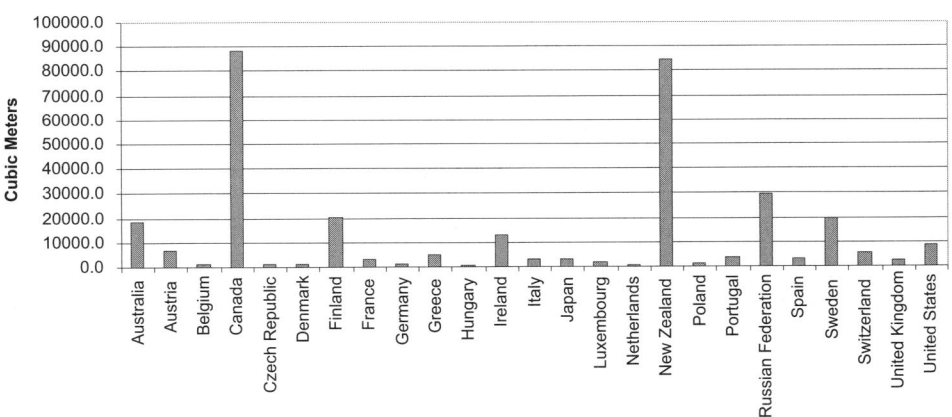

Fig. 7.2B. Annual internal renewable water resources per capita, 2000. (Data from World Resources Institute 2001.)

there may be greater cause for pessimism about water depletion. Many southern nations exceeded the 20 percent threshold, and some Middle Eastern nations do so to a degree indicating a rapidly approaching or occurring drawdown of nonrenewable water resources (e.g., Egypt, Iraq, Israel, Jordan, Libya, Mauritania, Oman, Saudi Arabia, and the United Arab Emirates) (World Bank 2001, World Development Indicators).

The results for the OECD countries must also be taken in the context of the data in the second graph in figure 7.2. This graph displays

Defensive Internationalism

the total freshwater per capita and shows the extreme variation that exists across the OECD countries. This graph also shows that the relatively high withdrawal rates from the first graph may be even more pronounced for those countries. Because each has lower per capita resources, higher withdrawal rates more directly threaten the supply. In essence, smaller internal water resources make larger drawdowns in any one year more threatening than they would be in a country with larger internal water resources.

For emissions of water pollutants, comparative data are available for

TABLE 7.11. Emissions of Organic Water Pollutants (kilograms per day per worker)

	1980	Any Year 1993–98
Less than .14	Bulgaria, Italy, Romania, Saudi Arabia, Singapore	Italy, Germany, **South Korea, Malaysia,** Romania, Singapore
Less than .18	Austria, Bangladesh, Belgium, Brazil, China, Denmark, Finland, France, Gabon, Greece, Hungary, Iran, Israel, Japan, Jordan, South Korea, Kuwait, Malaysia, Morocco, Nigeria, Poland, Portugal, South Africa, Spain, Sweden, Tunisia, United Kingdom, United States	**Austria,** Bangladesh, Belgium, ***Bulgaria,*** **Canada, *Central African Republic,*** China, *France,* **Ghana,** Hungary, ***Indonesia,*** Iran, *Iraq, Ireland, Israel,* Japan, Kuwait, **Lesotho, Mauritius, Mexico, Nepal,** Poland, **Portugal,** *Saudi Arabia,* South Africa, Spain, **Sri Lanka,** Sweden, **Thailand,** Tunisia, **Turkey,** United Kingdom, *United States*
Less than .22	Algeria, Argentina, Australia, Canada, Chile, Colombia, Egypt, Ghana, India, Iraq, Ireland, Kenya, Mauritius, Mongolia, Netherlands, New Zealand, Norway, Pakistan, Peru, Philippines, Sri Lanka, Syria, Tanzania, Trinidad and Tobago, Turkey, Uruguay, Venezuela, Zimbabwe	Australia, ***Brazil,*** **Botswana,** Colombia, *Denmark,* **Egypt,** ***El Salvador, Finland, Greece,*** **Honduras,** India, *Jordan,* Mongolia, *Morocco,* Netherlands, *Nigeria,* Norway, *Pakistan,* Peru, Philippines, *Venezuela,* Zimbabwe
Less than .26	Botswana, Burundi, Ivory Coast, Ecuador, El Salvador, Guatemala, Honduras, Indonesia, Jamaica, Lesotho, Mexico, Nepal, Sierra Leone, Thailand, Zambia	*Algeria,* Argentina, ***Burundi, Cameroon,*** *Chile,* Ivory Coast, ***Kenya, New Zealand, Syria, Uruguay,*** **Zambia**
Less than .30	Cameroon, Central African Republic, Panama	*Ecuador, Gabon, Guatemala, Jamaica,* **Malawi,** *Tanzania, Trinidad and Tobago*
Greater than or equal to .30	Gambia, Malawi, Senegal	*Gambia, Panama,* Senegal, *Sierra Leone*

Source: Data from World Bank, *World Development Indicators,* 2001.
Note: Countries in bold italics have reduced their emissions enough to move into a lower category. Countries in bold have reduced while remaining in the same category. Countries in italics underlined have increased enough to move into a higher category. Countries in italics have increased while remaining in the same category.

organic pollutants but not for metals, minerals, or toxic wastes. For organic pollutants, our approach resembles that for energy efficiency in using a measure relative to economic activity. Using kilograms of emissions per day per industrial worker, we categorize countries in those terms when data were available for two time periods. For this measure, unlike energy efficiency, a low value indicates restraint in the production of environmental bads. The national performance information appears in table 7.11. As with energy efficiency, the data do not reflect absolute amounts but rather relative ones.

To a lesser extent than for energy efficiency, the data again suggest some grounds for muted optimism, given the number of states and the size of their economies whose performances are improving relative to the number of those that are worsening. Shifts toward reduction were often small, however. Once again, reductions were hardly the monopoly of the OECD countries; indeed, a number of them worsened their performance, although they still lodged in the low-emission categories. Among the OECD countries, Italy turned in a particularly and persistently impressive performance. When data were available in the later period for Germany, it too was in the lowest-emission category. South Korea and Malaysia were especially impressive in the change in their behavior.

Turning to national volumes of such emissions, comparisons between the two periods for the largest national emitters (500,000 kilograms per day) are mixed (World Bank 2001, *World Development Indicators*). Substantial reductions were achieved by Brazil, France, and the United Kingdom, and Japan and the United States achieved small percentage reductions. India and especially China recorded large increases. The differences between the national aggregate emissions measure and those per industrial worker in table 7.11 indicate that a country could in fact emit more in aggregate while reducing the rate per industrial worker, a phenomenon exhibited by Malaysia and South Korea. Such patterns qualify the muted optimism suggested by table 7.11.

ATMOSPHERIC POLLUTANTS

We will start this discussion with global aggregate data on atmospheric concentration of greenhouse and ozone-depleting gases (World Bank 2001, *World Development Indicators*). Most concentrations increased from 1980 through 1995. The exceptions were carbon tetrachloride and methyl chloroform, which declined after 1990. From 1990 to 2000, those two continued to decline and were joined by CFC-11a and total gaseous chlorine. CFC-113a concentrations had also leveled off. Other gases, including carbon dioxide, nitrous oxide, and CFC-12a, continued to increase. These results warrant some optimism about reductions but also significant pessimism given that the 1990s had the onetime gains in emissions reductions associated with changes in the formerly communist economies of Central and Eastern Europe and the shorter interval between the last two data points.

In the context of the Kyoto agreement and the U.S. withdrawal from it, carbon dioxide has become an especially salient issue for the prospects of international collective action aimed at reducing environmental bads as well as an issue for which substantial comparable data over time are available, permitting us to characterize reduction—and the lack of it—in three ways (World Bank 2001, *World Development Indicators*). The first is again in relation to economic activity (kilograms emitted per dollar of purchasing-power-parity GDP), the second focuses on national aggregate emissions in total metric tons, and the third uses national shares of emissions of this global environmental bad. Efficiency improvements, the first measure, may or may not be accompanied by total reductions in emissions (the second measure). Even if such is the case, some countries may still stand out for production of global atmospheric bads (the third measure).

For emissions relative to economic activity, table 7.12 uses the same approach as in tables 7.10 and 7.11 for countries with data were available for 1980 and 1997. The lower the ratio of emissions to economic activity, the less the environmental damage associated with it. These results suggest a picture that shows obvious progress in reducing carbon dioxide bads per unit of economic activity, as indicated by the large number of countries showing reductions relative to units of GDP. Reductions were on the order of half, with an even greater reduction in the somewhat overlapping categories of high-income countries and the members of the European Monetary Union, a group whose cuts were matched by the United States. Compared to those two groupings, reductions were even greater in percentage terms per unit of economic activity in the low- and middle-income countries of East Asia and the Pacific (World Bank 2001, *World Development Indicators*). The last reduction was in large measure a function of a Chinese cut in relation to unit of economic activity of more than 70 percent.

With regard to national levels of emissions per unit of GDP in the more recent period (1997), the better performers tend to be poorer, slower-growing southern countries. Among the countries of the North, exceptional efficiency in limiting release of this environmental bad was shown by a number of West Europeans (Switzerland, Austria, Belgium, Denmark, France, Italy, Portugal, Spain, Sweden, and the United Kingdom) and Japan.[36] No EU member appeared in the three higher relative

TABLE 7.12. Carbon Dioxide Emissions per Unit of Purchasing Power Parity GDP (kilograms per $)

	1980	1997
0.2 or less	Bangladesh, Burkina Faso, Burundi, Central African Republic, Chad, Democratic Republic of Congo, El Salvador, Ethiopia, Ghana, Haiti, Mali, Nepal, Niger, Paraguay, Rwanda, Sri Lanka, Togo, Uganda	Bangladesh, **Benin**, Burkina Faso, Burundi, **Cameroon**, Central African Republic, Chad, Democratic Republic of Congo, *Congo, Costa Rica*, El Salvador, Ethiopia, **Gambia**, Ghana, *Guinea-Bissau*, Haiti, **Kenya**, **Madagascar**, Malawi, Mali, **Mauritius**, *Mozambique*, Nepal, Niger, *Papua New Guinea*, Paraguay, Rwanda, **Sierra Leone**, Sri Lanka, *Switzerland*, Togo, Uganda, *Uruguay*
0.4 or less	Benin, Brazil, Cameroon, Costa Rica, Gambia, Honduras, Madagascar, Malawi, Mauritania, Mauritius, Nicaragua, Philippines, Sierra Leone	**Argentina**, *Austria, Belgium,* **Botswana**, Brazil, **Colombia, Dominican Republic,** *France,* Honduras, *Indonesia, Italy, Japan,* **Morocco**, Nicaragua, **Pakistan**, **Peru**, Philippines, **Portugal**, *Senegal, Spain, Sweden, Tunisia, Zambia*
0.6 or less	Argentina, Bolivia, Botswana, Colombia, Congo, Ivory Coast, Dominican Republic, Guinea-Bissau, Morocco, Pakistan, Papua New Guinea, Panama, Peru, Portugal, Switzerland, Thailand, Uruguay	Bolivia, Ivory Coast, *Ecuador,* **Egypt,** *Finland, Gabon, Greece, Hungary,* **India,** **Ireland,** Israel, *South Korea,* **Mexico,** **Netherlands, Norway,** Panama, Thailand, **Turkey,** *Zimbabwe*
0.8 or less	Austria, Egypt, India, Indonesia, Israel, Italy, Japan, Kenya, Mexico, Mozambique, Senegal, Spain, Sweden, Tunisia, Turkey	*Algeria, Australia, Canada,* **Malaysia,** <u>**Mauritania**</u>, *Romania, United States*
1.0 or less	Chile, Ecuador, France, Greece, Jordan, Malaysia, Zambia, Zimbabwe	**China, Iran,** Jordan, **Nigeria**, **South Africa**
Greater than 1.0	Algeria, Australia, Belgium, Bulgaria, Canada, China, Finland, Gabon, Hungary, Iran, Ireland, Jamaica, South Korea, Kuwait, Mongolia, Netherlands, Nigeria, Norway, Romania, Saudi Arabia, Singapore, South Africa, Syria, Trinidad and Tobago, United Arab Emirates, United States, Venezuela	Bulgaria, Jamaica, Kuwait, Mongolia, Saudi Arabia, Singapore, Syria, Trinidad and Tobago, United Arab Emirates, Venezuela

Source: Data from World Bank, *World Development Indicators,* 2001, table 3.8.
Note: Countries that lowered their emissions by more than one category appear in bold italics, those that lowered emissions by one category appear in bold, those that remained in the same category appear in standard type, and those that worsened by one or more categories appear in bold underlined.

TABLE 7.13. Carbon Dioxide Emissions: National and Group Aggregates

	Change in Metric Tons National Emissions 1980–97 (%)	Share of World Emissions 1980 (%)	Share of World Emissions 1997 (%)	Change in Share of World Emissions 1980–97 (%)
Argentina	27	0.8	0.6	−0.2
Australia	56	1.5	1.3	−0.2
Belgium	−19	0.9	0.4	−0.5
Brazil	56	1.4	1.3	−0.1
Canada	17	3.0	2.1	−0.9
China	137	10.8	15.1	4.3
Czech Republic			0.5	
Egypt	153	0.3	0.5	0.2
France	−30	3.5	1.5	−2.0
Germany			3.6	
India	199	2.5	4.6	2.0
Indonesia	158	0.7	1.1	0.4
Iran	147	0.9	1.2	0.3
Italy	8	2.8	1.8	−1.0
Japan	25	6.9	5.0	−1.9
Kazakhstan			0.5	
North Korea	102	0.9	1.1	0.2
South Korea	244	0.9	1.9	1.0
Malaysia	371	0.2	0.6	0.4
Mexico	46	1.9	1.6	−0.3
Netherlands	6	1.1	0.7	−0.4
Poland	−23	3.3	1.5	−1.8
Romania	−46	1.4	0.5	−0.9
Russian Federation			6.1	
Saudi Arabia	107	0.9	1.1	0.2
South Africa	50	1.5	1.3	0.2
Spain	20	1.5	1.1	−0.4
Thailand	431	0.3	1.0	0.7
Turkey	161	0.6	0.9	0.3
United Kingdom	−11	4.2	2.2	−2.0
United States	19	32.9	22.9	−10.0
Ukraine			1.6	
Uzbekistan			0.4	
Venezuela	108	0.7	0.8	0.1
Groupings				
Low income	218	5.7	10.6	4.9
Middle income	132	30.7	41.9	11.2
High income	27	63.6	47.5	−16.1
Low and middle income of				
East Asia Pacific	151	14.4	21.3	6.9
Europe and Central Asia	259	6.5	13.8	7.3

TABLE 7.13—Continued

	Change in Metric Tons National Emissions 1980–97 (%)	Share of World Emissions 1980 (%)	Share of World Emissions 1997 (%)	Change in Share of World Emissions 1980–97 (%)
Latin America and Caribbean	53	6.3	5.7	−0.6
Middle East and North Africa	119	3.7	4.7	1.0
South Asia	198	2.9	5.0	2.1
Sub-Saharan Africa	40	2.6	2.1	−0.5
European EMU	52	11.2	10.0	−1.2

Source: Data from World Bank, *World Development Indicators,* 2001, table 3.8.
Note: Countries listed are those emitting 100 million or more metric tons of carbon dioxide in one or both of the observation years.

emissions categories, but Australia, Canada, the United States, China, and the Russian Federation did.[37]

The muted optimism of the previous paragraphs is, however, not sustained by changes in the absolute amounts of national emissions shown in the first column of table 7.13. For the 1980–97 period, world emissions increased by 70 percent, with much of that increase driven more by carbon dioxide emissions by a number of larger developing-country economies—that is, low- and middle-income countries—and less by emissions by the most underdeveloped nations. That is especially pessimistic news as the relevant time period encompassed the collapse of much of Central and Eastern Europe's "dirty" industry, which helped to reduce emissions by major sources such as Poland and Romania (as shown in table 7.13) and the newly reunified Germany.[38]

More specifically, changes in the absolute volume of emissions by the large-emissions countries listed in the table fall into four groups: reducers (Belgium, France, the United Kingdom, Poland, Romania, and [from other data] Germany); limited increasers of 25 percent or less (Canada, Italy, Japan, the Netherlands, Spain, and the United States); large increasers of more than 25 but less than 100 percent (Argentina, Australia, Brazil, Mexico, and South Africa); and multipliers, with increases of more—often much more—than 100 percent (China, Egypt, India, Indonesia, Iran, both Koreas, Malaysia, Saudi Arabia, Thailand, Turkey, and Venezuela). The result of these different patterns of change has been a shift in shares of global emissions, as shown in the last three columns of table 7.13. That shift carries with it substantial implications for international collective action aimed at reducing carbon dioxide emissions. Those implications do not imply excluding the rich nations of the North. Along these lines, the very large, if declining, U.S. share is noteworthy, as are the implications for emissions of fast-growth countries of the global South (e.g, in China's share and in that of the low- and middle-income countries of East Asia and the Pacific, Europe and Central Asia, and South Asia).

We conclude our discussion of atmospheric pollutants by considering four additional kinds; sulfur dioxide, nitrous oxide, volatile organic compounds, and carbon monoxide. For these, we limit our attention to emissions relative to GDP and the absolute volume of emissions.[39] Comparative time-series data for most of the OECD countries and a few others appear in figures 7.3–7.6. The values in the figures are index numbers and should not be compared across emissions types.

In general, emissions of sulfur dioxide and nitrous oxide show marked reductions relative to economic activity over the last decades of the twentieth century. Romania and Russia provide the only persistent exceptions to the overall patterns of improvement. Further, most countries, including the United States, also reduced their absolute volumes of emissions of these two pollutants, although the United States remained the largest national emitter. With slightly more fragmentary data, largely similar patterns can be seen for emissions of volatile organic compounds and carbon monoxide in figures 7.5 and 7.6. Russia and Romania again stand out for their lagging in reductions of these two types of emissions. These data, then, show substantial gains and some reason for optimism for the reduction of atmospheric bads.

PUTTING THE PIECES TOGETHER

Our discussion of public opinion on the environment yielded the following conclusions. Environmental quality concerns were widespread globally but not to the point of reliable support for protecting the environment at a major price to economic prosperity and growth. This does not suggest opposition to policy aimed at environmental quality in general, although Americans' sense of urgency about additional measures has declined. This finding does suggest, however, that support in much of the North and South will go to policies that seem to combine environmental protection with economic achievements. At most, only in some European countries would public sentiment tolerate substantial economic costs for the sake of environmental quality. As for a government's willingness to do more than others for environmental quality, a number of West European publics stood out in terms of opinion and ac-

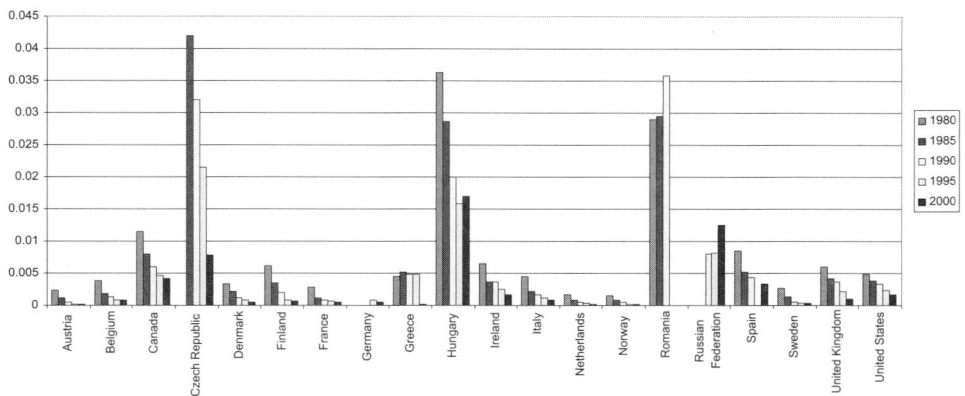

Fig. 7.3. Emissions of sulfur dioxide relative to gross domestic product. (Data from World Resources Institute 2001.)

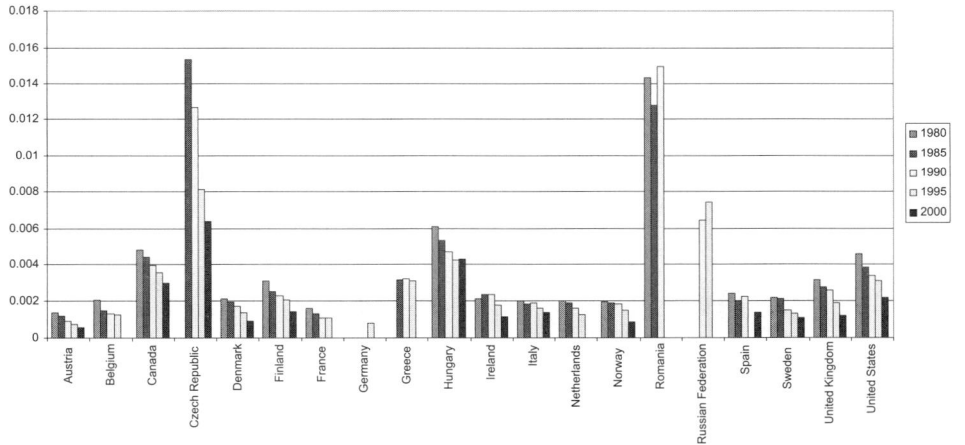

Fig. 7.4. Emissions of nitrous oxide relative to gross domestic product. (Data from World Resources Institute 2001.)

tivist voluntary organizations. The American public tended to deny any special obligation for exceptionally large U.S. contributions, while the Japanese public took an intermediate position emphasizing private-element benefits.

The contribution patterns we found in general seem to fit with these public opinion patterns, showing widespread achievements in reducing the environmental depletion and polluting impacts per unit of economic

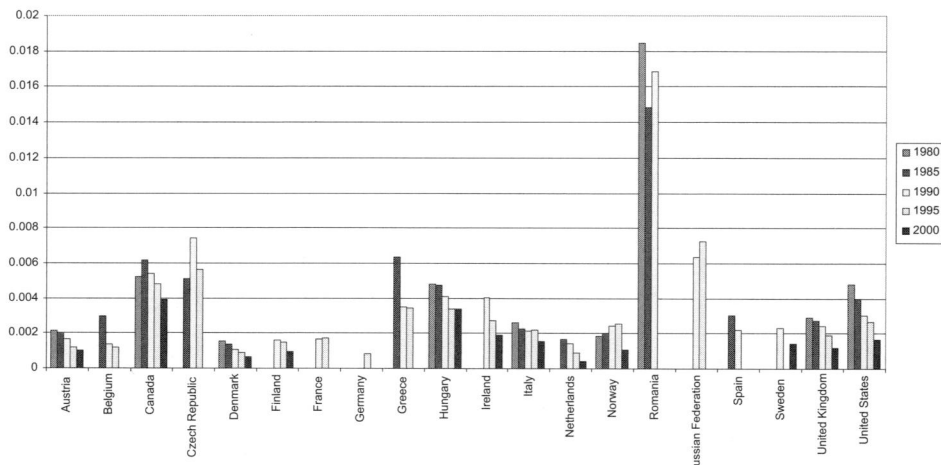

Fig. 7.5. Emissions of volatile organic compounds relative to gross domestic product. (Data from World Resources Institute 2001.)

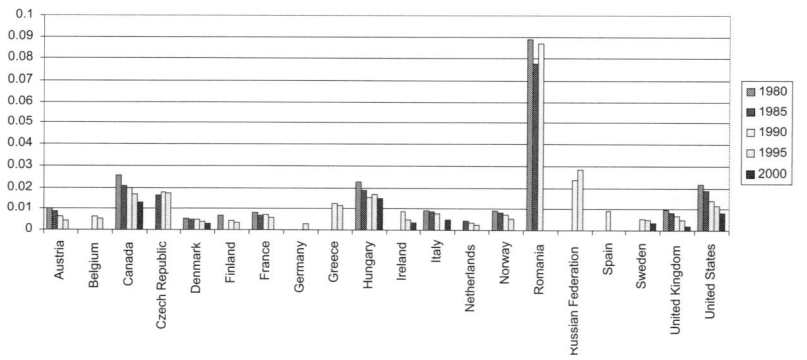

Fig. 7.6. Emissions of carbon monoxide relative to gross domestic product. (Data from World Resources Institute 2001.)

activity. We also have found widespread, if far from universal, protection of large parts of national territory, prevention of deforestation, and noncrisis levels of water withdrawals. In most of these respects, contributors ranged widely across categories of geography, level of economic development, and economic growth rate.

If, however, we consider aspects of the production of environmental bads that pose harsher tensions between prosperity and growth, our findings are less encouraging for the muted optimism perspective and more differentiating across countries and types of contributions. Among the largest emitters of organic water pollutants, Brazil, France, the United Kingdom, Japan, and the United States cut their volumes, but China and India and some smaller fast-growth countries (Malaysia and South Korea) increased the volumes emitted. For carbon dioxide emissions, only a few European nations made reductions (Belgium, France, Germany, the United Kingdom, Poland, and Romania). While other northern countries increased their emissions only to a moderate degree (the United States, Canada, Japan, Italy, the Netherlands, and Spain), emissions by some large developing economies multiplied (again China, India, Malaysia, and South Korea as well as Egypt, Indonesia, Iran, Saudi Arabia, Thailand, and North Korea). The record is hardly encouraging if the reduction of international environmental bads is viewed as a summation problem in public goods terms.

If we look at differences in national levels of efficiency as distinct from improvements in it, we get a better sense of contribution leaders and laggards. We define leaders as countries that are in the two least environmentally burdensome categories with respect to our three measures of global coverage in 1997 (energy, water, and carbon dioxide). In the North, Japan, Austria, Italy, Portugal, and Switzerland met that criterion for all three measures while Belgium, France, Spain, Sweden, and the United Kingdom met the criterion for two measures. The large representation of EU countries is in line with our previous discussion of public opinion. The U.S. absence on these measures also fits with the public opinion data. Japan's record is neither predicted nor contradicted by its public opinion. For our more general argument, it is important to note that some southern countries—and not merely the least developed ones—stood out for relatively modest environmental burdens per unit of economic activity. Bangladesh, Sri Lanka, and Tunisia met the criterion for all three measures, and a much larger number of southern countries (Argentina, Brazil, the Central African Republic, Colombia, Costa Rica, the Dominican Republic, El Salvador, Ghana, Indonesia, Mauritius, Nepal, Morocco, Panama, Peru, and the Philippines) met the criterion for two measures. And no West European country was in the bottom two categories on any of the three measures. The United States was not a leader or even a near-leader; the United States, Australia, and Canada almost met the laggard level for carbon dioxide emissions in our most recent observation.[40]

Financial contributions in terms of R&D, pollution abatement and control, and funding for environmental international organizations were examined only for some northern countries. Once again, a number of the Europeans stand out, as does Japan in recent years for R&D

and more continuingly for international organization funding. Germany joins those ranks for all three types of contributions after falling just short of being a near-leader on the efficiency measures. A number of smaller European countries are also prominent. The United States is the largest contributor on all three financial measures but is not a robustly increasing contributor.

Any integrated assessment will have elements of both muted optimism and pessimism. The balance between them seems to us to involve two judgments. The first is about the extent that the road to production of environmental goods and reduction of bads should emphasize what we introduced in chapter 2 as best shot, weakest link, or summation. The second, related to the first, is about the need and prospects for North-South cooperation on environmental quality.

A best-shot emphasis would yield a more optimistic verdict given the growth in R&D spending and the efficiency gains we have reported. Weakest-link approaches would come to a mutedly optimistic conclusion if they assumed that the improvements in efficiency we found would continue and would occur faster than economic growth in the world regions generating the largest absolute amounts of environmental bads. The weakest-link approaches would then make much of the improvements found in the largest source countries. Focusing on the growth in the amount of environmental bads being produced by large emitters and emphasized the onetime nature of reductions following regime changes in East and Central Europe, however, these approaches would come to a far more pessimistic conclusion. A summation approach would in large measure parallel the weakest-link perspective.

Each approach is affected by prospects for international cooperation, whether it is aimed at diffusing environmentally friendly technology, putting pressure on the largest sources of bads in the North and the South, or fostering a regime for environmental quality that would span the globe. Recent history, as in the Montreal Protocol, suggests that such forms of cooperation are possible. They also can be elusive, as with the Kyoto agreement. Nevertheless, the widespread signing on to relevant international agreements and the persistent striving for cooperation even in the face of U.S. negativism on greenhouse gases and biodiversity suggests that it would be premature to reject a muted optimism prospect. The biggest question mark in this regard is the low level of participation in environmental agreements by developing countries, which represent some of the largest potential threats to environmental quality. Strides need to be made in this regard to pump up optimistic prospects. This conclusion is bolstered by world public opinion, much of which demonstrates more in the way of concern about than indifference to environment quality. The impetus such opinion may provide for contributions is more likely to be expressed strongly in a context of dramatic environmental crises rather than in a context of more attention to threats to economic prosperity and growth.

8 A GLOBAL PROGNOSIS OF MUTED OPTIMISM?

The events of the relatively recent past have sensitized citizens and policymakers to the ways global phenomena can quickly and dramatically impact our lives. From the 9/11 attacks, with their roots in perceptions of injustice and privilege, to the fall of the Soviet Union and its devolutionary effects throughout much of Europe and Asia to the growing transboundary environmental impacts, the global is increasingly becoming the local in contemporary life. We began this project convinced that policymakers and citizens in the advanced industrialized countries of the global North were increasingly losing the capacity to isolate and insulate themselves from international and indeed global circumstances and events. Realistically, what was happening and what would continue to happen in the global South would increasingly have consequences for those in the North. At the same time, the South would lack even more the capacity—and perhaps the will—to isolate and insulate itself from northern actions of commission and omission. For us, 9/11, the many other recent dramatic events, and the responses and reactions to those events have been forceful confirmations of our expectations about the need for provision of global public goods and the reduction of global public bads.

Because of our desire to understand the dynamics of public-goods provision in our increasingly global society, we then set out to see if the shared fate produced by the realities of complex interdependence would lead to internationally focused "giving" that might improve the prospects for global order and progress. Was it possible that the North would increasingly turn to policies that aimed at producing global public goods and reducing public bads? Would policies aimed at producing public goods come especially from those northern countries where public opinion indicated a relatively more favorable domestic political context for global giving? To what extent would contributions come from those with the most to lose, motivated by defensive internationalism?

A GLOBAL PROGNOSIS OF MUTED OPTIMISM?

This chapter considers to what extent the previous analyses support our muted optimism position about cooperative efforts to enhance our global future and suggests some policy expectations and suggestions for contributions in the future.

Our exploration of contributions to global order and progress began with the joint implications of impure public goods theory, identity-based domestic beliefs, and multilateral institutionalism. From that conceptual foundation, we argued that in the post–Cold War world, the quantity and quality of global giving would warrant muted optimism for the future of global order and progress, an ameliorist perspective. We expected that more extremely optimistic or pessimistic perspectives would have little basis in the reality of who has been giving what to whom in the contemporary world system. While we expected more support for mutedly pessimistic interpretations, we thought it would be in general weaker than for mutedly optimistic ones. More concretely, we expected two general patterns.

The first was that giving in aggregate would increase over time both in volume and in the extent of the public goods element associated with it. Those trends would not take the form of linear increases but rather intermittent increases that would not stabilize at levels as low as those before the end of the Cold War. Put simply, policies conducive to the provision of global public goods and the amelioration of public bads would have grown stronger, not weaker. If those intermittent shifts toward pro-giving policies were instead followed by retrenchment below past levels, a muted pessimism interpretation would be more warranted.

The second expected pattern was that of diversity. The general policy shift associated with muted optimism would not occur uniformly for all the potential contributors among the nations of the Organization for Economic Cooperation and Development (OECD). Nor would national patterns of relative and absolute giving be the same from issue to issue or across recipient geographic regions. Contribution initiatives and leadership (at least in terms of volume) would sometimes come from states and groups of states distinct from the United States, but there would not be a prolonged, accelerating, generalized American withdrawal from contributions or a reduction in the public element associated with American action. Further, variety in northern national giving policies would crudely track with the relative degree that domestic beliefs supported contributions based in shared identities, national values and roles (self-realization), perceived external threats (defensive internationalism), and the perceived efficacy of various forms of contributions and the multilateral vehicles for them. In particular, we expected that positive domestic views of international institutions and clubs would be associated with tendencies to contribute to collective action. Those motivations would not be absent for the nations of the South, but whatever contributions they would make would lag behind those of the North and have a larger private element.

Our conjecture was that these expectations would on balance hold for contributions to the production of regional and even global public goods and the reduction of such public bads. We also suggested that defensive internationalism would tend to increase efforts to reduce perceived public bads with nonexcludable, negative national consequences for contributor states and would do less to induce contributions emphasizing the production of global public goods. Even those policies arguably designed and chosen to increase the provision of public goods might well also have rationales featuring the avoidance or reduction of private bads for contributors.

In the following pages, we first summarize the extent to which our findings about the contributions made in our four issue areas support our first general expectation. In that way, we identify outstanding contributors. We then consider the extent to which differences in national and club contributions tend to fit with differences in prevailing domestic beliefs within the potential contributors (our second general expectation). Finally, and more speculatively, we suggest some implications for progiving global policies in the coming years and the likely role of particular national contributors in those policy efforts.

CONTRIBUTION PATTERNS

The record of contributions we presented does not warrant extremes of optimism or pessimism about the production of global public goods or the amelioration of global public bads. Be it for development assistance, debt management and relief, peacekeeping, or environmental quality, deciding on the most warranted umbrella perspective about the current state of world affairs comes down to a choice between muted optimism and muted pessimism.

This conclusion has three bases. First, each of our issue areas was increasingly recognized in policy statements as having public consequences (good or bad) even beyond club-level concerns as well as private consequences for contributors or recipients. These joint product identifications, by shaping public debates about needed provision, have worked against the policy inclinations associated with full-blown contribution optimism or pessimism. Partly as result of the growing public policy attention to our four issue areas, vigorous debate about contribution options has increased and has worked both to curtail some previously pursued forms of giving and to generate support for increases in different forms of giving. That is, debate has shifted from whether each issue merits attention to the more operational level of what sorts of contributions, to whom, and with what conditions would have desirable global consequences.

Second, in each issue area, multilateral arrangements (formal, informal, and in between) have come to play an increasingly large role over the past few decades of the twentieth century. That development has worked to impel contributions rather than to eliminate or reduce them but has also generated some resistance to increases as contributions have become salient and often complex policy matters for constituents and the officials they elect.

Third, each issue area shows clear signs of contribution improvements, even if intermittent and with qualified commitments. But there is also ample evidence of continuing inadequacies in achieving public goods outcomes and eliminating public bads. The evidence in support of each of the muted perspectives varies among issue areas, and we thus briefly review some major aspects in the following paragraphs. Also, as we shall see, the policies of various national contributors differ in the support they provide for each muted umbrella interpretation.

Development Assistance

For development assistance, as chapter 4 reported, total OECD contributions fell during the 1990s but did better than one might expect when the analysis expands to include categories of aid other than official developmental assistance (ODA). By the end of the decade, growth rates were increasing, and the 2002 Monterrey summit provided hope that further increases in absolute amounts and growth rates would be forthcoming. Those tendencies also apply to ODA as a share of gross national product if the Monterrey promises are met. The Monterrey pledges were justified by the need to ameliorate looming public and donor bads from underdevelopment. As for the size of the public element in development aid, the grant element tended to increase, and untied ODA did so even more distinctly (at least for a while). Conversely, the share of bilateral aid going to the least-developed countries (with its relatively small private element) decreased in a continuing fashion. Aid provided through multilateral institutions (with its relatively large public element) declined beginning in 1980 but by the end of the century was moving slowly upward from its 1994 low. Specialization both in terms of functional purposes and recipient regions and growing dispersion among developing countries and regions favor muted optimism somewhat more than its pessimistic mate. The first pair shows specialization with possible efficiency gains and linkages to joint product incentives. The second pair suggests a wider sharing in the goods-producing and bads-reducing results aid can provide and suggests less of a tendency to favor recipients that are especially linked to private consequences for the donor.

In sum, aggregate development-assistance patterns for the OECD contributors do not provide clear support for muted optimism versus muted pessimism. The latter seems more in line with reductions in amounts of aid and contributor priorities as reflected in share of gross national product, although fulfillment of the Monterrey promises would lead to the muted optimist position if unaccompanied by requirements excluding many of the most needy countries and people. Further, some grounds for excludability based on the prospects that aid would be diverted from development purposes do not argue against muted optimism but instead may be conducive to confidence that contributions will indeed have internationally positive consequences.

Within these general policy patterns, donor behavior varied substantially. As summarized in table 4.10, in both the degree of national contribution effort and the size of the public element, the performances of Denmark, the Netherlands, Norway, and Sweden were particularly impressive. A second tier of pro-contribution policies includes other West European countries (e.g., Belgium, France, Germany, and Switzerland). Some additional states that were less than outstanding in the proportion of national resources devoted to aid performed relatively well in terms of a public goods emphasis in their giving (e.g., Italy, Portugal, the United Kingdom, and Canada). Yet the two largest donors in terms of the absolute amount of funds offer less ground for optimism. Japan's level of effort was relatively low throughout, and its policies were not outstanding in their conduciveness to a public goods element. In addition, there are recent signs of tighter limits on the absolute amount of its contributions, as evidenced by Japan's significant aid reductions in the past few years. The U.S. contributions were especially limited in terms of national resource allocation and the public element, even in the pledges made by American officials at and since Monterrey. However, particular crises continue to drive at least a portion of American giving, as was seen in President George W. Bush's signing of a $15 billion global AIDS bill in May 2003.

International Debt Management and Relief

For international debt management and relief, chapter 5 reported a clear increase, whatever its limitations, in contributions intended to improve the debt sustainability of the most heavily indebted low-income countries. It is difficult to interpret to the contrary the succession of Paris club terms, with their increasing focus on debt and debt-service reduction. The growing importance of multilateral creditors for that class of debtor countries suggests increased recognition of the public element in providing development financing to them. Those developments were justified largely by rhetoric citing the negative spillovers (i.e., global public bads) from continuing development failures. Such policy shifts, however, support only a muted degree of optimism, given the limited application of the more recent sets of terms, the continuing number of debt-vulnerable poor countries, and the controversies over increasing the mandates and funds of creditor international financial institutions.

As for heavily indebted middle-income developing countries, a comparison of the 1990s to the 1980s shows a considerable policy shift away from firm insistence on full and timely repayment and from severe austerity practices as conditions for further credit. The same period was also marked by increased provision of massive bailouts and concessionary "work-outs" (at least for those debtors thought too important geopolitically to fail). Both of these policy trends support a muted optimist perspective and follow from recognition of the nonexcludability of creditors from negative economic and other consequences of financial turbulence in middle-income debtors. In addition, heightened creditor consideration of additional mechanisms to deal with the debt-sustainability problems in the past, present, and future also argues in support of muted optimism.

The case for muted pessimism rests on interpreting the successive terms as in fact providing less relief than appears on their surface, signs of increased debtor fatigue, creditor resistance to further large bailouts, a reluctance to turn away from continuing use of debt-increasing loans, and little concrete movement toward changing the international financial architecture. Nevertheless, when we compare the debt-relief and -management contributions of the 1990s with those of the 1980s, the bulk of the evidence is more supportive of muted optimism. This is especially true when we consider the changes in expert understandings of debt-sustainability problems. The most dramatic recent negative case, Argentina, does not for us invalidate this conclusion, given the lack of rapid contagion from recent Argentinian troubles, the possible moral-hazard-reducing consequences of harsh treatment, and the continuing attempts to renew lending to Argentina. The lack of fast contagion argues against the Argentine breakdown posing a global public bad. The moral-hazard precedents associated with readily provided additional debt relief to an Argentina that had not met previous reform promises could themselves increase rather than reduce an international public bad and jeopardize possible gains from future contributions toward the goal of debt sustainability. Further, other Latin American middle-income countries have not experienced the same degree of rejection as Argentina, arguably because their practices have not made additional relief as much of a moral hazard.

In contrast to foreign aid, debt management and relief does not readily offer clear, sustained differences in national tendencies to lead, engage in, or refrain from pro-contribution policies. At various points in time, some West European countries, the United States, and Japan have been especially forthcoming for some debtors and on some relief instruments. At other times over the past two decades and for other debtors, those countries have been particularly resistant to making contributions. The absence of a generally differentiating policy stance from one to another creditor country is not strongly contradicted by the most recent behavior reported in table 5.8. All that more recent behavior suggests is the possibility of emerging differences, with more of a pro-contribution emphasis by some countries (i.e., France, Italy, and Portugal followed by Austria, Belgium, Canada, Germany, and the United Kingdom) in contrast to the United States and (controlling for stocks of relevant debt) Japan.

Fluctuation in relative national contribution postures suggests to us that those for debt relief and management, in contrast to foreign aid, are especially driven by the changing perceived private goods and bads associated with specific forms of relief at particular times for particular debtor countries and regions. The bads often had a private and creditor club element, including damage to creditors' financial institutions, export prospects, and spheres of historical influence. Even the George W. Bush United States has swung back and forth with respect to support for collective action clauses that would subordinate a private bad for commercial creditors and international-bankruptcy—like mechanisms. Those suggested steps do, of course, move toward reducing the public bads from debt default and severe austerity conditionalities.

United Nations Peacekeeping Operations

The aggregate evidence in chapter 6 straightforwardly supports muted optimism with regard to peacekeeping, even though our analysis focused only on United Nations efforts. If our analysis had included other multilateral and unilateral peacekeeping ventures, the evidence would be even stronger. An early post–Cold War increase was followed by a decline that stopped short of historical levels but subsequently returned to higher levels in terms of the number of cases, funding, and personnel. A broadening club or public element is suggested as UN peacekeeping became more globally widespread and the number of actively contributing countries increased. While those contributing a more than token share of personnel did decline for a while, there was an increase in the share of personnel contributions born by more than the same few countries, with more important roles in personnel contributions being borne by countries outside of the U.S. alliance system and lodged in the global South.

UN rules for authorizing and funding peacekeeping have meant that it would happen only if acceptable to the small club with veto power (the permanent members of the Security Council) and the somewhat larger club on which most of the remaining financial costs would be levied. These rules, even in their recently modified form, suggest that the aggregate activity patterns mentioned previously could not have occurred unless the members of both clubs saw substantial club and private goods being furthered or bads reduced. Failure to pay obligations, particularly by the United States and Russia, has at times posed great difficulties, and if this behavior continues, it argues for muted pessimism. Yet that obstacle seems to have lessened in a variety of ways in recent years. While contributing states and their volumes of contribution have varied with the private element involved, there are few signs of a reduction in their ranks for the set of cases active at any one point in time, and dropouts seem more than balanced by replacement contributors. This may well reflect joint product characteristics of international peacekeeping operations, especially when considering the potential for reducing negative spillovers from conflicts relevant to particular contributors and the payments obtained for troop commitments. In any event, we also think that the case for UN intervention versus standing aside has increasingly involved amelioration of international public and private bads. The latter have included the consequences of tolerating inhumane behavior, with its corollary of unwanted emigration, and de facto moral complicity. Such motives are part of the argued basis for muted optimism.

Unlike development assistance and debt relief and management, the possibility of contributions to peacekeeping extends to most countries and is not primarily limited to those most well-off and economically advanced. Also, we consider two distinct types of contributions: money (relative to UN-levied obligations) and people. Using the criteria introduced in chapter 6, contribution policy tendencies of particular countries are readily distinguished. Those now standing out for positive behaviors on both aspects are Australia, Austria, Canada, Denmark, France, Finland, Germany, India, Ireland, Italy, Japan, Norway, Poland, Slovakia, Spain, Sweden, and the United Kingdom, followed by Belgium, China, the Czech Republic, the Netherlands, New Zealand, Portugal, and Turkey. On the personnel side alone, we would add the following countries to the set of sustained contributors: Argentina, Brazil, Ghana, Indonesia, Nepal, Pakistan, the United States, and the USSR/ Russian Federation. Since 1987, they have been joined by many more countries than have retreated from that role, including many states in Central and Eastern Europe and in the global south.

Our optimism is muted by three primary considerations. First, while as many countries have recently taken on a contributor role as have withdrawn, the financial significance of those withdrawing is far greater (the United States and Brazil). That pessimistic note, however, may be a matter more of the past than of the future in light of changes in UN peacekeeping levies, the payment of U.S. arrears, and the substantial U.S. financing of non-UN operations. Second, recent U.S. legislation imposes especially severe conditions on participation, especially an exemption from proceedings against U.S. participants in the International Criminal Court. Third, repeated calls to bolster UN capabilities for rapid, large-scale peacekeeping operations have not been put into practice. That situation, however, is far different from one of reducing UN capabilities and at least preserves their growth in recent years.

Global Environmental Quality

On the subject of global environmental quality, any general conclusion about the fit with muted optimism relative to muted pessimism must be highly contingent for two reasons. The first is because of the evolution of scientific and technological understanding of threats to environmental quality and the measures that can be used to reduce those threats. This is especially a concern when considering measures that soften trade-offs with economic growth. If history is any guide, we can expect substantial additional understanding in the future. Second, if we adopt summation or weakest-link perspectives on challenges to environmental quality, the future conduct of large developing-country economies will play a crucial role. The future of environmental quality is only to a moderate extent in the hands of the OECD countries. Economic growth is an imperative in the South and is unlikely to be sacrificed to environmental integrity if a direct economic/environment trade-off is perceived. Southern politicians are unlikely to adopt policies that require their countries to forgo improved standards of living while the global North can adopt such policies and maintain high standards of living. Thus, the prospects for muted optimism depend on what will emerge in terms of southern assessments of the compatibility between economic growth and proenvironment policies. Those assessments, in turn, will be significantly affected by what the global North provides in terms of both best-shot proenvironment technologies and economic incentives for environmentally friendly practices. Some of those incentives can be related to policy areas we have discussed—that is, development assistance and debt relief and management—but others extend well beyond them to trade, investment, and technology transfer.

With these caveats, we think that the balance of evidence in chapter 7 favors muted optimism, but narrowly so. For best-shot research-and-development contributions, most of the countries with the most advanced science and technology capabilities have increased their efforts to make relevant contributions. Spending on pollution abatement and control, while not marked by clear increases in general, did show such a pattern in a number of West European countries and in the United States. Financial contributions to international environmental programs either were persistent for the major economies of the OECD (the United States, Japan, Germany, France, the United Kingdom, and Italy), or, in the case of the Environmental Fund, rebounded from declines in the first half of the 1990s. A number of smaller OECD economies persistently increased their contributions and were joined in more recent years by Russia and China. The number of proenvironment international agreements surged with especially high degrees of participation by West Europeans and a middling level of participation by the United States and Canada. Southern countries participated less in these agreements but did not uniformly abstain from them. Unilateral protections of substantial shares of national territory were rather widespread in OECD member countries in Western Europe, in Oceania, and in some developing countries (especially in Latin America).

With respect to reductions of bads, muted optimism is supported by proenvironment efficiency gains in energy use relative to economic activity around the world and to a more limited extent in emissions of organic water pollutants relative to industrial employment. As for greenhouse and ozone-depleting gases, some countries decreased in overall volumes of global emissions. Carbon dioxide emissions relative to economic activity were cut sharply in much of the North and the South, including China and the United States, with exceptional efficiency levels achieved by many West European countries and Japan. Other air pollutants showed declines in relation to economic activity for the OECD countries as well as in absolute volumes of emissions.

Muted pessimism finds most of its support in the absolute amounts of environmental bads generated, but even in this case some countries seem to have taken a course we associate with a more optimistic perspective. Here is where the role of the developing countries is and will continue to be particularly crucial in determining the future course of environmental quality. For example, the substantial reductions in organic water pollutant emissions by France, the United Kingdom, Japan, and the United States were accompanied by substantial increases by China and India. Changes in carbon dioxide emission volumes are especially informative in this respect, as shown in table 7.13. The reductions by a few northern countries that did not benefit from wall-fall changes (Belgium, France, the United Kingdom), those in some that did, and the only modest percentage increases by many others were swamped by the large increases in major southern economies.

Taken together, we think the balance tenuously favors muted optimism given the (at worst) mixed record of the United States, Canada, Australia, and the larger southern economies and the possible leadership shown by some West Europeans. Contributions to environmental quality are in a race with factors working to counter them, but we see more signs that the race is at least not being lost, even if it is hardly decisively won. If we assume, as international relations structuralists do, that the developed world creates the rules of the game for the world system, then it may be a reasonable conclusion that the least developed countries will be offered carrots and sticks to follow the rules. The rules suggested by West European behavior work in favor of environmental quality. While recent U.S. actions suggest a substantial chance that the North will not unify around those rules, the American record we have reviewed and American public opinion in support of environmental quality suggest that the future of American global environmental policy is more likely to be contested than already determined.

In sum, we conclude first that there is a clear core of countries that stand out for recent contributions to global order and progress. That finding is based on inspection of the detailed results reported earlier for development assistance, debt relief and management for low-income countries, international peacekeeping, and environmental quality.[1] For all four of those issue areas, these countries are Belgium, France, Germany, Italy, Portugal, and the United Kingdom. Others do so for three of the issue areas: Austria, Canada, Denmark, the Netherlands, Norway, and Sweden. Finland, Spain, and Switzerland arguably stand out for two of our issue areas. Japan has a strong record on the environment and, more recently, on UNPKO contributions. It is noteworthy that most of the mentioned states are located in Western Europe and that the United States is absent from the list. The pattern runs counter to the expectations of hegemonic-stability theory and the classic version of public goods theory. In sum, we believe that the balance of evidence supports muted optimism more than muted pessimism for international debt relief and management, international peacekeeping, and, in a more precarious way, environmental affairs. No verdict between the two perspectives is yet strongly warranted for foreign aid.

BELIEFS AND POLICY DIFFERENCES

Our expectation that some countries are more inclined than others to adopt policies—in general or for particular issues—in pursuit of global order has been confirmed. We turn now to the extent that such variation seems to match with the general domestic public opinion beliefs presented in chapter 3 and more specifically with those about foreign aid, international peacekeeping, and environmental quality reported in chapters 4, 6, and 7, respectively. Our assessment of the degree of matching, however, covers only the countries for which substantial pertinent public opinion data were reviewed in those chapters. For those countries, we asked whether public opinion provides support for or resistance to contributions and collective action on the same issues where actual contributions were reported.

Part of the answer about the degree of correspondence between opinion and policy action appears in chapter 3. Those data suggest substantial pessimism about the prospects for collective action if support for contributions has to be based on broader-than-national identities. Yet much of the other data in that chapter suggest muted optimism about support for contributions based on the interests that would be served by making them, their fit with national values and role conceptions, and support for international collective action arrangements.

In the comparative section of chapter 3, we argued that several kinds of public propensities were generally conducive to contributions: (1) closeness to some international construction broader than that of one's own nation; (2) low sense of national superiority; (3) low support for economic protectionism; (4) low support for risking international conflict by assertion of national interests; and (5) high support for authoritative international institutions (as reported in table 3.1). Of the twenty-three countries polled, three or more of those criteria were met mostly by European states (current European Union (EU) members Italy, Germany, the Netherlands, Spain, and Sweden) and some accession countries (the Czech Republic, Hungary, Poland, Slovenia, and Slovakia). Japan, Canada, and Norway were on the edge of meeting that cutoff. Belgium, France, and Greece met several of the criteria. Of the other OECD countries polled, the results suggested a less positive tendency for the United

States, Australia, Austria, Ireland, and New Zealand, and the Russian public showed the pattern we view as less conducive to contributions.

When data were available, most of the contribution-inclined publics were also those strongly in favor of their regional club, while those less contribution inclined had more reservations about it. States that tended to meet these criteria are heavily represented in the summary of outstanding contributors, but several other outstanding contributors whose publics were polled did not meet the criteria—Austria and the United Kingdom. Perhaps such exceptions can be attributed to the dynamics of multilateral institutionalism and the permissiveness provided by defensive internationalism and self-realization beliefs. Comparison of the cited public opinions with national contributions by Japan supports the view that public opinion may provide permission for giving but does not guarantee it.

The comparative data showed substantial reservations in many northern and southern publics about American international policies (table 3.2). This finding suggests some inclinations to depart from American policy preferences about contributions. Since actual American contributions, especially relative to national resources, often were and are less than those of some other countries, this may imply a willingness for some other publics to support contributions greater than the U.S. supplies. More conjecturally, there may even be better prospects for contributions by others if they are couched not in a Washington-led perspective but rather in one led by West European or middle and small OECD member states. In any event, the findings in table 3.3 suggest first that some of those others are more likely to give priority for public bads reduction to the environment and the rich-poor gap than the United States is. Second, there is a significant chance of collective action with the United States to curb the dangers posed by nuclear weapons and religious and ethnic hatred.

Our examination of opinion in the EU found the patterns we associate with muted optimism among EU member countries (summarized in table 3.8) to be especially present in Denmark, Germany, Italy, the Netherlands, Sweden, and the United Kingdom. Those broad internationalist publics may be joined in contribution-conducive inclinations by the publics of Belgium, France, Greece, Luxembourg, and Spain if a perceived EU club good is salient. The Japanese public also seems well disposed in terms of beliefs we interpret as defensive internationalism (e.g., when asked about concerns of isolation) and self-realization (e.g., when asked about what sort of world role Japan ought to play). Beliefs bearing on contributions with a military element, however, have been less supportive. The American public and elites presented less of a picture rejecting contributions and more of an image of selectivity and conditionality toward such involvement in world affairs. Their beliefs seemed most likely to yield support for contributions that could be interpreted as defensive internationalism (e.g., when focusing on reducing perceived threats to the United States) or as needed to realize a national self-image of humanitarian generosity and international importance. Contributions seen as useful ways of advancing those goals would seem likely to receive support, while contributions thought to be unrelated or inimical to such aims probably would not.

Most European publics, as well as those of Japan and the United States, were relatively well disposed toward the United Nations and other multilateral institutions with a more than regional purview. This finding suggests substantial permissiveness for contributions to collective action providing global public goods and limiting global public bads beyond the club of the global North. It also indicates that the use of multilateral organizations and agreements continues to be more widely supported in the United States than American policies imply. This stock of currently unused or underused permissions suggests that there are politically feasible possibilities for a future shift toward greater multilateralism and collective action commitments by the American government.

The evidence in chapter 3 leads us to expect a generally forthcoming stance on contributions in a number of West European countries, including support for some initiative taking. With such public support—especially if it was well received by the United States—we expect that it would be emulated in Japanese opinion, especially for nonmilitary contributions bearing on Asia. We expect no clear pattern of domestic support for U.S. leadership until perceived threats to American domestic well-being and the preservation of superior international status and influence become salient. Both are embedded in views of what defensive internationalism and self-realization entail. In other words, constraints from public opinion may well be relaxed if and when the American public sees major, direct threats to itself or perceives that others are making contributions greater than or equal to American ones. How contribution policy options are framed and perceived in those terms will matter a great deal in terms of the constraint or permission provided by American public opinion.

The affinity views of Americans and of Japanese suggest to us substantial sensitivity to each other's policies toward contributions and to those of West Europeans as well. Europeans, however, will have less inclination to emulate American and Japanese actions. With the evolution of the EU, more importance may well go to the policy preferences and actual contributions of other members of that club.

In sum, West European publics tend to present the upper end of support for national effort relative to resources for improving the production of global public goods and reduction of public bads. Given the scale of Japan and America in national resources and activity, that finding is compatible with absolute volumes of some types of contributions by the United States and Japan that will be larger than those of any single European state. When West European publics are inclined toward massive and growing contributions of a sustained and generalized nature, we expect a substantial and continuing growth in global goods production and bads reduction, as the publics of the United States and Japan will not treat such European behavior as justifying a reduction of their otherwise supported national contributions. Indeed, such developments might well yield greater domestic support for some increases. Yet European publics' priorities may tend to emphasize other policy issues and thus provide constraints that call this prospect into serious doubt. That seems probable and leads us into a present and future conducive to only a mutedly optimistic pattern of contribution maintenance and growth.

Additional insight into the implications of these general policy inclinations can be gained from the more specific issue-oriented opinions reported for development assistance, international peacekeeping, and environmental quality, to which we now turn.

Development Assistance

Pro-contribution opinions about development assistance are more the rule than the exception in Western Europe. Although a shrinking set of publics supports increases in such spending, most support maintenance of current levels. Compared to the United States and Japan, a number of current EU members have relatively large activist movements supporting development assistance. This activism might provide a constraint against reductions and could produce pressure for increases in contributions by invoking declared values and self-conceptions to counter the higher priority allotted to other issues.

Development assistance also fits well with declared Japanese values and self-conceptions but was not a priority relative to other issues. The Japanese public seems to support maintenance of its current large volume of assistance with a shrinking minority in favor of increasing it. Aid was seen as useful both for its public element and private returns, fitting with conceptions emphasizing good relations with Asia and with other donors. It was also conditionally supported on the prospect that it would induce stability-enhancing behavior by the recipients. When that was thought unlikely (e.g., by North Korea and Russia), support faded sharply.

As for the U.S. public, government development assistance programs were at best tolerated, with sustained preferences for reductions. Much of this negative view was based on beliefs that aid did little for the needy and on rejection of development assistance as a tool to support political-military objectives. In other words, the public doubted that aid would in general enhance public goods or reduce public bads. Support, and thus a much weaker constraint, was more present if the content and delivery mechanisms were thought to provide relief of immediate human suffering (along a charity model) and to insure that aid would get to the deserving poor (along welfare reform lines). Providing aid with those characteristics then would be in line with self-realization of U.S. values. In recent years, those criteria have led to a split in public opinion about assistance to Africa, in contrast to more opposition to aid to other recipients. When aid seemed to be part of a defensively internationalist portfolio to deal with critical threats with a large private element for the United States—for example, terrorism—the public became more supportive. In contrast to public preferences, elites have recently been more positive about the development assistance policy instrument and have continued to be more supportive of using aid to advance particular political-military foreign policy objectives, such as the consolidation of post–Cold-War Central and Eastern Europe (a joint product outcome). But elites were still hardly enthusiasts and desired others to bear the primary burden of aid provision.

In sum, the burden of public justification will lie in Europe and Japan on those favoring reductions and in the United States on those favoring increases or even maintenance of contributions. The relative degree of public support for development assistance fits in general with the actual contribution patterns discussed earlier in this chapter and in chapter 4. This crude ordering of public propensity to support contributions also seems compatible with the conclusions drawn previously from chapter 3.

International Peacekeeping

The more limited public opinion data on international peacekeeping, reported in chapter 6, suggest little general enthusiasm among the OECD countries but some acceptance for contributions to some situations, especially when the United Nations is involved. At most, our opinion data suggest the absence of a general rejection of contributions rather than a general commitment to making them. Put simply, the publics were open to persuasion about the need to make contributions. They would, however, not be easy to persuade except in cases of perceived threats to their domestic well-being and great foreign human suffering. In effect, peacekeeping operations were seen at best as a regrettable necessity when other modes of conflict limitation and resolution failed. Given the importance attached to "local conflicts" and "religious and ethnic hatred" as world problems (in chapter 3), action will seemingly be required when local conflicts flare. But the publics of the western members of the UN Security Council did not give international peacekeeping a high priority for their countries or for the UN itself.

The "regrettable necessity" view was associated for Europeans with proximity and negative spillovers, as in the former Yugoslavia. But even such cases were not attributed high priority until after conflicts had persisted for a lengthy time. Steps to achieve the capabilities to discharge the EU Petersburg missions, if and when fully implemented, would enable more effective action against "regrettable necessity" cases but would not guarantee that such actions would be taken in a timely fashion. For the U.S. public, regrettable necessity was associated mostly with perceived threats to strategic interests, including homeland defense, and ending barbarism and human suffering, rationales that might be more persuasive after rather than before violence. Even then, the necessity was for short-term intervention rather than long-term presence. For the Japanese, the necessities were those of avoiding strains in relations with other contributors or the weakening of international institutions. These considerations in general warranted some financial contributions but not more than the most limited military ones. In sum, OECD publics offered little support for substantial anticipatory commitments to international peacekeeping or acceptance of a blanket obligation to participate in UN or other international peacekeeping operations

These beliefs, with their lack of enthusiasm for peacekeeping operations, were accompanied by strong preferences for multilateral operations with the United Nations or other international support and participation. Multilateral auspices such as those would, of course, serve to spread the contribution burden around and would certify that a peacemaking/peace restoration/peacekeeping mission did indeed have a large public element. There would be a stronger prima facie case that the peacekeeping operation was about more than private payoffs to the United States. Absent the most persuasively immediate private bads foreign situations seemed to pose to the United States, multilateral involvement was a requirement for public and elite support. UN auspices were a sine qua non for the Japanese public. The U.S. stance was buttressed by American public skepticism about the efficacy of such interventions in terms either of providing international public goods or of reducing international public bads. On the private side of the ledger, peacekeeping operations were thought to hold out the possibility of increasing an image of American power but not of gaining greater international respect.[2] The importance of multilateral participation and international mandate factors introduces significant uncertainty about whether public opinion will be more compatible with muted optimism or muted pessimism. On these counts, any summary judgment rests on whether the prospects for meeting both requirements are growing or shrinking.

Finally, there are issues of public permissiveness toward peacekeeping operations that involve the application of force to make and enforce peace (biased, coercive interventions) and thus can involve substantial loss of life to personnel contributors and to bystanders in the conflict locale. These hot conflict situations are, of course, ones that increasingly face the international community when peacekeeping possibilities are posed. Fragmentary data suggest a contradiction between U.S. public support for such "harsh" interventions and tolerance for American casualties. This is a contradiction avoidable only by getting others to do the job for an extended period of time or by limiting the U.S. role to military means that make it almost impossible to avoid immediate or continuing "collateral damage" to the local population. Given the professed values in chapter 3, the latter seems acceptable only in circumstances of highly salient, extremely bad behavior by the target of the intervention. Yet taking actions that hurt noncombatants clashes with Japanese and European views about the warrant for the peacekeeping operation and thus their continuing participation in it. Getting others to do the temporally extended part of the job may be difficult (see table 6.1A) if the primary American policy motivation seems to be reducing a private bad for the United States. We are left with the paradox that those cases where the United States has the strongest contribution appeals to its domestic public may be precisely those where the publics of potential partners have the greatest ambivalence about contributions.

The limited public opinion data specifically on peacekeeping do not allow for a clear conclusion about the relative fit with a muted optimist or pessimist position, although they do run counter to more extremely optimistic or pessimistic alternatives. We suggest that a tentative conclusion in favor of muted optimism can be drawn from the more general attitudes in chapter 3, but only if we are willing to make three inferential jumps. The first is that the publics we categorized as generally having a pro-contribution stance will apply it to peacekeeping matters in general and to specific cases in particular. The second is that, given the previous inference, affinity considerations will lead to satisfying the multilateral participation and international mandate requirements for many cases. The third is that the first two will be reinforced for pro-contribution publics as international participation and mandates are seen as ways to bolster desirable constraints on suspect American policy tendencies.

Environmental Quality

The large body of public opinion data on environmental protection reviewed in chapter 7 more strongly supports the mutedly optimistic perspective than does the contribution record. There are a demand for national and international action in many West European countries, permissiveness for such moves in Japan, an activist environmental constituency in the United States, and concerns about environmental hazards in much of the South as well as in the North. In sum, domestic support is widespread for proenvironmental activity in principle, and there is a substantial prospect of domestic political risk for governments seemingly unconcerned about environmental quality. Most of the polled publics are not willing to leave environmental quality to the invisible hand of the market; most want governmental intervention. Public desires are, however, restrained to varying degrees by lack of priority for the environment, satisfaction with results achieved, unwillingness to bear a substantial economic cost, or reluctance to abandon some consumption preferences. The effect of these factors fluctuates depending on the specific environmental issues under consideration, the perceived lack of direct impact and imminence of environmental harms, and the prevailing degree of concern about prosperity. Domestic support tends to be strongest for action against those environmental hazards thought to have immediate local impacts (such as air and water pollution), with less urgency for those thought to have geographically remote and temporally distant impacts (such as global warming). The factors possibly supporting muted pessimism have been less present in the perceptions of a number of West European publics. While these factors seem recently to have gained strength in the United States, especially for elites, support for proenvironment action retains majorities in the public. A crucial swing factor in public support will be the extent that specific forms of contributions seem to avoid policies that win environmentally and lose economically.

Many publics have seen the global environment as more threatened than their local environment. Yet publics differ in degree about their national responsibility to act for global amelioration of environmental challenges. Few publics, however, have either denied any national or club responsibility or accepted primary responsibility in a sustained way. These opinions again suggest widespread support for some contribution-oriented actions but leave open questions of leadership and acceptable burden sharing. Those most supportive of leadership and least concerned with the burden borne by others are found in some West European countries (particularly Germany, the Netherlands, the Nordic countries, and the United Kingdom) and emphasize an EU role. The Japanese public seems strongly attracted to the environment as an emphasis for their country's international activity. The U.S. public seems less motivated in that direction, perhaps because environmental damage is not as prominent as other threats from abroad. Yet the American public does not reject contributions but rather tends to want assurances of matching contributions by others, particularly in the fast-growth parts of the South.

As events surrounding the Kyoto Protocol suggest, the patterns discussed previously provide a domestic political basis for West European and Japanese governments to keep pushing proenvironment contributions in the face of U.S. resistance. These patterns also provide a basis on which the governments of many southern economies can seek such contributions from the North. And American politicians who would oppose contributions will face continuing and evidentially hard to meet pressures to demonstrate that threats to environmental quality can be avoided by their stance and that others will free ride on whatever contributions the United States makes. In our view, such justifications are increasingly subject to challenge from growing scientific understanding about the nonexcludability of the United States from global environmental bads and the policy stance of other OECD governments.

Among the OECD countries, those with particularly impressive environmental quality contribution records are Austria, Denmark, France, Germany, Italy, the Netherlands, Sweden, and the United Kingdom. With the clear exception of Austria and less so of France, these states also had relatively high support in terms of citizen activism and public opinion for environmental protection. Yet once again, others with equal domestically supportive conditions were not equally outstanding contributors.

In sum, our public opinion analysis supports muted optimism with regard to most OECD countries in terms of a general pro-contribution bias, especially for the reduction of bads seen to have a private as well as a public element. More specifically, the data support muted optimism with regard to public support in Western Europe and Japan for foreign aid and environmental quality. This is less the case for peacekeeping, especially coercive peacemaking. Those general proclivities are lower in the United States for foreign aid and for environmental quality but are relatively greater than for other countries with respect to coercive peace-making (if not protracted peace restoration and maintenance). The major reservations to a mutedly optimistic conclusion center on the United States. Yet those reservations should not be overblown. The American public is neither generally unilateralist or isolationist. Our evidence suggests that the United States will contribute to the production of global public goods and the reduction of global public bads when the American public perceives a threat to well-being and safety at home, feels affinity to the other actively involved countries, and views positively the relevant international organizations. There are also substantial indications of willingness to provide temporary surges in contributions in reaction to episodic massive humanitarian disasters (such as for the fight against AIDS). There surely have been, are, and will be numerous situations for which the U.S. public is averse to major contributions to reduce what are seen as predominantly bads for others in the world. This does not warrant a conclusion that there will be a paucity of situations where the U.S. public will provide permission for or even demand collective action.

EXPECTATIONS AND POLICY NEEDS

What does our work suggest for the pursuit of global order and progress and the prospects for giving in the coming years? For us, much of the answer lies in four general expectations about constructive collective action and five policy needs that, if met, will increase the chances of more optimistic international futures.

Expectation 1: Positive Incrementalism Pushed by Events

Our first expectation is that any broad progiving policy will develop in an incremental way. For any student of politics and organizations, this expectation should come as no surprise. Nonetheless, it leaves us with the troubling possibility that the pursuit of global order and progress will develop in ways that are too little, too late to cope effectively with the problems that face the contemporary world system. That is by and large what we found with respect to the debt-sustainability problems of middle-income developing countries. On a more positive note, however, the data we examined in our four policy areas demonstrate that progress has been made and that states can cooperate, albeit imperfectly, in pursuit of reduction in impure public bads. It is also hardly out of the question that significant shocks in world affairs will push the incremental engine faster than it would otherwise go. If nothing else, responses to the events of 9/11 and to SARS have shown how quickly the United States and other states can muster their collective energies to advance a particular, apparently urgent international goal. Incrementalism may actually be punctuated by landmark fits and starts of activity that help move policy to a higher contribution and reduction level more quickly than straightforward trend analysis would suggest.

Expectation 2: Greater Multilateral Institutionalism

An additional spur to pro-contribution incrementalism will be provided by the growing reliance of major actors in the international system on multilateral institutions. Whether sovereign states like it or not, more and more issues present transboundary challenges that cannot be dealt with effectively or efficiently without multilateral action. The evolution of G-8 summitry offers a case in point. Growing out of the Rambouillet summit in 1975 in the aftermath of the first oil shock, G-8 summitry has evolved from informal discussions of common economic problems among heads of governments to annual consultations on a wide range of issues with recurrent lower-level policy work throughout the year. In our cases, the growing collaboration in debt management, aid guidelines and collective policy pronouncements; multilateral peacekeeping efforts; and significant and widespread participation in international environmental agreements suggests a pattern of multilateralism that is far from perfect, efficient, and purely cooperative but nonetheless exists and appears to be growing in institutional stature, scope, and regularity.

Expectation 3: Growing Importance of Nongovernmental Organizations

In much of what we know about globalization and its impacts, the role of nonstate actors (NGOs and international nongovernmental organizations, or INGOs) shows continuing growth. This holds for the foreign policies of local governments and their "paradiplomats" (see Aldecoa and Keating 1999), shaping agendas for international collective action by governments and international governmental organizations, and implementing and monitoring their contribution and reduction programs and projects. NGOs and INGOs will increasingly play crucial roles in facilitating policy decisions, identifying potential and existing policy problems, and lobbying for preferred courses of action. Even if states wish to remain staked to sovereignty (a very likely scenario), state leaders will need to navigate (or maybe manipulate) better the array of nonstate actors to remain in office and effectively deal with problems. Those realities are already evident in terms of the number and importance of NGOs and INGOs involved in the four issue areas we surveyed as well as in many others. The growth of NGO and INGO importance stands, whatever one's judgments about the extent that particular organizations (e.g., religious fundamentalist or business ones) make positive or negative contributions to public goods provision and bads reduction.

Expectation 4: Persisting Importance of Domestic Politics

The previous expectations will not eliminate the tendencies for different states to follow different giving patterns, tendencies embedded in the varieties of permissions, preferences, and representation that characterize their domestic politics. For example, even though Japanese decision makers have moved toward favoring a greater operational peacekeeping role in recent years, more significant direct military involvement will be difficult for Japan to pursue because of domestic constraints. Aid will probably remain a tough domestic sell in the United States, regardless of what anyone thinks about the wisdom of prevailing opinions about it. More generally, accepting the crucial role of domestic politics does, as we have shown, direct our attention to sources of support or at least tolerance of more robust policies to produce global goods and reduce global bads and not just resistance to greater giving. We did find some indications of greater support for some forms of giving, especially in Japan and the United States, than contribution records indicate.

Any success in capitalizing on the opportunities that domestic politics provides will, however, depend on a variety of political elite motivations, rationales, and skills in framing issues in domestic politics.[3] Yet, at best, effective framing will produce only what are for us positive policy developments if the "givers" will be doing more than providing private benefits to some narrow set of foreigners or domestic constituencies. Further, as we discussed in earlier chapters, attention to differences in domestic politics can call attention to comparative political advantages for various forms of giving and thus to the greater efficiencies offered by specialization in global giving.

Most broadly, our expectations do not yield unlimited confidence in a bright future for global order and progress. They do warrant the more modest claim that some elements of a conducive policy context for global order are now present and are likely to remain with us for quite a while. Adding to and strengthening those fragments seems highly doubtful without sustained, substantial, and successful transnational action to fill five currently unmet sets of policy needs.

Policy Need 1: Improved "Global Governance" Capacity

Developments away from purely state centered global politics drive home the need for greater capacity in designing and managing governance arrangements of more than a national, public-sector kind. But as Murphy (2000, 780) has argued, the broadest of such global governance arrangements are "poorly done and poorly understood." Multilateralism per se and NGO activism do not guarantee efficient and effective giving policies and can even inhibit and delay contributions with a public element. On occasion, multilateralism and NGO activism may even lend themselves to inflated illusions about what the parties have committed to contributing.

The consequences for global order and progress can be no better than our competence and commitment in two respects. The first involves our understanding of the factors that determine the performance of arrangements for global and transnational governance, their current status, and their future prospects. Such improved understanding can provide reasons directly to engage issues of feasibility and desirability of public goods provision rather than simply to talk about them in the many regional and global forums relevant to the issues. The second respect involves the policy conduct of national governments and NGOs in international governance. Both need to emphasize more than lip service to multilateralism (commitments to consult and dialogue) and vague paper pledges of good intentions. Pursuit of multinational and transnational arrangements for ameliorating global public goods shortfalls and public bads oversupply needs far greater resource priority and career incentives for politicians and bureaucrats than are now present. These needs are hardly easy to meet in a world of parochial partisan politics, even with the occasional spurs of policy necessity presented by salient, dramatic threats that produce the perceived need for action at a level broader than the state.

Policy Need 2: Improved Education about Global Interdependence

Since we expect no decline in the role of domestic politics, increases in effective global giving will need increased and higher-priority net domestic support. The challenge is how to meet that need in the face of developments that can provide impetus in the opposite direction, such as job-threatening import competition, cultural-identity-threatening immigration, and physical-safety-threatening terrorism. For us, an important part of a portfolio of strategies for the pursuit of global order and progress is education of two kinds. The first emphasizes awareness on the part of politicians and citizens of the manifold ways in which global developments can create direct problems for them (i.e., nonexcludable global bads). Such "relevance education" is of course facilitated by all the secular trends making transborder interactions more likely and more significant. Growing awareness of the inevitability of impacts from external and global developments can increase incentives for national leaders to work to shape global and international developments proactively rather than only to resist reactively and wall off their countries. Yet awareness per se can fuel demands for the latter sorts of responses by anxious publics and responsive politicians.

Accordingly, a second educational emphasis is necessary for successful collective action. This far more difficult challenge deals with understanding how to shape inherent interdependence to produce win-win outcomes—in our earlier language, to produce impure public goods and reduce impure public bads. Education along these lines does not deny the importance of national interests or patriotism but rather provides both negative and positive lessons. The negative ones concern the dubious prospects of private (national) payoffs from policies that scant the international public element of consequences. The positive lessons concern the substantial prospects of success for policies that emphasize the significant positive consequences from collective action.

Education strategies, of course, seldom provide immediate gains. When conducted in primary and secondary schools, colleges, and universities, such education can, however, shape successor generations of politicians, officials, and publics. Educational success is, then, not a fix for immediate problems but rather a long-term way to raise the chances that policies will truly focus on ameliorating the underlying causes of threats to global order and progress. Education will likely also increase the chances that policies can become more than ad hoc attempts to react to ugly events, reactive palliatives often coming after grave damage and then evaporating and fading away with the next headline.

Policy Need 3: Improved Policy Quality—Anticipatory, Sustained, Timely

Improved multilateralism and education can create a more receptive context for policies that shape the future by investing in public goods creation and forestalling public bads. Improvements will also help to sustain policy initiatives for the length of time required for them to have hard-to-reverse impacts. The actual making of contributions that effectively and efficiently produce those outcomes calls for policies whose quality is improved in several ways. One of the prevailing aspects of the efforts we have analyzed in the post–Cold War period is that active steps to increase contributions have often been reactive rather than preventive and have been marked by a burst of activity and ambitious goal setting followed by a fallback toward the status quo ante and a loss of momentum. That pattern provides much of the basis for muted pessimism. Analogous to treating high fevers and medical emergencies but not their underlying causes, such an approach is inadequate for achieving desirable long-term results. Unwarranted expectations about the payoffs from sporadic crisis-driven contributions can foster skepticism among northern governments and publics about the merits of making even those sorts of contributions in the future.

Failure to adopt and sustain the proclaimed goals of those operational programs can foster skepticism among southern governments and publics about the North's true intentions and the reliability of its pledges. We have seen grounds for that lack of confidence that are hard to dismiss and that cast doubt on contribution prospects with regard to development assistance, debt management, international peacekeeping, and environmental quality. In short, too much is often promised and too little is often delivered. Perhaps we can do more for global order and progress if we go on the wagon with respect to sunset deadlines for cutting back any surges in contributions, commitments to frequent reauthorization and appropriation for contributions to continue, signing on to international agreements with dubious domestic ratification prospects, and trumpeting agreements on goals without binding timetables and firm and feasible plans for implementation.

Even if policy quality improves by becoming more anticipatory and sustained, it is unrealistic to expect perfect foresight about opportunities for and threats to global order and progress. Nor is it any more realistic to expect that what foresight is available usually will triumph in contests for policy attention and resources. Accordingly, shocks and surprises will continue, even with the improvements in policy quality just discussed. This unfortunate truth suggests a third respect where policy quality needs to be improved—fast response collective action capabilities.

Multilateralism does not inherently guarantee such capabilities and can even work against them unless such arrangements are given the standing authority and resources to act quickly, predictably, and effectively when red lines on the international temperature chart are crossed. Selfish efforts to retain state sovereignty above all other considerations will then equate to denying the needed authority and resources to multilateral arrangements. Those denials, in turn, feed the self-fulfilling prophecy of sluggish and helpless multilateral institutions. Confirmations of that prophecy strengthen the case for continuing mandate and resource denials. Globalized education as discussed previously becomes an even more pressing long-term policy need if we hope to break out of the vicious spiral of sovereignty assertion and defense.

Policy Need 4: Broaden Participation in Pursuing Global Order

Our issue area analyses and the public opinion context reported in chapter 3 found signs of support, albeit mixed ones, in much of the global North for increased contributions to the production of global public goods and reduction of public bads. The public beliefs we discussed show substantial, if often conditional, sources of domestic permission for at least some pro–global order and progress policies. Yet we also found that northern contributions were hindered in important ways by skepticism about the necessary commitments by one or another part of the global South and, indeed, by developments in the South that might counterbalance or even outweigh any gains from northern contributions. Those contribution and production limitations applied to development assistance, debt relief and management, international peacekeeping, and environmental quality. Yet we also found fragmentary signs that some southern governments and publics sought to participate in ameliorative collective action.

This means that substantial gains in net contributions and movement toward global order and progress will require southern participation to a much greater extent than is now the case. Meeting that need has several elements. First, proactive southern proposals to identify and address global challenges must receive serious consideration by northern governments. This is more likely as the South offers to the North some private as well as public benefits and bads reductions. Proposals that focus primarily on northern "compensation" for historical behavior are unlikely to get such a response and thus are likely to be counterproductive. Second, particular southern governments, nonstate actors, and publics that are inclined to cooperate along lines favored by the North must in actuality and in southern perceptions gain private benefits. Failure to receive such side payments makes cooperation appear primarily as a vehicle that provides private goods and reduces private bads solely for the North. Third, northern policymakers and publics must become aware of southern contributions and the legitimate basis for some southern reservations about northern proposals. The North must also acknowledge and reward southern success stories. Meeting these needs calls for greater intellectual effort and policy action in both the South and the North, including commitments to the more anticipatory and sustained policies and the faster multilateral crisis response mechanisms discussed previously.

Policy Need 5: More Comprehensive and Consistent American Contributions

We have previously argued that American leadership is not a necessary condition for continued and growing contributions to global order and progress. Our issue area analyses suggested that in many ways, contribution leadership has not resided in Washington. This did not lead us to mutedly pessimistic conclusions, because we also found substantial, if selective and tardy, support in Americans' self-conceptions, affinities, and defensive interests for some contributions and indeed also for some degree of multilateralism. These potential sources of domestic support for contributions were accompanied by a record in our four issue areas that was more mixed than totally negative with respect to actual contributions.

Yet the lack of a requirement for American leadership does not equate to the lack of a need for American contributions. A forthcoming American role is needed for several reasons. One is the sheer magnitude of tangible American impacts on the rest of the world in terms of the extent that global public goods are produced or bads reduced. Contribution niggardliness in absolute or relative terms will continue to have more than neutral consequences. Another reason is the internationally perceived importance of what America does in terms of the judgments others make about the utility of their possible contributions. It is hard to imagine, for example, that much progress can be achieved in meeting the needs for more global multilateralism in the face of determined, official U.S. opposition. It is no less hard to imagine a surge in southern cooperation with the North if potential cooperators feel that Washington will leave them swinging in the wind. Nor are we likely to get massive contribution increases by others countries if their leaders are left exposed to domestic charges of being gullibly exploited by a free-riding United States. For these and other reasons, there are grounds to think that the United States plays a crucial role in supporting or frustrating movement to meet better the needs for global order and progress.

As of this writing, the George W. Bush administration seems to show a level of resistance (indeed, hostility) to contributions and other American obligations to genuinely multilateral collective action and international cooperation that has not been seen since before World War II. That is matched by the far-from-obviously-true presumption that current American policy preferences are reliably excellent in what they will generate in terms of international public goods and reduced bads. Such a "my way or the highway" posture hardly seems to commend muted optimism.

Yet we think that the practices we label as warranting muted optimism are hardy and resilient enough to make an obituary premature. While massive increases in contributions to global amelioration may require that the United States come through, maintaining current volumes for many types of contributions and keeping existing institutions alive may not. For regional as distinct from global amelioration, many parts of the world have and will turn to multilateral institutionalism without the United States and will pursue their own sense of club goods and impure public goods. Further, U.S. policies may well be pulled and pushed back to multilateralism and contributions on a host of issues, whatever the prevalence of supremacist rhetoric.

Examples are readily at hand. Washington has not hesitated to call quickly for multilateral institutions and NGOs to pick up burdens in Afghanistan and Iraq. It finds itself bogged down in international economics without the consent of numerous others in the World Trade Organization Millennium Round and the formation of a Free Trade Area of the Americas. In the environmental arena, the U.S. government has little choice in the face of an EU precautionary regime for chemicals but to negotiate with Brussels or invoke the processes of the World Trade Organization. Even the "war on terrorism" and its repeated flurries of incidents make the adequacy of unilateral measures hard to defend.

This current American deviation from Cold War and post–Cold War patterns, then, is not immediately fatal to global public goods provision and bads reduction. Furthermore, Washington will have difficulty sustaining this deviation, although we offer no expectations about when and for what particular issues it will be erased. We are sure that it is far from becoming an embedded consensus and remains very vulnerable to erosion from foreign actions and domestic evaluations of the bottom line yielded by assertive unilateralism.

So where does this leave us? We set out to see if there were grounds for muted optimism about the prospects for the sorts of northern giving that would advance global order and progress. On conceptual and empirical grounds, we have argued that the grounds for muted optimism have existed based on the historical record and continue to exist today. Yet we also recognize that such steps have hardly won the race with the evolution of international and global ills and the complexity of timely and effective responses to them. Nor can we assert with confidence that the world is set on a course that will provide effective and timely policy responses. Whether muted optimism or muted pessimism is more warranted for the present and future remains not just to be seen but to be shaped. Neither is a foregone conclusion, and neither is fully under the control of the wealthy and powerful North. The expectations introduced earlier in this chapter suggest only the possibility of the sorts of evolution in international affairs that muted optimism envisions. The extent to which those possibilities will become probabilities will depend on meeting the five policy needs we outlined. We hope that those needs will be met, and we think our findings imply that it can happen with the maintenance and diffusion of the policy stance we found in a core of mostly West European nations. We are not so utopian as to expect that these needs will be fulfilled quickly or without major setbacks and delays, and we believe that the long-term outcomes will depend on continuing battles in the trenches of domestic politics, especially in the global South and in the United States. While we do not know if those battles will be won, we have found reasons to reject any conclusion that they have in general been or inevitably will be lost.

NOTES

Chapter 1

1. We do not, however, assume that their understandings are necessarily wise.

2. Some inclined to this view emphasize political economy aspects (e.g., Gilpin 1981, 1987; Kindleberger 1973). Others emphasize military, physical security aspects (e.g., Mearsheimer 2001).

3. In this vein, Cox 2002 argues that 9/11 has highlighted the renaissance of American world power.

4. In *Ruling the World*, Gruber (2000) argues that the primary explanation for the growth of supranational institutions in recent years and what is apparently increasing international cooperation is that the powerful winning states have moved ahead with many cooperative institutions and ventures in a go-it-alone way. In an argument that resembles Olson's privileged-group argument for public goods provision, Gruber contends that the powerful cooperate because it is beneficial to themselves to do so and that others (the losing states, or weaker parties) eventually follow. As we and many others have noted, much of what has gone on in international cooperation since World War II has apparently followed this model, with the United States in the lead.

5. For discussions of the validity of assumptions about state decline, see, e.g., Doremus et al. 1998; Evans 1997; Hirst and Thompson 1996; Spruyt 1994; Strange 1998.

6. For a discussion of the likely responses to 9/11 and their consequences, see Bobrow 2002.

Chapter 2

1. Along these lines, Bobrow 1999b provides a recent example of how different theoretical single-lens starting points lead to very different visions for the future of international affairs. Although starting from the same temporal vantage point, the conclusions reached by the single-lens essays differ dramatically.

2. Consider, for example, Lyndon Johnson's statement about increased American military commitments in Vietnam: "We did not choose to be the guardians at the gate, but there is no one else" (Johnson 1965).

3. If such goods were largely rival and available to all club members, we would have problems of common pool resources at the club level of governance.

4. The strength of those incentives will depend on club rules for consumption of the good involved, the tying of membership to contributions, and the costs to particular members a particular contribution level involves.

5. This recognition underlies substantial work building on and departing from the pure public goods approach on such international relations matters as alliance burden-sharing (see Olson and Zeckhauser 1966; Oneal 1990a, b; Palmer 1990; Sandler 1977; Sandler and Forbes 1980; Sandler and Hartley 1995; Sandler and Murdoch 1990), the management of international environmental affairs (Sandler 1997; Sandler and Sargent 1995), and international peacekeeping and peacemaking (Khanna, Sandler, and Shimizu 1998, 1999).

6. As Wolfers (1962, 74) observes, "A nation may hope to increase its prestige or its security by making sacrifices for the establishment and maintenance of international organizations."

7. For example, NATO burden-sharing has been analyzed in these terms (Sandler 1977; Sandler and Forbes 1980; Sandler and Hartley 1995; Sandler and Murdoch 1990). In this body of work, it is assumed that during the Cold War a strong conventional defense posture by the alliance provided a public good with some degree of nonrivalry and nonexcludability for NATO members. At the same time, conventional forces offered private benefits. Conventional forces deployed in one country provided that country with higher levels of privately consumable defense than those forces provided to others in the NATO collective because of limited force mobility and bounded geographic force coverage. The state where the weapons were deployed had a private goods incentive to spend on conventional forces assigned to its protection because it stood to consume more of their benefits than its fellow allies did. More subtly, the state may also have had such private incentives for forces stationed between it and an enemy on the territory of a buffer state if doing so placed the zone of wartime destruction more firmly outside the state's borders.

8. We believe that absent any sense of shared identity, a pure *They* formation, multilateral clubs will not exist or continue to exist.

9. The appropriately realistic benchmark for them in term of private benefits will not be the world as it used to be without the institution but the world as it is or might become with the institution. For a more negative view of the effects of international institutions on smaller members, see Gruber 2000.

10. We think the North American Free Trade Area meets those conditions since we view it as an expansion of the previously established Canada–United States trade arrangement and the ongoing explorations of a free trade area of the Americas would in effect enlarge the agreement.

11. See Jervis 1999 for a set of arguments similar to the ones that follow from our framing of the three schools.

12. Such a situation occurs either when there is a majority-determining body of defensive internationalist opinion or a stalemate in the face of worsening threats between opinions supportive of general offensive realist or neoliberal policy inclinations.

Chapter 3

1. We recognize that international cooperation and contributions may well involve the complicated interplay of identities, interests, and institutional representation (Bartolini, Risse, and Strath 1999). Rather than denying the importance of organized agents within and across nations (Checkel 1999), we think that identity and normative beliefs can be conducive to creating agents, not just their consequence. Further, our view of the public opinion–policy nexus suggests that after agents are created, they pay some heed to prevailing identities and norms (Risse-Kappen 1992).

2. We are indebted to Aaron Hoffman for stimulating our thinking about trust in international affairs.

3. Our argument resembles those in the early integration literature (Deutsch et al. 1957; Hoffman 1966; Sinnott 1995a), which emphasized the importance of public opinion about such matters (E. B. Haas 1971; Nye 1971; Schmitter 1971). Also, public opinion support for multilateral internationalism provides evidence of "diffuse values" and attitudes toward specific "interdependence" and "transnational" issues (Hoffman 1966; Krasner 1983; Rosenau and Czempiel 1992).

4. Because of a lack of specific opinion data on debt management policy, we assume that some general conceptions can be extrapolated from the more general opinion data about foreign aid and economic cooperation.

5. Of particular importance with regard to quality are sampling and question and response-alternative wording in terms of bias and clarity. Yet even with high quality, pressure for selectiveness is inherent in the polling situation, the limited time for which respondents will consent to participate, and the costs associated with lengthy surveys.

6. As a crude rule of thumb, it is conservative to reject the significance of differences of less than 5 percent. We think a 10 percent threshold for making much of differences provides warranted inferential caution.

7. Results were in the 10–19 percent range in Argentina, Belgium, Bulgaria, Canada, Chile, the Czech Republic, Finland, France, Germany, Mexico, the Netherlands, Portugal, Russia, South Africa, Spain, Switzerland, the United Kingdom, and the United States. They were even lower for publics in Austria, Belarus, China, Denmark, Estonia, Hungary, Iceland, India, Ireland, Japan, Latvia, Lithuania, Norway, Poland, Romania, Slovenia, Sweden, and Turkey.

8. With the exception of Russia, the mean, multi-item scores on national superiority (column D) conform to this pattern.

9. The national public samples were taken in Germany, France, the United Kingdom, Italy, Spain, Turkey, Croatia, Albania, Macedonia, Bulgaria, Poland, Romania, Hungary, the Czech Republic, Slovakia, Estonia, Lithuania, Latvia, Serbia, Azerbaijan, Armenia, Belarus, Georgia, Kazakhstan, Uzbekistan, Russia, Ukraine, El Salvador, Panama, Mexico, Bolivia, Peru, Colombia, Venezuela, Chile, Brazil, Argentina, Israel, Morocco, Australia, Japan, Korea, Thailand, and South Africa. Urban or elite samples were taken in Guatemala, Honduras, Nicaragua, Costa Rica, Jordan, Lebanon, India, Kenya, Nigeria, Tanzania, Cameroon, Ghana, and Senegal.

10. The countries were the United States, Austria, Denmark, Finland, France, Germany, Italy, Luxembourg, the Netherlands, Portugal, Spain, Great Britain, Norway, Switzerland, Bosnia, Bulgaria, Czech Republic, Croatia, Estonia, Latvia, Lithuania, Romania, Ukraine, Argentina, Colombia, Ecuador, Mexico, Panama, Peru, Venezuela, India, Israel, South Korea, Pakistan, South Africa, and Zimbabwe.

11. National public samples were taken in the United States, Canada, Argentina, Mexico, Peru, Great Britain, France, Italy, Germany, Bulgaria, the Czech Republic, Poland, Russia, the Slovak Republic, Ukraine, Ghana, Kenya, Nigeria, South Africa, Tanzania, Uganda, Bangladesh, Japan, the Philippines, South Korea, Jordan, Lebanon, Turkey, and Uzbekistan. Primarily urban samples were used in Angola, Bolivia, Brazil, China, Egypt, Guatemala, Honduras, India, Indonesia, Ivory Coast, Mali, Pakistan, Senegal, Venezuela, and Vietnam.

12. In the 1993–94 and 2002 polls, not all questions were asked in all countries. Except for the activism item, responses were sorted into positive when views of the United States exceeded negative ones by 10 percent or more, divided when the gap between them was less than 10 percent, and negative when negative views exceeded positive ones by 10 percent or more. For the activist item, positives are those with 40 percent or more finding the activity level about right, divided when the number was between 30 and 39 percent, and negative when the number was less than 30 percent. Negatives are the sum of those responding that the U.S. activity level was either too great or too small.

13. The question was, "Do you see yourself in the near future as: (a) European only; (b) European and nationality; (c) nationality and European; or (d) nationality only."

14. With varying wording, the question asked if they think of themselves as citizens not only of their own countries but also of Europe (Eurobarometer, nos. 24, 45).

15. Respondents were asked to agree or disagree that "there is a European cultural identity shared by all Europeans" (Eurobarometer, nos. 50, 52).

16. Data were for 1990, 1996, 1999, 2000, 2001, and 2002 (Eurobarometer, nos. 33, 46, 51, 53, 56, 57, 58).

17. Data were for 1990 and 1996 (Eurobarometer, nos. 33, 46).

18. The membership question has been, "Generally speaking, do you think that [your country's] membership in the [Common Market/European Community/European Union] is a good thing, a bad thing, or neither good nor bad?" The benefit question asked, "Taking everything into consideration, would you say that [your country] has on balance benefited or not from being a member?"

19. Publics in the United Kingdom, France, Italy, Germany, Bulgaria, the Czech Republic, Poland, and the Slovak Republic were asked to evaluate the EU's influence in their countries. Large absolute majorities were positive except for the United Kingdom and Poland (Pew Research Center 2002c).

20. The question was, "How is the European Union/European Community, the European unification, advancing now, and which corresponds best to what you would like?"

21. While the number and substance of the policy areas queried has varied,

the question about them has remained constant from 1990 onward: "Some people believe that certain areas of policy should be decided by [national] government, while other areas of policy should be decided jointly with the European Community. Which of the following areas of policy do you think should be decided by the [national] government, and which should be decided jointly within the European Community?"

22. Eighteen issues were included in the 1997 polling, twenty-five in the 2000 poll, and twenty-seven in 2002 (Eurobarometer, nos. 47, 53, 58).

23. The question was, "Should the right to veto be retained in order to preserve essential national interests or be given up in order to make the EU more efficient?" (Eurobarometer, nos. 57 and 58).

24. The questions asked respondents whether they supported or opposed the proposition that "The EU should be enlarged and include new countries." Data for four observation points (1997, 1998, 2000, 2002) are available for twelve candidate countries (the Czech Republic, Slovakia, Poland, Hungary, Romania, Slovenia, Estonia, Latvia, Lithuania, Bulgaria, Cyprus, and Malta); for Turkey for 1997, 2000, and 2002; and for Switzerland and Norway for 1997 and 2000.

25. Questions from 1990 to 1994 asked about "security and defense" together. Since 1994, questions have asked solely about "defense."

26. The question was worded somewhat differently at that time.

27. When polled in late 2001, with regard to responses to international terrorism, sole EU or joint action received substantial majority support in each of the EU-15 (European Commission, "Europeans and the International Crisis" 2001).

28. That predominant opinion held true in 2002 for the current member publics of the United Kingdom, France, Germany, the Netherlands, and Italy (Chicago Council and Marshall Fund 2002).

29. Supporting the low priority for the assertion of global importance, that for enlargement persisted even though it was overwhelmingly viewed as a step that would increase the EU's importance in the world (Eurobarometer, nos. 56, 2001; *Flash Eurobarometer*, no. 132/2, 2002).

30. The question was, "Here is a list of things that some people say they are afraid of. For each of these, please tell me if, personally, you are afraid of it or not" (Eurobarometer, no. 58).

31. The British public margin was quite small.

32. The question was, "With respect to our relationship with the great powers (like the USA, Russia, China), do you think that the European Union and its institutions play a too important role, a too small role, the role they should play?"

33. Respondents were asked, "I am now going to read out some possible threats to the vital interests of Europe for the next ten years. Could you please tell me on a scale from 1 to 10 to what degree you view the respective points as threats."

34. Multiple responses were allowed.

35. The confidence question was, "Do you have a great deal, a fair amount,

not very much, or no confidence in NATO to deal effectively with European problems? What about the EU?" The common European force question asked, "There have been a number of proposals for actions the European Union could take in the next several years. For the following, please tell me whether you are strongly in favor, somewhat in favor, somewhat opposed or strongly opposed—or haven't you heard enough to say: The development of a common European defense force?" The 1999 assessment asked for an evaluation of NATO's contribution to European peace and security. The replacement question then was, "Do you agree or disagree that: The European Union should develop a new defense and peacekeeping force consisting only of European troops, to replace NATO?"

36. Categories were "both NATO and EU participation," "one or the other," "none," or "doubtful about both international clubs."

37. The indicators were drawn from our previous discussion and are referred to subsequently. For each, we use the most recent data point cited earlier.

38 The other powers were Russia, Japan, China, India, Germany, Great Britain, France, and the EU (Chicago Council and Marshall Fund 2002).

39. Forty-four country publics were polled (Pew Research Center 2002c).

40. The answers were (1) "regardless of the interests of other nations"; (2) "modify its national security interests to take into consideration the interests of other nations"; or (3) "to maintain its national security interests, the U.S. should avoid becoming involved with other nations as much as possible."

41. The question was, "Should the U.S. restrict imports to protect [domestic jobs and industry]?"

42. The coexistence may reflect the negative view of effects on jobs and workers predominant in numerous polls between 1992 and 2000 (Americans and the World 2002a; PIPA 2000b).

43. It is widely recognized that advanced industrial country openness to agricultural and textile imports would probably do more for the developing (i.e., low-wage) world than the totality of foreign aid and debt relief programs discussed in later chapters.

44. Majorities in four polls (1991, 1992, 1998, 1999) supported the World Court with regard to its having compulsory jurisdiction, stronger powers, and U.S. compliance with adverse judgments (PIPA 2000b).

45. The question was, "I'm going to read you a list of possible threats to the vital interests of the U.S. in the next ten years. For each one, please tell me if you see this as a critical threat, an important but not a critical threat, or not an important one at all."

46. The concern with nuclear arms fits with the threat salience reported in table 3.3. The salience of religious and ethnic hatred in that poll may reflect the fact that hatred was viewed as including international terrorism and Islamic fundamentalism.

47. Assessments of Israel may have benefited from generally negative ones of most of its declared enemies. Numerous questions asked from 1989 through 2002 found Americans giving their "sympathies" far more to Israelis than to Palestinian Arabs (Americans and the World 2002f; Gallup Poll Release, August 31, 1999).

48. There has been especially extensive polling on China in the past decade (Americans and the World 2002d). Judgments have been very volatile but have never been strongly positive, and many respondents often chose a neutral response when it was available.

49. See Americans and the World 2000e; Gallup Poll Release, August 31, 1999; Gallup and Yomiuri Shimbun, as cited in Richman 1993a, 1994a.

50. That may be because of the high affinity expressed with a number of EU member countries and the relatively accepting view of European trade behavior. In any event, other data suggest that the EU was not seen as a threat (e.g., by a majority of elites with respect to the European Monetary Union in 1998) or by the public (only 6 percent saw the "European Community" as the "biggest challenge to America's world power status in the next one hundred years" in 1999) (Americans and the World 2001b; Reilly 1999).

51. The question asked was, "Do you think the United States and other UN member countries should provide the United Nations with more money than it has right now to [listed items], or less money, or are they providing the UN with the right amount of money for the purpose?"

52. We list them with the net percentages favoring increased over decreased funding in declining order: health care (43); narcotics trafficking and abuse (35); the environment (32); food production (28); disaster relief (25); population (17); human rights (10); regional conflicts (4); a defense force to stop aggression (4); democracy promotion (0); LDC economic development (2); weapons production and diffusion (3); world economy management (9).

53. Majorities responded "don't know" in 1994.

54. Given low public levels of information, there probably is little awareness of the different timetables and other differentiating conditions the WTO agreements permit.

55. Unless otherwise indicated, data are from polls archived in the Japan Public Opinion Location Library (JPOLL).

56. The question asked for agreement or disagreement that each possibility was a national characteristic.

57. Net evaluations were used.

58. In 1993, the operative polling phrase was a "group of advanced countries in North America and Europe."

59. The questions differed slightly: "Which of the following roles do you think Japan should play in the international community?" and "What do you think should be Japan's primary role in international society?" Each question permitted two responses.

60. Again, the questions differed slightly: "Which of the following areas are important for Japan to promote international cooperation through the United Nations?" and "What kinds of international cooperation through the United Nations are important for Japan to actively promote?" Each question permitted multiple responses.

61. The decline in China's position seems temporally related to its nuclear tests, events viewed very negatively by large majorities of the Japanese public (in three questions in 1995).

62. That possibility does not account for the 1991 majority believing it likely that the United States would become an enemy. That poll occurred during a period of serious economic frictions between Japan and the United States when majorities in Japan viewed the United States as engaging in unfair trade practices and unwarrantedly blaming its problems on Japan.

63. One type of question does not have the listed actors competing for importance (either because multiple responses were allowed or separate questions were posed about each). Another forces priority judgments by allowing respondents only to choose one entity from a list provided to them. Another asks either about priority between a pair of nations or regions. Still another type of question asks only about agreement that one country should have top priority. Questions of several of these types have been asked about relations in general and about political, national security, and economic importance more specifically.

64. The questions asked: "Are United States–Japan relations . . . ?" And "Do you think the current relations between Japan and [country] are . . . ?"

65. The questions were: "Do you think economic frictions between the United States and Japan are likely to increase, decrease, or remain about the same during the coming year?" and "Do you think Japan–United States relations are headed in a good direction, bad direction, or staying the same?"

Chapter 4

1. The DAC excludes two types of flows that fail to meet these criteria and thus have less obvious public goods or club goods elements (other official flows and private flows), even if both have development implications.

2. The DAC also includes Australia, Austria, Belgium, Canada, Denmark, Finland, France, Germany, Ireland, Italy, Japan, Luxembourg, the Netherlands, New Zealand, Norway, Portugal, Spain, Sweden, Switzerland, the United Kingdom, and the United States.

3. See Bobrow and Boyer 1996 for a more thorough discussion of public goods and foreign aid. In that article we developed a continuum of aid categories and their relative public goods/private goods elements.

4. Statistical Annex to *Development Cooperation* (www.oecd.org).

5. In the early post–Cold War years, declaratory G-2 policy statements emphasized a public goods rationale for foreign aid with a stronger coordination emphasis. The 1992 United States–Japan Global Partnership signed by President George H. W. Bush and Prime Minister Kiichi Miyazawa pledged the governments to "enhance collaboration to promote democratization and stability in the developing world" ("Fact Sheet" 1992, 45). Miyazawa interpreted the partnership as being "aimed at confirming the global responsibility of both Japan and the United States in constructing a framework of a new world order of peace and democracy" (quoted in Langdon 1993, 84).

6. The problem remains that many of the "weakest link" states in international affairs (e.g., Afghanistan) are precisely those least able or willing to make the domestic changes now thought to be necessary for aid to have positive development effects.

7. Recipient characteristics are held to feature policy reforms and policy

reformers, both of which benefit from a strong civil society. Unfortunately, experiences in using foreign aid to build civil society are no less checkered than those for other development-through-aid objectives (e.g., Ottaway and Carothers 2000).

8. Ruling parties with a large margin of support have less to fear from domestic opposition to foreign aid, suggesting that their "generosity" fluctuates with their support margin. This relationship has been demonstrated to hold for Japan from 1970 to 1992 (Katada and McKeown 1998).

9. In Western Europe, the questions asked whether aid to developing countries by their national government and that by the EU should increase or decrease and whether "humanitarian aid" to non-EU countries should be increased or maintained at its current level. In the United States, the question was whether U.S. spending on foreign aid was too much, just right, or too little. In Japan, the question was, "Most developed countries help developing countries through cooperation in finance and technology. Do you think Japan should increase its current levels of economic cooperation with developing countries or not?" and the response options were increase, maintain, decrease, or eliminate.

10. "Net support" refers to the percentage of respondents answering "too little being spent" minus those answering "too much."

11. Those majorities have recently been declining, however, in much of the EU, especially Denmark, Austria, Sweden, and Finland.

12. The 1996 polling was of publics in the EU-15 and that in the earlier years of those in the EC-12. The question in the two earlier years asked about the Third World and mentioned no particular regions.

13. The other EU-related publics polled were in Great Britain, France, Italy, Bulgaria, and the Czech and Slovak Republics.

14. In 2002, overwhelming public and elite majorities supported in the context of efforts to combat terrorism "helping poor countries to develop their economies" (Chicago Council and Marshall Fund 2002).

15. In a 1998 poll, the biggest international problems for the public were, in declining order, disease and hunger abroad, spread of nuclear weapons, and threat to the global environment (Adamson et al. 2000).

16. The 1995 questions asked for a list of possible emphases: "Assuming changes in spending increasing and reducing taxes accordingly, do you favor increasing or reducing . . ." The 1998 questions asked for judgments about the importance of each of a list of goals for foreign aid. In each instance, the posed emphases were not in explicit competition with each other.

17. That skepticism was, for example, present with regard to a collective effort to reduce world hunger.

18. The questions asked about "feelings toward each of these kinds of aid," evaluations of "reasons for giving aid to other countries," and favoring types of aid. In each set, the response alternatives were not in explicit competition with each other.

19. Responses to aid for the same general purposes (e.g., reducing hunger) that omitted *needy* received a less favorable response in that poll and others.

20. Those who thought Japan should increase or maintain its current aid

were asked, "Why do you think Japan should increase or maintain its current levels of economic cooperation with developing countries?" Multiple responses were permitted.

21. The polling was done in 1991 and 1994–97 of urban populations in China, South Korea, India, Indonesia, Malaysia, Thailand, the Philippines, and Vietnam (Hastings and Hastings 1991–92, 566; 1995–96, 593, 601; 1997–98, 531).

22. Foreign aid contributions from Japan to the developing world were wanted by large minorities in the U.S., British, French, and German publics (Hastings and Hastings 1987–88, 592; 1989–90, 714; 1990–91, 632; 1993–94, 661).

23. For reasons of data availability, here and elsewhere in this chapter we discuss only development assistance by the DAC. Nevertheless it is important to recognize the existence of other contributors, even if their combined efforts would have added only a small percentage to total annual DAC contributions. Two sets of other countries are notable here: non-DAC members of the OECD, and Arab states. For the former, Greece prior to membership, the Republic of Korea, and Turkey all tended to increase their ODA contributions after 1994, post–Cold War Poland became a contributor in 1998, and the Czech Republic returned to that status after a hiatus of several years. Kuwait and Saudi Arabia were substantial contributors in the late 1990s. Other contributors in the 1997–98 period included Estonia, Iceland, China, and Taiwan. Contributions by Arab donors fell sharply during the 1990s in terms of current-year amounts and relative to DAC aid provision (about 10 percent in 1990 to less than 1 percent in 1999) (World Bank 2001a, 88).

24. The ODA surge does not include most of the funding in the Miyazawa Plan discussed in chapter 5, which the DAC placed in the other official flows rather than ODA category. It is important to note that Tokyo's original intent in the pertinent fiscal year budget was to cut ODA by 10 percent, and the Japanese government did end its practice of proclaiming five-year financial-contribution goals for its aid programs (Castellano 1999c, 2000c).

25. Exact figures in yen terms are a .2 percent decrease in fiscal year 2000, a 3 percent decrease in fiscal 2001, a 10.3 percent decrease for fiscal 2002, and a 5.8 percent decrease for fiscal 2003 (Ohno 2003, 4).

26. Some of these measures follow from an assumed and debatable theory of development rather than different volumes of national contributions to development. For example, Japan's aid has tended to be focused more on loans than grants, thus lowering the public element by our measure. If one believes, as Japan's policy states, that loans instill in the recipient the development-conducive discipline of repayment, they may actually have a higher public element over the long term.

27. That reasoning underlies the analysis of Chang, Fernandez-Arias, and Serven 1999, which concludes that in the first half of the 1990s the grant element in concessional loans was radically overstated because of an interest rate higher than was available domestically to the largest donors. We instead follow

established DAC reporting for two reasons. The first is conceptual. The proper comparison between the aid interest rate and the market one needs to include risk, and Chang, Fernandez-Arias, and Serven do not. The second is empirical—the unavailability to us of comparable over-time, cross-national data applying the alternative measurements.

28. A decline in formal tying may not indicate that the share of ODA funds going to the donor economy has shrunk. Formal tying may simply no longer be as necessary to secure private benefits because of other advantages on the part of donor country aid project performers. An appropriate way to check this possibility looks at the nationality of the contractors who receive ODA funds. Comparative data were not available, but there was a major cut in the channeling of ODA loan funds to Japanese firms as primary contractors from 1983 to 1994, with a corollary increase in the share going to developing-country firms (Islam 1993, 346; *JEI Report* 1994; Johnstone 1995, 10).

29. For example, from 1980–81 to 1990–91, the ratio of Japanese to U.S. aid supplies in the region changed from about 2.5:1 to about 6:1 (Islam 1993, 336).

30. It is important to bear in mind the full caveats about changing definitions.

Chapter 5

1. Up to now, they have not had an option analogous to that which bankruptcy provides in some domestic legal systems.

2. By way of definition, the former is the "system under which credit is created, allocated, and used" (Stopford and Strange 1991, 35), and a financial crisis is "a disturbance of financial markets, associated . . . with falling asset prices and insolvency among debtors and intermediaries, which ramifies through the financial system, disrupting the market's capacity to allocate capital within the economy. In an international financial crisis, disturbances spill over national borders, disrupting the market's capacity to allocate capital internationally" (Eichengreen and Portes 1987, 10).

3. In principle, trade and investment liberalization might close the gap as well or better, yet those strategies may encounter more political obstacles at home or abroad (Armijo 2000).

4. The impossible trinity with its incompatibility of exchange rate stability, monetary independence, and financial market integration makes this an unavoidable bet (Frankel 1999).

5. The devil lies in the details of case-specific applications, as with the pricing and additionality associated with debt-equity swaps (Husain and Mitro 1989; Krugman 1989a; Sung and Troia 1992; United Nations 1993) and the immediate costs to debtor governments of buybacks (Claesens and Diwan 1989).

6. The declared American emphasis on austerity was accompanied by hegemonic pressure on Japan to provide capital to the debtors in which the United States had other private-element considerations. That Japanese provision may have been important in whatever success the austerity emphasis had. For example, South Korea's debt during the 1980s was one of the largest in the

world, but servicing it was feasible at least partly because in 1983 the Japanese government provided its neighbor with a $4 billion package of loans and credits. This resulted from strong behind-the-scenes pressure from the United States for such burden bearing to balance Japan's low defense spending (Cumings 1987–88, 81). The results of pressure from Washington have also been confirmed in Stallings's (1990) analysis of Japan's role in helping to manage Latin American debt problems in the 1980s.

7. Perhaps most prominent was the 1988 Omnibus Trade and Competitiveness Act, which called for an international debt-adjustment facility to buy back sovereign loans at a discount and pass the benefits to the debtor country, stimulating capital-surplus-country investment in debtors and aiding creditor banks' disposal of sovereign loans.

8. For a summary of the Toronto and successive series of terms, see table 5.2.

9. Miyazawa's proposal also included incentives for voluntary debt reduction on the part of private creditors by giving exit bonds seniority over other claims and for guarantees from the IFIs.

10. After the fall of 1990, lower-middle-income countries could avail themselves of the extended grace and maturity periods of the G-7 Houston terms.

11. Initially forgiving donors were Canada, Denmark, Finland, France, Germany, the Netherlands, Sweden, Switzerland, and the United Kingdom—with the notable absence of the United States.

12. For details on which countries were eligible and the lengthy and demanding process before they would get relief beyond Naples terms, see Abrego and Ross 2001.

13. According to a German foreign aid expert, the motivation was largely a matter of elite competition in his ruling party and an inducement for a smaller party to take part in a governing coalition. Germany had previously been reluctant to espouse forgiveness.

14. The Mexican crisis treatment involved emergency provision of $12 billion from the United States (over European objections). This was accomplished through executive branch authority that has since been revoked. Terms were not concessional, and repayment was guaranteed by compelling Mexican oil revenues to be deposited in the Federal Reserve Bank of New York until full payoff (which was quickly made). U.S. commercial creditors benefited substantially, and the administration's stakes in NAFTA were protected.

15. Warnings about Russia were abundant. Japan tried to get the G-7 to address looming East Asian problems prior to the full-blown crisis. Washington ignored pleas by Thai officials as well as more recent pleas from Argentina (Rohter 2001;Wedel 1998).

16. Extrapolated from the ninety noted in "Global Finance" 1999.

17. U.S. support for forgiveness of Iraqi debt is, of course, facilitated by the fact that the U.S. holds little such debt.

18. European banks had the greatest exposure to East Asia, followed by those of Japan. Japan's economy and security were sensitive to the health of others in East Asia. Germany was a massive source of Russian debt. Even the

original American position on Argentina (2001–2) that "nobody forced them to be what they are" faced adjustment given the implications for the desired future achievement of a Free Trade Area of the Americas. Spanish banks were especially exposed in Argentina, and Spain was assuming the EU presidency.

19. The World Bank found the IMF responsible for worsening the East Asian financial collapse (Sanger 1998a).

20. For a useful review, see "Global Finance" 1999; for a particularly demanding set of suggestions, see Wyplosz 1999.

21. As proposed by Anne Krueger of the IMF, in the bankruptcy court procedure a country would "come to the Fund and request a temporary standstill on the repayment of its debts, during which time it would negotiate a rescheduling or restructuring with its creditors" (Blustein 2001). During that time, creditor claims would not be honored and capital exit blocked. The new bankruptcy body would be empowered to decide "when a country could stop paying its lenders and how much their loans should be reduced [and would] deprive lenders of the option of suing borrowers" ("Bankruptcy Court" 2001).

22. The April 2002 G-7 "action plan" only hedged on limiting the size of future IMF bailouts and on future reliance on grants rather than loans to avoid future debt sustainability problems. The plan did favor the sort of collective action clauses that would make it easier to harness private creditors to debt crisis "work out" schemes.

23. As of this writing, the recent treatment of Argentina—especially, but not only, by the United States—shows a combination of the factors just discussed, including an emphasis on moral hazard in a case felt to be lacking in other grounds of foreign policy importance. Nevertheless, the Argentine crisis has not had substantial contagion effects on other emerging-market debtors in spite of its continuing severity.

24. The data were for the most part obtained from various years of the World Bank's *Global Development Finance* (formerly titled *World Debt Tables*).

25. Thresholds for category placement of developing countries are summarized in the notes to table 5.1.

26. We do not report share of cutoff-date obligations consolidated, since from 1980 through 2000 that number was usually 100 percent and dropped below 85 percent in only three cases in the 1980s.

27. Debt-relief efforts are defined as "grants for forgiveness of ODA, Other Official Flows (OOF) or private claims; other action on debt such as debt conversions, debt buybacks or service payments to third parties; and new ODA resulting from concessional rescheduling operations; net of offsetting entries for the cancellation of any ODA principal involved and . . . contributions to the HIPC Trust Fund" (Organization for Economic Cooperation and Development, "Development Cooperation," 2002, table 34).

Chapter 6

1. As Boutros-Ghali put it, "supervision of cease-fires, the regroupment and demobilization of forces, their reintegration into civilian life and the destruction

of their weapons; the design and implementation of demining programmes; the return of refugees and displaced persons; the provision of humanitarian assistance; the supervision of existing administrative structures; the establishment of new police forces; the verification of respect for human rights; the design and supervision of constitutional, judicial and electoral reforms; the observation, supervision and even organization and conduct of elections; and the coordination of support for economic rehabilitation and reconstruction" (1995, supplement p. 6).

2. That has happened in the United States, Japan, Germany, Russia, the United Kingdom, France, Canada, and Norway (Ku and Jacobson 2001).

3. We shall not deal with important operational issues, such as command and staff organization, force capabilities, and rules of engagement. Each has been the subject of extensive analyses elsewhere. A recent pragmatic assessment can be found in United Nations 2000. The literature on peacekeeping operations is large and growing; see, e.g., Diehl 1988, 1993a, b; Dobbie 1994; Durch 1993; Goulding 1993; James 1990; MacFarlane, Minear, and Shenfield 1996; Mingst and Karns 1995; Ratner 1995; Roberts 1994; Ruggie 1993b; Warrington 1995. Most studies have focused either on operational and tactical issues or on the politics of approving and conducting peacekeeping operations. For country-specific profiles of peacekeeping operations, see the series of articles published in the spring 1995 *International Journal:* Baranyi 1995; Inoguchi 1995; James 1995; MacFarlane and Schnabel 1995; P. Martin and Fortmann 1995; Sokolsky 1995.

4. Major examples are the IFOR and KFOR operations in Bosnia and Kosovo.

5. They identify twelve cross-cutting categories of PKOs: (1) traditional peacekeeping, (2) observation, (3) collective enforcement, (4) election supervision, (5) humanitarian assistance during conflict, (6) state/nation building, (7) pacification, (8) preventive deployment, (9) arms control verification, (10) protective services, (11) intervention in support of democracy, and (12) sanctions enforcement (Diehl, Druckman, and Wall 1998, 39–40).

6. For example, contrast Lindley's (1997) analysis of the UNPKO in Cyprus with that of Diehl, Reifschneider, and Hensel (1996).

7. A public majority recently was willing to extend aid to a future African Union PKO capability (PIPA 2003a).

8. As with funding, the public had very exaggerated ideas about the U.S.-provided share of troops in UNPKOs (Kull 1995–96).

9. The latter was also true for the public in 1995.

10. The military campaign in Afghanistan is of course different in its framing and presidentially provided expectations. It is framed more as a war along the lines of World War II or the Cold War than as a PKO. From the beginning, the duration of administration commitments has been open-ended, unlike the declarations about many PKO cases. Perhaps for those reasons, a large majority has expected it to last "longer than . . . months" and still favored it and other counterterrorist military actions (Americans and the World 2002b; *New York Times*/CBS News 2001).

11. Canadian opinion strongly favored participation for both Bosnia and Kosovo (Hastings and Hastings 1994–95, 294; "NATO" 1999).

12. The lack of Japanese public support for its Self-Defense Forces emphasizing any form of international contribution (PKOs and humanitarian relief) did not change much between 1992 and 2000 (*Government Poll Yearbook* 1998, 120; 2001, 98; JPOLL, various years).

13. Polls in 2001 and 2002 had public majorities linking a resolution of the Israeli-Palestinian conflict to prosecuting the war on terrorism (Americans and the World 2003).

14. The U.S. public found it appropriate (72 percent to 20 percent); the Japanese public found it inappropriate (26 percent to 70 percent) (Hastings and Hastings 1991–92, 629).

15. That may fit with the prevailing British view (1995) that until that point, the United Nations had not been a key actor in achieving peaceful resolution of international disputes (Hastings and Hastings 1995–96, 198).

16. Some clues about the preferred American role in multilateral action lie in opinion about troop participation under a foreign commander. The public and civilian elites do not seem to require having an American in command but view UN or NATO command as acceptable; military elites view only the NATO alternative as acceptable (Americans and the World 2001a; Gallup Poll Release, June 24, 1999; O. R. Holsti 1998–99; Reilly 1995).

17. The participation-supportive majority or plurality in poll after poll is that Self Defense Force units (1) be either unarmed or very lightly armed with high-level authorization required even for self-defense; (2) their tasks essentially be civil ones (logistics, medical care, road construction); and (3) avoid taking part in peace-imposition missions (*Government Poll Yearbook* 2001, 490; Hastings and Hastings, various years; JPOLL, various years).

18. On Bosnia, the British public (1993–95) never had a majority thinking that an international force could "achieve peace" (Hastings and Hastings 1993–94, 292; 1995–96, 272–73).

19. UNMOP, UNTAES, and UNOMSIL were not included in this size evaluation for lack of data on personnel levels.

20. If anything, the situation worsened because developing countries moved to prohibit accepting unlimited free experts because they were coming too abundantly from Western military organizations (Crossette 2000d).

21. Information for 1988 on initiations and actives excludes UNASOG because of lack of information.

22. That peak was built on two unusually large operations, Somalia and Cambodia. Of course, the personnel numbers do not include non-UN peacekeeping, peace consolidation, or peace enforcement operations.

23. We use UN data to facilitate comparisons over time and countries. The UN practice totals the incremental and ongoing costs of the military involved. The World Bank has suggested, we think correctly, that a better sense of the public element of contributions would look only at incremental costs. That of course would yield a much smaller amount (World Bank 2001a, 117). Our choice does not inherently distort the contributions of member states relative

to the total to UNPKO, or to state gross national product or gross domestic product.

24. Iran is not included in these correlations because of lack of reliable World Bank GDP data for 1995. Thus, $n = 37$ rather than the $n = 38$ of table 6.9. These correlations were calculated using World Bank *World Development Report* GDP data and UN PKO data. Significance tests for the data were not included because the 37 states used to calculate the correlation represent almost the entire relevant population for study rather than a random sample of that population.

25. Spill-in data are from Khanna, Sandler, and Shimizu 1999, 361. Their analysis does not include India.

26. The Japanese government continues to interpret the UNPKO law in a restrictive fashion with regard to personnel contributions. Japan has been unwilling to send police officers to Kosovo or troops to East Timor but in both cases has been willing to provide substantial funds (Castellano 1999b; Wanner 1999). In the non-UN Iraqi presence, combat has carefully been avoided.

27. The Pentagon rationale cites other missions for an active duty force reduced by 36 percent in the past ten years and calculates the burden as three soldiers, not one—one fielded in a PKO, one preparing to go, and one just returned.

28. That sort of contribution may of course be overstated. UN Secretary-General Annan has noted that for the 2000 Sierra Leone UNPKO crisis, the United States was willing to supply peacekeeper airlift transport only at three times market commercial rates (Crossette 2000b).

29. For example, in 1997, the US had thousands of military personnel in NATO former Yugoslavia IRPKOS compared to only a few hundred in UNPKOs. U.S. personnel assigned to the Multilateral Observer Force to monitor the Egyptian-Israeli Sinai peace agreement exceeded those assigned to UNPKOS (International Institute 1998).

30. The congressional requirement for fifteen days advance notice of any UN Security Council PKO vote has not always been met.

31. A full menu of enhancements can be found in the Brahimi Report (United Nations 2000).

Chapter 7

1. For some recent discussions of the economics/environment trade-off, see Hochstetler, Clark, and Friedman 2000; Thomas and Belt 2000. For a review of earlier estimates of damage versus restraint costs for ozone and global warming emissions, see Barrett 1999.

2. For a unique perspective on the summation aspects of environmental problems and the impact of individuals and localities on helping to solve them, see Barlow and Rifkin 2002; Coordinadora 2002; Research Foundation 2002.

3. Although the United States eventually took the lead (Paarlberg 2001), it could have done so earlier than it did (Sell 1996) instead of leaving leadership to Australia, Canada, Denmark, Finland, Norway, Sweden, and Switzerland (Sprinz and Vaahtoranta 1994).

4. Data are drawn from Hastings and Hastings 1987–88, 518–19; 1991–92, 320; 1992–93, 657; 1993–94, 106, 108, 656–57; 1995–96, 674–75; Inglehart, Basañez, and Moreno 1998, V26, V290; ISSP1995.

5. In the United States in 2000, a substantially larger share of the public trusted environmental groups to "protect the quality of our nation's environment" than trusted elements of government, either political party, or the private sector. In another question at that time, one about on whose scientific opinion respondents would rely most on environmental issues, more than a quarter chose "environmental groups," and less than 10 percent opted for government or industry ("Gallup Poll Topics: A–Z Environment" 2000). In 2002, international environmental groups had a positive thermometer reading (Chicago Council and Marshall Fund 2002). In the EU, polls in 1995, 1999, and 2002 showed a similar pattern of greater trust in information from such NGOs than from other sources (European Commission, *What Do Europeans Think* 1999; European Opinion Research Group 2001). That was also true in Japan in 2000 (*Government Poll Yearbook* 2002, 555).

6. The U.S. erosion may well not apply to specific program spending. For example, in 2001, a very large majority favored increased spending on the development of solar and wind power (Gallup Poll Release, March 16, 2001). We reported in our discussion of public opinion on foreign aid more support for spending focused on environmental protection than for many other purposes.

7. Data are drawn from Gallup Poll Topics A–Z: Environment; Government Poll Yearbook 2002, 555; Hastings and Hastings 1989–90, 105–6, 137; 1991–92, 96–97; 1992–93, 107–8, 110; 1993–94, 109, 120; 1997–98, 364–65.

8. Of course, the question of whether regulatory activity should emphasize market incentives or administrative and legal restraints remains open.

9. These opinions are consistent with the view of industry as at the heart of environmental problems in the United States (1990, 1991, 1997, 1999), the United Kingdom (1990, 1992, 1996), and Japan (1992, 1993) (CBS News Poll in Public Agenda Online; Gallup Poll Release, April 22, 1999; Hastings and Hastings 1991–92, 108–9; 1992–93, 107; 1993–94, 117; 1996–97, 129; JPOLL, various years).

10. Japanese public support remained at about the 60 percent level in 1995 (JPOLL, various years).

11. For relevant polling, see Eurobarometer, no. 46, 1996; European Commission, *What Do Europeans Think* 1999; European Opinion Research Group 2002; Gallup Poll Release, March 16, 2001; *Government Poll Yearbook* 2001, 506; 2002, 553–55; Hastings and Hastings 1989–90, 108, 117–18; 1991–92, 93, 100–101, 105–6, 111–12, 123–24, 618; 1992–93, 90–91; 1993–94, 103, 106, 109; 1994–95, 122; 1996–97, 126–28; 1997–98, 112, 521, 524; ISSP 1995; PIPA 2000c.

12. By 2000, Japanese rejection of the view that the economy was underemphasized had increased greatly (*Government Poll Yearbook* 2002, 553–54).

13. For the U.S. polls in 1984 and 1990–2002, see Americans and the World 2003a; Gallup Poll Topics: A–Z Environment, 2001; PIPA 2000b); for

Japan in 1992, 1996, and 1997, see Hastings and Hastings 1992–93, 103; 1996–97, 617; 1997–98, 114; for Western Europe in 1986 and 2002, see European Commission 2002; Hastings and Hastings 1986–87, 588–89; for the others in the mid-1990s, see Hastings and Hastings 1992–93, 94–95; 1995–96, 126–27, 622–23; 1996–97, 617; 1997–98, 524).

14. Specifically, the environment was chosen only once by respondents in one nation by more than a low double-digit percentage. It usually ranked highly for only a smaller part of the publics in the United States, Japan, Canada, India, Latin America, and some European countries. For U.S. data for 1987–2002, see Gallup Poll Release, April 22, 1999; Hastings and Hastings 1989–90, 136–37; 1991–92, 129–30; 1993–94, 136–38; 1995–96, 123; 1997–98, 148; Chicago Council and Marshall Fund 2002; for six Japanese queries 1989–96, see Hastings and Hastings 1989–90, 133–34; 1994–95, 142, 144; 1996–97, 147–48); for six Canadian queries 1989–96, see Hastings and Hastings 1989–90, 126; 1991–92, 109, 119; 1993–94, 131; 1994–95, 140; 1995–96, 118; 1996–97, 144–45; for fewer polls taken in other countries in the mid-1990s, see Hastings and Hastings 1993–94, 134–35; 1995–96, 120, 621; 1997–98, 145–46; for six European countries in 2002, see Chicago Council and Marshall Fund 2002.

15. Additional data are for the United Kingdom in 1986, 1990, 1991, 1992, 1993, 1995; Japan in 1993; Canada in 1987, 1989, 1990; and the EC-12 in 1989 and 1991 (Hastings and Hastings 1985–86, 586; 1986–87, 139; 1989–90, 104, 106, 630; 1991–92, 107–8, 530; 1992–93, 128; 1993–94, 132–33; 1994–95, 121–22, 139–40, 538–39; 1995–96, 119, 361).

16. Data are for Japan in 1989, 1990, 1991, 1993, 1994, 1996, 1997; for the United Kingdom in 1989, 1990, 1991, 1996; for Germany in 1990; for Australia in 1987, 1989, 1991, 1992, 1994, 1995; for the EC-12 in 1986 and 1994; and for the United States as shown in polling discussed in chapter 3 on the "very important foreign policy goal" list l (Chicago Council and Marshall Fund 2002; Hastings and Hastings 1989–90, 129–30, 133–34; 1991–92, 112, 115–16, 119–22, 126, 309; 1993–94, 134; 1994–95, 144; 1995–96, 118–19; 1996–97, 146–47, 674; 1997–98, 607.

17. Support for proenvironmental actions by the UN asked in the United States, Japan, the United Kingdom, Germany, and France show the pattern noted earlier for national action—that is, the priority declines when the question is posed in the context of multiple issues (Hastings and Hastings 1994–95, 628).

18. The data are from Prime Minister's Information Office annual surveys on "Social Consciousness" (1990–97). Respondents were asked for each of a list of aspects of Japan whether the country "was headed" in a good or bad "direction." In each survey, the environment was one of the aspects with the highest negative percentage, and only once was it less than 45 percent. In 1993, more than 90 percent of Japanese thought that global environmental problems would have serious effects on Japan in the future (Hastings and Hastings 1993–94, 113).

19. Those were taken in the EU-15 in 1999; Germany in 1991; the United Kingdom in 1992 and 1996; Japan in 1989, 1992, 1993, 1997; the United States in 1993, 1994, 1995; India in 1992; Thailand in 1994; and urban China

in 1994 (European Commission, *What Do Europeans Think* 1999; Hastings and Hastings 1992–93, 90, 95, 97; 1993–94, 95–96, 103–4, 111, 117–19; 1994–95, 125–26; 1995–96, 105–6; 1996–97, 129; 1997–98, 112, 522–23).

20. We tentatively suggest that the difference stems from beliefs that remedial actions are feasible and likely. Thus, we expect strong negative reactions by many publics to international policy actions that throw that belief into doubt— e.g., the recent U.S. rejection of the Kyoto agreement.

21. For data, see European Commission, *What Do Europeans Think* 1999; European Commission, "Sustainable Development" 2002; European Opinion Research Group 2002; Chicago Council and Marshall Fund 2002 (on biotechnology and genetic modification polled in the United Kingdom, France, Germany, the Netherlands, Italy, and Poland).

22. For data, see *Government Poll Yearbook* 2002, 555; Hastings and Hastings 1989–90, 104; 1992–93, 98, 124; 1994–95, 120–21.

23. The problems posed were ozone depletion, global warming, loss of rain forests, ocean pollution, species loss, and desertification (Hastings and Hastings 1991–92, 177–78; 1992–93, 102; 1997–98, 110–11).

24. In 1993, the German public also provided a plurality for "rich countries" paying for "Third World environment protection" (Hastings and Hastings 1993–94, 113).

25. See Hastings and Hastings 1991–92, 126, 191–92, 645–46; 1992–93, 305–6, 326–27; 1993–94, 193, 336; 1994–95, 212; 1995–96, 304; 1997–98, 199; JPOLL, various years.

26. Another stimulus to support may have been a 1992 poll that found substantial minority support in the United States, United Kingdom, Germany, and France for Japan making international environmental contributions and much smaller ones (in 1995) perceiving Japanese activism in that regard (Hastings and Hastings 1991–92, 645–46; 1994–95, 611–12).

27. The candidate countries' publics were, however, less so disposed (Applicant Countries Eurobarometer 2001).

28. These views were in polls accompanied by signs of willingness to assist the developing countries in reducing emissions through debt waivers, technology transfers, and other fund transfers (Americans and the World 2003a).

29. American elites also favored participation by a large majority when polled in 2002 (Chicago Council and Marshall Fund 2002).

30. Four polls in the second half of 2002 and early 2003 failed to show strong support for the administration's global warming foreign policy, and two of the polls found substantially negative pluralities (Chicago Council and Marshall Fund 2002; PIPA 2003e).

31. We have included both global and regional agreements. Although regional agreements will likely have a lower public goods component than global ones, they do signify a state's willingness to sign on to environmental action. In addition, given the spillover effects that exist for many environmental problems, even regional agreements can have global impacts.

32. The International Union management categories are (1a) Strict Nature Reserve (managed mainly for science); (1b) Wilderness Area (managed mainly

for wilderness protection); (2) National Park (managed mainly for ecosystem protection and recreation); (3) Natural Monument (managed mainly for conservation of specific natural features); (4) Habitat/Species Management Area (managed mainly for conservation through management intervention); (5) Protected Landscape/Seascape; and (6) Managed Resource Protected Area (managed mainly for the sustainable use of protected ecosystems). The values in figure 7.1 do not include category 6 areas, which are not reported in a fashion allowing aggregation with the other areas. In addition, the values also exclude protected areas that are part of global agreements. Although significant in size, such areas are uniformly smaller in size than the International Union–protected areas created through national action. In addition, we argue that the national areas are more reflective of commitment to such action than is participation in the smaller global agreements on protected areas. For more details on the underlying data, see World Resources Institute 2001, 244–45.

33. We think that using purchasing-power-parity terms provides a more indicative measure than does using exchange-rate dollars.

34. The 1997 data from the same source placed Germany in the "five or more" category and Russia in the "one or more category."

35. The World Bank and the World Resources Institute data on these indicators are for the most part relatively close in values. In some instances, however, the data from the two sources diverge. In those instances, World Resources Institute data have been used. World Bank data were used where noted.

36. Data for Denmark and the United Kingdom do not appear in table 7.12 but were available using the same source for 1997, where they appeared in the "0.4 or less" category.

37. The 1997-only data available for Germany placed it in the "0.6 or less" category and the Russian Federation in the "greater than 1.0" category.

38. The degree of post-1990 German reductions related to the demise of East Germany have been estimated as being on the order of 15 percent.

39. GDP is measured in constant purchasing-power-parity terms.

40. Our findings about superior records by EU members are in general in line with those of Scruggs 1999.

Chapter 8

1. No contributors were outstanding on a sustained basis for debt matters involving middle-income countries.

2. The Afghan campaign has been an exception to the cases discussed in chapter 6 in two respects: the trigger of an attack on the American homeland, and the associated perceived need to reestablish perceptions of American strength.

3. For a detailed discussion of policy framing, see, e.g., Gitlin 1980; C. Smith 1996; Snow and Benford 1988.

REFERENCES

Abbott, Kenneth, and Duncan Snidal. 1998. "Why States Act through Formal International Organizations." *Journal of Conflict Resolution* 42:3–32.

Abrego, Leandro, and Doris C. Ross. 2001. *Debt Relief under the HIPC Initiative: Context and Outlook for Debt Sustainability and Resource Flow.* Working Paper wp/01/144, September. Washington, DC: International Monetary Fund.

Adamson, David M., Nancy Belden, Julie DaVanzo, and Sally Patterson. 2000. *How Americans View World Population Issues: A Survey of Public Opinions.* Santa Monica, CA: RAND.

Adler, Emanuel, and Michael Barnett, eds. 1998. *Security Communities.* Cambridge: Cambridge University Press.

Aggarwal, Vinod K. 1996. *Debt Games: Strategic Interaction in International Debt Negotiations.* New York: Cambridge University Press.

Aggarwal, Vinod K., ed. 1998. *Institutional Designs for a Complex World: Bargaining, Linkages, and Nesting.* Ithaca: Cornell University Press.

Aggarwal, Vinod K., and Cedric Dupont. 1999. "Goods, Games, and Institutions." *International Political Science Review* 20 (4): 393–409.

Aldecoa, Francisco, and Michael Keating, eds. 1999. *Paradiplomacy in Action: The Foreign Relations of Subnational Governments.* London: Frank Cass.

Alesina, Alberto, and David Dollar. 1998. *Who Gives Foreign Aid and Why?* Working Paper 6612. Cambridge, MA: National Bureau of Economic Research.

Almond, Gabriel. 1950. *The American People and Foreign Policy.* New York: Harcourt, Brace.

Altbach, Eric. 1998. "Tokyo May Increase Asian Aid: Congress Passes IMF Funding." *JEI Report,* October 23, 9–10.

Alvarez, Lisette. 2001. "Senate Ends Its Feud with U.N., Voting for $582 Million Payment." *New York Times,* p. A1.

Americans and the World. 2001a. "Global Issues: United Nations." Available at www.americans-world.org/digest/global_issues/un.

Americans and the World. 2001b. "Regional Issues: China." Available at www.americans-world.org/digest/regional_issues/china.

References

Americans and the World. 2002a. "Global Issues: International Trade." Available at www.americans-world.org.
Americans and the World. 2002b. "Global Issues: Terrorism." Available at www.americans-world.org/digest/global_issues/terrorism.
Americans and the World. 2002c. "Global Issues: United Nations." Available at www.americans-world.org.
Americans and the World. 2002d. "Regional Issues: China." Available at www.americans-world.org.
Americans and the World. 2002e. "Regional Issues: Conflict with Iraq." Available at www.americans-world.org.
Americans and the World. 2002f. "Regional Issues: Israel and the Palestinians." Available at www.americans-world.org.
Americans and the World. 2002g. "Regional Issues: Russia." Available at www.americans-world.org.
Americans and the World. 2003a. "Global Issues: Global Warming." Available at www.americans-world.org.
Americans and the World. 2003b. "Regional Issues: Israel and the Palestinians." Available at www.americans-world.org.
Anderson, Benedict. 1991. *Imagined Communities: Reflections on the Origin and Spread of Nationalism.* London: Verso.
Annan, Kofi. 1999. "Two Concepts of Sovereignty." *Economist*, September 18, 49–50.
Arase, David. 1994. "Public-Private Sector Interest Coordination in Japan's ODA." *Pacific Affairs* 67:171–99.
Arase, David. 1995. *Buying Power: The Political Economy of Japan's Foreign Aid.* Boulder, CO: Lynne Rienner.
Arce, M., G. Daniel, and Todd Sandler. 2001. "Transnational Public Goods: Strategies and Institutions." *European Journal of Political Economy* 17:493–516.
Armijo, Leslie Elliott. 2000. "Skewed Incentives to Liberalize Trade, Production, and the Capital Account." Paper presented at the World Congress of the International Political Science Association, Quebec, August 1–5.
"ASEAN has Invited Howard's Bravado." 1999. *Bangkok Post*, September 24. See www.bangkokpost.net.
Atwood, J. Brian. 1998. "The Future of United States Foreign Assistance." In *The Global Crisis in Foreign Aid*, ed. Richard Grant and Jan Nijman, 147–51. Syracuse: Syracuse University Press.
Axelrod, Robert. 1984. *The Evolution of Cooperation.* New York: Basic Books.
Balakrishnan, Uma. 2002. "The Kyoto Protocol on Climate Change: A Balance of Interests." In *Contemporary Cases in U.S. Foreign Policy*, ed. Ralph G. Carter, 317–38. Washington, DC: CQ Press.
Bank for International Settlements, World Bank, International Monetary Fund, and Organization for Economic Cooperation and Development. 1994. *Debt Stocks, Debt Flows, and the Balance of Payments.* Paris: Bank for International Settlements, World Bank, International Monetary Fund, and Organization for Economic Cooperation and Development.

REFERENCES

"A Bankruptcy Court." 2001. *International Herald Tribune*, December 12, p. 8.

Baranyi, Stephen. 1995. "Peace Missions and Subsidiarity in the Americas: Conflict Management in the Western Hemisphere." *International Journal* 50:343–69.

Barlow, Maude, and Jeremy Rifkin. 2002. "The Treaty Initiative: To Share and Protect the Global Water Commons." In *Global Backlash*, ed. Broad, 274.

Barrett, Scott. 1999. "Montreal versus Kyoto: International Cooperation and the Global Environment." In *Global Public Goods*, ed. Kaul, Grunberg, and Stern, 192–219.

Bartolini, Stefano, Thomas Risse, and Bo Strath. 1999. *Between Europe and the Nation State: The Reshaping of Interests, Identities, and Political Representation*. Florence: Robert Schuman Centre for Advanced Studies, European University Institute.

Beattie, Alan. 2002. "EU Close to Deal on Help for World's Poor." *Financial Times*, March 12, p. 8.

Benedick, Richard Elliot. 1991. *Ozone Diplomacy*. Cambridge: Harvard University Press.

Bergerson, Helge Ole, and George Parmann, eds. Various years. *Green Globe Yearbook of International Co-operation on Environment and Development*. Oxford: Oxford University Press.

Berthélemy, Jean-Claude, and Ann Vourc'h. 1994. *Debt Relief and Growth*. Paris: OECD.

Biersteker, Thomas J. 1992. "The 'Triumph' of Neoclassical Economics in the Developing World: Policy Convergence and Bases of Governance in the International Economic Order." In *Governance without Government: Order and Change in World Politics*, ed. James N. Rosenau and Ernst-Otto Czempiel, 102–31. Cambridge: Cambridge University Press.

Bite, Vita. 1996. "U.N. System Funding: Congressional Issues." *CRS Issue Brief* (Congressional Research Service), January 2.

Blair, James. 1998. "Newest Item on Black Market: Refrigerator Coolants." *Christian Science Monitor*, January 21. Available at www.csmonitor.com.

Blaney, David L., and Naeem Inayatullah. 2000. "The Westphalian Deferral." In *Continuity and Change*, ed. Caporaso, 29–64.

Blechman, Barry M. 1995. "The Intervention Dilemma." In *The United Nations, Peace-Keeping, and American Foreign Policy*, ed. Dick Clark. Washington, DC: Aspen Institute.

Blustein, Paul. 2001. "IMF Plan Takes Corporate Approach." *International Herald Tribune*, November 29, p. 12.

Blustein, Paul. 2002. "U.S.-British Standoff Stalls World Bank Aid for Poorest Countries." *International Herald Tribune*, January 15, p. 9.

Bobrow, Davis B., 1989. "Japan in the World: Opinion from Defeat to Success." *Journal of Conflict Resolution* 33 (4): 571–604.

Bobrow, Davis B., ed. 1999a. *Prospects for International Relations: Conjectures about the Next Millennium*. Malden, MA: Blackwell.

Bobrow, Davis B. 1999b. "Hegemony Management: The U.S. in the Asia-Pacific." *Pacific Review* 12 (2): 172–96.

Bobrow, Davis B. 2002. "A Changing American World Role?" *Zeitschrift fur Politikwissenschaft* 12 (1): 83–96.
Bobrow, Davis B., and Mark A. Boyer. 1996. "Bilateral and Multilateral Foreign Aid: Japan's Approach in Comparative Perspective." *Review of International Political Economy* 3 (1): 94–121.
Bobrow, Davis B., and Mark A. Boyer. 1997. "Maintaining System Stability: Contributions to Peacekeeping Operations." *Journal of Conflict Resolution* 41 (6): 723–48.
Bobrow, Davis B., and Robert T. Kudrle. 1999. "Understanding Regional Arrangements: From Occam to Gillette." Paper presented at the conference on After the Global Crises: What Next for Regionalism? University of Warwick, September 16–18.
Bonner, Raymond. 1995. "Job Done, UN Troops Stay on in Croatia." *New York Times,* August 25, p. A5.
Bouchet, Michel H., and Jonathan Hay. 1989. "The Rise of the Market Based 'Menu' Approach and Its Limitations." In *Dealing with the Debt Crisis,* ed. Husain and Diwan, 146–58.
Boulding, Kenneth E. 1973. *The Economy of Love and Fear: A Preface to Grants Economics.* Belmont, CA: Wadsworth.
Boulding, Kenneth E. 1989. "An Apologia." In *Journeys through World Politics: Autobiographical Reflections of Thirty-four Academic Travelers,* ed. Joseph Kruzel and James N. Rosenau, 105–17. Lexington, MA: Lexington Books.
Boutros-Ghali, Boutros. 1995. *An Agenda for Peace.* New York: United Nations.
Boutros-Ghali, Boutros. 1996. "UN Peacekeeping: An Introduction." *Brown Journal of World Affairs* 3 (1): 17–21.
Boyer, Mark A. 1993. *International Cooperation and Public Goods: Opportunities for the Western Alliance.* Baltimore: Johns Hopkins University Press.
Bradlow, Daniel D., ed. 1994. *International Borrowing: Negotiating and Structuring International Debt Transactions.* 3d ed. Washington, DC: International Law Institute.
Brady, Nicholas F. 1989. "Third World Debt." In *Alternative Solutions,* ed. Dornbusch, Makin, and Zlowe, 115–21.
Broad, Robin, ed. 2002. *Global Backlash: Citizen Initiatives for a Just World Economy.* Lanham, MD: Rowman and Littlefield.
Browne, Marjorie Ann. 1994. "United Nations Peacekeeping Operations, 1988–1993: Background Information." *CRS Issue Brief* (Congressional Research Service), February 28.
Browne, Marjorie Ann. 1995. "United Nations Peacekeeping: Issues for Congress." *CRS Issue Brief* (Congressional Research Service), December 21.
Bryant, Ralph. 1987. *International Financial Intermediation: Issues for Analysis and Public Policy.* Washington, DC: Brookings.
Bumiller, Elisabeth. 2002. "Bush, in Monterrey, Speaks of Conditional Global Aid." *New York Times,* March 23. Available at www.nytimes.com.
Burley, Anne-Marie Slaughter, and Carl Kaysen. 1993. "Introductory Note." In *Emerging Norms of Justified Intervention,* ed. Laura W. Reed and Carl Kaysen, 7–14. Cambridge, MA: American Academy of Arts and Sciences.

REFERENCES

"Bush Vows Aid for Poor as Antidote to Terrorism." 2002 *International Herald Tribune,* March 23–24, p. 1.

Buzan, Barry. 1993. "From International System to International Society: Structural Realism and Regime Theory Meet the English School." *International Organization* 47:327–52.

Caporaso, James A., ed. *Continuity and Change in the Westphalian Order.* Malden, MA: Blackwell.

Carnegie Commission on Preventing Deadly Conflict. 1997. *Preventing Deadly Conflict: Final Report with Executive Summary.* Washington, DC: Carnegie Commission.

Castellano, Marc. 1999a. "G-7 Agrees to Debt Relief Plan for Poorest Nations." *JEI Report,* June 25, pp. 4–5.

Castellano, Marc. 1999b. "Japan Contributes Funds, Not Troops, to East Timor Peacekeeping Force." *JEI Report,* September 24, pp. 10–11.

Castellano, Marc. 1999c. "Japan Remains World's Largest Aid Donor." *JEI Report,* June 18, pp. 8–10.

Castellano, Marc. 1999d. "Japanese Aid to Focus on National Interests, East Asia." *JEI Report,* August 20, pp. 9–10.

Castellano, Marc. 2000a. "Forgiving Poor—Country Debt: Will Japan Lead the Way?" *JEI Report,* May 5, pp. 1–10.

Castellano, Marc. 2000b. "Japan Again Claims Top Donor Spot." *JEI Report,* June 16, pp. 6–8.

Castellano, Marc. 2000c. "Japan's Foreign Aid Program in the New Millennium: Rethinking 'Development.'" *JEI Report,* February 11, pp. 1–10.

Castellano, Marc. 2000d. "More of Japan's Aid Has Strings Attached." *JEI Report,* June 23, pp. 8–9.

Center for Strategic and International Studies. 1998. *The United States and the Multilateral Development Banks.* Washington, DC: Center for Strategic and International Studies.

Center on Policy Attitudes. 2000. "Americans on the Federal Budget." Available at www.policyattitudes.org/OnlineReports.

Chang, Charles C., Eduardo Fernandez-Arias, and Luis Serven. 1999. *Measuring Aid Flows: A New Approach.* Working Paper 2050. Washington, DC: World Bank.

Chanley, Virginia A. 1999. "U.S. Public Views of International Involvement from 1964 to 1993." *Journal of Conflict Resolution* 43 (1): 23–44.

Chase, Robert S., Emily Hill, and Paul Kennedy. 1996. "Pivotal States and U.S. Strategy." *Foreign Affairs* 75 (1): 33–54.

Chayes, Abram, and Antonia Handler Chayes. 1995. *The New Sovereignty: Compliance with International Regulatory Agreements.* Cambridge: Harvard University Press.

Checkel, Jeffrey T. 1999. "Norms, Institutions, and National Identity in Contemporary Europe." *International Studies Quarterly* 43 (1): 83–114.

Chicago Council on Foreign Relations and the German Marshall Fund. 2002. "Worldviews 2002." Available at www.worldviews.org.

Chin, Ji Young, and Christopher Marsh. 1999. "Public Opinion, Congressional

Policymaking, and Congruence: The Case of U.S. Policy towards the United Nations." Paper presented at the annual meetings of the International Studies Association, Washington, DC, March 16–20.

Chongkittavorn, Kavi. 1999. "ASEAN Splits over East Timor Crisis." *Nikkei Weekly,* October 4, p. 14.

Claessens, Stijn. 1994. "Alternative Forms of External Financing for Developing Countries." In *International Borrowing,* ed. Bradlow, 49–62.

Claessens, Stijn, and Ishac Diwan. 1989. "Market-Based Debt Reduction." In *Dealing with the Debt Crisis,* ed. Husain and Diwan, 258–73.

Claessens, Stijn, and Ishac Diwan. 1994. "Recent Experience with Commercial Bank Debt Reduction: Has the 'Menu' Outdone the Market?" *World Development* 22:201–13.

Claessens, Stijn, Daniel Oks, and Rossana Polastri. 1998. *Capital Flows to Center and Eastern Europe and the Former Soviet Union.* Working Paper 1976. Washington, DC: World Bank.

Claessens, Stijn, and Sweder van Wijnbergen. 1993. "Secondary Market Prices and Mexico's Brady Deal." *Quarterly Journal of Economics* 108:965–82.

Clark, Richard, and Kenneth Dautrich. 2000. "Who's Really Mis-Reading the Public? A Rejoinder to Kull and Ramsay's 'Challenging US Policy Makers' Image of an Isolationist Public.'" *International Studies Perspectives* 1 (2): 195–98.

Cline, William R. 1989. "The Baker Plan and Brady Reformulation: An Evaluation." In *Dealing with the Debt Crisis,* ed. Husain and Diwan, 176–93.

Cline, William R. 1995. *International Debt Reexamined.* Washington, DC: Institute for International Economics.

Cohen, A. 1985. *The Symbolic Construction of Community.* London: Routledge.

Cohen, Benjamin J. 1996. "Phoenix Risen: The Resurrection of Global Finance." *World Politics* 48:268–96.

Cohn, Jonathan. 1999. "Irrational Exuberance: When Did Political Science Forget about Politics?" *New Republic,* October 25. Available at http://www.tnr.com/magazines/tnr/current/coverstory102599.html.

Coklas, Toula. 1995. "Finance and Administration." In *A Global Agenda: Issues before the 50th General Assembly of the United Nations,* 285–366. New York: New York University Press.

Cook, Lisa D., and Jeffrey Sachs. 1999. "Regional Public Goods in International Assistance." In *Global Public Goods,* ed. Kaul, Grunberg, and Stern, 436–49.

Coordinadora de Defensa del Agua y de la Vida. 2002. "The Cochahamba Declaration on Water: Globalization, Privatization, and the Search for Alternatives." In *Global Backlash,* ed. Broad, 273.

Corbridge, Stuart. 1993. *Debt and Development.* Oxford: Blackwell.

Cortell, Andrew P., and James W. Davis Jr. 2000. "Understanding the Domestic Impact of International Norms: A Research Agenda." *International Studies Review* 2 (1): 65–87.

Cox, Michael. 2002. "American Power before and after 11 September: Dizzy with Success?" *International Affairs* 78 (2): 261–76.

REFERENCES

Cronin, Bruce. 1999. *Community under Anarchy: Transnational Identity and the Evolution of Cooperation.* New York: Columbia University Press.
Crossette, Barbara. 1997. "U.S. Offers Third World a Wider Role in the U.N." *New York Times,* September 13, p. A7.
Crossette, Barbara. 1999a. "U.N. Chief Issues a Call to Speed Interventions and Halt Civil Wars." *New York Times,* September 21, p. A1.
Crossette, Barbara. 1999b. "U.N. Details Its Failure to Stop '95 Bosnia Massacre." *New York Times,* November 16, p. A3.
Crossette, Barbara. 1999c. "U.N. Moving ahead to Organize Force for Eastern Timor." *New York Times,* September 14, p. A1.
Crossette, Barbara. 2000a. "Japan Asks for an End to Debate on U.N. Security Council's Shape." *New York Times,* February 22, p. A3.
Crossette, Barbara. 2000b. "U.N. Chief Faults Reluctance of U.S. to Help in Africa." *New York Times,* May 13, p. A1.
Crossette, Barbara. 2000c. "U.N. Reform Group Assesses U.S. Candidates." *New York Times,* August 20, p. Y12.
Crossette, Barbara. 2000d. "The U.N.'s Unhappy Lot: Perilous Police Duties Multiplying." *New York Times,* February 22, p. A3.
Crossette, Barbara. 2000e. "Washington Takes a Blast from Its Envoy at the U.N." *New York Times,* July 2, p. A9.
"Crossroads on Global Warming." 2002. *New York Times,* June 3. Available at www.nytimes.com.
Cuddington, John T. 1989. "The Extent and Causes of the Debt Crisis of the 1980s." In *Dealing with the Debt Crisis,* ed. Husain and Diwan, 15–41.
Cumings, Bruce. 1987–88. "Power and Plenty in Northeast Asia: The Evolution of U.S. Policy." *World Policy Journal* 5:79–106.
Dao, James. 2003. "With Rise in Foreign Aid, Plans for a New Way to Give It." *New York Times,* February 3, p. A6.
Dawes, Robyn M. 1980. "Social Dilemmas." *Annual Review of Psychology* 31: 169–93.
Delanty, Gerard. 1995. *Inventing Europe: Idea, Identity, Reality.* London: Macmillan.
Dempsey, Judy, and Alan Beattie. 2002. "Germany Urged to Fall in Line on Aid Package." *Financial Times,* March 14, p. 4.
Deutsch, Karl W., et al. 1957. *Political Community and the North Atlantic Area.* Princeton: Princeton University Press.
Devarajan, Shantayanan, Margaret J. Miller, and Eric V. Swanson. 2002. *Goals for Development: History, Prospects, and Costs.* Working Paper 2819. Washington, DC: World Bank.
Development Cooperation. Various years. Paris: Organization for Economic Cooperation and Development.
"Development Minister Lauds EU for Aid Resolution." 2002. *Frankfurter Allgemeine Zeitung* (English ed.), March 16, p. 2.
Diehl, Paul F. 1988. "Institutional Alternatives to Traditional UN Peacekeeping: An Assessment of Regional and Multinational Options." *Armed Forces and Society* 19 (2): 209–30.

References

Diehl, Paul F. 1993a. *International Peacekeeping.* Baltimore: Johns Hopkins University Press.

Diehl, Paul F. 1993b. "Peacekeeping Operations and the Quest for Peace." *Political Science Quarterly* 103 (3): 485–507.

Diehl, Paul F., Daniel Druckman, and James Wall. 1998. "International Peacekeeping and Conflict Resolution: A Taxonomic Analysis with Implications." *Journal of Conflict Resolution* 42 (1): 33–55.

Diehl, Paul F., Jennifer Reifschneider, and Paul R. Hensel. 1996. "UN Intervention and Recurring Conflict." *International Organization* 50 (4): 683–700.

Dobbie, Charles. 1994. "A Concept for Post–Cold War Peacekeeping." *Survival* 36 (3): 121–48.

Dombrowski, Peter. 1997. "A Principal-Agent Approach to Foreign Economic Policy: State-Business Relations during U.S. Debt Crisis Management." *Competition and Change* 2 (3): 259–98.

Dombrowski, Peter. 1998. "Haute Finance and High Theory: Recent Scholarship on Global Financial Relations." *Mershon International Studies Review* 42:1–28.

Doremus, Paul N., William W. Keller, Louis W. Pauly, and Simon Reich. 1998. *The Myth of the Global Corporation.* Princeton: Princeton University Press.

Dornbusch, Rudiger. 1993. *Stabilization, Debt, and Reform: Policy Analysis for Developing Countries.* Englewood Cliffs, NJ: Prentice Hall.

Dornbusch, Rudiger, John H. Makin, and David Zlowe, eds. 1989. *Alternative Solutions to Developing Country Debt Problems.* Washington, DC: American Enterprise Institute.

Downs, George W., David M. Rocke, and Peter N. Barsoom. 1998. "Managing the Evolution of Multilateralism." *International Organization* 52 (2): 397–419.

Doyle, Michael W., and Nicholas Sambanis. 2000. "International Peacebuilding: A Theoretical and Quantitative Analysis." *American Political Science Review* 94 (4): 779–801.

Duchesne, Sophie, and Andre-Paul Frognier. 1995. "Is There a European Identity?" In *Public Opinion and Internationalized Governance,* ed. Niedermayer and Sinnott, 193–226.

Dunlap, Riley E. 1994. "International Attitudes towards Environment and Development." In *Green Globe Yearbook,* ed. Bergerson and Parmann, 115–26.

Durch, William J. ed. 1993. *The Evolution of UN Peacekeeping.* New York: St. Martin's.

Durch, William J. 2000. *Discussion of the Report of the Panel on UN Peace Operations: The "Brahimi" Report.* Washington, DC: Stimson Center.

Easterly, William. 2001. "Debt Relief." *Foreign Policy,* November–December, pp. 20–26.

Eatwell, John. 1997. *International Financial Liberalization: The Impact on World Development.* UNDP Office of Development Studies, Discussion Paper Series.

"Ecuador Becomes First Country to Default on 'Brady Bonds.'" 1999. *Japan Times,* October 2, p. 13.

Eichenberg, Richard C. 1998. "Domestic Preferences and Foreign Policy: Cumulation and Confirmation in the Study of Public Opinion." *Mershon International Studies Review* 42 (supp. 1): 97–105.

Eichengreen, Barry. 1999. "The Baring Crisis in a Mexican Mirror." *International Political Science Review* 20:249–70.

Eichengreen, Barry, and Ricardo Hausmann. 1999. "Exchange Rates and Financial Fragility." In *New Challenges for Monetary Policy*, 329–68. Kansas City: Federal Reserve Bank of Kansas City.

Eichengreen, Barry, and Richard Portes. 1987. "The Anatomy of Financial Crises." In *Threats to International Financial Stability*, ed. Richard Portes and Alexander K. Swoboda, 10–66. Cambridge: Cambridge University Press.

Eisenstadt, S. N., and B. Giesen. 1995. "The Construction of Collective Identity." *Archives Européenes de Sociologie* 36:72–102.

Ensign, Margee M. 1992. *Doing Good or Doing Well? Japan's Foreign Aid Program*. New York: Columbia University Press.

European Commission. Various years. "Eurobarometer: Public Opinion in the European Union." Available at europa.eu.int/comm/public_opinion.

European Commission. 1999. *What Do Europeans Think about the Environment?* Luxembourg: Office for Official Publications of the European Communities.

European Commission. 2001. "Europeans and the International Crisis." *Flash Eurobarometer* 114. Available at europa.eu.int/comm/public_opinion/archives/flash_arch.htm.

European Commission. 2001. *Green Paper: Towards a European Strategy for the Security of Energy Supply*. Luxembourg: Office for Official Publications of the European Communities.

European Commission. 2002. "Applicant Countries Eurobarometer." December, Report no. 2. Available at europa.eu.int/comm/public_opinion.

European Commission. 2002. *Flash Eurobarometer* 132/2, "Enlargement of the European Union." Brussels: European Commission.

European Commission. 2002. "Perception du Développement Durable et Préoccupations Environmentales des Européens." *Flash Barometer* 123. Available at www.europa.eu.int/comm/public_opinion/archives/flash_arch.htm.

European Commission. (2002). "Sustainable Development." http://europa.eu.int/comm/environment/barometer/results.pdf.

European Opinion Research Group. 2001. *Les Européens, la Globalisation, et la Liberalisation*. Brussels: European Commission.

Evans, Peter. 1997. "The Eclipse of the State? Reflections on Stateness in an Era of Globalization." *World Politics* 50:62–87.

Everts, Philip. 1995. "NATO, the European Community, and the United Nations." In *Public Opinion and Internationalized Governance*, ed. Niedermayer and Sinnott, 402–29.

"Fact Sheet: U.S.-Japan Global Partnership Action Plan." 1992. *U.S. Department of State Dispatch*, January 20, pp. 45–46.

Fearon, James D. 1998. "Bargaining, Enforcement, and International Cooperation." *International Organization* 52 (2): 269–305.

References

Ferguson, Yale H., and Richard W. Mansbach. 1996. *Polities: Authority, Identities, and Change.* Columbia: University of South Carolina Press.

Finnemore, Martha. 1996. "Norms, Culture, and World Politics: Insights from Sociology's Institutionalism." *International Organization* 50 (2): 325–47.

Finnemore, Martha, and Kathryn Sikkink. 1998. "International Norm Dynamics and Political Change." *International Organization* 52 (4): 887–917.

Foyle, Douglas C. 1994. "Public Opinion in Foreign Policy Decision Making: Insight from Comparative Case Studies." Presented at the annual meetings of the American Political Science Association, New York, September 1–4.

Frankel, Jeffrey A. 1999. "The International Financial Architecture." Brookings Policy Brief 51. Available at Brook.edu/comm./PolicyBriefs/pb051.

Friedman, Thomas L. 2000. *The Lexus and the Olive Tree: Understanding Globalization.* New York: Farrar Straus Giroux.

Fukuyama, Francis. 1992. *The End of History and the Last Man.* New York: Free Press.

Funabashi, Yoichi. 1989. *Managing the Dollar: From the Plaza to the Louvre.* 2d ed. Washington, DC: Institute for International Economics.

Gabel, Matthew J. 1998. *Interests and Integration: Market Liberalization, Public Opinion, and European Union.* Ann Arbor: University of Michigan Press.

Gallup International. 2001. "Gallup International Poll on Terrorism in the U.S." Available at www.gallup-international.com/terrorismpoll_figures.

Gallup Poll Archives. Various years. Available at www.gallup.com/poll/archives.

Gallup Poll Releases. Various years. Available at www.gallup.com/poll/releases.

"Gallup Poll Topics: A–Z Environment." 2001. Available at www.gallup.com/poll/indicators.

"Gallup Poll Topics: A–Z Kosovo." 2000. Available at www.gallup.com/poll/indicators.

"Gallup Poll Topics: A–Z Russia." 2000. Available at www.gallup.com/poll/indicators.

"Gallup Poll Topics: A–Z Military and National Defense." 2001. Available at www.gallup.com/poll/indicators.

"Gallup Poll Topics: A–Z Russia." 2001. Available at www.gallup/com/poll/indicators.

Gardner, Roy, Eleanor Ostrom, and James Walker. 1990. "The Nature of Common-Pool Resources." *Rationality and Society* 2:335–58.

"Gifts with Strings Attached." 2000. *Economist,* June 17, p. 21.

Gilpin, Robert. 1981. *War and Change in World Politics.* Cambridge: Cambridge University Press.

Gilpin, Robert. 1987. *The Political Economy of International Relations.* Princeton: Princeton University Press.

Gitlin, Todd. 1980. *The Whole World Is Watching: Mass Media in the Making and Unmaking of the New Left.* Berkeley: University of California Press.

Gleditsch, Nils Petter. 1998. "Armed Conflict and the Environment: A Critique of the Literature." *Journal of Peace Research* 35 (3): 381–400.

REFERENCES

Gleditsch, Nils Petter. 2000. "Armed Conflict and the Environment: A Critique of the Literature." *Journal of Peace Research* 35 (3): 381–400.
Gleick, Peter H. 1993. "Water and Conflict." *International Security* 18 (1): 79–112.
"Global Finance—Time for a Redesign?" 1999. *Economist*, January 30, pp. 3–18.
Global Policy Forum. 2003. Available at www.globalpolicy.org.
Goldgeier, James M., and Michael McFaul. 1992. "A Tale of Two Worlds: Core and Periphery in the Post–Cold War Era." *International Organization* 46: 467–91.
Goldstein, Judith. 1993. *Ideas, Interests, and American Trade Policy*. Ithaca: Cornell University Press.
Goulding, Marrack. 1993. "The Evolution of United Nations Peacekeeping." *International Affairs* 69 (3): 451–64.
Government Poll Yearbook [Yoron Chosa Nenkan]. Various years. Tokyo: Printing Bureau, Ministry of Finance.
Grant, Richard, and Jan Nijman. 1998. "The Foreign Aid Regime in Flux: Crisis or Transition?" In *The Global Crisis in Foreign Aid*, ed. Richard Grant and Jan Nijman, 3–10. Syracuse: Syracuse University Press, 1998.
Green, Donald, and Ian Shapiro. 1994. *Pathologies of Rational Choice Theory*. New Haven: Yale University Press.
Grimmett, Richard F. 1996. "Multinational Peacekeeping Operations: Proposals to Enhance Congressional Oversight." *CRS Issue Brief* (Congressional Research Service), January 23.
Gruber, Lloyd. 2000. *Ruling the World: Power Politics and the Rise of Supranational Institutions*. Princeton: Princeton University Press.
Haas, Ernest B. 1971. "The Study of Regional Integration: Reflections on the Joy and Anguish of Pre-Theorizing." In *Regional Integration: Theory and Research*, ed. Leon Lindberg and Stuart Scheingold, 3–44. Cambridge: Harvard University Press.
Haas, Peter M. 1992. "Banning Chlorofluorocarbons: Epistemic Community Efforts to Protect Stratospheric Ozone." *International Organization* 46 (1): 187–224.
Hamburg, David A., and Jane E. Holl. 1999. "Preventing Deadly Conflict: From Global Housekeeping to Neighborhood Watch." In *Global Public Goods*, ed. Kaul, Grunberg, and Stern, 366–81.
Hardin, Russell. 1982. "Collective Action as an Agreeable n-Prisoners' Dilemma." In *Rational Man, Irrational Society? An Introduction and Sourcebook*, ed. Brian Barry and Russell Hardin, 121–36. Beverly Hills, CA: Sage.
Hastings, Elizabeth Hamm, and Philip K. Hastings. Various years. *Index to International Public Opinion*. Westport, CT: Greenwood.
Heal, Geoffrey. 1999. "New Strategies for the Provision of Global Public Goods: Learning from International Environmental Challenges." In *Global Public Goods*, ed. Kaul, Grunberg, and Stern, 220–39.
Held, David. 1996. "The Decline of the Nation State." In *Becoming National*:

A Reader, ed. Geoff Eley and Ronald Ginger Suny, 407–16. New York: Oxford University Press.

Hernandez, Leonardo, and Saori N. Katada. 1996. *Grants and Debt Forgiveness in Africa: A Descriptive Analysis*. Working Paper 1653. Washington, DC: World Bank.

Herring, Richard, and Robert E. Litan. 1995. *Financial Regulation in a Global Economy*. Washington, DC: Brookings.

Herron, K. G., H. C. Jenkins Smith, and S. D. Hughes. 2000. *Mass and Elite Views on Nuclear Security: U.S. National Security Surveys, 1993–1999*. Vol. 1, *General Public*. Albuquerque: University of New Mexico Institute for Public Policy Studies.

Hill, Stephen H., and Shahin P. Malik. 1996. *Peacekeeping and the United Nations*. Aldershot, UK: Dartmouth.

Hirst, Paul, and Grahame Thompson. 1996. *Globalization in Question*. Cambridge: Polity.

Hochstetler, Kathryn, Ann Marie Clark, and Elisabeth J. Friedman. 2000. "Sovereignty in the Balance: Claims and Bargains at the U.N. Conferences on the Environment, Human Rights, and Women." *International Studies Quarterly* 44 (4): 591–614.

Hoffman, Stanley. 1966. "Obstinate or Obsolete? The Fate of the Nation-State and the Case of Western Europe." *Daedalus* 95:862–915.

Hoffman, Stanley. 1989. "A Retrospective." In *Journeys through World Politics: Autobiographical Reflections of Thirty-four Academic Travelers*, ed. Joseph Kruzel and James N. Rosenau, 263–78. Lexington, MA: Lexington Books.

Holsti, K. J. 1995. "War, Peace, and the State of the State." *International Political Science Review* 16 (4): 319–40.

Holsti, Ole R. 1992. "Public Opinion and Foreign Policy: Challenges to the Almond-Lippmann Consensus." *International Studies Quarterly* 36:439–66.

Holsti, Ole R. 1996. *Public Opinion and American Foreign Policy*. Ann Arbor: University of Michigan Press.

Holsti, Ole R. 1998–99. "A Widening Gap between the U.S. Military and Civilian Society: Some Evidence, 1976–96." *International Security* 23 (3): 5–42.

Holsti, Ole R., and James N. Rosenau. 1993. "The Structure of Foreign Policy Beliefs among American Opinion Leaders—After the Cold War." *Millennium* 22 (2): 235–78.

Holt, Victoria K. 1996. "Reforming U.N. Peacekeeping: The U.S. Role and the U.N. Financial Crisis." *Brown Journal of International Affairs* 3 (1): 125–34.

Homer-Dixon, Thomas. 1991. "On the Threshold: Environmental Changes as Causes of Acute Conflict." *International Security* 16 (2): 76–116.

Homer-Dixon, Thomas. 1994. "Environmental Scarcities and Violent Conflict." *International Security* 19 (1): 5–40.

Hook, Steven W. 1995. *National Interest and Foreign Aid*. Boulder: Rienner.

Huizinga, Harry. 1989. "The Commercial Bank Claims on Developing Countries: How Have Banks Been Affected?" In *Dealing with the Debt Crisis*, ed. Husain and Diwan, 129–43.

REFERENCES

Huntington, Samuel P. 1993. "The Clash of Civilizations." *Foreign Affairs* 72 (3): 56–73.

Huntington, Samuel P. 1996. *The Clash of Civilizations and the Remaking of World Order*. New York: Simon and Schuster.

Husain, Ishrat, and Ishac Diwan, eds. 1989. *Dealing with the Debt Crisis*. Washington, DC: World Bank.

Husain, Ishrat, and Saumya Mitro. 1989. "Future Financing Needs of the Highly Indebted Countries." In *Dealing with the Debt Crisis*, ed. Husain and Diwan, 199–208.

Ikenberry, G. John, and Charles A. Kupchan. 1990. "Socialization and Hegemonic Power." *International Organization* 44: 283–315.

IMF [International Monetary Fund]. Various years. *Official Financing for Developing Countries*. Washington, DC: International Monetary Fund.

IMF [International Monetary Fund]. 1992. *Private Market Financing for Developing Countries*. Washington, DC: International Monetary Fund.

"I.M.F. and World Bank Blueprint." 2000. *New York Times*, March 9, p. A28.

Independent Advisory Group on UN Financing. 1993. *Financing an Effective United Nations: A Report of the Independent Advisory Group on U.N. Financing*. New York: Ford Foundation.

Inglehart, Ronald, Miguel Basañez, and Alejandro Moreno. 1998. *Human Values and Beliefs: A Cross-Cultural Sourcebook*. Ann Arbor: University of Michigan Press.

Inoguchi, Takashi. 1986. "Japan's Images and Options: Not a Challenger, but a Supporter." *Journal of Japanese Studies* 12:95–119.

Inoguchi, Takashi. 1995. "Japan's United Nations Peacekeeping and Other Operations." *International Journal* 50:324–42.

International Institute for Strategic Studies. 1998. *The Military Balance, 1998–1999*. London: Oxford University Press.

Islam, Shafiqul. 1993. "Foreign Aid and Burdensharing: Is Japan Free Riding to a Coprosperity Sphere in Pacific Asia?" In *Regionalism and Rivalry: Japan and the U.S. in Pacific Asia*, ed. Jeffrey A. Frankel and Miles Kahler, 321–72. Chicago: University of Chicago Press.

ISSP [International Social Survey Program]. 1995. *International Social Survey Program 1993: Environment, Codebook ZA Study 2450*. 2d ed. Cologne: Zentral Archiv fur Empirische Sozialforschung.

James, Alan. 1990. *Peacekeeping in International Politics*. New York: St. Martin's.

James, Alan. 1995. "Peacekeeping in the Post–Cold War Era." *International Journal* 50:241–65.

"Japan: Comparative Aid Performance." 1993. *DAC Aid Review: Press Releases*. SG/Press, 17.

Japan Information Network. Various years. Available at www.Jin.jcic.or.jp/stat/stats.

Jayaraman, Rajshri, and Ravi Kanbur. 1999. "International Public Goods and the Case for Foreign Aid." In *Global Public Goods*, ed. Kaul, Grunberg, and Stern, 418–35.

JEI Report. 1994. No. 44A. Washington, DC: Japan Economic Institute, November 18.

Jentleson, Bruce W. 1992. "The Pretty Prudent Public: Post Post-Vietnam American Opinion on the Use of Military Force." *International Studies Quarterly* 36:49–74.

Jentleson, Bruce W., and Rebecca L. Britton. 1998. "Still Pretty Prudent: Post–Cold War American Public Opinion on the Use of Military Force." *Journal of Conflict Resolution* 42:395–417.

Jervis, Robert. 1999. "Realism, Neoliberalism, and Cooperation." *International Security* 24 (1): 42–63.

Johnson, Lyndon Baines. 1965. White House News Conference, July 28.

Johnstone, Christopher B. 1995. "The Challenge of Transition." *JEI Report*, December 15.

JPOLL [Japan Public Opinion Location Library]. Various years. www.roperweb.ropercenter.uconn.edu.

Kahn, Joseph. 2001. "IMF's Bankruptcy Plan Gains." *International Herald Tribune*, December 26, p. 10.

Kameyama, Yasuko. 2001. "Japan: Struggling to Achieve 6%." *German Foreign Policy in Dialogue* 2 (6): 19–21. Available at www.deutsche-aussenpolitik.de.

Kammler, Hans. 1997. "Not for Security Only: The Demand for International Status and Defence Expenditure, an Introduction." *Defence and Peace Economics* 8:1–16.

Kanbur, Ravi, and Todd Sandler. 1999. *The Future Of Development Assistance*. Policy Essay 25. Washington, DC: Overseas Development Council.

Kaplan, Robert D. 2000. *The Coming Anarchy: Shattering the Dreams of the Post Cold War*. New York: Random House.

Kapstein, Ethan B. 1996. "Shockproof: The End of the Financial Crisis." *Foreign Affairs* 75:2–8.

Karns, Margaret P., and Karen A. Mingst. 1995. "The Past as Prologue: The United States and the Future of the U.N. System." In *The United Nations System: The Policies of Member States*, ed. Chadwick F. Alger, Gene M. Lyons, and John E. Trent, 410–60. Tokyo: United Nations University Press.

Katada, Saori N., and Timothy J. McKeown. 1998. "Aid Politics and Electoral Politics: Japan, 1970–1992." *International Studies Quarterly* 42:591–600.

Kaufmann, Chaim D., and Robert A. Pape. 1999. "Explaining Costly Moral Action: Britain's Sixty-Year Campaign against the Atlantic Slave Trade." *International Organization* 53 (4): 631–68.

Kaul, Inge, Isabelle Grunberg, and Marc A. Stern, eds. 1999. *Global Public Goods: International Cooperation in the 21st Century*. New York: Oxford University Press.

Kegley, Charles W., Jr. 1996. "International Peacemaking and Peacekeeping: The Morality of Multilateral Measures." *Ethics and International Affairs* 10: 25–45.

Keller, William W., Theodore J. Lowi, and Gerry Gendlin. 2000. "Negative Capital and the Wealth of Nations." *International Studies Perspectives* 1: 75–88.

REFERENCES

Keohane, Robert O. 1984. *After Hegemony: Cooperation and Discord in World Political Economy.* Princeton: Princeton University Press.

Keohane, Robert O. 2001. "Governance in a Partially Globalized World: Presidential Address, American Political Science Association, 2000." *American Political Science Review* 95 (1): 1–13.

Kerr, Elizabeth, and Jonathan Mercer. 1996. "Setting Precedents in Anarchy: Military Interventions and Weapons of Mass Destruction." *International Security* 20 (4): 77–106.

Khanna, Jyoti, Todd Sandler, and Hirofumi Shimizu. 1998. "Sharing the Financial Burden for U.N. and NATO Peacekeeping, 1976–1996." *Journal of Conflict Resolution* 42 (2): 176–95.

Khanna, Jyoti, Todd Sandler, and Hirofumi Shimizu. 1999. "The Demand for U.N. Peacekeeping, 1975–1996." *Kyklos* 52:345–68.

Kindleberger, Charles P. 1973. *The World in Depression, 1929–1939.* Berkeley: University of California Press.

Kindleberger, Charles P. 1986. *The World in Depression, 1929–1939.* Rev. ed. Berkeley: University of California Press.

Krasner, Stephen D., ed. 1983. *International Regimes.* Ithaca: Cornell University Press.

Kristof, Nicholas D., and David E. Sanger. 1999. "How U.S. Wooed Asia to Let Cash Flow In." *New York Times,* February 16, p. A1.

Kristof, Nicholas D., and Edward Wyatt. 1999. "Who Went under in the World's Sea of Cash." *New York Times,* February 15, p. A1.

Krugman, Paul R. 1988. "Financing versus Forgiving a Debt Overhang: Some Analytical Notes." *Journal of Development Economics* 94:287–307.

Krugman, Paul R. 1989a. "Market Based Approaches to Debt Reduction." In *Alternative Solutions,* ed. Dornbusch, Makin, and Zlowe, 43–63.

Krugman, Paul R. 1989b. "Private Capital Flow to Problem Debtors." In *Developing Country Debt and the World Economy,* ed. Jeffrey D. Sachs, 285–98. Chicago: University of Chicago Press.

Ku, Charlotte, and Harold K. Jacobson. 2001. "Using Military Forces under International Auspices and Democratic Accountability." *International Relations of the Asia-Pacific* 1:21–50.

Kull, Stephen. 1995–96. "What the Public Knows and Washington, DC Doesn't." *Foreign Policy* 101:102–15.

Kull, Stephen, and I. M. Destler. 1999. *Misreading the Public: The Myth of a New Isolationism,* Washington, DC: Brookings.

Kupchan, Charles A. 1998. "After Pax Americana: Benign Power, Regional Integration, and the Sources of a Stable Multipolarity." *International Security* 23:40–79.

Kydd, Andrew. 2000. "Trust, Reassurance, and Cooperation." *International Organization* 54 (2): 325–58.

Lacey, Marc. 2001. "House Warns U.N. of Pocketbook Revenge." *New York Times,* May 11, p. A8.

Lake, David. 1983. "International Economic Structures and American Foreign Economic Policy, 1887–1934." *World Politics* 35:517–43.

References

Lancaster, Carol. 2000a. "Redesigning Foreign Aid." *Foreign Affairs* 79 (5): 74–88.

Lancaster, Carol. 2000b. *Transforming Foreign Aid: United States Assistance in the 21st Century*. Washington, DC: Institute for International Economics.

Langdon, Frank. 1993. "The Posthegemonic Japanese-U.S. Relationship." In *Japan in the Posthegemonic World*, ed. Tsuneo Akaha and Frank Langdon, 69–90. Boulder, CO: Rienner.

Lapid, Yosef. 1995. *The Return of Culture and Identity in International Relations Theory*. Boulder, CO: Rienner.

Lasswell, Harold D. 1936. *Politics: Who Gets What, When, and How*. New York: Whittlesey, McGraw-Hill.

Lavrov, Sergei. 1996. "The Russian View of Peacekeeping: International Activity for Peace." *Brown Journal of World Affairs* 3 (1): 23–33.

Lee, Boon-Chye. 1993. *The Economics of International Debt Renegotiation: The Role of Bargaining and Information*. Boulder, CO: Westview.

Lehman, Howard P. 1993. "Strategic Bargaining in Brazil's Debt Negotiations." *Political Science Quarterly* 108:133–55.

Levinson, Jerome I. 1994. "A Perspective on the Debt Crisis." In *International Borrowing*, ed. Bradlow, 455–79.

Lewis, Paul. 1997. "How U.N. Keeps Pace as Fewer Keep Peace." *New York Times*, May 4, p. 4.

Lewis, Paul. 1999. "Debt-Relief Plan Is Flawed, 5 Nations Say." *New York Times*, April 24, p. B2.

Lieberman, Bernhardt. 1967. "I-Trust: A Notion of Trust in Three-Person Games and International Affairs." *Journal of Conflict Resolution* 8:271–80.

Lindberg, Leon N., and Stuart A. Scheingold. 1970. *Europe's Would-Be Polity: Patterns of Change in the European Community*. Englewood Cliffs, NJ: Prentice-Hall.

Lindley, Dan. 1997. *UNFICYP and a Cyprus Solution: A Strategic Assessment*. Security Studies Working Paper 97-1. Cambridge, MA: Defense and Arms Control Studies Program, MIT, May.

Lippmann, Walter. 1955. *Essays in the Public Philosophy*. Boston: Little, Brown.

Lipschutz, Ronnie D. 1989. *When Nations Clash: Raw Materials, Ideology, and Foreign Policy*. New York: Harper and Row.

Lissakers, Karin. 1991. *Banks, Borrowers and the Establishment: A Revisionist Account of the International Debt Crisis*. New York: Basic Books.

Lowi, Miriam R. 1993. "Bridging the Divide: Transboundary Resource Disputes and the Case of West Bank Water." *International Security* 18 (1): 113–38.

Lumsdaine, David Halloran. 1993. *Moral Vision in International Politics: The Foreign Aid Regime, 1949–1989*. Princeton: Princeton University Press.

Luterbacher, Urs, and Detlef F. Sprinz, eds. 2001. *International Relations and Global Climate Change*. Cambridge: MIT Press.

MacFarlane, S. Neil, Larry Minear, and Stephen D. Shenfield. 1996. *Armed*

REFERENCES

Conflict in Georgia: A Case Study of Humanitarian Action and Peacekeeping. Occasional Paper 21. Providence, RI: Thomas J. Watson Institute for International Studies, Brown University.

MacFarlane, S. Neil, and Albrecht Schnabel. 1995. "Russia's Approach to Peacekeeping." *International Journal* 50:294–324.

Manigart, Philippe. 2001. "Public Opinion and European Defense." Special Eurobarometer 146. Available at europa.eu.int/comm/public_opinion/archives/ebs/ebs_146_en.pdf.

Mansfield, Edward D., and Helen V. Milner. 1997. *The Political Economy of Regionalism.* New York: Columbia University Press.

Maoz, Zeev, and Dan S. Felsenthal. 1987. "Self-Binding Commitments, the Inducement of Trust, Social Choice, and the Theory of International Cooperation." *International Studies Quarterly* 31:177–200.

March, James G., and Johan P. Olsen. 1998. "The Institutional Dynamics of International Political Orders." *International Organization* 52 (4): 943–70.

Martin, Lisa L. 1992a. *Coercive Cooperation: Explaining Multilateral Economic Sanctions.* Princeton: Princeton University Press.

Martin, Lisa L. 1992b. "Interests, Power, and Multilateralism." *International Organization* 46 (4): 765–92.

Martin, Lisa L. 1999. "The Political Economy of International Cooperation." In *Global Public Goods,* ed. Kaul, Grunberg, and Stern, 51–64.

Martin, Pierre, and Michel Fortmann. 1995. "Canadian Public Opinion and Peacekeeping in a Turbulent World." *International Journal* 50:370–400.

Maruoka, Yasushi. 1999. "The Policy of Burden Sharing in Japan's ODA 1987–1997." *Journal of International Studies* 44 (July): 1–24.

Matthews, Jessica Tuchman. 1989. "Redefining Security." *Foreign Affairs* 68: 162–77.

Mattli, Walter. 1999. *The Logic of Regional Integration: Europe and Beyond.* New York: Columbia University Press.

McCormick, John. 1999. "The Role of Environmental NGOs in International Regimes." In *The Global Environment: Institutions, Law, and Policy,* ed. Norman J. Vig and Regina S. Axelrod, 52–71. Washington, DC: CQ Press.

McDermott, Anthony. 1994. *United Nations Financing Problems and the New Generation of Peacekeeping and Peace Enforcement.* Occasional Paper 16. Providence, RI: Thomas J. Watson Jr. Institute for International Studies, Brown University.

McKean, Margaret A. 1992. "Success on the Commons: A Comparative Examination of Institutions for Common Property Resource Management." *Journal of Theoretical Politics* 4 (3): 247–81.

Mearsheimer, John J. 1993. "Back to the Future: Instability in Europe after the Cold War." In *The Cold War and After: Prospects for Peace,* expanded ed., ed. Sean M. Lynn-Jones and Steven E. Miller, 141–92. Cambridge: MIT Press.

Mearsheimer, John J. 2001. *The Tragedy of Great Power Politics.* New York: Norton.

Meernik, James, Eric L. Krueger, and Steven C. Poe. 1998. "Testing Models of U.S. Foreign Policy: Foreign Aid during and after the Cold War." *Journal of Politics* 60 (1): 63–85.

Mendez, Ruben P. 1999. "Peace as a Global Public Good." In *Global Public Goods,* ed. Kaul, Grunberg, and Stern, 382–416.

Mills, Susan R. 1989. *The Financing of United Nations Peacekeeping Operations: The Need for a Sound Financial Basis.* Occasional Paper 3. Washington, DC: International Peace Academy.

Milner, Helen. 1991. "The Assumption of Anarchy in International Relations Theory: A Critique." *Review of International Studies* 17:67–85.

Mingst, Karen A. 1996. "State Participation in International and Regional Peacekeeping: A Comparative Analysis." Paper presented at the annual meeting of the International Studies Association, San Diego, April.

Mingst, Karen, and Margaret Karns. 1995. *The United Nations in the Post–Cold War Era.* Boulder, CO: Westview.

Mitchell, Ronald B. 2001. "Institutional Aspects of Implementation, Compliance and Effectiveness." In *International Relations and Global Climate Change,* ed. Luterbacher and Sprinz, 221–44.

Miyashita, Akitoshi. 1999. "Gaiatsu and Japan's Foreign Aid: Rethinking the Reactive-Proactive Debate." *International Studies Quarterly* 43 (3): 695–732.

Moravcsik, Andrew. 1989. "Disciplining Trade Finance." *International Organization* 43:173–205.

Morgenthau, Hans J. 1962. "A Political Theory of Foreign Aid." *American Political Science Review* 56 (2): 301–9.

Morgenthau, Hans J. 1978. *Politics among Nations.* New York: Knopf.

Morrison, Alex. 1996. "U.N. Peacekeeping Reform: Something Permanent and Stronger." *Brown Journal of World Affairs* 3 (1): 95–110.

Murphy, Craig N. 2000. "Global Governance: Poorly Done and Poorly Understood." *International Affairs* 76 (4): 780–803.

Murray, Shoon Kathleen. 1996. *Anchors against Change: American Opinion Leaders' Beliefs after the Cold War.* Ann Arbor: University of Michigan Press.

Mydans, Seth. 1999. "Peacekeepers Stake Claim to Capital of East Timor." *New York Times,* September 21, p. A1.

Myers, Stephen Lee. 1999. "Full-Time U.S. Force in Haiti to Leave with Peace Unsure." *New York Times,* August 26, p. A1.

"NATO and the War in Kosovo/Yugoslavia: A Report on International Public Opinion." 1999. *Economist*/Angus Reid World Poll. Available at www.angusreid.com.

Nau, Henry R. 1990. *The Myth of America's Decline: Leading the World Economy in the 1990s.* New York: Oxford University Press.

Neack, Laura. 1995. "U.N. Peace-Keeping: In the Interest of the Community or Self?" *Journal of Peace Research* 32 (2): 181–96.

Neack, Laura. 1997. "Multilateral Responses to Risky States: The Case of U.N. Peacekeeping." In *Enforcing Cooperation: "Risky" States and Intergovernmental Management of Conflict,* ed. Gerald Schneider and Patricia A. Weitsman, 262–82. New York: St. Martin's.

REFERENCES

New York Times/CBS News Poll. 2001. October 30. Available at www.nytimes.com.
Niedermayer, Oskar. 1995. "Trust and Sense of Community." In *Public Opinion and Internationalized Governance*, ed. Niedermayer and Sinnott, 227–45.
Niedermayer, Oskar, and Richard Sinnott, eds. 1995. *Public Opinion and Internationalized Governance*. Oxford: Oxford University Press.
Nimcic, Miroslav. 1992. *Democracy and Foreign Policy: The Fallacy of Political Realism*. New York: Columbia University Press.
Noël, Alain, and Jean-Philippe Thérien. 1995. "From Domestic to International Justice: The Welfare State and Foreign Aid." *International Organization* 49 (3) 523–53.
Nye, Joseph S. 1971. *Peace in Parts: Integration and Conflict in Regional Organization*. Boston: Little, Brown.
Nye, Joseph S. 1990. *Bound to Lead: The Changing Nature of American Power*. New York: Basic Books.
Nye, Joseph S. 2001. "The 'Nye' Report: Six Years Later." *International Relations of the Asia-Pacific* 1 (1): 95–103.
Nye, Joseph S. 2002. "The American National Interest and Global Public Goods." *International Affairs* 78 (2): 233–44.
O'Brien, Phil. 1993. "The Latin American Debt Crisis." In *The Politics of Global Debt*, ed. Stephen P. Riley, 85–112. New York: St. Martin's.
OECD [Organization for Economic Cooperation and Development]. Various years. *Development Cooperation*. Paris: OECD.
OECD [Organization for Economic Cooperation and Development]. Various years. *OECD Environmental Data: A Compendium*. Paris: OECD.
O'Hanlon, Michael. 2003. *Expanding Global Military Capacity for Humanitarian Intervention*. Washington, DC: Brookings.
O'Hanlon, Michael, and Carol Graham. 1997. *A Half Penny on the Federal Dollar: The Future of Development Aid*. Washington, DC: Brookings.
Ohno, Izumi. 2003. "Japan's ODA at the Crossroads: Striving for a New Vision." *Japan Economic Currents*, April, pp. 4–7.
Olson, Mancur. 1965. *The Logic of Collective Action*. Cambridge: Harvard University Press.
Olson, Mancur, and Richard Zeckhauser. 1966. "An Economic Theory of Alliances." *Review of Economics and Statistics* 48:266–79.
Oneal, John R. 1990a. "Testing the Theory of Collective Action: NATO Defense Burdens, 1950–1984." *Journal of Conflict Resolution* 34:426–48.
Oneal, John R. 1990b. "The Theory of Collective Action and Burden-Sharing in NATO." *International Organization* 44: 379–402.
Oppenheimer, Joe. 1979. "Collective Goods and Alliances: A Reassessment." *Journal of Conflict Resolution* 23:387–407.
Orr, Robert M. Jr. 1988. "The Aid Factor in U.S.-Japan Relations." *Asian Survey* 28:740–56.
Orr, Robert M. Jr. 1989–90. "Collaboration or Conflict? Foreign Aid and U.S.-Japan Relations." *Pacific Affairs* 62:476–89.

Ostrom, Elinor. 1990. *Governing the Commons*. New York: Cambridge University Press.
Ostrom, Elinor. 1992a. "Community and the Endogenous Solution of Commons Problems." *Journal of Theoretical Politics* 4 (3): 343–51.
Ostrom, Elinor. 1992b. "Institutions and Common-Pool Resources: Editor's Introduction." *Journal of Theoretical Politics* 4 (3): 243–45.
Ostrom, Elinor, Roy Gardner, and James Walker. 1994. *Rules, Games, and Common-Pool Resources*. Ann Arbor: University of Michigan Press.
Ottaway, Marina, and Thomas Carothers, eds. 2000. *Funding Virtue: Civil Society Aid and Democracy Promotion*. Washington, DC: Carnegie Endowment for International Peace.
Paarlberg, Robert. 2001. "The Eagle and the Global Environment: The Burden of Being Essential." In *Eagle Rules? Foreign Policy and American Primacy in the Twenty-first Century*, ed. Robert J. Lieber, 324–41. Upper Saddle River, NJ: Prentice Hall.
Page, Benjamin I., and Jason Barabas. 2000. "Foreign Policy Gaps between Citizens and Leaders." *International Studies Quarterly* 44:339–64.
Page, Benjamin I., and Robert Y. Shapiro. 1992. *The Rational Public: Fifty Years of Trends in American Policy Preferences*. Chicago: University of Chicago Press.
Palmer, Glenn. 1990. "Corralling the Free-Rider: Deterrence and the Western Alliance." *International Studies Quarterly* 34:147–64.
Paterson, Matthew. 2001. "Principles of Justice in the Context of Global Climate Change." In *International Relations and Global Climate Change*, ed. Luterbacher and Sprinz, 119–26.
Patterson, Rubin. 1997. *Foreign Aid after the Cold War: The Dynamics of Multipolar Economic Competition*. Trenton, NJ: Africa World.
Payne, Rodger A. 1998. "The Limits and Promise of Environmental Conflict Prevention: The Case of the GEF." *Journal of Peace Research* 35 (3): 363–80.
Pew Research Center for the People and the Press. 2001. "Bush Unpopular in Europe, Seen as Unilateralist." Available at www.people-press.org.
Pew Research Center for the People and the Press. 2002a. "Americans and Europeans Differ Widely on Foreign Policy Issues." Available at www.people-press.org.
Pew Research Center for the People and the Press. 2002b. "Public More Internationalist Than in 1990s." Available at www.people-press.org.
Pew Research Center for the People and the Press. 2002c. "What the World Thinks in 2002." Available at www.people-press.org.
Pew Research Center for the People and the Press. 2003. "America's Image Further Erodes, Europeans Want Weaker Ties." Available at www.people-press.org.
Pharr, Susan J. 1994. "Japanese Aid in the New World Order." In *Japan: A New Kind of Superpower?* ed. Craig C. Garby and Mary Brown Bullock, 159–80. Washington, DC: Woodrow Wilson Center Press; Baltimore: Johns Hopkins University Press.
Powlick, Philip J. 1991. "The Attitudinal Basis for Responsiveness to Public

Opinion among American Foreign Policy Officials." *Journal of Conflict Resolution* 35:611–41.
Powlick, Philip J., and Andrew Z. Katz. 1998. "Defining the American Public Opinion/Foreign Policy Nexus." *Mershon International Studies Review* 42 (supp. 1): 29–62.
PIPA [Program on International Policy Attitudes]. 2000a. "Africa Summit Plan Likely to Elicit Sympathetic but Guarded Response from U.S. Public." Available at www.pipa.org.
PIPA [Program on International Policy Attitudes]. 2000b. "Americans on Globalization: A Study of U.S. Public Attitudes." Available at www.pipa.org.
PIPA [Program on International Policy Attitudes]. 2000c. "Americans on the Global Warming Treaty." Available at www.pipa.org.
PIPA [Program on International Policy Attitudes]. 2001. "Americans on Foreign Aid and World Hunger: A Study of U.S. Public Attitudes." Available at www.pipa.org.
PIPA [Program on International Policy Attitudes]. 2002. "PIPA Bulletin: October Polling on Iraq." Available at www.pipa.org.
PIPA [Program on International Policy Attitudes]. 2003a. "PIPA–Knowledge Networks Poll: Americans on Africa." Available at www.pipa.org.
PIPA [Program on International Policy Attitudes]. 2003b. "PIPA–Knowledge Networks Poll: Americans on America's Role in the World after the Iraq War." Available at www.knowledgenetworks.com.
PIPA [Program on International Policy Attitudes]. 2003c. "PIPA–Knowledge Networks Poll: Americans on North Korea, I and II." Available at www.pipa.org.
PIPA [Program on International Policy Attitudes]. 2003d. "PIPA–Knowledge Networks Poll: Americans on the Iraq War and the Future of the United Nations." Available at www.knowledgenetworks.com.
PIPA [Program on International Policy Attitudes]. 2003e. "PIPA–Knowledge Networks Poll: U.S. Foreign Policy Performance Ratings and Priority Rankings." Available at www.pipa.org.
Public Agenda Online. Various years. Available at www.publicagenda.prg/issues.
Qin, Huasun. 1996. "The Importance of Observing U.N. Peacekeeping Norms." *Brown Journal of World Affairs* 3 (1): 35–40.
Ratner, Steven R. 1995. *The New U.N. Peacekeeping*. New York: St. Martin's.
Rattinger, Hans. 1991. "The Development and Structure of West German Public Opinion on Security Issues in the 1980s." In *Debating National Security: The Public Dimension*, ed. Don Munton and Hans Rattinger, 301–41. Frankfurt: Lang.
Reilly, John. Various years. *American Public Opinion and Foreign Policy*. Chicago: Chicago Council on Foreign Relations.
Research Foundation for Science, Technology, and Ecology. 2002. "Jaiv Panchayat: Biodiversity at the Village Level." In *Global Backlash*, ed. Broad, 269–72.
Revise, Nicolas. 1999. "East Timor the Test for 'Kinder, Gentler' Thai Army." *Mainichi Daily News*, September 30, p. 2.

Revkin, Andrew C. 2002. "Climate Changing, U.S. Says in Report." *New York Times*, June 3. Available at www.nytimes.com.

Richman, Alvin. 1993a. "Key Findings from Recent Polls in the U.S., and Japan." Unpublished memorandum to Ann Pincus, U.S. Information Agency, March 6. In possession of author.

Richman, Alvin. 1993b. "Key Findings from Recent Polls in the U.S., and Japan." Unpublished memorandum to Ann Pincus, U.S. Information Agency, September 17. In possession of author.

Richman, Alvin. 1994a. "American Public's Attitudes toward U.S. International Involvement in the Post–Cold War Era." Paper presented at the meeting of the International Studies Association, Washington, DC, March 29.

Richman, Alvin. 1994b. "The American Public's 'Rules of Military Engagement in the Post–Cold War Era." Paper presented at the meeting of the American Political Science Association, New York, September 2.

Richman, Alvin. 1994c. "American Views of Japan: Key Findings from Recent Polls." Unpublished memorandum to Ann Pincus, U.S. Information Agency, March 6. In possesion of author.

Richman, Alvin. 1994d. "Trends in Internationalist Sentiment." Unpublished memorandum, March 28. In possession of author.

Riddell, Roger C. 1999. "The End of Foreign Aid to Africa? Concerns about Donor Policies." *African Affairs* 98:309–35.

Rieffel, Alexis. 1994. "The Role of the Paris Club in Managing Debt Problems." In *International Borrowing*, ed. Bradlow, 481–506.

Riggs, Fred W. 1995. "Ethnonational Rebellions and Viable Constitutionalism." *International Political Science Review* 16 (4): 375–404.

Riley, Stephen P., ed. 1993. *The Politics of Global Debt*. New York: St. Martin's.

Risse-Kappen, Thomas. 1992. "Public Opinion, Domestic Structure, and Foreign Policy in Liberal Democracies." *World Politics* 43:479–512.

Roberts, Adam. 1994. "The Crisis in U.N. Peacekeeping." *Survival* 36 (3): 93–120.

Rodrik, Dani. 1997. *Has Globalization Gone Too Far?* Washington, DC: Institute for International Economics.

Rohter, Larry. 2003. "Some Fault U.S. for Argentina's Fall." *International Herald Tribune*, December 26, p. 9.

Rosecrance, Richard N. 1999. *The Rise of the Virtual State: Wealth and Power in the Coming Century*. New York: Basic Books.

Rosecrance, Richard N., and Jennifer Taw. 1990. "Japan and the Theory of International Leadership." *World Politics* 42:184–209.

Rosenau, James. 1990. *Turbulence in World Politics*. Princeton: Princeton University Press.

Rosenau, James. 1997. *Along the Domestic-Foreign Frontier*. Cambridge: Cambridge University Press.

Rosenau, James N., and E. O. Czempiel, eds. 1992. *Governance without Government: Order and Change in World Politics*. Cambridge: Cambridge University Press.

REFERENCES

Ruggie, John Gerard, ed. 1993a. *Multilateralism Matters: The Theory and Practice of an Institutional Form.* New York: Columbia University Press.

Ruggie, John Gerard. 1993b. "Wandering in the Void." *Foreign Affairs* 72 (5): 26–31.

Ruggie, John Gerard. 1996. *Winning the Peace: America and World Order in the New Era.* New York: Columbia University Press.

Russett, Bruce. 1970. *What Price Vigilance?* New Haven: Yale University Press.

Russett, Bruce. 1985. "The Mysterious Case of Vanishing Hegemony; or, Is Mark Twain Really Dead?" *International Organization* 39:205–31.

Russett, Bruce. 1990. *Controlling the Sword: The Democratic Governance of National Security.* Cambridge: Harvard University Press.

Russett, Bruce. 1993. *Grasping the Democratic Peace.* Princeton: Princeton University Press.

Ruttan, Vernon W. 1996. *United States Development Assistance Policy: The Domestic Politics of Foreign Economic Aid.* Baltimore: Johns Hopkins University Press.

Sachs, Jeffrey D. 1986. "Managing the LDC Debt Crisis." *Brookings Panel on Macroeconomic Activity* 2:397–431.

Sachs, Jeffrey D., ed. 1989a. *Developing Country Debt and the World Economy.* Chicago: University of Chicago Press.

Sachs, Jeffrey D. 1989b. "Efficient Debt Reduction." In *Dealing with the Debt Crisis,* ed. Husain and Diwan, 239–56.

Saideman, Stephen M. 1997. "Explaining the International Relations of Secessionist Conflicts: Vulnerability versus Ethnic Ties." *International Organizations* 51:721–54.

Sandler, Todd. 1977. "The Impurity of Defense: An Application to the Economics of Alliances." *Kyklos* 30:443–60.

Sandler, Todd. 1993. "Tropical Deforestation: Markets and Market Failures." *Land Economics* 69 (3): 225–33.

Sandler, Todd. 1997. *Global Challenges: An Approach to Environmental, Political, and Economic Problems.* Cambridge: Cambridge University Press.

Sandler, Todd. 1999. "Intergenerational Public Goods: Strategies, Efficiency, and Institutions." In *Global Public Goods,* ed. Kaul, Grunberg, and Stern, 20–50.

Sandler, Todd, and John F. Forbes. 1980. "Burden-Sharing, Strategy, and Design of NATO." *Economic Inquiry* 18:425–44.

Sandler, Todd, and Keith Hartley. 1995. *The Economics of Defense.* Cambridge: Cambridge University Press.

Sandler, Todd, and James Murdoch. 1990. "Nash-Cournot or Lindahl Behavior? An Empirical Test for the NATO Allies." *Quarterly Journal of Economics* 105:875–94.

Sandler, Todd, and Keith Sargent. 1995. "Management of Transnational Commons: Coordination, Publicness, and Treaty Formation." *Land Economics* 71:145–62.

Sanford, Jonathan E. 2000. *IB96008: Multilateral Development Banks: Issues* for the 106th Congress. CRS Issue Brief. Washington, DC: Congressional Research Service, October 6.

Sanger, David E. 1998a. "U.S. and IMF Made Asia Crisis Worse, World Bank Finds." *New York Times,* December 3, p. A1.

Sanger, David E. 1998b. "Wealthy Nations Back Plan to Speed Help to the Weak." *New York Times,* October 31, p. A1.

Santiso, Javier. 1999. "Analysts Analyzed: A Socio-Economic Approach to Financial and Emerging Markets." *International Political Science Review* 20: 307–30.

Schafers, Manfred. 2002. "Rejuvenating Relief Aid." *Frankfurter Allgemeine Zeitung* (English ed.), February 7, p. 3.

Schmitter, Philip C. 1971. "A Revised Theory of Regional Integration." In *Regional Integration: Theory and Research,* ed. Leon Lindberg and Stuart Scheingold, 232–64. Cambridge: Harvard University Press.

Schnabel, Albrecht. 1994. "Utopia or New Order? State Sovereignty, Humanitarian Intervention, and the Emergence of a Global Society: A Theoretical Analysis on the Prospects for Global Governance." Paper presented at the annual meeting of the Academic Council on the United Nations System, the Hague, June 23–25.

Schraeder, Peter J., Steven W. Hook, and Bruce Taylor. 1998. "Clarifying the Foreign Aid Puzzle: A Comparison of American, Japanese, French, and Swedish Flows." *World Politics* 50:294–323.

Schreuers, Miranda A. 2001. "A View from the United States: COP-7 and the Kyoto Protocol." *German Foreign Policy in Dialogue* 2 (6): 22–25. Available at www.deutsche-aussenpolitik.de.

Sciolino, Elaine. 2000. "Bush Adviser Hints Military Isn't Best Tool to Keep Peace." *New York Times,* November 17.

Scroggins, Deborah. 1996. "Finance and Administration." In *A Global Agenda: Issues before the 51st General Assembly of the United Nations,* 303–31. New York: New York University Press.

Scruggs, Lyle. 1999. "Institutions and Environmental Performance in Seventeen Western Democracies." *British Journal of Political Science* 29:1–31.

Sell, Susan. 1996. "North-South Environmental Bargaining: Ozone, Climate Change, and Biodiversity." *Global Governance* 2:97–118.

Shulman, Stephen. 2000. "Nationalist Sources of International Economic Integration." *International Studies Quarterly* 44: 365–90.

Sinnott, Richard. 1995a. "Bringing Public Opinion Back In." In *Public Opinion and Internationalized Governance,* ed. Niedermayer and Sinnott, 11–32.

Sinnott, Richard. 1995b. "Policy, Subsidiarity, and Legitimacy." In *Public Opinion and Internationalized Governance,* ed. Niedermayer and Sinnott, 246–76.

Sinnott, Richard. 1996. "Problems and Priorities in Comparative Research on Public Opinion and Foreign and Security Policy." Paper presented at the World Association for Public Opinion Research Regional Conference, Tokyo, November 8–9.

Smith, Christian. 1996. *Resisting Reagan: The U.S. Central American Peace Movement.* Chicago: University of Chicago Press.

REFERENCES

Smith, Tom W. 2001. "Trends in National Spending Priorities, 1973–2000." Available at www.norc.uchicago.edu.
Smith, Tom W., and Lars Jarkko. 1998. *National Pride: A Cross-National Analysis*. National Opinion Research Center/University of Chicago, GSS Cross National Report 19.
Smouts, Marie-Claude. 1998. "Political Aspects of Peace-Keeping Operations." In *United Nations Peacekeeping Operations*, ed. Stern, 7–39.
Snidal, Duncan. 1985. "Coordination versus Prisoner's Dilemma: Implications for International Cooperation." *American Political Science Review* 79: 923–42.
Snider, Lewis W. 1996. *Growth, Debt, and Politics: Economic Adjustment and the Political Performance of Developing Countries*. Boulder, CO: Westview.
Snow, David, and Robert Benford. 1988. "Ideology, Frame Resonance, and Participant Mobilization." In *International Social Movement Research*, ed. Bert Klandermans, Hanspeter Kriesi, and Sidney Tarrow, 197–218. Greenwich, CT: JAI.
Sobel, Richard. 2001. *The Impact of Public Opinion on U.S. Foreign Policy since Vietnam*. New York: Oxford University Press.
Sokolsky, Joel J. 1995. "Great Ideals and Uneasy Compromises: The United States' Approach to Peacekeeping." *International Journal* 50:266–93.
Solingen, Etel. 1998. *Regional Orders at Century's Dawn: Global and Domestic Influences on Grand Strategy*. Princeton: Princeton University Press.
Soroos, Marvin S. 1999. "Global Institutions and the Environment: An Evolutionary Perspective." In *The Global Environment: Institutions, Law and Policy*, ed. Norman J. Vig and Regina S. Axelrod, 27–51. Washington, DC: CQ Press.
Spence, Jacqueline M. 1996. *The European Union, "A View from the Top": Top Decision Makers and the European Union*. Brussels: EOS Gallup Europe.
Sprinz, Detlef. 2001. "Climate Change after Marrakech: The Role of Europe in the Global Arena." *German Foreign Policy in Dialogue* 2 (6): 6–8. Available at www.deutsche-aussenpolitik.de.
Sprinz, Detlef, and Tapani Vaahtoranta. 1994. "The Interest-Based Explanation of International Environmental Policy." *International Organization* 48 (1): 77–105.
Spruyt, Hendrik. 1994. *The Sovereign State and Its Competitors*. Princeton: Princeton University Press.
Spruyt, Hendrik. 2000. "The End of Empire and the Extension of the Westphalian System: The Normative Basis of the Modern State Order." In *Continuity and Change*, ed. Caporaso, 65–92.
Stallings, Barbara. 1990. "The Reluctant Giant: Japan and the Latin American Debt Crisis." *Journal of Latin American Studies* 22:1–30.
Steinbruner, John. 1998. "Can the United States Lead the World?" In *Statecraft and Security: The Cold War and Beyond*, ed. Ken Booth, 135–48. Cambridge: Cambridge University Press.
Stern, Brigitte, ed. 1998. *United Nations Peacekeeping Operations: A Guide to French Policies*. Tokyo: United Nations University Press.

References

Stolberg, Sheryl Gay. 2002. "AIDS Fund Falls Short of Goal and U.S. Is Given Some Blame." *New York Times*, February 13. Available at www.nytimes.com.

Stopford, John M., and Susan Strange. 1991. *Rival States, Rival Firms: Competition for World Market States*. Cambridge: Cambridge University Press.

Strange, Susan. 1998. "Globaloney?" *Review of International Political Economy* 5 (4): 704–20.

Sung, Woonki, and Rosaria Troia. 1992. *Developments in Debt Conversion Programs and Conversion Activities*. World Bank Technical Paper 170. Washington, DC: World Bank.

Thacker, Strom C. 1999. "The High Politics of IMF Lending." *World Politics* 52:38–75.

Thomas, Vinod, and Tamara Belt. 2000. "Growth and the Environment: Allies or Foes." In *Globalization and the Challenges of a New Century*, ed. Patrick O'Meara, Howard D. Mehlinger, and Matthew Krain, 377–82. Bloomington: Indiana University Press.

Titmuss, Richard M. 1971. *The Gift Relationship: From Human Blood to Social Policy*. New York: Pantheon.

Triandafylliou, Anna. 1998. "National Identity and the Other." *Ethnic and Racial Studies* 21 (4): 593–612.

Trilateral Commission. 2001. *London 2001: The Annual Meeting of the Trilateral Commission*. Trialogue: 55.

Ullman, Richard. 1983. "Redefining Security." *International Security* 8:129–53.

U.S. Department of State. 1995. "Focus on the United Nations: U.N. Peacekeeping Operations." *U.S. Department of State Dispatch*, 6 (18): 377–79.

U.S. Information Agency. 1995. *America as a Global Actor: The U.S. Image around the World*. Washington, DC: Office of Research and Media.

UNCTAD [United Nations Conference on Trade and Development]. 1994. *Final Report of the Ad Hoc Working Group on Investment and Financial Flows: Non-Debt Creating Finance for Development; New Mechanisms for Increasing Investment and Financial Flows*. New York: United Nations.

UNDP [United Nations Development Program]. Various years. *Human Development Report*. New York: Oxford University Press.

UNDP [United Nations Development Program]. 1996. *Debt Management: A Report on the Joint Programme of Debt Management, 1991–96*. Discussion Paper 4. New York: UNDP in cooperation with UNCTAD and the World Bank.

United Nations. 1990. *The Blue Helmets: A Review of United Nations Peace-Keeping*. New York: United Nations.

United Nations. 1993. *Debt-Equity Swaps and Development*. New York: United Nations.

United Nations. 1996. *The Blue Helmets: A Review of United Nations Peace-Keeping*. New York: United Nations.

United Nations. 2000. *The Report of the Panel on UN Peace Operations*. New York: United Nations. Available at www.un.org/peace/reports/peace_operations.

United Nations Centre on Transnational Corporations. 1992. *Transnational Banks and the External Indebtedness of Developing Countries: Impact of Regulatory Changes.* New York: United Nations.

United Nations General Assembly. 1995. *The Financial Situation of the United Nations—Report of the Secretary General.* New York: United Nations.

United Nations General Assembly. 1997. *Improving the Financial Situation of the United Nations—Report of the Secretary-General.* New York: United Nations.

United Nations Military Adviser's Office. 1991–97. *Monthly Summary of Troop Contributions to Peace-Keeping Operations.* New York: United Nations.

United Nations Secretariat. 1995. *Status of Contributions as at 30 November 1995.* New York: United Nations.

United Nations Secretariat. 1997. *Status of Contributions as at 28 February 1997.* New York: United Nations.

United Nations Secretariat. 2003. *Status of Contributions as at 1 January 2002.* New York: United Nations.

Vos, Rob. 1994. *Debt and Adjustment in the World Economy.* New York: St. Martin's.

Waever, Ole. 1996. "European Security Identities." *Journal of Common Market Studies* 34 (1): 103–32.

Wallander, Celeste A., Helga Haftendorn, and Robert O. Keohane, eds. 1999. *Imperfect Unions: Security Institutions over Time and Space.* New York: Oxford University Press.

Walzer, Michael. 1983. *Spheres of Justice: A Defense of Pluralism and Equality.* New York: Basic Books.

Wan, Ming. 1995. "Spending Strategies in World Politics: How Japan Has Used Its Economic Power in the Past Decade." *International Studies Quarterly* 39 (1): 85–108.

Wang, T. Y. 1999. "U.S. Foreign Aid and U.N. Voting: An Analysis of Important Issues." *International Studies Quarterly* 43:199–210.

Wanner, Barbara. 1996. "United Nations Reform Shines Spotlight on Japan's Leadership Potential." *JEI Report,* April 19.

Wanner, Barbara. 1999. "Tokyo Shies away from U.N. Request for Kosovo Police Support." *JEI Report,* July 9, pp. 11–12.

Warrington, Robert D. 1995. "The Helmets May Be Blue, but the Blood's Still Red: The Dilemma of U.S. Participation in U.N. Peace Operations." *Comparative Strategy* 14:23–34.

Wedel, Janine. 1998. *Collision and Collusion: The Strange Case of Western Aid to Eastern Europe, 1989–1998.* New York: St. Martin's.

Weiner, Tim. 2000a. "One G.O.P. Senator Blocks Spending on Peacekeepers." *New York Times,* May 20, p. A1.

Weiner, Tim. 2000b. "G.O.P. Senator Frees Money for U.N. Mission in Sierra Leone." *New York Times,* June 7, p. A14.

Wellons, Philip A. 1987. *Passing the Buck: Banks, Governments, and Third World Debt.* Boston: Harvard Business School Press.

References

Wells, Robin. 1993. "Tolerance of Arrearages: How IMF Loan Policy Can Effect Debt Reduction." *American Economic Review* 83:621–33.

Wendt, Alexander. 1994. "Collective Identity Formation and the International State." *American Political Science Review* 88 (2): 384–96.

Wendt, Alexander. 1999. *Social Theory of International Politics*. Cambridge: Cambridge University Press.

Wiegandt, Ellen. 2001. "Climate Change, Equity, and International Negotiations." In *International Relations and Global Climate Change*, ed. Luterbacher and Sprinz, 127–50.

Wisnumurti, Nugroho. 1996. "The United Nations and Peace Enforcement: Prescription for Disorder or Path towards a New World Order?" *Brown Journal of World Affairs* 3 (1): 67–76.

Wittkopf, Eugene. 1986. "On the Foreign Policy Beliefs of the American People: A Critique and Some Evidence." *International Studies Quarterly* 30: 425–45.

Wittkopf, Eugene. 1990. *Faces of Internationalism: Public Opinion and American Foreign Policy*. Durham, NC: Duke University Press.

Wittkopf, Eugene. 1996. "What the Public Really Thinks about Foreign Policy." *Washington Quarterly* 19 (2): 91–106.

Wolfers, Arnold. 1962. *Discord and Collaboration: Essays on International Politics*. Baltimore: Johns Hopkins Press.

World Bank. Various years. *World Debt Tables*. Washington, DC: World Bank.

World Bank. Various years. *World Development Indicators*. Washington, DC: World Bank.

World Bank. 1998. *Assessing Aid: What Works, What Doesn't, and Why*. Washington, DC: World Bank.

World Bank. 2001a. *Global Development Finance: Building Coalitions for Effective Development Finance*. Vols. 1–2. Washington, DC: World Bank.

World Bank. 2001b. "World Development Indicators." Available at www.worldbank.org.

World Resources Institute. 2001. *World Resources, 2000–2001*. Washington, DC: World Resources Institute.

World Trade Organization. 2002. "Governments Pledge CHF 30 Million to Doha Development Agenda Global Trust Fund." Press Release 279. March 11. Available at www.wto.org/english/news.

Wren, Christopher S. 1999a. "U.N. Role in Enforcing Peace Is Changing." *New York Times*, October 3, p. 12.

Wren, Christopher S. 1999b. "U.S. Told It Must Pay $550 Million or Risk Losing U.N. Vote." *New York Times*, October 6, p. A10.

Wyplosz, Charles. 1999. "International Financial Instability." In *Global Public Goods*, ed. Kaul, Grunberg, and Stern, 152–89.

Young, Oran R. 1997. "Rights, Rules, and Resources in World Affairs." In *Global Governance: Drawing Insights from the Environmental Experience*, ed. Oran R. Young, 1–24. Cambridge: MIT Press.

Zacher, Mark W. 1992. "The Decaying Pillars of the Westphalian Temple: Implications for International Order and Governance." In *Governance without Government: Order and Change in World Politics,* ed. James N. Rosenau and Ernst-Otto Czempiel, 58–101. Cambridge: Cambridge University Press.

Zielonka, Jan. 1998. *Explaining Euro-Paralysis: Why Europe Is Unable to Act in International Politics.* New York: St. Martin's.

INDEX

accommodationists, 97
Adler, Emanuel, 26, 49
adoption spillovers, 23, 29
American elites, 96, 112, 145, 146, 148, 289
American international affairs culture, 98
American internationalism, 110
American public opinion, 52, 88, 89–91, 94–95, 98, 103, 106, 108, 111–12, 114, 143, 145, 147, 149, 179, 232, 234–35, 237, 238, 239, 280, 282, 289, 291, 293, 295, 297, 298, 299, 321, 336, 338–39, 342, 345–46
Annan, Kofi, 132
Arce, M., 275
Argentine crisis (2002), 203, 206
Asia-Pacific Economic Cooperation (APEC), 59, 120
Atwood, J. Brian, 137
Axis of Evil, 85

Baker initiative, 191
Bank of International Settlements, 205
bargaining linkages, 26
Barnett, Michael, 26, 49
Bono/O'Neill trek, 149
Boulding, Kenneth, 1
Brady Plan, 191, 197
Brandt, Willy, 135
Brandt Commission, 191

Brazilian debt, 196
Bryce, Lord, 51
Bush administration, 2, 203, 206, 263, 277

capital availability, 186
casualty aversion, 241
citizen activism, 279, 345
Clinton administration, 264
club bads, 23, 35, 43, 154, 228; amelioration, 43
club goods, 19, 22, 23, 27, 29, 35, 36, 44, 87, 133–34, 137, 154, 165, 177–78, 188, 191, 197, 207, 229, 230, 231, 266, 354
club membership, 15, 34, 48, 117, 129, 130; common, 49
club norms, 48
club theory, 181
collateral damage, 14, 239, 343
collective action, 11, 15–16, 21, 24, 30, 35–36, 38, 40–41, 45, 49, 50–51, 56, 70, 73, 74–75, 79, 81, 83, 86, 90, 102, 111–12, 114, 124, 129, 130, 182, 186–87, 202, 205, 207, 270, 273, 276, 282, 290, 291–92, 296, 304, 312, 316, 319, 328, 332, 337–38, 339, 346– 47, 350, 351–53
Cologne summit (1999), 199, 200
common cultural identity, 68
common pool resources, 22, 23, 273

Contingent Credit Facility, 206
cooperative internationalism, 88

Daniel, G., 275
debt, 4, 47, 55, 67, 112, 131, 134, 138, 139, 169, 171, 180–213, 216–21, 231, 252, 271, 279, 328, 331, 332, 333, 335, 336, 346, 347, 351, 352. *See also* international debt
debt management, 4, 47, 55, 112, 131, 134, 138, 139, 182, 184–92, 196, 199, 207, 220, 231, 271, 328, 332, 347, 351. *See also* international debt management
debt relief, 182–85, 221
defensive internationalism, 1, 2, 12, 42–43, 46, 50, 89, 130, 223, 229, 326, 327, 328, 338, 339
democratic peace theorists, 222
Development Assistance Committee (DAC), 133–34, 136, 142, 152, 155, 157, 158, 159–60, 161–62, 165, 167, 169, 171–72, 173, 175, 177–78, 219
diplomatic studies, 49
domestic parochialism, 15
domestic permissiveness, 56, 152

economic nationalism, 190
economic theory of behavior, 28
economic unilateralism, 94
Enhanced HIPC Initiative, 200
environment, 6–7, 40, 67, 76, 85, 96, 98, 112, 119, 121, 145, 226, 272, 274, 279, 280–83, 286–89, 291–98, 300–302, 310–11, 320, 325, 334–35, 338, 344–45
European citizenship, 68
European Commission, 70, 78–79, 84, 278, 280–81, 283, 286, 292, 297
European cultural identity, 68
European integration, 72
European Monetary Union, 316
European Parliament, 144
European project, 86, 87

European public opinion, 52, 69, 76, 84, 85–86, 144, 179, 233, 236, 237, 286, 288–89, 296–97, 299, 339–40. *See also* West European public opinion
European supranational identity, 67
European Union, 5, 22, 35, 73, 77, 110, 113, 122, 135, 141, 175, 178, 229, 235, 298, 338; collective action, 67, 70; elites, 80; entry, 75; membership, 70; multilateral giving, 141; multilateralism, 71; publics, 67–69, 70, 76–79, 81, 84, 88, 144, 236, 283, 286
external debt sustainability, 182

foreign aid, 26, 51, 55, 85, 90, 112, 121, 131–37, 139–52, 154–55, 161, 167, 177–80, 182, 219, 231, 235, 271, 278–79, 296, 332, 337, 345–46
foreign negativism, 242
Framework Convention on Climate Change, 270, 277

G-2 club good element, 137
G-7, 22–23, 38, 135, 159, 181, 191–92, 200–201, 203, 205, 347
G-77, 191–92
G-8, 23, 135, 161
G-10, 23, 205
Gallup International, 59–60
game theory, 49
German public opinion, 293
global interdependence, 3
global North, 17, 43, 129, 186, 210, 279, 326, 334–35, 339, 352
good stewardship, 139

Halifax G-7 summit (1988), 205
hegemon, 8–9, 12–13, 154, 165, 167
hegemonic decline, 12, 21, 221
hegemonic optimism, 9, 12–13, 15
hegemonic pessimists, 163, 165
hegemonic stability, 8–9, 21, 136, 154, 157, 243, 261, 263, 265, 336

INDEX

Helms, Jesse, 180
Highly Indebted Poor Countries (HIPCs), 199–201, 206, 210, 219; HIPC Enhanced Initiative, 200; HIPC initiative, 191, 219; HIPC Trust Fund, 200
Hill, Stephen H., 173, 251
Hoffman, Stanley, 1

identity-based domestic beliefs, 327
identity constructions, 31, 49
Ikenberry, G. John, 9, 26, 178
impure public goods, 19, 24–25, 28, 41, 44, 46, 136–37, 151, 179, 181, 188, 207, 229, 242, 250, 253, 257, 261, 264–66, 271, 276, 327, 350, 354
interdependence, 26–27, 42, 273–74, 326, 350
international activism, 89, 98, 100, 117, 237
International Court of Justice, 96
international debt, 180–82, 186, 188–90, 194, 330, 337
international debt management, 180–82, 186, 188, 190, 330
international development assistance, 4, 132, 134
international financial institutions (IFIs), 181–82, 185–88, 193–95, 202, 204, 206–7, 210, 220, 331
international governance, 138, 349
International Monetary Fund (IMF), 84, 181; concessionality, 196; conditionality, 192, 196; credits, 182
international public good, 45, 47, 137, 225, 229, 343, 354
isolationists, 8, 88, 89, 92, 346

Japanese imperfection, 117
Japanese political leadership, 119
Japanese public opinion, 52, 116–22, 124, 126, 128–29, 143, 146, 148, 150–52, 232–33, 236, 239–40, 291, 293, 295–96, 299, 300, 338, 340, 342, 345

Japanese public affinity, 122
joint products, 22–23, 38, 44, 46, 229, 230, 242, 256

Kennedy, Paul, 173
Kissinger Commission report on Latin America, 195
Kupchan, Charles A., 9, 26, 178

London club, 181, 193
London Inter-bank Offered Rate (LIBOR), 192
Lumsdaine, David H., 26, 135, 147
Luterbacher, Urs, 271, 274, 275
Lyon terms, 199

March, James G., 18, 91, 97, 112, 280, 281, 294
Marrakech agreements, 278
McCormick, John, 274
McWorld, 9
Mexican crisis (1982), 182, 191, 202, 221
Mexican payment moratorium declaration, 192
militant internationalism, 88
minilateralism, 36
Mitchell, Ronald, 275
Monterrey UN Conference on Financing for Development (2002), 178
Montreal Protocol on the Ozone, 270
Morgenthau, Hans, 134
Morgenthau, Henry, 180, 186
multilateral institutionalism, 4, 37, 44, 181, 327, 338, 354
multilateralism, 11, 34, 36, 38, 48, 49–50, 90, 102, 148, 224, 297, 339, 347, 349–50, 353–54
multilateral liberalism, 18
Murphy, Craig N., 349
muted optimism, 1–2, 8–9, 11–12, 14, 16, 56, 67, 129–31, 154, 157, 159, 162, 171–72, 177, 179, 187, 190, 207, 209, 211, 221, 265–66, 273, 278, 312, 315, 319, 322, 324, 327–38, 343–44, 345–46, 354–55

muted pessimism, 327–28, 330–31, 333–34, 337, 343–44, 351, 355

Naples terms, 199, 201
National Opinion Research Center, 142
Nau, Henry R., 9, 26, 178
negative spillovers, 271, 272, 331, 333, 342
neoliberal state decline, 15
nongovernmental organizational aid (NGOA), 134–35, 153, 155, 159, 177
North American Free Trade Area (NAFTA), 35
North Atlantic Treaty Organization (NATO), 35

official development assistance (ODA) planning guidelines, 173, 175
Okinawa G-7 summit (2000), 200
Okinawa G-8 summit (2000), 161
Olson, Mancur, 20
O'Neill, Paul, 139
Oppenheimer, Joe, 52
optimistic hegemonic stability, 9
Organization for Economic Cooperation and Development (OECD), 14–15, 17, 45–46, 55, 67, 124, 133, 135, 140, 147, 154, 203, 219, 242, 279, 280, 283, 294, 301–3, 312–15, 320, 327, 329, 330, 334–35, 337–38, 341–42, 345. *See also* Development Assistance Committee
Ostrom, Elinor, 22, 273, 274

Paris club, 181, 192–93, 196, 198, 200–201, 210–11, 331
parochial assertiveness, 154
parochial national interests, 187
patented goods, 23
Peace Corps, 148
peacekeeping, 4, 19, 25, 47, 51, 55, 67, 85, 90, 96, 111–12, 122, 131, 133, 222–25, 227–29, 231, 235–36, 237–38, 243, 244–45, 256, 262, 265–66, 271, 278, 328, 332, 336, 341–42, 345, 347–48, 352
Pearson, Lester, 135
perverse incentives, 3
Pew Research Center, 59, 85, 91–92, 102, 110–11, 113
Poverty Reduction Strategy Paper, 201
private goods view, 227–28
procyclical private flows, 184
public bads, 20–23, 25–27, 32, 35, 38, 43, 46, 66, 115, 129, 135, 154, 186, 193, 222, 230, 266, 270–72, 275–78, 310, 326–29, 331–33, 338–41, 343, 346, 349, 350, 352
public goods: conducive emphasis, 165, 167; provision, 20, 188, 326, 349; theory, 4, 22, 25, 27, 154, 157, 253, 256, 337. *See also* impure public goods; international public goods; pure public goods
public opinion, 48–55, 60, 70, 81, 84, 91, 93, 113–14, 128, 132–33, 135, 140–41, 149–50, 152, 182, 225, 231, 234–35, 238–39, 264, 271, 278–79, 281, 293, 297, 299, 320–21, 323–24, 326, 336–39, 341, 343–45, 352; constructions, 48, 51
pure public goods, 19–20, 22–25, 26, 44, 136, 160, 225, 227, 243, 256, 260; pure public good conception, 227. *See also* impure public goods

Rambouillet summit (1975), 347
rational choice perspectives, 18
rethinking of aid, 139
Rieffel, Alexis, 180, 181
Russian Federation, 250, 256, 258, 261, 319, 334

Sandler, Todd, 22, 133, 226–27, 229, 230, 253, 254, 256, 260, 275
Schroeder, Gerhard, 200
Shimizu, Hirofumi, 226–27, 229, 253–54, 256, 260

Shulman, Stephen, 29
Sierra Leone, 264, 266
Sikkink, Kathryn, 18
soft hegemony, 222
soft power, 9, 15, 65, 124
Soroos, Marvin S., 274
Special Programme of Assistance (SPA), 208
state decline optimists, 8, 10–12, 14
Stockholm conference (1972), 270
supranational governance, 139

Toronto G-7 summit (1988), 196
Toronto terms, 196, 198
Trilateral Commission, 45
Trinidad terms, 198

unilateralist internationalism, 96
United Nations, 35, 39, 45, 51, 55, 83, 86, 96–97, 110, 120–21, 135, 192, 195, 222, 224, 227, 243–44, 249–51, 260, 275, 277, 302, 332, 339, 341–42; Conference on Trade and Development (UNCTAD), 191, 198, 199; Development Program (UNDP), 138, 302; Millennium Summit, 178; Security Council, 111, 120, 228, 231–34, 237, 252–53, 264, 333, 342
U.S. Congress, 192

U.S. Department of Defense, 263
U.S. Treasury Department, 192

Venice G-7 summit (1987), 196
Venn diagrams, 40

Wan, Ming, 137
war on terrorism, 97, 103, 111, 179, 204, 225, 264, 354
Warsaw Pact, 247
weapons of mass destruction (WMD), 79, 106, 108
West European public opinion, 141, 146, 152, 280, 282, 287, 289–300, 320, 340, 344
Wolfers, Arnold, 3
World Bank, 23–24, 45, 54, 84, 134–35, 138–39, 157, 160–61, 167, 171–72, 178, 181, 183, 186, 188, 191–92, 197, 200–203, 205–6, 210, 307, 312–13, 315–16; International Development Assistance (IDA) Debt Reduction Facility, 197
World Trade Organization, 35, 39, 83, 114, 178

Young, Oran R., 273–74

zero-sum game, 31